Pastimes and Politics

Eastern African Studies

Revealing Prophets
Edited by DAVID M. ANDERSON & DOUGLAS H. JOHNSON

Swahili Origins
JAMES DE VERE ALLEN

Being Maasai
Edited by THOMAS SPEAR & RICHARD WALLER

A History of Modern Ethiopia 1855–1991
Second edition
BAHRU ZEWDE

Ethnicity & Conflict in the Horn of Africa
Edited by KATSUYOSHI FUKUI & JOHN MARKAKIS

Conflict, Age & Power in North East Africa
Edited by EISEI KURIMOTO & SIMON SIMONSE

Jua Kali Kenya
KENNETH KING

Control & Crisis in Colonial Kenya
BRUCE BERMAN

Unhappy Valley
Book One: State & Class
Book Two: Violence & Ethnicity
BRUCE BERMAN & JOHN LONSDALE

Mau Mau from Below
GREET KERSHAW

The Mau Mau War in Perspective
FRANK FUREDI

Squatters & the Roots of Mau Mau 1905–63
TABITHA KANOGO

Economic & Social Origins of Mau Mau 1945–53
DAVID W. THROUP

Multi-Party Politics in Kenya
DAVID W. THROUP & CHARLES HORNSBY

Decolonization & Independence in Kenya 1940–93
Edited by B. A. OGOT & WILLIAM R. OCHIENG'

Penetration & Protest in Tanzania
ISARIA N. KIMAMBO

Custodians of the Land
Edited by GREGORY MADDOX, JAMES L. GIBLIN &
ISARIA N. KIMAMBO

Education in the Development of Tanzania 1919–1990
LENE BUCHERT

The Second Economy in Tanzania
T. L. MALIYAMKONO & M. S. D. BAGACHWA

Ecology Control & Economic Development in East African History
HELGE KJEKSHUS

Siaya
DAVID WILLIAM COHEN & E. S. ATIENO ODHIAMBO

Uganda Now
Changing Uganda

Developing Uganda
From Chaos to Order

Religion & Politics in East Africa
Edited by HOLGER BERNT HANSEN & MICHAEL TWADDLE

Kakungulu & the Creation of Uganda 1868–1928
MICHAEL TWADDLE

Controlling Anger
SUZETTE HEALD

Kampala Women Getting By
SANDRA WALLMAN

Slaves, Spices & Ivory in Zanzibar
ABDUL SHERIFF

Zanzibar Under Colonial Rule
Edited by ABDUL SHERIFF & ED FERGUSON

The History and Conservation of Zanzibar Stone Town
Edited by ABDUL SHERIFF

East African Expressions of Christianity
Edited by THOMAS SPEAR & ISARIA N. KIMAMBO

The Poor Are Not Us
Edited by DAVID M. ANDERSON & VIGDIS BROCH-DUE

Alice Lakwena & the Holy Spirits
HEIKE BEHREND

Property Rights & Political Development in Ethiopia & Eritrea
SANDRA FULLERTON JOIREMAN

Revolution & Religion in Ethiopia
ØYVIND M. EIDE

Empire State-Building
JOANNA LEWIS

Brothers at War
TEKESTE NEGASH & KJETIL TRONVOLL

From Guerrillas to Government★
DAVID POOL
★forthcoming

Pastimes and Politics

Culture, Community, and Identity in Post-Abolition Urban Zanzibar, 1890–1945

Laura Fair

Ohio University Press
Athens

James Currey
Oxford

Ohio University Press
Scott Quadrangle
Athens, Ohio 45701

James Currey Ltd
73 Botley Road
Oxford
OX2 0BS

Published in the United States of America by Ohio University Press, Athens, Ohio 45701

Library of Congress Cataloging-in-Publication Data

Fair, Laura.
   Pastimes and politics : culture, community, and identity in post-abolition urban Zanzibar, 1890–1945 / Laura Fair.
      p.   cm. — (Eastern African studies)
   Includes bibliographical references (p.) and index.
   ISBN 0-8214-1383-X (Ohio University Press : alk. paper) — ISBN 0-8214-1384-8 (Ohio University Press : pbk. : alk. paper)
   1. Zanzibar—Social life and customs—20th century. 2. Popular culture—Tanzania—Zanzibar.
   3. Identity (Psychology)—Tanzania—Zanzibar. 4. Group identity—Tanzania—Zanzibar.
   5. Leisure—Tanzania—Zanzibar. 6. Ethnicity—Tanzania—Zanzibar. I. Title. II. Eastern
   African studies (London, England)

   DT499.Z28 F35 2001
   967.8'103—dc21

                                                                    00-067756

British Library Cataloguing in Publication Data

Fair, Laura
   Pastimes and politics : culture, community, and identity in post-abolition urban Zanzibar, 1890–1945.—(Eastern African studies)
   1. Sociology, Urban—Zanzibar 2. Zanzibar—Social life and customs 3. Zanzibar—Social conditions—To 1964
   I. Title
   306'.096781'09041

   ISBN 0-85255-795-7 (paper)
   ISBN 0-85255-796-5 (cloth)

Chapter 2 appeared in an earlier version as "Dressing Up: Clothing, Class and Gender in Post-Abolition Zanzibar" in the *Journal of African History* 39(1). Copyright 1998 by Cambridge University Press.

Chapter 5 appeared in an earlier version as "Kickin' It: Leisure, Politics and Football in Colonial Zanzibar, 1900s–1950s" in *Africa* 67(2). Copyright 1997 by the International African Institute.

*In memory of
my grandparents,
Margaret and Richard Gall,
and my great-aunt and uncle,
Frances and Howard Gustafson,
whose fascinating and never-ending stories about the
"old days" inspired my study of the past and gave me an
appreciation for the value of oral history.*

Contents

List of Illustrations   xi

Acknowledgments   xiii

Chapter 1. Introduction   1

Zanzibar History, Slavery, and Abolition   10
Culture and Community in Urban Zanzibar   20
Ethnicity, Identity, and Belonging   28
Being and Becoming an Arab: Citizenship,
    Consumption, and Race   41
Methodology   56

Chapter 2. Dressing Up: Clothing, Class, and
Gender in Post-Abolition Zanzibar   64

Dress, Class, and Ethnicity in the
    Nineteenth Century   67
Dressing Up: New Identities and New Clothes   74
Islam, Veiling, and Respectability   85
Gender, Politics, and Cultural Change   96
Conclusion   108

Chapter 3. "The Land Is Ours! Why Should
We Pay Rent?": Land, Law, and Housing
in Colonial Ng'ambo   110

From Kiungani to Ng'ambo   113

Hut Tax, Ground Rent, and Resistance
    to World War I   129
Transformations in Urban Land Tenure and
    the Early Years of Ground Rent in Ng'ambo   133
Growing Tensions over Ground Rent   140
The Ground Rent Strike of 1928   148

Chapter 4. The Music of Siti binti Saad:
Creating Community, Crafting Identity, and
Negotiating Power through Taarab   169

Taarab and the Creation of a Zanzibari Identity   171
Background on the Band and the Role of Religion
    in Their Rise to Fame   175
The Creative Context of Siti's Songs   182
Continuity and Change in the Constellations of
    Colonial Power   185
Gender and the Colonial Courts   195
"When you wanted me I stayed with you / Now
    you do not want me I have no need for you":
    Love, Sex, and Rejection between the Wars   209
Conclusion   223

Chapter 5. Colonial Politics, Masculinity,
and Football   226

The Early Years of Football in Zanzibar   228
The Politics of Sport in Colonial Zanzibar   240
Ethnicity, Nationalism, Masculinity, and
    Community: The Multiple Meanings of
    Football in Island Life   248
Conclusion   264

Chapter 6. Conclusion   265

Notes   273
Glossary   331
Bibliography   335
Index   365

Illustrations

Figures

Fig. 1.1. Ng'ambo from Stone Town, with creek
at high tide, 1903　　21
Fig. 1.2. Stone Town from Mnazi Mmoja, with creek
at low tide, c. 1900　　23
Fig 2.1. A male Arab of Zanzibar wearing a kilemba,
kanzu, waist scarf, jambia, and short jacket　　65
Fig. 2.2. Male slaves wearing winda made of
merikani cloth　　66
Fig. 2.3. Female vibarua employed as construction workers
wearing kaniki, merikani, and early kanga designs　　67
Fig. 2.4. A suria of Seyyid Said wearing a barakoa and
shela, accompanied by a young Nyasa slave attendant
wearing merikani　　69
Fig. 2.5. Seyyida Salme Said (later known as Emily Ruete)
wearing marinda pants and a barakoa　　70
Fig. 2.6. Aziza, the niece of Governor Seyyid Suleiman　　71
Fig. 2.7. A Zanzibari Arab wearing a kilemba, joho,
and jambia　　72
Fig. 2.8. A Swahili man of Zanzibar wearing a kofia　　72
Fig. 2.9. A Swahili family from Mombasa　　73
Fig. 2.10. A Swahili woman of Zanzibar
wearing an ukaya　　73

Fig. 2.11. Swahili women wearing kangas
and grinding grain   79
Fig. 2.12. Women wearing kangas and men wearing
kanzus and kofias in Zanzibar, c. 1910   87
Fig. 2.13. Zanzibari women wearing buibuis   88
Fig. 2.14. Zanzibari women wearing buibuis in the
ghubighubi style and marinda pants   89
Fig. 2.15. Siti binti Saad   95
Fig. 2.16. Swahili woman of Zanzibar wearing a kilemba,
kanga, and marinda pants   102
Fig. 2.17. Seyyida Salme Said (later known
as Emily Ruete)   103
Fig. 2.18. Amina Seif Othman (BiAmina Mapande),
nyakanga (leader) of mkinda initiation, during a
performance of ndege   104
Fig. 3.1. A street in Ng'ambo, c. 1900   114
Fig. 3.2. Swahili women at a well   136
Fig. 3.3. Ng'ambo, c. 1920   137
Fig. 3.4. A street in Ng'ambo and a woman
wearing a kaniki   142
Fig. 5.1. Malindi Sports Club, 1950, with the Rankine Cup   227
Fig 5.2. Miembeni Sports Club, 1952, with the
Jinnah Cup and the Rankine Cup   239
Fig 5.3. African Sports Club, 1952   249
Fig. 5.4. Arab Sports Club, 1949, with the Kettles-Roy
and Zeigler Cup and the Jinnah Cup   253
Fig. 5.5. Kikwajuni Sports Club, 1943, with
the Kettles-Roy and Zeigler Cup   254

Maps
Drawn by the author
1.1. Western Indian Ocean and East African Trade Routes   11
1.2. Zanzibar and Selected Towns   12
1.3. The Growth of Urban Zanzibar   17
3.1. Nineteenth-Century Land Control and
Major Wakf Properties   119
3.2. Control of Land in Ng'ambo, c. 1928   138
3.3. Housing in Urban Zanzibar, c. 1939   151
5.1. Selected Urban Neighborhoods, c. 1940   232

Acknowledgments

The research for this work was generously funded by grants from the Joint Committee on African Studies of the Social Science Research Council and the American Council of Learned Societies, the Fulbright-Hays Doctoral Dissertation Research Program and the University of Minnesota's Frances E. Andrews-Hunt Bequest. Subsequent research was made possible by the University of Oregon's Summer Research Award, the Junior Professor Development Grant, and a fellowship awarded by the department of history, which was generously funded by one of our former history graduates, Spencer Brush. I thank the University of Oregon's Humanities Center for a fellowship which gave me time to think and write about this project during the early stages of revision, and Jim Mohr and Quintard Taylor, chairs of the department of history, who graciously agreed to reduce my teaching load slightly after the births of my children, thus providing me with critical time to concentrate on writing while my babies slept. I have been lucky to have spent the last several years surrounded by a group of warm and encouraging colleagues at the University of Oregon. They have offered not only intellectual support but friendship and many pleasant diversions.

My warmest thanks goes out to the numerous people in Zanzibar who made the research and writing of this book possible. I would especially like to thank the women and men who agreed to be interviewed for this project for their generous willingness to share their thoughts and memories of the past. Mwalim Idd, Mzee Bingwa, and Nasra Mohammed Hilal deserve to be commended for their efforts to maintain personal archival collections and for their interest in sharing their knowledge of Zanzibar's history. I wish to thank the staff at the Zanzibar National Archives for their skillful and efficient efforts in collecting, preserving, and organizing material and for their enthusiastic support and encouragement of foreign researchers. Working in the Zanzibar archives and with the archival staff has always been a rewarding and pleasurable experience.

As I sit here on a gray, wet, and gloomy Eugene afternoon I am warmed by my memories of friends and family in Zanzibar who filled my days in the isles with friendship, laughter, and light. Mwanakhamis Said Amour and Khamis Kombo welcomed me into their home and remain supportive friends. My adoptive family from the Flamingo Guest House, including Bibi Saumu and Mzee Omar Msuo, Saloum, Abdullah, Sam, Amour and Mwanaisha enriched my life in ways I cannot express. My teammates from the Women Fighters, Zanzibar's only female soccer team, continue to inspire me with their relentless dedication to the game and their continued pursuit of equality for female football enthusiasts. My friends from Women Fighters and my mothers from the taarab group Sahib el-Arry allowed me to develop a first-hand appreciation for the fun and importance of popular pastimes in urban life and to grasp the significance of the life-long friendships that can be made through such clubs. My husband's family, particularly Aunti Ajba, Bibi Saumu, Aesha and Rashid have repeatedly displayed boundless hospitality. Your kind willingness to provide housing, childcare, and moral support has allowed me to do the research I needed to complete this book. A special thanks to Amina, who provided love and gentle care for Sabri during the final stages of completing this book.

Intellectually I owe a great debt to Jan Vansina, Steven Feierman,

Allen Isaacman, Luise White, and Susan Geiger for their efforts to mold an unprepared graduate student into an historian. Allen's unyielding support and relentless encouragement saw me through many moments of doubt. Susan has always been willing to read and offer critical comments on anything I ask her to, and has provided great personal inspiration through her willingness to express ambivalence about academia and her insistence that there are often more important things in life than work. My thoughts and prayers are with her. I again thank Susan, along with Ann Waltner, MJ Maynes, Jodi Vandenberg-Daves, and Christine Walley, for urging me to recognize that universities should be places that welcome anyone with intellectual questions or the desire to learn and not simply sites for the perpetuation of privilege. Luise White has been an engaged and supportive mentor from beginning to end and has consistently offered the kind of critical advice and backing that one can only expect from the best of friends.

I first met Garth Myers, Christine Walley, Bill Bissell, and Gary Burgess while doing research in Zanzibar and each of them has repeatedly offered insights and suggestions that have made this a better book. I thank them, as well as Sheryl McCurdy and Kelly Askew, for their critical reading of my dissertation and earlier versions of parts of the book, and for their supportive friendship over the years. Asanteni sana. I also wish to thank Charles Ambler, Jonathon Glassman, Phyllis Martin, as well as several of my colleagues at the University of Oregon, including Jeff Hanes, Bryna Goodman, Michael Pebworth, and Barbara Pope, for their willingness to read and offer comments on drafts of various chapters. The criticisms and suggestions offered by the anonymous readers for Ohio University Press and Cambridge University Press also forced me to sharpen my arguments, refine my language, and pull the pieces together in ways that I couldn't have done without their help. (Muchai) Misheck Mureithi helped me create the maps.

Gillian Berchowitz has been the best editor an author could possibly have. From the beginning she has been not only interested in this book, but also supportive, honest, and determined to keep things moving along. The production staffs at Ohio University and James

Currey have also been impressive and a pleasure to work with. A special note of thanks to Nancy Basmajian and Bob Furnish for their very thorough copyediting.

And to my two sons, Nassir and Sabri, who have infused my life with laughter and play and who continuously remind me what a joy it is to be living.

Pastimes and Politics

Chapter 1

Introduction

In March 1928 a Zanzibari woman by the name of Siti binti Saad traveled with her *taarab* band to Bombay, where they became the first East Africans to have their voices and music recorded on gramophone disc. Siti's popularity as a local performer had been increasing steadily for well over a decade as she grew from a casual performer of quaint colloquial tunes to an accomplished vocalist and reciter of the Qur'an, ultimately becoming the most widely praised and revered taarab performer in coastal history. The music of Siti binti Saad's band, based on a Swahili tradition of *shairi* poetry[1] combined with new musical and linguistic innovations, was in wide demand. The band performed from the inner rooms of the sultan of Zanzibar's palace—where they were introduced to the HMV (His Master's Voice) agent responsible for arranging the recording session in Bombay—to the neighborhoods of the isles' urban poor, where they were applauded for their ability to transform local debates about class, gender, and political inequality into poetic verse and song. The recorded version of the band's music was equally popular. Over the course of three sessions, Siti and her band recorded and released some one hundred songs with the Bombay branch of HMV, which were major hits back home, selling nearly 72,000 copies by 1931.[2]

Siti's recordings marked a breakthrough not only for industry executives anxiously searching for new markets, but also for coastal East Africans looking for cultural affirmation in an era of colonial hegemony. Prior to the release of Siti's 1928 recordings, the only gramophone discs available in East Africa were in the languages of the colonies' economic and political overlords: English, Arabic, Hindi, and Gujarati. According to both island residents and company executives, Siti's records served to elevate the social and cultural position of Kiswahili speakers and affirm their status among the "civilized" and "modern" peoples of the world. A contemporary of African-American blues legends Bessie Smith and Ma Rainey, who were also among the first blacks to have their work produced commercially in North America, Siti binti Saad has been heralded for her ability to open up a space within a commercial culture industry that had previously been content to largely ignore people of African descent. Seventy years after her recordings were first released, it is still difficult to find anyone in coastal East Africa who does not recognize her name. Like Smith and Rainey, Siti's lyrics offered a view of contemporary life from a distinctively working-class, female perspective, yet unlike Smith and Rainey her music was also widely respected among the dominant members of Swahili society, making her legacy much more akin to that of Billie Holiday or Duke Ellington than any of the classic blues singers. Her success as a recording artist, combined with the deep and profound mark she left on East African music culture, has led her to be memorialized by generations of East Africans as "giving voice to the voiceless."[3] Her voice is in fact one of the only Swahili voices recorded from this era; with the onset of the depression, all the major recording companies pulled out of East Africa and most did not return until well after World War II.[4] Nonetheless, Siti's recordings made it possible for Swahili music and poetry to be heard not only domestically but internationally for the first time. Sold from the Swahili coast to up-country Tanganyika, Kenya, the Belgian Congo, and throughout the Indian Ocean, Siti's records also helped to temporarily renew Zanzibar's waning position as the cultural capital of East Africa. According to one of her contemporaries, these recorded songs gave new and decidedly modern meaning to the old saying, "When the pipes play in Zanzibar, they dance on the lakes."[5]

This phrase was first coined in reference to Zanzibar's position as the finance and market center of the East African slave trade. Its application to Siti's success is highly ironic, as Siti's ancestors were themselves forcibly brought to the isles in the preceding century as slaves. Unlike the majority of famed Swahili-language poets, descended from learned Islamic scholars or urban families that ranked among the most economic and socially prestigious on the coast,[6] the woman who created this treasure of songs was born into a family of poor, servile farmers from Zanzibar's countryside. After the abolition of slavery, in 1897, Siti binti Saad joined Zanzibar's version of the Great Migration from the countryside to the city—searching for economic opportunity as well as new possibilities for social and personal autonomy in the post-abolition era. While few urban migrants achieved the economic and social success of Siti, for many of her contemporaries, her life story served as a poignantly powerful example of the transformative potential of the era. Here was a poor woman who had risen above her servile beginnings to become the most acclaimed musician in Swahili history. Here was the daughter of rural slaves being received, both locally and internationally, as the cultural icon of Swahili civilization. Members of the coastal elite, from Ali bin Salim in Mombasa to patricians in Pangani and Seyyid Khalifa, the sultan of Zanzibar, regularly hired Siti and her band as the star performers at their families' weddings and celebrations.[7] Although dominant coastal ideologies continued to deny the cultural and intellectual contributions of "women, slaves and foreigners" to high Swahili society, Siti's recordings and widespread popularity among all classes of coastal people were living proof of the significant impact women and persons of low birth had in shaping the very core of coastal culture.[8]

Siti's life history and her musical career highlight several of the themes that are at the core of this book: the often dramatic transformations in personal identities that were negotiated in post-abolition island society, as well as the importance of popular culture as a central stage on which these new identities were played out before a range of diverse audiences. One of the goals of this book is to illustrate the numerous ways in which marginal members of society actualized emancipation at both the ideological and practical levels, as well as the ways that new identities were performed and contested in the course of daily urban life.

The public performance of poetic verse served as an important venue for Siti to display the rich contributions that descendants of African slaves could make to coastal culture, yet poetry and song were also used to deride her growing stature, and by extension that of all newcomers, to the "civilized" ranks of urban coastal society. Public debates of personal status and respectability had a long history within Swahili communities of being verbalized through dialogic poetry exchanges or through the performance of verse in the course of larger drum and dance performances known as *ngoma*. It was as a performer of such verse that Siti binti Saad first became known in Zanzibar Town and it is perhaps not surprising that the circulation of such verse also served as one of the principal means of contesting Siti's newly acquired status among the cultural elite of Zanzibar. Although none of Siti's numerous biographers identify either the composer or performers of the following songs, they have become a cornerstone of Siti binti Saad narratives. They are used by some to illustrate the importance of moral fortitude, perseverance, and wit for the attainment of success, while other authors use them to illustrate the pervasiveness of *choyo* (avarice) and *wivu* (envy) in Swahili society. What these songs also illustrate is the difficulty that many early-twentieth-century urban migrants had in distancing themselves from their heritage as slaves. As this book will illustrate, the islands' underclass seized the limited, but important, opportunities available in this period of transformation from a political economy based in plantation slavery to one dominated by colonial capitalism to improve their class and status positions. Nonetheless, institutions and individuals that benefited from keeping upstarts like Siti "in their place" continued to hold great institutional as well as discursive power. As the following songs suggest, becoming a respected "someone" was no simple task.[9]

Siti binti Saadi
Ulikuwa mtu lini?
Ulitoka shamba
Na kaniki mbili chini.
Kama si sauti
Ungekula nini?

∎

Siti binti Saad,
When did you become someone?
You came from the countryside
Wearing only the cloth of slaves [*kaniki*].[10]
If it wasn't for your voice,
What would you be eating?

Another tune that circulated as a critique of Siti again drew attention to her slave origins as well as her African physical features—traits that were valued negatively by the dominant coastal elite.

Jakazi jeusi halina maana
Mchache wa nyusi hata kope hana
Hakika nuhusi kasuhubiana.

∎

A black female slave has no meaning.
She has few eyebrows and no eyelashes.
It is certainly bad luck to make friends with her.

As urban legend would have it, Siti was traumatized by these songs, yet with the support and encouragement of her fellow performers and friends in town she composed a song in response to her detractors. Although this mockery of Siti's poverty and origins was intended to undermine her growing popularity, it allegedly produced the opposite effect, spreading knowledge of her presence in town as well as her skill as a dialogic poet who could debate through verse. Her willingness to engage and challenge these discourses of subordination no doubt also earned her numerous fans among the thousands of other former slaves living in Zanzibar, who were presumably subjected to similar torments. Siti responded to her detractors in the course of her next public performance, allegedly drawing scores of potential new fans to her show to hear her sing the following song.[11]

Si hoja uzuri
Na sura jamali,
Kuwa mtukufu
Na jadi kubeli,
Hasara ya mtu
Kukosa akili.

∎

It is not good enough
To appear gracious,
To be an exalted person
With a noted genealogy,
The true deprivation of a person
Is to be without intelligence.

The lyrics in this competitive song exchange suggest that despite the growing affluence and independence of the formerly servile, issues of pedigree, property, and intellectual accomplishment, three of the cornerstones of Swahili "civilization," remained central to contestations over social status. Siti's adversaries questioned her very identity as a "someone," reminding all who heard or repeated these songs that she was, in reality, only a poor servile woman with no wealth beyond that provided by daily labor. On the other hand, in her response to her tempters Siti questioned the very basis of dominant coastal ideology which granted authority and power to individuals from certain families, particularly those with social, economic, and religious ties to the Arabian peninsula, regardless of personal integrity or capabilities. Siti may have been the subject of these particular songs but the resonance of their lyrics and tunes within the hearts and minds of her contemporaries suggest that this competitive verse exchange reflected much wider debates over the nature of status and the means by which it was achieved that were taking place in urban Zanzibar during the early decades of the twentieth century.

The importance of *earning* the respect of the community would become a hallmark refrain of many of Siti's songs. While those taking advantage of new opportunities lauded the importance of cleverness (*ujanja*), wit (*akili*), and perseverance (*uvumilivu*) for success, many established island residents, as well as the new British colonial authorities, continued to place excessive weight on the importance of old money and blue blood for social status and political power. In one of the songs performed by Siti's band, "The Poem of What Poverty Does," the band once again gives poetic form to the notion that personal skill, integrity, and piety should be weighed much more heavily than inherited status when evaluating an individual's worth. The band calls upon its listeners to grant respect to those who have earned it through their deeds, and chastises the still prevalent habit of treating adults like children or ignoring their thoughts as though they were those of an animal, simply because they were born poor and servile.

Hufanyani la kufanya akapendeza fakiri
Machoni akalingana kwa mfano wa tajiri
Hayana jihad hayana nimekwisha takibiri.

Ufakiri ni dhaifu mfano wake kama nasi
Japo uwe mtukufu uwake kama johari
Lazima hufanywa dufu huwi katika shauri.

Ufakiri kama kiza na kiza hakina nuru
Jamii hukufukuza na uwe mtu fakiri
Huna litalopendeza kwa saghiri na kabiri.

Na akili halingani sawa na mwenye kururi
Zaliwa bitakweni safi minal kadiri
Watu hukufanya nyani aula hinziri.

Ufakiri jambo zito aliloumba Kakhari
Mkubwa huwa mtoto na rijali huwa thori
Usemalo kama ndoto mwema hufanya ayari.

Tajiri ahalii makadirie pasipo mtu kusema.

∎

There is nothing you can do to make a poor person look good
If you compare him/her with the example of someone who is
    rich.
There is no struggle that can overcome it, I have finished,
    God is great.

Poverty is powerlessness, its example is like a reed.
Even if you should become an honored person and you shine
    like a jewel,
You are always treated as dumb and useless, you are never
    consulted.

Poverty is like darkness and darkness has no light.
Society will disregard you as if you were a beggar;
You have nothing that will please the young or the old.

Your intelligence does not compare to someone with money
Born with more good manners than wealth and power,
You will always be treated like a baboon, or worse, like a
    female slave.

Poverty is a heavy thing, the one who created it Confusion.
An adult is always considered a child, and the manliest of
    men a mere animal.
Your words are treated like a dream, an honest person is
    always made out to be a rogue.

A rich person is always among those who are counted
    without even having to speak.

Siti and her band were keenly aware of how deeply the roots that
gave preference to the elite extended into coastal culture, but through
their music they urged the need for change. Like their friends and
neighbors involved in the rent strike of 1928 (see chapter 3), the band
members questioned the justice of a political system that ignored the
thoughts and concerns of poor tenants, but seemed to grant a willing
ear to the voices of wealthy landlords. Many things were in flux during
the first decades of the twentieth century, but there were other things
that were simply not changing quick enough from the perspective of
former slaves. Many poor women and men obviously objected to being
treated like animals and having their ideas disregarded, while the rich
remained among those whose thoughts and concerns "counted," without even having to speak.

Leisure and popular culture, including taarab, were extremely
important vehicles through which the poor and working-class members of urban society engaged each other, urban patricians, and their
new colonial masters in debates to define the social, economic, and political principles around which twentieth-century island society
should be built. Although the majority of those who lived in urban
Zanzibar were excluded from formal participation in the political institutions of the colonial state, they were nonetheless actively involved

in formulating the debates that constituted civil society. Though institutionally feeble, the poor of urban Zanzibar used "the weapons of the weak" to affect social change.[12] Attempts to ascertain the economic, political, and social goals of the islands' underclass were rarely undertaken by members of the new colonial administration. Yet Siti and her contemporaries used the media over which they had control to make their voices heard. Whether performing for the sultan and the British resident or the urban poor among whom they lived, Siti's band members used their music to offer trenchant critiques of the economic, social, and gender inequalities that framed island life and to protest their further institutionalization through British administrative policy and colonial law. In addition to critiquing the status quo, they also used the space provided by popular pastimes to articulate alternative visions of the new society they hoped to build.

Pastimes and politics were not discrete categories of experience in the lives of Siti's contemporaries; they were intimately connected. In providing a social history of this urban community, one of my goals is to integrate "traditional" historical accounts of changes in social status, economic patterns, and colonial politics with a less traditional examination of changes in dance, music, fashion, and sport. Although explorations of these two sets of issues and practices tend to be treated separately in the historiography, they were deeply intertwined in lives of the women and men who made the islands' history during these years. In some ways chapter 3, which documents transformations in urban land tenure and the resistance of the urban poor to the imposition of ground rents, appears not to fit, sandwiched between a chapter that focuses on changes in fashion after abolition and one that analyzes the lyrics and performance contexts of the taarab songs performed by Siti binti Saad's band. But this organizational strategy reflects both a subtle chronological development that evolves throughout the book and the need to recognize that cultural and material issues were deeply intertwined. Siti and her contemporaries strove to assert and secure a place within the complex social cartography of urban Zanzibar in numerous and varied ways. And all these things took place in the space that was Zanzibar Town. The men and women who asserted their place within cultural space by donning previously forbidden clothing and transforming taarab were the same men and women who boycotted landlords' demands for ground rent and broke neighbors out of colonial courts and jails in an effort to protect their access to physical space within the town. By integrating a political and economic history of the islands with social and cultural history I have attempted to highlight the various issues that occupied people's attention during the 1910s, 1920s, and 1930s and to illustrate the numerous ways that leisure and political economy informed each other.

Zanzibar History, Slavery, and Abolition

Like the numerous other Swahili settlements located along the East African coast, the group of islands commonly known as Zanzibar (including Unguja, Pemba, and Tumbatu) were widely known throughout the ancient and medieval worlds due to the involvement of their inhabitants in international trade, linking the peoples and products of the African interior with markets and goods from the Red Sea, Persian Gulf, and wider Indian Ocean world. East African merchants and the ruling classes of Swahili towns maintained centuries of close commercial and extended familial ties with maritime traders from Oman and others in the Persian Gulf, whose ports occupied a central position within the monsoon-powered trade routes of the Indian Ocean.[13] In the mid-seventeenth century, the Omanis came to play an increasingly significant role in the political, economic, and military situation along the coast. Beginning in the 1650s, political and mercantile leaders from various Swahili towns began enlisting Omani naval support to defeat the Portuguese, who had maintained military garrisons, demanded taxes, and generally disrupted a once lucrative trade along the coast for more than a century. Once the Portuguese were defeated by the combined Swahili-Omani forces, however, the leadership in many of the Swahili towns became reluctant to accept Omani overlordship and a further series of uprisings aimed at asserting Swahili autonomy began.[14] Unable to defeat the commercially im-

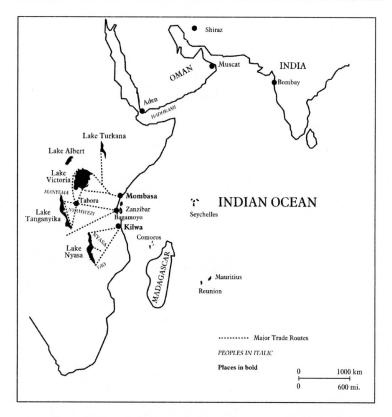

Map 1.1. *Western Indian Ocean and East African Trade Routes*

portant centers of eighteenth-century trade in Mombasa and the
Lamu archipelago, the Omanis located the base of their East African
operations in Zanzibar, on the island of Unguja. Zanzibar was favored because of its deep and protected ports, its ideal position within
the monsoon trade patterns, as well as its relatively weak ruling dynasty and small indigenous population.

From their base in Zanzibar the al-Busaidi ruling family of
Oman gradually extended their trading empire, over the course of
nearly a century, redirecting the bulk of East African trade through
the island. Other ports continued to trade, but the al-Busaidis' military, commercial, and diplomatic strength allowed them to claim
annual payments of customs duties from rival Swahili towns that

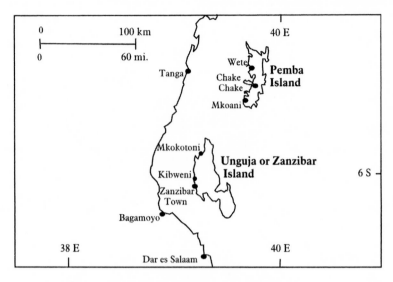

Map 1.2. *Zanzibar and Selected Towns*

were eventually required to accept Omani suzerainty. This process of commercial centralization was exacerbated in the 1830s, after the reigning sultan of Oman, Seyyid Said bin Sultan al-Busaidi, decided to move his capital to Zanzibar. The commercial and political importance of Zanzibar to Indian Ocean trade expanded dramatically after this move. Caravans financed and directed from Zanzibar became the principal sources of ivory and slaves for the world market, as well as the primary avenues through which East Africans gained access to European-, American-, and Indian-made cotton goods and other trade items.[15] By the mid-nineteenth century these tiny islands off the East African coast had earned a worldwide reputation as the trading entrepôt linking East African producers of ivory and slaves with a bullish international market. As of 1859, more than four million dollars worth of goods were being traded through the port at Zanzibar annually.[16] Slaves, and the profits derived from both their sale and their labor, were at the very heart of Zanzibar's transformation from a small and relatively unimportant Swahili town to the center of a vast trading empire stretching from central Africa halfway around the globe.

The rapid expansion of trade in Zanzibar during the early nineteenth century resulted in the booming growth of a new urban town as merchants, traders, diplomats, artisans, sailors, porters, and a vast population of slaves flocked to what became known as Zanzibar Town. An area that had been occupied primarily by a small fishing village in the eighteenth century became the home of an estimated 10,000 people by 1830, 50,000 people by mid-century, and somewhere between 70,000 and 80,000 inhabitants by the 1870s.[17] As economic opportunities expanded after the 1830s, increasing numbers of immigrants from across the Indian Ocean opted to make Zanzibar their permanent home. Arab traders who accumulated capital from caravans and commerce diversified their holdings and began investing in plantation agriculture, including clove and coconut plantations on Zanzibar's two largest islands, Unguja and Pemba. The number of Omanis settled in Zanzibar, the majority of whom were involved in plantation agriculture, grew from an estimated 1,000 in 1819 to 5,000 by the 1840s. South Asians, who dominated the commercial sector of the economy by mid-century, also began to settle permanently in Zanzibar. Their numbers grew from a mere 200 in 1819 to 3,000 by the 1870s.[18] Swahili immigrants from the mainland coast, Hadhramis from present-day Yemen, and others from the Comoro Islands and Madagascar also moved to Zanzibar in large numbers, in hopes of striking it rich in this rapidly expanding commercial center. The largest segment of the island's urban and rural population, however, were slaves captured from the East African mainland.[19] On the eve of the twentieth century, some three-fourths of the Zanzibar Protectorate's estimated population were either slaves or recently manumitted slaves.[20] Brought to the isles during the height of East Africa's involvement in the international slave trade, these men, women, and children transformed the forest- and scrub-covered coral islands of Unguja and Pemba into the most productive clove plantations in the world.

As the nineteenth century drew to a close, however, the political economy of the isles began to undergo a series of rather dramatic transformations. In 1890, Zanzibar became an official protectorate of the British Empire, meaning that the reigning sultan of Zanzibar retained his power as the figurative political head of the protectorate, but in practical terms the status of the protectorate was little different from that of a colony. The real power governing the isles was located in the hands of British members of the Foreign and (later) Colonial Offices. Seven years later, in 1897, the British forced the enactment of an abolition decree, proclaiming the legal, but not necessarily economic or social freedom of slaves.[21] The impact of the abolition decree was at first fairly imperceptible. Slaves were not summarily granted their freedom, but were required to apply for it in court, where they had to prove that they had not only a place to live, but a means of earning a living as well. Caustic vagrancy laws were drafted and imposed at the same time as the abolition decree, with the aim of preventing slaves from confusing *freedom* with freedom from work. Only some ten percent of island slaves went to court to claim their freedom papers, yet many others utilized the option to strengthen their bargaining position vis-a-vis owners. Within a year of the decree, British administrators were already complaining, "The masters have no power now and the slaves know it and act accordingly."[22] Although the decrees marking the inauguration of the protectorate and the abolition of slavery can be precisely dated, the establishment of colonial control and the emancipation of former slaves were not events, but rather elaborate, drawn-out, and often contradictory processes. This book examines these processes as they were played out in Zanzibar Town, focusing in particular on the ways in which colonialism and abolition influenced and were in turn influenced by the goals and actions of several generations of former slaves who were at the core of a growing urban population.

One of the central concerns driving the early chapters of this book is an exploration of the myriad processes and practices of individual and societal transformation encapsulated in the terms *abolition* and *emancipation*. As Frederick Cooper's landmark book *From Slaves to Squatters* illustrated some twenty years ago, contestations over labor and economic power were central to these processes. Yet much more ephemeral and much less easily quantifiable struggles to enhance personal autonomy, improve one's social status, and gain the respect of the community were no less important to slaves and their descendants in the decades following abolition. It is by elaborating on the varied ways in which the men and women of Zanzibar sought to actualize their desires for autonomy, status, and respect in the course of daily practice that this study makes its greatest contribution to the existing literature on emancipation in Africa.[23] What clothes one chose to wear, how one expressed religious devotion, whether one spent one's leisure time dancing in public, playing football in the streets, or exchanging news with friends and neighbors in private, who one slept with as well as where one slept—these basic choices of daily life played a critical role in framing the day-to-day definitions of emancipation. The new forms of popular music, religious ritual, and fashion created in the early twentieth century were not mere idle pastimes, but central components of the process of producing new kinds of self and collectivity, as well as new images of individual and collective identity.[24]

This study illustrates the numerous and manifold changes which took place in urban life from 1890 to World War II as former slaves, their children, and a host of other recent immigrants to the town fought to establish an urban community that recognized and respected their rights in and contributions to society.[25] The turn of the century was a time of immense social, economic, and political flux in the isles. Former slaves, as much as any other social group, played a major role in forging the shape of these new relationships. Although similar processes were at work throughout the Swahili coast, one of the things that makes Zanzibar unique is the fact that, compared to Lamu or Mombasa, it was a relatively new urban settlement. The social "rules" were generally similar to those in operation elsewhere along the coast, but the century from 1830 to 1930 witnessed the complete transformation of island society, so that the "rules" were not nearly as rigid as they were in more established Swahili settlements, perhaps giving slaves more freedom to move than elsewhere on the coast.

During the first three decades of the twentieth century the size of Zanzibar's working-class quarter, generally referred to as Ng'ambo, more than doubled, as tens of thousands of slaves left their owners' plantations and moved to the city in search of new economic opportunities and a place to make a new start in life. By 1931, some forty-five thousand people, or one-third of Unguja's total population, lived in town, with roughly half of those living in Ng'ambo.[26] The men and women who migrated to town joined the existing Ng'ambo community, comprised of former urban slaves, boathands, fishermen, traders, and laborers, from the isles and across the Indian Ocean, and together they created a vibrant, exciting, and transformative urban culture. Through music, dance, football (soccer), and other popular pastimes, these men and women forged a social community from a mélange of immigrants and in the process redefined both themselves and Zanzibar as a whole.

Part of the attraction of moving to the city was the ancient association in Swahili culture between urbanity and civilization. It was inside the numerous Swahili towns which ran up and down the East African coast that the families of wealthy traders and planters patronized the schools of Islamic scholarship, poets, musicians, and splendors of urban life which distinguished the *mwungwana*—freeborn, well-bred, Muslim patrician—from the *mshenzi*—non-Muslim, rural, or slave. In reality the divisions between town and countryside, civilization and savagery were rarely so stark, yet discourses which equated urbanity and civilization were nonetheless a cornerstone of patrician Swahili ideologies.[27] The favored domestic slaves of urban patricians also promoted aspects of this ideology. As one knowledgeable, nineteenth-century European resident noted, town slaves "look down on their country cousins and consider themselves a superior class."[28] In many ways they were a superior class, as they often enjoyed economic and social opportunities that were unavailable to plantation slaves.[29] Urban slaves, particularly those who served the wealthiest members of Swahili society, were encouraged to partake in the joys of urban living, though sometimes only vicariously. Slave women and girls delivered greetings to the friends of their mistresses, who were often confined to home during the day as a result of domestic obligations or a combination of class and religious prescriptions which required elite women to observe *purdah* during the daylight hours.[30] Slave messengers often spent hours in the homes of their owner's friends soaking up news and information which they would

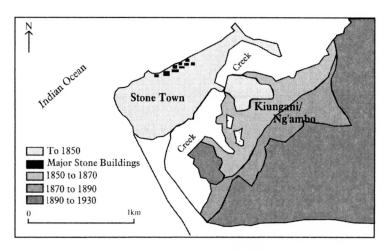

Map 1.3. *The Growth of Urban Zanzibar*

report back home, while simultaneously developing their own social and economic networks among other domestic slaves. In some instances favored domestic slaves were also encouraged to participate in religious rituals, musical performances, or dances sponsored by their owners, though slaves' participation in such events typically served to reify rather than eliminate hierarchy by placing slaves in subordinate positions within the ritual or dance.[31] Trusted male slaves participated in these cultural events as well, while they also often served as the business envoys and emissaries of their owners. Elite women, in particular, often relied on trusted and experienced male slaves to carry out business and personal missions which they did not want to trust to male family members and could not conduct themselves because such matters were concluded within spaces deemed inappropriate for women of status.[32] The economic and social opportunities available in town also expanded somewhat in the early twentieth century as a result of colonial schemes to expand the port and other facilities which in turn provided new options for waged work to urban men. After abolition many slaves moved to the city in hopes of integrating themselves into these networks, which afforded their city cousins certain social options and economic opportunities unavailable in the countryside.

By the early years of the twentieth century, as former slaves pushed for further integration into urban society, they began to reformulate urban popular culture in ways that granted them a more central place in performance. Expanding the boundaries of belonging within the community of Islam was one of their central concerns during this era. While the majority of coastal slaves were already Muslims, they strove to reform a variety of cultural and ritual practices in ways that made pious living a more important evaluative criterion of a "good" Muslim than scholarly achievement. Servile women also introduced reforms in coastal Islamic practices that served to undermine the alleged superiority of free women. In the nineteenth century slave women were forbidden from veiling, but during the 1910s distinctive new forms of female dress (ch. 2) were created that literally veiled slave bodies in a cloth of Islamic respectability. Elderly women explained the widespread adoption of the now ubiquitous *buibui* veil during these years as a sign of slave women's growing knowledge of Islam as well as a symbol of their spiritual equality with patrician women, who had always covered their bodies entirely while in public. The veil was seized by formerly servile women as one very visible sign of their new identities as socially autonomous, adult Muslim females. The widespread adoption of the buibui was one component of new definitions of femininity that were developed during these years. As one woman remarked about her own decision to wear the buibui during these years, "If I went out naked [*uchi*, without a buibui] people would say, 'She is not a woman, that one.' " Unlike her mother, who was prohibited from veiling by her owners, Bibi Adija said that by the 1910s, "you could dress like a lady, a truly respectable woman ... No one [i.e., an owner] could stop you."[33] Earlier cultural practices that attempted to distinguish "respectable" patrician women from allegedly sexually promiscuous slaves also began to disintegrate during these years. By the turn of the century there were hundreds if not thousands of urban women who were either slave concubines (*masuria/ suria*) of patrician men or children born of such unions. Having lived at the margins of a nebulous line dividing patrician and slave culture, they were at the forefront of helping to create a new form of female initiation, known as *mkinda*, which urban patrician, free, manumitted, and slave women participated in together. This form of initiation was known by the dances *kunguiya* and *ndege*, which incorporated the joys and sexual lessons of slave puberty initiation ceremonies with the pomp and piety of elite dance culture.[34]

New forms of Islamic ritual and devotional practice, such as *tariqa*, or Sufi brotherhoods, also became widely popular among former slaves who sought to move from the margins to the center of the islands' religious community.[35] The tariqa (literally, the path or the way [leading to communication with God]; also, faith, creed) represents a mystical tradition in Sunni Islam. Drawing on the mystical experiences of the Prophet Muhammad, Sufis encourage their followers to practice ascetic devotion and intense spiritual concentration, believing that such practices, combined with pious living, can lead to direct communication with God. By as early as the third century after the death of the Prophet Muhammad (roughly A.D. 900), Sufi orders had spread widely throughout the Muslim world, bringing the poor and nonliterate into the fold of Islam and earning Sufism its reputation as the religion of the masses. When the brotherhoods began organizing in Zanzibar their messages of piety, frugality, and equality found a willing ear among the islands' large slave and immigrant populations.[36] Sufism's tolerance of local custom also appealed to nonliterate and poor coastal Muslims. The religious brotherhoods incorporated elements of African religious ritual, including the use of drums and Kiswahili, making tariqa a more attractive ritual experience for the islands' African populations. Unlike more orthodox religious traditions, many religious brotherhoods based in Zanzibar also allowed for female participation in public ritual. Furthermore, Africans, former slaves, and women were allowed to seek leadership positions within the brotherhoods, a form of status and authority unavailable within earlier orthodox institutions.[37] The broadening of Islamic ritual to include former slaves and women had become so commonplace by the 1910s that formerly servile women, like Siti binti Saad, were able to earn a reputation as well as a living performing Qur'anic cantellations and *maulid* religious poems not only for the poor in Ng'ambo but for the island's patrician families as well. The new forms of religious ritual that were created during this era transformed many aspects of Islamic practice in Zanzibar while simultaneously creating new spaces and opportunities for the formation of community.[38]

Culture and Community in Urban Zanzibar

At its most basic level the Ng'ambo "community" was defined by physical geography; Ng'ambo (literally, the other or opposite side) was the quarter of town located on the eastern side of a tidal creek, opposite the "center" of town, known as Stone Town. There were extensive gradations of relative wealth and poverty on both sides of the creek, gradations that meant a lot to those who knew how to read them, but there was a distinct tendency for the wealthiest urbanites to live in Stone Town and for the poorest to live in Ng'ambo.[39] The cultural heterogeneity of the urban population, the majority of whom were first- or second-generation immigrants, meant that there was not always or necessarily a uniformity of vision and purpose which enveloped either half of town. Class, cultural, language-, and gender-based differences could just as easily lead to conflicts between neighbors as unity among them. Neighborhood-based rivalries were also as endemic in Zanzibar as in any other coastal Swahili town. Shared feelings of belonging, beliefs, and behaviors did not emerge naturally among those who found themselves living on either side of the creek. Community, as an affective unit, required not only imagining but work; community had to be created and re-created on a continuous basis.[40] Daily, face-to-face contact between residents, in their neighborhoods *(mitaa)*, during the course of work, or at places of worship was an essential component of this process of crafting social community. The numerous social and cultural clubs that criss-crossed urban Zanzibar were also central to the generation of shared feelings of belonging, ties of support, and perceptions of commonality that grew among established residents and immigrants to town.

Group membership and perceptions of community also changed dramatically over time. In the late nineteenth and early twentieth centuries, kinship and patron-client ties were often the nodes around which community was built, and dance groups, football clubs, and religious associations often drew their members from both sides of the creek, thereby creating competitive rivals among neighbors in Ng'ambo. However, as the twentieth century progressed and the political economy of the isles continued to change, class and ethnicity came to be perceived as increasingly important in defining community. It is not that patronage networks necessarily came to play any less significant role, but that ethnic associations, work gangs, football clubs, and eventually political parties came to assume the role of patron, helping men, in particular, find their ways about the town.[41] In the course of the colonial era the economic and political divisions between Stone Town and Ng'ambo were reified, and by the 1930s men and women became less and less interested in "crossing-over" to participate in cultural groups or political associations that spanned the creek. Although a few performers, like Siti binti Saad, could still play to both sides, football clubs and dance associations that incorporated members from Stone Town as well as Ng'ambo became increasingly rare. New clubs, such as African Sports, Arab Sports, or PWD (the Public Works Department), grew in

Fig. 1.1. *Ng'ambo from Stone Town, with creek at high tide, 1903. Courtesy of Zanzibar National Archives.*

importance as class and ethnicity became increasingly salient elements of people's twentieth-century social identities.

Whereas late-nineteenth and early-twentieth-century Ng'ambo residents were often divided among themselves as a result of their allegiance to competing leisure and devotional groups or their ties to the Stone Town patrons on whose land they lived, the unanimity of action displayed during the ground rent strike of 1928 (discussed in ch. 3) suggests that by the late 1920s the women and men of Ng'ambo had grown to perceive themselves as members of a unified class—at least when defined in opposition to ground landlords and the colonial state. In the course of the 1928 strike, Ng'ambo tenants not only boycotted the demands of avaricious landlords for ever-increasing rents, they also broke friends and neighbors out of colonial courts and jails after they were convicted for refusing to abide by court-enforced eviction orders. This strike, which involved thousands of Ng'ambo tenants, was an exceptional event in the generally peaceful history of colonial Zanzibar, yet these attacks on landlords, courts, and jails illustrate the lengths to which Ng'ambo residents would go to defend their rights to live in the city. The near unanimous adherence to the call to strike also suggests that this hodgepodge of urban immigrants, many of whom had moved to the city in the period following abolition, had managed to create a fairly cohesive community by the late 1920s; a community that could be mobilized to protect a core set of economic and political principles. This study does not take community as a given, but aims to illustrate how a variety of social, cultural, and political practices were mobilized in urban Zanzibar to foster shared visions of communal identities, albeit identities that were always shifting, sometimes in conflict, and that changed dramatically over the decades.

The forms of leisure and popular culture that were created in town during this era were extremely important vehicles through which the members of urban society debated and defined their communities. Membership in one or more of the numerous music and dance societies (ngoma troops) that permeated urban life was key to integrating oneself into the social and political networks that defined urban society. Music was a vital part of urban communal life. Archival records and

Fig. 1.2. *Stone Town from Mnazi Mmoja, with creek at low tide, c. 1900. Anglican Church of Christ Cathedral, built on top of the former slave market, is in center of photo. Courtesy of Zanzibar National Archives.*

conversations with women and men who spent their youths in Ng'ambo create the impression that participating in the nightly dances that pervaded Ng'ambo was one of the great joys of urban living. As Salum Baraka recalled of his youth, "I lived here in [the neighborhood of] Miembeni and everywhere, everywhere there were ngoma!"[42] Nunu binti Salum had similar memories of her youth: "Life was good, we were young, and every night we danced!"[43] Archival records suggest that nearly every night someone danced. In 1931, for instance, there were 2,450 licensed ngoma, or roughly seven different ngoma each night in urban Zanzibar.[44] Many elders wistfully recalled the fun of their youths; following the performances of their favorite bands, hopping from party to party several nights a week, and in the process making friends and meeting lovers from neighborhoods across the town.

Football (soccer), discussed in chapter 5, was one leisure pursuit that became extremely popular among urban men in the years following World War I. While the form of football was new to the isles, having been introduced at the beginning of the twentieth century by missionaries and other employees of the empire, it quickly grew to become one of the premier pastimes of urban men. By the late 1920s, key matches drew over 10,000 spectators. Football resonated with the aesthetics of indigenous ngoma, providing the opportunity for individuals to display their virtuoso skills before a crowd of spectators while simultaneously supplying a ritualized space for the public display and dispute of social cleavages. Ngoma and football were leisure activities that allowed urban residents to really enjoy themselves, while at the same time making connections and establishing networks that could help in finding a job, marketing one's produce, or negotiating marriage for one's child. Playing football was not simply a passing diversion for urban youth, but a passionate part of becoming an adult male in Zanzibar society. The friendships men made through these teams lasted a lifetime. Sponsors, siblings, mothers, friends, and fans were also integrated into the lifelong networks that grew out of urban football clubs. Conversations between club members and fans held during practices, after games, or while relaxing in their neighborhoods at night also played a crucial role in creating bonds of community.

The music of Siti binti Saad (ch. 4) illustrates the importance of talk, as well as leisure, in helping to formulate discourses of social and political values among community members. Gossip *(udaku)* and rumor *(uvumi)* have long occupied a central place in Swahili society and Siti's band drew on these traditions as it crafted its performance style. Gossip—about civil servants caught stealing money, husbands neglecting their wives, unfaithful lovers, and a host of other timely scandals—provided the core material for much of the band's music. In one of Siti's songs, *Ukisemwa* (If people tell malicious tales about you), the power of gossip to mold social behavior was commemorated. A key verse of the song portrays an individual who is so embarrassed by local gossip that she hates to even leave the house.

> Nimechoka kuzikwa ningali hai
> Wenzangu wananisema kwa jirani sitembei
> Ningeona ajabu komba kuwacha papai.
>   Kibwagizo: Kuwacha papai, kuwacha papai . . .

∎

I am tired of being buried, even though I am still alive.
People are telling malicious tales about me, I do not visit my
   neighbors.
I would be astonished to see a bushmonkey leave a papaya.
REFRAIN: Leave a papaya, leave a papaya. . . .

The importance of being able to visit neighbors and participate
in the social community of the neighborhood is a theme that runs
throughout much of the band's work, as neighborliness *(ujirani)* is
also central to Swahili definitions of communal identity. A person
who stuck to themselves was not a good member of the community.
The final line from the verse—I would be astonished to see a bushmonkey leave a papaya—also alludes to the irresistible temptation
that repeating juicy gossip presented to most island residents. Talking, about themselves as well as others, helped to establish the values
which bound this community of immigrants together. As Siti's band
and their audiences told and retold the stories on which their songs
were based they formulated and negotiated boundaries between the
acceptable and the deviant in twentieth-century society.[45]

Songs intended to shock and scandalize focused not only on the
deeds and misdeeds of neighbors and members of the Ng'ambo community but also on the actions of leading members of the aristocracy
as well as members of the colonial service. Decisions by members of
the colonial judiciary were the subject of some of the band's most
trenchant critiques of the state. Lines such as, "You shouldn't live in
hopes that there will be an appeal of your case / The aim of these appeals is merely to deceive you . . . / Nor is it any use to have a lawyer
who studied in London / He will eat your wealth for nothing, and you
will be sent to jail," voiced the general lack of confidence in the colonial court system that pervaded Ng'ambo. Although British magistrates were undoubtedly less effected by the circulation of catchy
verses critical of their judgments than were typical community members, the dissemination of discourses that openly questioned and
chastised still served to undermine the overall image of colonial authority. Each time such songs were repeated, be it by Siti, a fisherman

hauling in a catch, or a gramophone disc being played inside a coffee house, alternative discourses of social and legal justice, as well as civil society, were advanced.

Popular leisure pursuits served as critical arenas in which public debate and critiques of colonial policy were formulated and expressed. Excluded from the meetings of the colonial administration as well as from the halls of the Legislative Council—formed in 1926 to allow the male Arab and South Asian elite a limited role in colonial governance—the women and men of Ng'ambo made their voices and opinions heard through less formal but no less powerful channels. Through music, dance, football, rallies, and mass public marches, Ng'ambo residents discussed, debated, and worked to transform core political values as well as social and economic practices. In a society where official politics was dominated by an Arab monarch under the tutelage of the British Empire, community-based popular culture was a centrally important component of the public sphere. The British and their domestic allies certainly controlled the institutions of domination but this exploration of popular pastimes and politics reveals their very limited ability to constrain debate regarding the reasonable, feasible, or just.[46]

Football clubs and taarab performances were popular because they were fun, but part of the fun was generated by the fact that here the men and women of Ng'ambo could openly challenge the "public transcript" of colonial power.[47] Unlike their counterparts in much of colonial Africa, in Zanzibar administrative officials took a chance and met their subordinates on the football, hockey, and cricket fields, where they were not infrequently trounced to the bold cheers of thousands of spectators. The symbolic importance of such defeats was minimized by the British, but winning went a long way toward affirming Zanzibaris' impressions that, when given an equal chance, they were as good as any other man in the empire. These cultural challenges to British authority were more than merely symbolic. They provided the discursive context as well as part of the organizational framework from which the 1928 ground rent strike as well as subsequent "political" actions were launched.

The relationship between popular culture and popular politics in early-twentieth-century Zanzibar was a dialectical one where, as George Lipsitz has argued, "Culture can seem like a substitute for politics, a way of posing only imaginary solutions to real problems, but under other circumstances culture can become a rehearsal for politics, trying out new values and new beliefs permissible in art but forbidden in social life."[48] Popular culture provided critical grounds for the "rehearsal" of new social values in post-abolition Zanzibar. These values included recognizing the central contributions of former slaves to the making of society as well as the right of the poor and disenfranchised to economic and social justice. And unlike the institutionalized forms of political expression that became dominant in the colonial era, these neighborhood-based cultural forms encouraged the participation of women. As they created new forms of art and adopted new leisure pursuits, the men and women of urban Zanzibar defined new images of themselves and reconceptualized the social and political categories that framed their lives.[49]

Public ritual, music, and dance had long played critical roles in establishing one's place in coastal society.[50] As Jonathon Glassman's study of the nineteenth-century Swahili coast suggests, participation in elaborate public rituals and dance societies was a central component in the process of being recognized and accepted as a member or "citizen" of urban society.[51] In twentieth-century island society as well, popular culture remained a prominent venue through which former slaves and new immigrants actualized their growing identities as citizens of the isles. New cultural forms and new leisure pursuits were created to articulate desires for recognition, first as free men and women, and later as Zanzibaris, women and men who thought of Zanzibar as home and who wanted to be recognized and respected as citizens. To borrow from Liisa Malkki, this pragmatics of identity "comprised a series of tactical moves and performative poses that were empowering in specific, sometimes fleeting, social contexts."[52] Bodily adornment, music, dance, and sport served not merely as reflections of identity but rather as central stages on which new forms of consciousness, community, and new individual and collective identities were created, debated, and explored.

Ethnicity, Identity, and Belonging

While the arts and various leisure pursuits served as vibrant articulations of former slaves' changing identities, articulations which were
visibly and audibly apparent to others at the time, it was by looking at
a comparison of census returns from the first half of the twentieth century that the importance of "belonging" and the dramatic shifts in
identity that followed from such desires first became apparent to
me. A comparison of these returns provides a stunning indication of
changes in self-identity over time, as former slaves sought to recast
themselves as members of island society who were deserving of the social and economic benefits that derived from such status. Institutions
organized around ethnicity, or "tribes," conceptualized as discreet and
exclusive social and biological categories, were the principal organizations through which the colonial state interpreted and attempted to direct African life.[53] Certain types of rights were reserved by the British
for members of particular ethnic categories, and distinct correlations
can be seen between ethnic shifts recorded in the census returns and
struggles by the disenfranchised to achieve specific kinds of rights.
These shifts in identity were communicated to other islanders primarily
through a range of popular pastimes which were at the core of public
life, and to the British through discourses of race, ethnicity, and tribe.

Coastal conceptions of ethnicity, much like coastal interpretations of kinship, emphasized the multivalent, malleable, and social nature of such identities.[54] These indigenous ideas contrasted strikingly
with British colonial perceptions which were based in the "immut-
able" biological traits of blood and genetics. Coastal residents, including former slaves, had always attempted to define themselves in ways
that allowed them to make claims on resources controlled by the widest range of social actors, and they continued to employ such strategies
during the colonial era. For instance, women and men in the isles responded quickly and overwhelmingly to administrative policies that
awarded economic benefits and selective citizenship "rights"—such
as the right to own land—only to members of particular ethnic categories. As individuals and groups sought access to particular forms of
power they pragmatically claimed belonging to the ethnic groups

deemed by the state to be "deserving" of such benefits. This does not necessarily mean that men and women simultaneously abandoned or disavowed earlier identities, but merely that they learned to manipulate the administration's own ethnic and racial categories as one means of making claims on resources now controlled by the colonial state. However, it is important to note that while census returns provide concrete data that illustrate important patterns, the following tables make these shifts in claimed ethnicity seem more sudden and certainly more stark than they really were. As the central chapters of this book suggest, these numbers illustrate only part of the picture, a picture whose form is much more fluid and whose lines are far more muted than the columns in the tables suggest.

Although British policy in colonial Africa was based on ideas that ethnicity, tribe, and race were fixed categories, even a cursory examination of tables 1.1 and 1.2 illustrates the practical fluidity of such identities in Zanzibar during the first half of the twentieth century. Ethnic and racial identities, at least as defined by census enumerators and interpreted by island residents, were clearly not fixed identities. Rather ethnicity was but one part of larger social identities, which were themselves constantly being created and recreated by individual and collective groups of women and men throughout this period. Unlike the British, individuals living in early-twentieth-century Zanzibar did not conceive of ethnicity as some primordial or genetic trait. Ethnicity could be inherited at birth, but it could also be adopted as necessary to meet the particular social, economic, and political goals of human actors as they negotiated their way through the complexities of real life.[55] Biology was by no means destiny for coastal East Africans, a point which a great deal of the existing literature makes quite clear. This is not to suggest that these identities did not "mean" anything to the men and women engaged in such practices; on the contrary, ethnic definitions meant a lot, which is precisely why people self-consciously deployed them in strategic ways.

Nineteenth-century estimates of Zanzibar's population routinely reported that between two-thirds and three-fourths of the islands' total population were slaves of mainland origin, primarily of the Nyasa, Yao, and Manyema ethnic groups.[56] In 1895 slaves and recently

Table 1.1

Changes in Claimed Ethnic Identity as Reported to Census Enumerators, Zanzibar
Island (Unguja)

Ethnic Category	1924	1931	Percent Change	1948	Percent Change
Comorian	2,244	2,101	-6%	2,764	+32%
"Indigenous" Africans					
Swahili	14,806	2,038	-86%	129	-94%
Hadimu	16,454	27,732	+69%	41,185	+49%
Tumbatu	21,288	27,663	+30%	38,548	+39%
Shirazi	13,602	8,642	-36%	disallowed as a census ethnicity	
Pemba	143	480	+235%	900	+88%
Mainland Africans					
Manyema	3,934	3,020	-23%	1,899	-37%
Nyasa and Yao	10,994	9,539	-13%	6,131	-36%
Other Mainland	23,662	31,933	+35%	29,374	-8%
Total African Population					
	107,127	113,148	+6%	118,652	+5%

manumitted slaves accounted for 85 percent of the total African population of the isles.[57] By the time that the first official census was taken
of the African population, in 1924, however, individuals who
identified as members of ethnic communities associated with slavery
constituted less than 13 percent of the protectorate's population.
While a certain number of former slaves left the isles after abolition, it
appears that the vast majority who remained in the isles reidentified
themselves as members of freeborn ethnic communities as one means
of establishing their identities as free men and women in the post-
abolition era.[58]

In turn-of-the-century East Africa, the Swahili were generally
identified as freeborn coastal Muslims, many of whom were of mixed
African and Arab descent, who lived primarily in urban areas and
spoke the Kiswahili language. Who exactly the Swahili "were," how-

Table 1.2

Percent Change in Overall Ethnic Category

	Zanzibar Island		Pemba Island		Protectorate	
	1924–31	*1931–48*	*1924–31*	*1931–48*	*1924–31*	*1931–48*
Swahili	-86%	-94%	-99.8%	*	-94%	-94%
Indigenous Africans	+47%	+44%	+6%	+246%	+34%	+96%
Ex-slave	-16%	-36%	-35%	-37%	-23%	-36%
Arabs	***	***	***	***	+77%	+33%
Shirazi	-36%	**	+151%	**	+55%	**
Mainland Africans	+35%	-8%	-11%	-34%	+15%	-17%
Overall Population	***	+8.5%	***	+17%	+8.5%	+12%

* Numbers too small to be of statistical significance.

** Claim of Shirazi ethnicity was disallowed in the 1948 census. All who identified as Shirazi were forced to claim either Hadimu, Tumbatu, or Pemba as their ethnicity.

*** The 1924 census enumerated only African households. Estimates of the "non-Native" population were made only for the Protectorate as a whole.

Based on *Report of the Native Census of Zanzibar, 1924*, BA 34/2; *The Report on the Census Enumeration of the Entire Population, 1931*, BA 34/3; *Notes on the Census of the Zanzibar Protectorate, 1948*, BA 34/4; R. R. Kuczynski, *Demographic Survey of the British Colonial Empire* 2 vols. (London: Oxford Press, 1949), 2:650-85.

ever, varied from town to town, and within each town over time. In the case of the island of Zanzibar (Unguja) in the nineteenth century, what differentiated the Swahili from other indigenous populations, including the Hadimu and Tumbatu, was the fact that the Swahili lived in town and worked largely in the commercial economy, while the Hadimu and Tumbatu lived in the eastern and northern parts of the island, respectively, and concentrated their labor in peasant agriculture. Throughout the East African coast the Swahili have historically been perceived as a very fluid population, both in terms of ancestry and residence. As the preeminent trading population of East Africa, Swahili families often had members living in numerous ports up and down the coast and as far away as Arabia. In addition to having many places to call home, as a community the Swahili have been known for centuries as tolerant hosts who were generally welcoming of outsiders wanting to settle in their midst, provided those outsiders were willing to adapt themselves to Swahili cultural habits.[59]

Europeans attempting to rigidly classify and encapsulate African "tribes" were frequently frustrated in their attempts to demarcate the boundaries of the Swahili, yet the very permeability of the boundaries of Swahili identity made it extremely attractive to East Africans seeking the benefits of belonging to urban coastal society. The following description of the Swahili, penned by Charles New in the 1870s, captures the essence of Swahili heterogeneity, if in rather pejorative nineteenth-century terms.

> The modern Msuahili is a medley of almost everything oriental, and perhaps not without a spice of something occidental in his blood. If any mortal could claim relationship with half the world, and a little more, the man is the Msuahili. . . . A race of half-castes . . . hybrids, or creoles, widely differing from each other according to their various parentage, yet coming under the one designation, Wasuahili. Every physical type is to be found among them. . . . There is also a great variety of colour among them, every shade between jet black and light brown. . . . Many distinctions of rank and station exist among them [as well].[60]

The openness of the Swahili as an ethnonym and the physical mobility of many Swahili as traders made identifying as a Swahili particularly suitable for former slaves, many of whom were on the move in the period after abolition and hoping to assert a new social identity distinct from their servile pasts. As the ranks of urban society swelled at the beginning of the twentieth century, many of those who moved to town began to identify themselves to others as freeborn Swahili.[61] While these men and women may have come to the isles in the nineteenth century from as far away as contemporary Mozambique, Malawi, or Congo, as New's comments suggest, the range of physical and social characteristics which "defined" the Swahili was elastic enough to allow room for almost anyone. Having spent many years living in Zanzibar, these men and women had also adopted many of the cultural characteristics that distinguished the Swahili: they were Muslim, they spoke Kiswahili, many of them had chosen to move to town, and above all, they were free. As subsequent chapters will illustrate, they also became very active participants in the performance of urban "Swahili" cultural forms. Women and men, like Siti binti Saad, adopted distinctly "Swahili" forms of dress, had their daughters initiated in puberty rituals that marked them as members of urban Zanzibar society, and forged friendships and integrated themselves into urban social networks through membership in religious brotherhoods, dance societies, and football clubs and through marriage.

An expanding urban colonial economy and relatively high wages added to the allure of Ng'ambo in the first decades of the twentieth century, while simultaneously enhancing the ability of former slaves to acquire the homes, clothing, and habits that marked them as Swahili urbanites. Colonial infrastructure projects such as the building and expansion of the wharf, the laying of the Bububu Railway, and the construction of roads leading from town to the countryside created hundreds of new jobs for urban residents. The wages offered to urban workers in Zanzibar were substantially higher than those available in the countryside. Men employed by the Public Works Department in 1911 earned an average monthly wage of 18 rupees, while rural wage laborers employed primarily as weeders of government clove plantations earned only 12 rupees (Rs). In 1913, skilled African carpenters were able to earn from Rs 35 to Rs 50 per month in Zanzibar town, while unskilled laborers averaged Rs 15 per month. The men who lived in Ng'ambo were also able to find employment in Stone Town as houseboys and cooks in European, Indian, and Arab homes, where they earned anywhere from Rs 15 to Rs 35 per month.[62] Urban labor was attractive not only because it paid well, but also because rural waged work consisted primarily of weeding and picking cloves, work that was directly associated with slavery.

However, the economic options available in town at the turn of the twentieth century were highly gendered. Whereas women accounted for at least fifty percent of the urban labor force in the nineteenth century, working not only as domestics but also sorting, loading, and packaging goods down at the port or in building construction, the British perceived these forms of wage labor as men's work. As the twentieth century progressed, women found it increasingly difficult to procure waged jobs in town. The few women who were employed by the Public Works Department (PWD) or Harbor Works as unskilled laborers also suffered wage discrimination, typically earning only one-half to two-thirds of the wage paid to their male counterparts.[63] However, men came to dominate these occupations, not only because of British gender stereotypes, but also because after abolition many women consciously chose not to look for jobs with the PWD or Harbor Works specifically because such jobs were associated with servility. Instead, many women sought to withdraw their labor from public view and refocus their energies in more "respectable" and independent forms of employment historically associated with free Swahili women, such as trade, entertainment, or the production and sale of food and crafts. Trade and home-based manufacturing gave women control over their own work rhythms and allowed them to combine domestic, child-rearing, and social obligations with income-generating activities.[64] While the profits earned from such enterprises were often fairly marginal, they nonetheless contributed to women's growing sense of economic and personal empowerment.[65] Living off income generated from rental housing was another urban option pursued by countless "Swahili" women and men. In the first two decades after abolition, women anxious to establish their economic and personal autonomy increasingly invested in urban housing.[66] Becoming a landlady was a lucrative and very respectable occupation to which many Swahili women in Zanzibar aspired.[67]

Men and women who gained access to property, either in town or the countryside after leaving their former owners' plantations, tended to be much more likely to redefine themselves as Swahili than those who continued to live and work on rural estates owned by someone else. An analysis of the 1924 census indicates that men who identified themselves to enumerators as Swahili were nearly five times as likely to own their own farms as those who identified themselves as Nyasa, Yao, or Manyema.[68] By 1924, 88 percent of those who continued to define themselves as members of ethnic communities associated with slavery still lived on someone else's land and performed work associated with slavery. Significantly, there were 25 percent more women than men who identified themselves as Nyasa, Yao, and Manyema in 1924, perhaps suggesting that, because of the way waged labor and the control of land were gendered, it was easier for men to establish themselves as property owners, especially in the countryside.[69] Economic mobility was apparently a key component of redefining one's identity. The Swahili had a reputation as East Africa's self-made men and women. As former slaves began to actualize their desires for economic and physical autonomy from former masters and mistresses, they too remade themselves as Swahili.

As increasing numbers of former slaves began to define themselves as Swahili, however, the term Swahili itself gradually became understood as a euphemism for former slave.[70] The pejorative connotations associated with the appellation grew in the 1910s and many former slaves once again began to redefine their ethnic identities in order to distance themselves from the stigma of slavery. Archival records and court testimonies indicate that by the end of the First World War many people were already moving away from their adoptive identities as Swahilis. Registers of births and deaths recorded in Zanzibar Town between 1914 and 1919 also reveal a reluctance on the part of Swahili parents to identify their children as such. While Swahili births accounted for 21 percent of total registered urban births between 1909 and 1913, between 1914 and 1919 Swahili births dropped to a mere 7 percent of total urban births. During this same five-year period, however, the Swahili accounted for a full 50 percent of registered urban deaths. Local administrators interpreted these statistics as evidence of the toll that Swahili "immorality" was taking on their mortality, but hindsight suggests that a more compelling interpretation is that Swahili parents were probably choosing to identify their children as members of another ethnic category at birth.[71]

This process of abandoning former identities as Swahili became overwhelmingly obvious in the 1920s. As tables 1.1 and 1.2 indicate, between 1924 and 1931 the number of people identifying themselves to census enumerators as Swahili declined by 86 percent in the island of Zanzibar (Unguja) and nearly 100 percent in Pemba. By 1930 the term Swahili had become "an epithet of reference," a label which people of higher social status used to identify their inferiors or implicate slave heritage, but a name which almost no one used to identify themselves.[72] The pejorative connotations associated with a Swahili ethnic identity remain today, as Zanzibar residents will frequently chastise someone's "bad manners" or "uncouth behavior" with an expression of contempt made by sucking air through the teeth, a practice known as *kufyonya,* followed by *"We, Mswahili we!"* (Ah, you Swahili, you!). The ancient Arabic-derived use of the term Swahili in reference to "the people of the coast" remained widely in use as a general category distinguishing coastal residents from those of upcounty Africa, but typically a free man or woman from the coast would define themselves as members of a particular clan, village, or town rather than vaguely as Mswahili, a Swahili person.[73] As growing numbers of Swahili gained access to property and confidence in their status as members of island society they began to reidentify themselves and their children as members of ethnic categories associated specifically with the isles.

Census records suggest that the majority of men and women who abandoned their identities as members of the elusive but all-encompassing category of Swahili reidentified themselves either as members of one of the islands' indigenous ethnic communities: Hadimu, Tumbatu, and Pemba or as Shirazi, a term used largely in reference to members of the indigenous ruling class, which also implied a distant, and largely fictive, ancestry in ancient Persia.[74] As the ranks of the self-identified Swahili plummeted in the late 1910s and early 1920s those of indigenous communities swelled. In 1895, the freeborn indigenous African population of the protectorate accounted for less than 15 percent of the total population. By 1924, those identifying themselves as either Hadimu, Tumbatu, Pemba, or Shirazi accounted for 45 percent of the population, a figure which grew to 62 percent by 1931, a growth pattern which suggests that factors other than simple human biological reproduction were at work. In Zanzibar (Unguja) the majority of those who switched their ethnic appellation chose to identify as either Hadimu or Tumbatu, while in Pemba the overwhelming choice of identification was as Shirazi. In either case, however, there was once again a strong correlation between property ownership and identification as an indigenous islander.

Property ownership in Zanzibar was rarely predicated on the holding of a paper title. Freehold tenure was also a foreign concept in the nineteenth century, though one could establish one's rights to a piece of soil and thus effectively assert ownership, by planting trees, building a home, or otherwise making improvements on the land. In post-abolition Zanzibar, former slaves were not given the proverbial forty acres and a mule. Yet because neither their former owners nor the new colonial state held title for unoccupied land, former slaves were able to move into unoccupied areas and gradually establish de facto "ownership" by planting trees, building homes, or cultivating annual food crops.[75] Turn-of-the-century tax policy further encouraged former slaves to plant clove trees, thus establishing themselves as landowners, by exempting from tax all those who moved to unoccupied land and planted and cultivated fifty or more clove trees.[76] In Zanzibar, the "clove zone" was confined to the central and western parts of the island. Although these areas had already largely been planted with cloves during the preceding century, numerous new small farms were planted between and adjacent to larger plantations in the early 1900s. In Pemba, however, most of the island was suitable for clove cultivation and vast tracts of new land were planted with clove trees in the immediate post-abolition period.[77]

While the ability of former slaves to open up new areas of Zanzibar island to clove cultivation was not great, many slaves acquired land and trees through other means. In 1905 the colonial state began leasing and selling some of its smaller and most overgrown clove and coconut plantations. As the problems of recruiting and maintaining labor intensified in the post-abolition era, the state began selling off even more of its plantations to smallholder peasants.[78] By 1910, the colonial administration had disposed of nearly half of the royal family's former clove plantations, which were now under the control of the Department of Agriculture. As the productivity and profitability of its remaining plantations continued to decline through the 1920s, the administration continued to sell off many of its more marginal holdings.[79] During the 1910s and 1920s many of the largest Arab-owned plantations were also divided up and sold to an emerging class of smallholders. Faced with declining profitability due to increased labor costs, declining productivity of old trees, a 25 percent in-kind duty charged by the state, and the continuous subdivision of estates among heirs, many members of Zanzibar's formerly wealthy clove-holding families began to sell or go bankrupt during this period.[80] The financial difficulties faced by the former landowning aristocracy and the new colonial state combined to yield a window of opportunity for the landless to acquire farms of cloves, coconuts, and other tree crops during the first three decades of the twentieth century, thus establishing their positions as property owners in the isles.[81]

Through various means Zanzibar Island's (Unguja) former slave population gained access to considerable amounts of land by the 1920s, and as they did so they increasingly came to identify themselves, at least to employees of the colonial administration, as indigenous Hadimu or Tumbatu rather than Swahili. According to the 1922 Clove Bonus Survey, nearly 75 percent of those engaged in clove production claimed to be indigenous islanders.[82] While Arabs controlled 69 percent of the bearing trees in that year, "indigenous" smallholders owned a full 50 percent of the total clove trees on the island. Arab holdings were not only older than those of indigenous Africans but also far larger, with the former owning an average of 394 trees per person and the latter only 33.[83] Regardless, the Clove Bonus Survey indicates that former slaves had succeeded in gaining control of significant amounts of land in the decades following abolition. In areas outside the fertile clove belt, "indigenous" islanders also became major tree holders. By the early 1930s, the majority of coconut farms were also in their hands.[84] Because former slaves were not encroaching on land occupied, claimed, or even desired by those who had historically identified as either Hadimu or Tumbatu, these moves appear to have generated little or no resistance from the latter.[85] It should also be noted that while the authors of these various colonial reports persistently referred to the smallholder populations as Swahili, indicating their understanding that they were in fact former slaves, 99 percent of these same smallholders identified themselves to the authors as members of indigenous ethnic communities. In the eyes of former slaves, their claims of "belonging" to island society were confirmed by their status as property owners.

Ex-slaves understood the importance of ethnic classifications to British authorities and they responded pragmatically to a series of colonial decrees, passed in the 1920s, that provided additional encouragement for identifying as indigenous Zanzibaris rather than as Swahili. According to the 1921 Public Lands Decree, only "native" or indigenous Zanzibaris were rightfully allowed to claim the waste and unoccupied land on which many former slaves had established their homes and farms in the preceding decades. "Indigenous" Zanzibaris were defined by this decree as Hadimu, Tumbatu, Pemba, or Shirazi. The Swahili were specifically defined as being "non-native" for the purposes of land acquisition.[86] How quickly word of this decree and an appreciation for its implications passed throughout the isles is unknown, but we can assume that such legislation contributed at least in part to the reluctance of landowning individuals to identify themselves as Swahili to employees of the colonial census projects. When the government began disposing of its clove plantations in the 1920s, it gave further incentive to former slaves and Swahili to declare themselves as indigenous Zanzibaris. Those who defined themselves as either Swahili or members of mainland ethnic groups were granted only "copy-hold tenure" to these estates, which amounted to little more than glorified squatting rights.[87] Those who defined themselves as Hadimu, Pemba, Tumbatu, and Shirazi, however, were given freehold tenure to the parcels of plantations sold to them. There were obvious legal advantages to defining oneself as a Zanzibari and these advantages did not escape the notice of former slaves who presumably found changing their claimed ethnicity to be a simple and effective means of protecting their legal right to established homes and farms. By the end of the 1920s, less than one percent of the non-Arab clove-owning population were defining themselves as Swahili.[88]

These identities as Zanzibaris were by no means fictive. We need to recognize that for the majority of former slaves who remained on the islands, by the 1920s, Zanzibar was in fact home. These men and women had spent the greater part of their lives in Zanzibar; they had built their homes, planted their farms, and watched both their children and their trees grow to maturity on Zanzibar's rich soil. In 1913 one man responded, when asked by a member of the colonial service if he would like to go back to Malawi, where he was captured and enslaved as a child, "Go back to those savages? No! Besides, I have my house here, and a small piece of land, and my son is a rich man, a silversmith in town. ..."[89] Regardless of where they had come from, many former slaves had grown accustomed to coastal life and culture. They had spent most, if not all, of their lives in the isles. They did in fact regard themselves and each other as islanders.

Gaining access to rural property did not necessarily stem the tide of urban migration, however. Island residents generally recognized the importance of rural land as a source of wealth and economic independence, but not everyone desired to remain in the countryside. In fact, many landholders—from the wealthiest plantation owners to the smallest peasant producers—used the wealth generated by their rural property to finance their move to town.[90] The coastal association of town life with "civilization" and status remained strong and was ascribed to by rural residents as well as urban patricians. These associations pervaded coastal culture and were conveyed in numerous subtle ways, including through children's rhyme-songs, such as the following, which was sung to the tune of "Yankee Doodle Dandy."[91]

> Mkulima mwenye shamba, alipanda viazi.
> Alichimbachimba chini, akaona almasi.
> Akatupa jembe upande, akaenda mjini.
> Kanunua nyumba zuri, sasa mtajiri.
>
> ▌
>
> The farmer who owned the land planted sweet potatoes.
> S/he dug and dug and dug deep down and discovered diamonds.
> [The farmer] then threw the hoe aside and went to town.
> S/he bought a beautiful house and now is a wealthy, powerful
>   person.

Although the source of wealth, in this case a cache of diamonds serendipitously found while planting sweet potatoes, came from land in the countryside, it was only after going to town and buying a nice house that this lucky individual became recognized as a person of wealth, power, and status. Judging by the coastal standards enshrined in this rhyme, buying a nice urban home is what made this person rich, not finding the diamonds. Wealth needed to be displayed in culturally appropriate ways in order to be recognized, and in coastal Swahili culture urban consumption and display, as opposed to rural production, is what conferred affluence and social power.

Being and Becoming an Arab: Citizenship, Consumption, and Race

Indigenous ideologies relating consumption and social display to notions of urban citizenship continued throughout the period covered in this book, yet they also interacted with British theories and practices that made race, gender, and class the defining criteria of potential citizenship within the colony. In early-twentieth-century Zanzibar, former slaves seeking to assert their status as citizens engaged in a wide range of new consumption habits that effectively displayed their economic and social autonomy to themselves and other members of island society. As subsequent chapters document, both women and men began dressing up in the latest local fashions, moving to the city and building nice, new homes, purchasing gramophone players, entertaining kin and neighbors with the latest release of Siti binti Saad's recordings, organizing themselves into football and ngoma clubs that created urban networks and reflected changing notions of belonging, as well as acquiring small farms in the countryside. However, as the power of the colonial administration solidified in the early twentieth century new definitions of citizenship, marked by rigid boundaries of race, class, and gender, increasingly came into play. In 1926 the administration's attempts to define and craft a citizenry was given institutional form through the creation of the Legislative Council, in which only wealthy Arab, Asian, and British men were allowed to participate.

A range of individuals and groups objected to their placement outside the boundaries of state-defined citizenship, and as subsequent chapters detail they made use of a wide variety of practices—from ground rent strikes, to jailbreaks, to taarab performances and football matches—to ensure that their ideas and concerns regarding key economic and social issues were part of the political debate. There are no archival records to suggest that the women and men engaged in these practices ever explicitly confronted either the British or other members of the Legislative Council about these new, exclusionary definitions of citizenship, but the constant debates and actions taking place in Ng'ambo demonstrate the pervasive persistence of alternative definitions of citizenship, definitions that were not based on masculinity or race.[92] The decades between the two world wars represented a critical period for the institutionalization of racial policies and politics in colonial Zanzibar. Although the British had long encouraged local communities to organize themselves into communal or "ethnic" associations, with the formation of the Legislative Council, in 1926, the relationship between racial identity and citizenship was formally institutionalized in the realm of colonial politics. The Arab Association and various organizations representing subsections of the islands' South Asian population were now allowed to nominate representatives to serve in the Legislative Council, the principal advisory and legislative body in the protectorate. Members of the islands' African communities were awarded no such representation in the Legislative Council until well after World War II. Although colonial policy was certainly full of contradictions, by and large the administrative aim in the isles was to preserve Omani hegemony, yet in clearly circumscribed form. As the author of one report on administrative policy issued in the 1930s argued,

> The situation in Zanzibar differs from that in Kenya or Tanganyika as Zanzibar is a Protectorate proper [as opposed to a colony] with a ruling Sovereign [the sultan] who has accepted the protection and suzerainty of the King. The ruler is not an African but an Arab. There can be no suggestion in Zanzibar of any form of devolution with the ultimate aim of teaching his Highness' African subjects to govern themselves.[93]

Throughout most of the colonial era, Africans were defined as subjects of the sultan rather than as citizens of Zanzibar.[94]

Reverence for "Arabness" was by no means purely a creation of the colonial era. For centuries coastal residents had painstakingly created and reinforced networks and kinship ties which linked them to the crossroads of world trade in the Middle East. Tangible marriage and economic ties between coastal and Middle Eastern peoples were often reinforced ideologically through foundation myths which linked the establishment of numerous coastal patrician communities and towns to settlement by mythical Muslim immigrants, often from Shiraz (in ancient Persia).[95] Coastal patricians, and other urban citizens, prided themselves on their civilized cultural habits, qualities that were signified by the Kiswahili terms *uungwana* (possessing refined urbanity and high social standing, free) and *ustaarabu* (civilized, like an Arab). Individuals who were regarded as possessing these traits referred to themselves, and hoped to be referred to by others, as *mwungwana* or *mstaarabu*—one who personified the attributes of civilization: good character, a respectable family background, social and economic wealth, and a deep knowledge of Islam. As the power and prestige of Omani Arabs based in Zanzibar grew in the eighteenth and nineteenth centuries, *mstaarabu* came to eclipse *mwungwana* in usage, suggesting the increasing need to become like an Arab or adopt the customs of the Arabs in order to be regarded as a civilized member of the urban citizenry.[96] While birth and descent could be important criteria for asserting one's status among the civilized, such status could also be achieved through the accumulation of wealth, the adoption of "civilized" or Arab dress and manners, integration in existing urban networks and institutions of public life, or by gradually establishing oneself as a patron of less fortunate members of society. There was certainly a clear emphasis on the desirability of being seen as an Arab within precolonial coastal patrician culture, but being recognized as such often rested more on an individual's creative fashioning of social and cultural materials than on genealogy, biology, or race.[97]

The British colonial framework of control and indirect rule was predicated on the state's ability to classify and differentiate the allegedly distinctive "tribes" and "races" of Africa. The importance of such distinctions was all the more critical in the case of Zanzibar, where the administration made a commitment early on to the preservation of Omani hegemony in the isles.[98] In the nineteenth century, economic wealth and political power were defined in relation to the number of

clients a patron had at their disposal. The importance of having a large
and extensive following encouraged Arab patriarchs to define kin in
the broadest possible terms. Clan names such as al-Busaidi, al-Harthi,
or al-Barwani distinguished the principal contenders for power, but
membership in the clan included the widest range of biological kin,
including the children of slave concubines, as well as free clients and
even slaves of the family who were often incorporated as *akina al-
Harthi,* or the followers (folk) of the al-Harthi. During the early years
of colonial rule British officials spent a great deal of time and energy
attempting to segregate the "true Arabs" from their numerous hangers-
on. These efforts were undertaken most explicitly in the case of the al-
Busaidi ruling family, where the new administration considered the
financial demands of the extended family and their clients to be an excessive drain on the national treasury, which was previously administered as the clan's personal account.[99] The British attempted to
separate what they defined as the "real" Arabs from those with but "a
drop of blue blood," whose actions and habits "besmirch the reputation of the true Arab."[100] Desires to "protect" the Arab population
from the "contaminating" and "degrading" influences of African
blood, culture, and habits framed discourses of administrative segre-
gation in the isles, yet much more practical concerns limiting the
number of people who were exempt from labor, vagrancy, and other
regulations directed at the "native African" but not the Arab population were often at the root of such concerns. For most colonial administrators, Arabness was something one was born with, not something
that could be acquired or achieved, yet the evidence suggests that they
were largely unsuccessful in convincing most islanders to adopt such
a perspective.

At the same time that the state attempted to circumscribe membership among "the Arabs," they intensified the economic and political in-
ducements for laying claim to such an identity.[101] That the local
populations understood the advantages to being classified as an Arab
rather than an African there can be no doubt. Despite administrative
attempts to "seal off" claims to an Arab identity, between 1924 and
1931 the number of individuals identifying themselves to census enu-

merators as Arabs increased nearly 80 percent (see table 1.2). During the 1920s, many individuals who could lay claim to a "racial" classification as an Arab—either by virtue of genealogy, education, cultural "refinement," marriage, patronage, property, or color—did so. In the 1920s substantial numbers of individuals, particularly on Pemba, also began defining themselves as Shirazi, or descendants of ancient fictive kin from the Persian town of Shiraz. Many of these Shirazi from Pemba were owners of small, but not insignificant, clove plantations. At this time, not only was representation on the Legislative Council restricted to Arabs and Asians, membership in the Clove Growers' Association (CGA) and the Land Alienation Board—two boards whose policies directly effected the economic position of clove-owning smallholders—was similarly restricted. In the late 1930s, the petit bourgeois Shirazi on Pemba founded the Shirazi Association, which had as one of its central aims securing smallholder representation on the board of the CGA and, by extension, access to credit and other membership benefits that were presently restricted to Omani (Arab) plantation owners. By defining themselves as Shirazi, Pemba smallholders were attempting to lay claim to certain citizenship rights currently reserved for Arabs, including a voice in the CGA and access to CGA credit and marketing schemes.[102] If "being" an Arab was the key criterion determining who had such rights, then they too were Arabs. The Shirazi Association later became active on Unguja as well, where it pushed for a further expansion of citizenship rights, including the development of additional educational facilities for children, the appointment of citizens other than Omanis and South Asians to positions within the civil service, and in the post–World War II era for Shirazi and African representation on the Legislative Council and other advisory bodies.

Members of the Shirazi Association were not the only group to attempt to secure the benefits of "Arab" status for their members. The Comorian Association, comprised of the economic and social elite of immigrants from the Comoro Islands in the Indian Ocean, also attempted to have their ethnic community officially defined as Arab, rather than African. The efforts of the Comorian Association began in

1930, when it petitioned the administration to have the entire Comorian population of the isles, amounting to some 2,400 individuals, legally reclassified from African to Arab. Although numerically small, immigrants from the Comoros had long played important economic, legal, and religious roles in urban Zanzibar society. In the 1930s, members of the Comorian Association were hoping to be reclassified as Arab, not only as an attempt to avoid certain regulations and restrictions being discussed under the Native Administration Regulations, but also because they too were aspiring to representation within the Legislative Council. Rather than challenging the British policy of excluding Africans from the Legislative Council they sought to have themselves and their membership reclassified as Arabs, arguing that Comorians were not only "less dark in color" but generally more intelligent than the "average Swahili native."[103] Certain members of the Legislative Council agreed. Upholding the principle that "backward races" (Africans) should be encouraged to "advance towards civilization," the argument was put forward by a minority on the council that allowing for reclassification provided tangible rewards for those who made such strides to "uplift" themselves and "their race." In the end, a compromise was reached that effectively evaded the issue of defining Comorians as either Africans or Arabs.[104] The Comorian Association persisted in its efforts at reclassification, however, and by the late 1930s had managed to secure key allies within the administration for its position. In 1939, in the context of further debates about "native" administration, the provincial commissioner asked his fellow administrators, "Why cause the Comorians to be termed Africans against their own wish and convictions?"[105] The astute response he received from a few unusually perceptive members of the local administration was that considering the economic and political implications of being classified as African, it would be difficult to find anyone in the isles wishing to be so defined.

Desires to be recognized by the British administration as Arab intensified during World War II, when access to rationed material commodities also became restricted along racial lines. Beginning in 1941, imported goods including sugar, matches, kerosene, flour, butter—and, most important, rice and *kanga* cloths—began to be rationed in the islands. The distribution of rations was facilitated by the allotment of color-coded cards distributed to the head of household that indicated whether a family was "officially" defined as South Asian (green card), Arab (brown), or African (tan).[106] Suddenly, British perceptions and definitions of an individual's race began to impact daily life and local understandings of citizenship that were rooted in consumption and display in immediate ways. A woman's official racial classification now determined whether she could purchase a new kanga, the colorful cloths worn by coastal women, or what kinds of food a family could eat. Africans, at the bottom of the colonial racial and ration hierarchy, had the most difficult time of any community in the isles gaining legal access to rationed goods. As Sidney Mintz and others have argued, historically consumption has served as a key means of displaying power throughout the globe, and Zanzibar was no exception to this general rule.[107] Consumption and display had long served critically important roles in demarcating the social position of individuals and groups in coastal society. With the imposition of rations the colonial state began to systematically affect consumption and make the impact of exclusionary racial classifications tangible in the course of daily consumer practice.

As chapter 2 documents in detail, one of the ways that slaves asserted their status as free citizens of post-abolition urban society was through their consumptive habits. Adopting new or previously forbidden forms of clothing gave women in particular a new power to alter their sense of and presentation of self. The ability to purchase and wear the latest patterns of kanga cloths remained an important public display of a woman's social and economic position throughout the period of this study. The problem, of course, was that as World War II intensified, the available supply of imported kangas became increasingly restricted. In 1939 one million yards of kanga cloth, or 500,000 pairs of kangas, were imported into Zanzibar for domestic consumption. However, by 1944 and 1945, the number of imported kangas available annually was reduced to 10,400.[108] In an apparent effort to avoid "riots" at the shops among women fighting to get their hands on one of the latest designs, access to kangas was rationed and distribution was controlled through lottery. The administration's decision to award access to rationed commodities based on race, however, undermined perceptions that such allocations were fair. A Ng'ambo woman defined by the state as an Arab had more than twice the chance of receiving a kanga than her neighbor who was defined as an African. Such disparities increased when rural versus urban residence was taken into account, meaning that an Arab woman living in Ng'ambo had a one-in-thirty chance of being awarded a kanga from a particular batch of imports, while a rural African woman's chances of receiving one of these same kangas was closer to one in a hundred.[109] The administration's attempts to convince African women that they should content themselves with the cheaper and more widely available off-white *merikani* sheeting—the dominant form of cloth worn by island slaves in the mid-nineteenth century, now used almost exclusively for wrapping the bodies of the dead prior to burial—only further enraged women at the bottom of the race-based rationing hierarchy. Island women who read the color, pattern, design, weight, texture, and commonness of cloth with a precision that defies Western comprehension refused to be caught dead walking around in either the cloth of a corpse or the cloth of slaves. Wearing merikani would have been tantamount to declaring their own social death as Zanzibaris. Their mothers and grandmothers had struggled decades ago for the freedom to choose what they would wear. The rationing of goods by race during the war marked the first time in the lives of many island women that they could really empathize with the ways in which their elders' sense of self, and of citizenship, was compromised by the denial of their ability to consume.

Rice was another consumer good that was made largely unavailable to the isles' "African" population during the war, and its importance cannot be understated. In fact, the entire period surrounding the war is known locally in Zanzibar as *wakati wa mchele wa kadi,* "the era of getting rice by ration cards," suggesting that the rationing of rice by color-coded card was in fact the most important effect of the war on the lives of those in the islands.[110] During the course of many oral interviews, I often began attempts to date various events by asking men and women if such-and-such happened before or after World War II. In many cases my question was met with a blank stare. I then rephrased the question, using the term many in mainland East Africa did, "the Italian war." It was only after one interviewee responded to such a question with, "Yes, during the era of getting rice by ration cards . . . ," that I discovered this local terminology, whose meaning I had yet to fully comprehend. In subsequent interviews I tested the pervasiveness of this phrase, generally drawing a blank or confused look when I referred to the period as "World War II," "the Italian war," or any number of other possible alternatives, but invariably getting an almost immediate response when I used the local term, which defined the war as a battle over rice.

Since at least the nineteenth century, rice was considered the quintessential Zanzibari food, and the administration's attempts to deny holders of African ration cards the right to purchase rice struck many as a direct attack on their identities as Zanzibaris. Having access to rice was not only a matter of being able to fill one's belly, but also an important indicator of status and respect *(heshima)* in local society.[111] Rice, 90 percent of which was imported by the time of World War II, was a status food eaten by all who could afford it. While most islanders supplemented or varied their diets through the inclusion of alternative staples such as breads, plantains, or cassava, even peasants typically resorted to eating locally produced staples, particularly cassava, only when the money needed to purchase rice had been exhausted.[112] As Amy Bentley argues in her study of wartime rationing in the United States, food, and particularly high-status foods, reinforce social roles, notions of power, and perceptions of citizenship in society.[113] Being *deprived* of highly valued foods because of one's class, gender, or race sent important—and not always appreciated—messages regarding one's "value" to the state. Ration policies had important implications that went beyond the dinner table, affecting the very core of people's perceptions of self. As Jamal Ramadhan Nasibu explained of the situation in Zanzibar, "[the rationing of rice by race] has a psychological effect, teaching you that you as a person are not equal to others."[114]

Women and men who defined themselves as Zanzibaris objected not only to the fact that they were being denied access to the most important dietary staple in the isles, but also to the fact that the one rationed staple they were allowed to buy was maize meal *(ugali* or *sembe)*, a type of food associated in the isles with migrant laborers.[115] Up-country, rural, non-Muslim Africans ate ugali, Zanzibaris did not. Anthropologists and historians of food have repeatedly noted that there is nothing more basic dividing "us" from "them" than what and how we eat.[116] Mintz contends that "food preferences are close to the center of . . . self-definition: people who eat strikingly different foods or similar foods in different ways are thought to be strikingly different, sometimes even less human. . . . What we eat [and] how we eat it . . . speak[s] eloquently to the question of how we perceive ourselves in relation to others." [117] By denying Zanzibari Africans access to rice, the administration was not only undermining their self-perception as civilized, rice-consuming islanders, but also subverting one of the key consumptive food habits that differentiated them from recent migrants from the mainland. In essence, the message that many "African" Zanzibaris heard was that they were not really islanders at all; eating maize meal meant that they really belonged on the mainland. The wartime rationing of food challenged the assimilationist practices and postures that former slaves and their children had put forth for nearly half a century. Each and every afternoon, when "African" Zanzibaris sat down to eat their rationed meal, they were confronted either by a plate of ugali that denounced their sense of belonging in the isles, or by a plate of cassava, the food of the rural poor. Being forced to eat ugali or cassava left a literal as well as a figurative bad taste in the mouths of many Zanzibaris who were denied the ability to legally purchase rice because of their race.[118]

The sense of outrage and injustice experienced by many Zanzibaris as a result of these rationing policies was enhanced by the fact that certain segments of the "African" population were selectively granted Arab rations. The Comorian Association's earlier efforts to be classified as Arab, rather than African, served them well when the rationing system was introduced. The provincial commissioner argued that Comorians had "never been looked upon or administratively treated" as Africans, and they were therefore awarded the brown ration cards of Arabs and granted access to all the rationed goods, including rice, that were withheld from their "African" neighbors. In Pemba, those who defined themselves as Shirazis were also given access to rationed goods being denied other segments of the "African" indigenous and mainland populations.[119]

As a result of the politics of rationing, many "indigenous" Africans in Zanzibar also began to assert their "Arabness" and once again redefine their identities, this time claiming, at least for the purposes of rations cards, ethnic identities as Shirazis, or descendants of immigrants from Persia. By 1943, thousands of people who formerly defined themselves as Hadimu or Tumbatu were appearing at government centers demanding that they be reregistered as Shirazi. Many people, particularly those from rural Zanzibar, began adopting Persian clan names, such as al-Shirazi, as a way to substantiate their claims to Persian ancestry, acquire rationed goods, and exempt themselves from forced cultivation policies also being directed against "African" but not "Arab" residents of the isles. Individuals whose parents and grandparents were known as Swahili, Digo, and Zaramu also began calling themselves Shirazi at this time. And membership in the Shirazi Association grew exponentially during this period, as many island residents began to perceive new and perhaps immediate material benefits from taking out a membership card.[120] When asked why so many people in Zanzibar began to call themselves Shirazis at this time, one member of the Afro-Shirazi Party, which came to rule Zanzibar in 1964, explained: "During the time of the Second World War . . . there was a lot of discrimination. Even getting food was based on racial discrimination. Africans were not getting the same rations as Arabs and Asians were . . . and that is in fact the reason they changed. If they changed their ethnicity they received full rations."[121] Many other Zanzibaris confirmed this view, arguing that either they themselves or others they knew began identifying as Shirazis and adopting Arab clan names during the war as a means of getting access to Arab rations, particularly rice. Although everyone denied access to rice, kangas, and other rationed commodities because of their "race" understood the reasons why their friends and neighbors began to lay claim to Arab status, there was considerable debate within the majority community of "Africans" as to whether this was the most appropriate strategy. One anonymous woman vividly recalled the resentment engendered by both the government's rationing policy and the choice of her neighbors to seek classification as Arab. "Are we not all human? Do we all not want our children to eat?" she asked, "Why should my child be denied food simply because I refuse to play their games and call myself Shirazi?" The political implications of these choices struck at the heart of the community, dividing not only neighbors from neighbors but often creating intense antagonisms within families, antagonisms which occasionally even split households apart.[122]

For many island residents, asserting an identity as a Shirazi was more about demanding respect as a citizen than about articulating a fundamental shift in self-perception regarding one's race. Like thousands before them, many Shirazi asserted their claims to Arabness as a step toward achieving political rights in a colonial situation that defined citizenship in racial terms. Staking a claim as a Shirazi was a political move intended to assert the rights of long-term residents to all the economic, social, and political benefits that the state restricted to those of Arab and Asian ancestry. As one man who self-identified on two separate occasions, first as a Shirazi and later as a Hadimu, explained, "Before you were asking about politics, and for the purpose of politics I am Shirazi. Now you are asking about traditions and for that purpose I am Hadimu." According to many island residents, to say that identities—even "racial" identities—are multiple, mutable, and situational is to state the obvious.

The articulation of identities as Shirazi took place not only in reaction to administrative policies that provided numerous benefits to Arabs, but also in the context of a growing presence of African immigrants from the mainland and their efforts to organize politically in the isles. As nationalist politics intensified after the war, two principle organizations competed for the right to represent the "African" population of the isles: the Shirazi Association and the African Association. While members of the former generally sought to claim "Arab" *privileges* for their members, the African Association encouraged its members to take pride in their African heritage and demand equal rights, as non-Arabs, but nonetheless deserving citizens of the isles. The differences in outlook and political philosophy taken by the leadership of the African Association and the Shirazi Association were in some respects rooted in the distinctive historical experiences of the two organizations' leadership. The Shirazi Association was generally dominated by individuals who were long-term residents of the isles and rural property owners, while the African Association was comprised largely of urban working-class men, many of whom were fairly recent immigrants to the isles and who maintained close ties to social, cultural, and nationalist organizations on the African mainland.

Migration from the African mainland was actively encouraged by the local colonial administration as one means of addressing a perceived labor shortage after abolition. Within a year of the abolition decree, rural slaves had successfully negotiated for a universal reduction in their work week, from five days to three, and over time the vast majority of labor needed to weed rural plantations came to be provided by migrants from the mainland.[123] The reliance on migrant laborers from the mainland increased in the 1910s, as the islands' "Swahili" population either became increasingly successful in their endeavors to establish themselves as peasant smallholders, or moved to town. In patterns similar to those seen elsewhere in colonial Africa, the preferences of Zanzibaris to avoid work associated with slavery and seek out options that allowed them to work for themselves gradually hardened into ethnic stereotypes regarding the "laziness" of the indigenous population and the "superior physique" and work ethic of men and women from the mainland.[124] The pervasiveness of such stereotypes fueled an administrative policy that encouraged rather than restricted immigration to the isles throughout the colonial era. By 1931, there were some 44,500 individuals who identified themselves as members of a mainland ethnic community living on the island of Zanzibar (see table 1.1), out of a total of 113,000 "Africans." Although the actual number of women and men identifying as mainlanders was fairly constant from the 1920s through the 1940s, their presence within the urban labor force and urban politics grew considerably over the decades.

The relatively high wages offered in Zanzibar combined with the isles' reputation as the Paris of the Indian Ocean made it an attractive place for many men and women from continental Africa. During the 1920s and 1930s, wages in Zanzibar were some of the highest available anywhere in East Africa. Laborers in Zanzibar earned more than twice the wage paid to squatters living in the so-called White Highlands of Kenya. Unskilled laborers working for the Public Works Department (PWD), the largest employer of men in urban Zanzibar, also earned 36 percent more than men performing comparable jobs in the neighboring Tanganyikan port of Dar es Salaam.[125] Zanzibar's reputation as a place where one could find work and enjoy a good quality of life was commemorated in the popular refrain from one of Siti's songs, *"Unguja ni njema, atakaye aje!"* (Zanzibar is wonderful, anyone who likes should come!). In the 1930s and 1940s, immigrants continued to heed the call. Whereas the majority of those living and working in Ng'ambo up through the 1920s identified themselves as Swahili or members of indigenous ethnic groups, by the time of the 1948 social survey of Zanzibar there were more than twice as many mainland Africans as indigenous Zanzibaris living in and around town. The majority of men with fairly steady waged jobs also identified as mainlanders.[126]

As recent immigrants, these men and women retained their identities and associations with others of their mainland communities and were generally less likely to assert identities as Arabs compared to members of the islands' "indigenous" African communities. Recent immigrants were generally less well integrated into the local urban networks which bridged the growing Arab-African divide, and in point of fact, many of the most significant social, cultural, and personal networks which brought Africans and Arabs together at the start of the twentieth century were largely defunct by the time of their arrival. Histories of the mainland communities from which these recent immigrants originated, be they in the Nyamwezi and Manyema regions of central and western Tanganyika or the Zaramu and Derengenko regions along the littoral, also had conflictual relations with the Omanis due to the latter's involvement in the slave trade as well as their efforts to assert political and economic control over coastal towns in the nineteenth century. For a variety of historical and contemporary reasons, "Arabs" were often perceived as exploiters and not as a category of persons one would want to emulate or claim as one's own. Although many of the men and women who migrated to Zanzibar after 1920 converted to Islam, adopted Swahili names, and gradually donned local clothing styles, they were much more likely to identify themselves as legitimate immigrants from the African mainland, rather than as indigenous islanders or Arabs. By and large, they were also unaccepting of a political discourse that required one to claim an identity as an Arab before one could lay claim to citizenship. This did not mean, however, that the leadership of the African Association eschewed the notion of race altogether. On the contrary, by the 1950s, the leadership of this organization had become prominent promoters of discourses of citizenship that reified rather than resisted the centrality of race—this time the "African" race—to the imagining of the postcolonial nation.[127]

In addition to being known as *wakati wa mchele wa kadi* the period of rations during the war is also widely remembered in Zanzibar as the beginnings of *zama za siasa*, or "the time of politics."[128] *Politics* in this case has largely negative connotations associated with the reification of ethnic boundaries, the deification of ethnic nationalism, and the hardening of associational political boundaries to the point where members of competing groups, even if members of the same family, often would not even speak to each other, let alone engage in meaningful debate. The "time of politics" culminated in a bout of state-sponsored ethnic cleansing—resulting in the murder and emigration of tens of thousands of the islands' Arab and Asian residents—following the 1964 revolution, in which the Afro-Shirazi Party, under the leadership of Abeid Karume, came to power.[129] Politics in postwar Zanzibar were markedly different from those of the 1910s, 1920s, and 1930s. In the earlier period, individuals' political affiliations, like their ethnic identities, were multiple, fluid, strategic, and situational. For reasons that lie beyond the scope of this book, after the war things began to change. By the eve of independence, ethnic boundaries and party allegiances had hardened to a degree unimaginable earlier in the century. If this book contributes anything to the historiography of the revolution or postcolonial conflict it is to illustrate that politics in the isles was not always, and perhaps need not continue to be, a politics based in essentialism, infused with a rhetoric of intolerance or a politics orchestrated by intransigent political parties whose leaders rarely engage the concerns of their members, let alone the critiques of their opponents.[130]

Methodology

Although I spent the better part of two years, from October 1990 to November 1992, doing archival research for this book, the oral histories I conducted during that and subsequent periods have played a much more fundamental role in shaping my understanding of the islands' history. In fact, without the information generously provided by the men and women of Zanzibar, large portions of this book could not have been written. Colonial administrators, whose records dominate the Zanzibar National Archives, were largely uninterested in Ng'ambo and even less interested in the pastimes and political debates of the men, women, and children who inhabited this largely African, working-class section of Zanzibar Town. The archival records focus on the concerns of the colonial powers, and while one can certainly read between the lines to assess the perspective of the colonized on any particular issue, relying exclusively on sources created by administrators provides a deceptive picture of the power and strength of the state in determining the course of the islands' history as well as average people's lives. As the chapter on football illustrates, the British may have written and administered the rules, but they had very little control over how the people of Ng'ambo played the game in the field. If I had only read the minutes of the annual meetings of the Sports Control Board, I would have been overwhelmed by the inherently political nature of sport in the colonies, but I would have completely missed the intensely social and personal feelings that sports generated for the men who played. Several of the men I interviewed shed tears as they recalled the friends, many of whom had since died, and the fun that football brought to their lives. Without the benefit of evidence gained from oral history I would have understood football only as a realm of contestation between colonizer and colonized. This was one important aspect of the social history of the sport, but football meant far more to the lives of the men who organized and played.

Histories of popular culture combined with oral histories also demonstrate the power, resilience, and agency of the colonized in ways that were often overlooked or intentionally downplayed in the written colonial record. If I had confined my analysis of political discourse to that summarized in the annual Blue Books, the debates of the Legislative Council, or the records of the provincial administration I would have been lead to conclude that the poor of Ng'ambo did not analyze or critique the impacts of various policy options and that they rarely voiced their opinions publicly. However, in the course of interviews about pastimes, as well as politics, I was awakened to the vibrant and seemingly endless debates about social, economic, and political policy that permeated Ng'ambo. As it turns out, sports contests, dance competitions, taarab performances, and evening gossip sessions were far more important in shaping public opinion and community action in Ng'ambo than the most heated debates of the Legislative Council. Looking beyond the realm of state-dominated, institutionalized politics also led me to see the numerous and critically important ways in which women—who were completely excluded from "official" politics—shaped these debates and actions. Oral evidence allows me to demonstrate the historical agency of those who remained nameless, faceless, and largely inactive in the written sources.

Almost as soon as I landed in Zanzibar female neighbors in the Ng'ambo neighborhood of Miembeni and friends from other parts of town began inviting me to the wedding celebrations of their friends and relatives. Wedding celebrations have historically been one of the most important social and personal rituals in coastal Swahili society, especially for women. Dance and music celebrations, known as ngoma, which accompany weddings are extremely important events that can draw hundreds of women from across the island together. It was also clear to me from the very beginning that weddings and ngoma played an extremely important role in the expression of class and status divisions within the island community. Inspired by the work of Margaret Strobel in Mombasa, I was also curious about the ways women's involvement in dance and music groups may have helped to mitigate ethnic and class divisions within the community or foster a gendered sense of political consciousness that was different from that generated by male-dominated ethnic associations.[131]

I therefore began collecting data from elderly men and women about ngoma and the histories of various ngoma groups. One of the most popular and important forms of music in Zanzibar is taarab and

I therefore focused, though not exclusively, on the historical development of this particular form of music. I found that weddings, ngoma, and taarab were things that women personally defined as meaningful and that they were particularly excited to talk about. Several months into my stay in Zanzibar, I was introduced to Nasra Mohamed Hilal, who heads the women's taarab group Sahib el-Arry, and I was subsequently invited to join the group. The women of Sahib, as it is locally known, took me in like a daughter and taught me not only about the history of taarab, but also how to dance, sing, and appreciate what it meant to be an adult woman in Zanzibar society. By attending the group's daily practices and traveling with them when they performed in town, in the countryside, and on the mainland I came to understand and appreciate how involvement with popular culture framed the lives of so many men and women in the isles. Many urban residents regularly attend activities organized by religious, ngoma, taarab, football, or other cultural groups. Both historically as well as in the present, popular culture has played a central role in giving shape to individual and collective urban lives.

The famed taarab musician and scholar Mwalim Idd Abdulla Farahan also taught me a vast amount about the history and importance of taarab. Mwalim Idd regularly invited me to the practices and performances of the two taarab groups of which he is a member: Ikhwan Safaa and Culture Music Club. In addition, he spent countless hours teaching me about instruments, scales, and the origins and development of taarab on the island. Mwalim Idd is a teacher in the true sense of the word and I am fortunate to have been one of the hundreds of students whose lives he has touched over the years. He happily answered my never-ending questions and unselfishly shared with me songbooks and his personal manuscript collection as well as the manuscripts of Shaib Abeid Barajab, one of the founding members of Ikhwan Safaa in 1905. Until quite recently there was scant mention of culture or cultural institutions in the collections of the Zanzibar National Archives. The only interest colonial officials seem to have had in ngoma or taarab was how to keep such performances from interfering with the clove harvest. Luckily, however, many clubs, organizations, and individuals have long recognized their own historical importance and have maintained personal archives as one means of passing on their legacy to future generations. I am greatly indebted to the following groups and individuals for their work in preserving such collections as well as their generous willingness to share: Mwalim Idd Abdulla Farahan and Ikhwan Safaa (a.k.a. Malindi), M. A. Ghassany, Abdulrahman Othman, Abdulrahman Ali Saleh, Nasra Mohammed Hilal and the women of Sahib el-Arry, Mwalim Rajab Mzee Ali and the members of Malindi Sports Club, Hamid Feruzi, Bibi Pili Jaha Ubwa, and Juma Aley.

In addition to information gained from written and pictorial archives preserved by Zanzibari historians I also conducted 116 formal interviews (in Kiswahili) with men and women, as well as a clothing survey. Most, but not all, interviewees were members of the Ng'ambo community or individuals who had spent a portion of their lives living in Ng'ambo. Most of these interviews were organized topically; that is, I identified respondents largely through various football, taarab, and ngoma groups. Each interview typically led me to at least one or two more. As most of these popular pastimes drew in people from a range of class, status, and ethnic backgrounds, I was able to interview people from all walks of island life. The topics discussed in the course of each interview varied as a result of interaction between myself and the person with whom I was talking. I began most interviews with a series of biographical questions about parents, siblings, children, marriage, living arrangements, work history, and so forth. Through these autobiographical statements I was able to learn about class and ethnic mobility as well as the gendered nature of power within a variety of family forms. While such information was rarely the aim of an interview, in the end it proved invaluable in allowing me to evaluate a number of cultural stereotypes against a lived domestic reality. The interview generally then proceeded to a topic such as music, dance, football, or particular historical events. Here I would ask various questions about particular groups, their histories, founders, social composition, and my respondent's personal involvement or their understanding of a particular event. From here interviews went off into hundreds of different directions as I tested the waters to see if a particular person knew and was willing to discuss other events and issues. Many respondents also had their own agendas and our discussions were therefore taken in directions that they found interesting or important for me to understand.

Most interviews lasted anywhere from forty-five to ninety minutes, a time structured as much by the length of the recording tapes I had bought as anything else. In most cases I would follow up the formal interview either with another interview, or more typically with informal meetings where I would ask questions that occurred to me later or where we would simply chat about life, history, and the state of the world. I never paid the people whom I interviewed. I did, however, make a conscious effort to return after the interview with a gift from the local market as an expression of my gratitude and appreciation for the respondent's willingness to set aside a part of his or her busy day to help an inquisitive student.

In addition to oral histories I also collected and analyzed nearly three hundred taarab and ngoma songs. Taarab songs form the bulk of this collection, with approximately half the songs representing the work of the members of Siti binti Saad's band. The lyrics to most of these songs were taken from transcriptions provided by a member of the band, Mwalim Shaaban, and published under the guidance of W. H. Whiteley, director of the Institute of Kiswahili, under the title *Waimbaji wa juzi*. Other lyrics were given to me by Nasra Mohamed Hilal and Mwajuma Ali of Sahib el-Arry, both of whom are Siti aficionados, taken from other published sources on Siti, such as Mgana's *Jukwaa la taarab* and Khatib's *Taarab Zanzibar*, or painfully transcribed by me with the aid of friends from poor-quality cassette recordings. Lyrics to an additional forty-seven songs recorded by the band with HMV/Gramophone were taken from catalogues published in 1929 and 1930. Siti binti Saad and her band transformed taarab music in the early decades of the twentieth century from a genre reserved almost exclusively for wealthy Arab men who lived in Stone Town into a musical genre which captured and expressed the daily life, hopes, and frustrations of those who inhabited Ng'ambo in the period between the two world wars. The profound importance that Zanzibaris attribute to Siti and her music, as well as the rich documentary evidence her songs provide about the social history of urban Zanzibar in the 1920s and 1930s, compelled me to devote an entire chapter of this book to her work. The translation of these songs and all other Kiswahili materials are my own. Translating these songs was not an easy task, as many contain not only archaic Kiswahili, but occasional words and phrases from Arabic.[132] These difficulties were compounded by the fact that taarab songs are composed as poems which typically conform to standardized patterns of rhyme and meter. In Kiswahili poetry it is accepted practice to manipulate both nouns and grammar to fit the constraints of rhyme and meter, which again compounds the troubles of a translator searching for the meaning of some archaic phrase. Swahili poetry, including taarab songs, is also extremely metaphorical, so that the precise meaning of a given line, stanza, or poem is open to a range of possible interpretations.[133] Translating anything is difficult, translating poetry all the more so. The greatest dilemma I faced came from my inability to capture the beauty and metaphor conveyed by the poet into the English translations. My goal in providing these translations has been to render the meaning conveyed by the poet, and I have occasionally strayed from a precise word-for-word translation in order to make the overall meaning clearer to English-speaking readers. For those who read and can appreciate Swahili poetry the originals have been included.

The choices, or more frequently accidents of acquaintance, that determine a researcher's residence can have a fundamental impact on the perspective from which society and history are seen.[134] In some respects foreign researchers are like children, who unconsciously grow to accept the worldviews, biases, and prejudices of the adoptive kin who welcome us into their homes; provide us with food and clothing; and nurture us physically, emotionally, and intellectually. While all good researchers evaluate their sources against established standards of evidence, take into account the class, gender, ethnic, and religious biases of oral as well as written sources, and actively attempt to gather evidence from a variety of perspectives, the people we live with and the places we live often frame our lives and our studies in subtle and unconscious ways. A fair amount of the material in this book contradicts earlier academic studies of Swahili society, no doubt because many of these studies were written by authors who lived and circulated among patricians and their descendants. Growing up as a working-class kid from the south of Chicago, I came to see, very early on, the numerous ways in which social rules and regulations were stacked to protect the interests of the wealthy. I owe a great debt to my friends, neighbors, and hosts, from my old neighborhoods as well as those from Zanzibar's "other side," who taught me not only the "rules" of society but, more important for this book, the ways in which codes intended to reify the dominance of the elite could be evaded, undermined, and overturned.

I hope that the diversity of the documentation I draw on has allowed me to begin to convey the richness and complexity of social life in colonial Zanzibar. As other scholars of colonial urban Africa have cautioned, although the struggles between capitalists, colonialists, and African laborers may seem like the dominant themes of the era's history, this was rarely the perception of city dwellers living at the time.[135] The rich sources provided by oral and cultural history help to illustrate the ways in which the colonized understood and experienced the period as well as their own attempts to structure and transform society. Because the population of Ng'ambo was largely nonliterate, there is very little written documentation of the intellectual debates and struggles taking place within this community. Even those who were literate were unlikely to have their reflections preserved in the national archives, which has few collections of personal papers. The memories of the men and women who participated in music, dance, and football groups, however, are an archive in themselves. I have only begun to tap into the rich and nuanced material available from these sources. A great deal more work on the history of leisure and urban society remains to be done.

I readily admit that there are both gaps and limits in the study which follows. I only hope that I have provided readers with a taste of daily life experienced by those who built and created the Ng'ambo community in the early decades of the twentieth century. Colonial history can at times be downright depressing, yet few of the men or women who lived through this period would describe their lives as being devoid of happiness. By focusing on the family, friends, and fun that were at the center of people's lives I hope to have humanized our understanding of the era. Although filled with struggle, the decades that witnessed the introduction of colonialism and the abolition of slavery were also years of immense satisfaction and accomplishment for the average men and women who made Ng'ambo's history.

Chapter 2

Dressing Up
Clothing, Class, and Gender in Post-Abolition Zanzibar

Pemba peremba
Ukija na winda, hutoka na kilemba
Ukija na kilemba, hutoka na winda.

(Proceed cautiously in Pemba / If you come wearing a loincloth, you leave wearing a turban. / If you come wearing a turban, you leave wearing a loincloth.)
—A Swahili adage c. 1900

Dress has historically been used as one of the most important and visually immediate markers of class, status, and ethnicity in East African coastal society. As one of many forms of expressive culture, clothing practice shaped and gave form to social bodies.[1] From 1900 to 1930 clothing styles and fashions, as well as class and ethnic identities, were dramatically remade in the isles. As former slaves and their children increasingly asserted their status as members of local society they gradually abandoned clothing associated with their servile heritage and adopted fashions which identified them first as free Swahili and later as indigenous Zanzibaris.

The turn-of-the-century aphorism *Pemba peremba*, cited above, succinctly depicts the popular understanding that the period following the abolition of slavery was a time of particular economic flux in the islands of Zanzibar, as well as the recognition of the importance of dress as a terrain for contesting social relations and articulating new social identities. This "terse little saying embodying a general truth" captures the social reality that many members of the islands' plantation-owning Omani aristocracy—whose status was publicly marked by a proudly worn turban (*kilemba*, fig. 2.1)—were being reduced to poverty during this period, while many of their former slaves— previously clad only in loincloths (*winda*, fig. 2.2)—were rising both in class and status. As the latter changed classes and fabricated new identities they also changed their clothes. Former slaves and their freeborn children began adopting elements of free dress that they had formerly been forbidden from wearing, particularly head coverings and shoes, as well as creating new forms of dress as a public and daily expression of their growing autonomy and economic might. New markets for imported cloth opened up, particularly in town, and consumerism was seized by former slaves as one means of articulating their aspirations for upward social mobility.[2] Examining transformations in dress and fashion illustrates one of the many ways that boundaries between ethnic categories, discussed in chapter 1, were negotiated, made visible, and traversed in the course of daily practice.

Historically, changing one's class or ethnicity in East Africa was never as easy as simply changing one's clothes, yet the power of magical clothing to transform poor African freepersons or slaves into Arab or Shirazi sultans served as a common trope in

Fig 2.1. *A male Arab of Zanzibar wearing a kilemba, kanzu, waist scarf, jambia, and short jacket. Reprinted from Guillain,* Documents sur l'Afrique orientale *(1856), vol. 3.*

Fig. 2.2. *Male slaves wearing winda made of merikani cloth. Reprinted from Guillain,* Documents sur l'Afrique orientale *(1856), vol. 3.*

nineteenth-century Swahili oral literature. Several of the stories contained in Edward Steere's *Swahili Tales, as Told by the Natives of Zanzibar,* originally published in 1869, have plots that center on a poor and despised character who dons the clothes of the elite and then is treated with all the pomp and respect of a sultan. There are also stories in this collection with alternative plots in which young men of the elite are dressed in the clothing of slaves or women and thus socially and materially disinherited.[3] In a very real way, dress embodied these characters' identities. While few members of the coastal East African underclass held illusions of succeeding in the transformation of their own identities to the degree of their fictional counterparts, the importance of dressing up to one's status—be it actual or aspirational—was widely recognized throughout East African society.[4]

Innovations in the use of dress, however, were highly gendered—reflecting, in part, the differential experiences men and women had of ethnicity, economic mobility, and political power. Poor women adopted a wider range of previously forbidden "Arab" dress than island men, and Zanzibari women also created entirely new fashions which, while leaving room for the expression of relative degrees of wealth through the choice of fabrics, blurred the distinctions of ethnicity that remained largely intact in male attire throughout the early twentieth century. Where men innovated in clothing fashions, it was through the incorporation of European clothing and accessories.[5] Although both men and women understood the fluidity of social categories, including class and ethnicity, they experienced and negotiated them in different ways and these differences were reflected in their choice of clothing and what they defined as fashionable.

Dress, Class, and Ethnicity in the Nineteenth Century

Travelers to Zanzibar in the nineteenth century regularly remarked on the importance of dress as a marker of class and status differences in society.[6] The fewer and less ornate clothes one wore, the lower was one's status. Slaves in nineteenth-century Zanzibar typically wore only the slightest of clothes, which were usually made of the rudest and cheapest white cloth, known as merikani because it came from the United States. Sources from this period indicate that male and female slaves often wore only one piece of cloth, which men wrapped around their waists (the winda) and women tied under their armpits. At mid-century the quantity, color, and quality of male and female cloth was identical. However, as the decades progressed servile women increasingly sought to differentiate their clothing from that of their male counterparts. By the 1870s, slave women were dyeing their merikani fabrics with locally produced indigo (fig. 2.3), changing the color from white to a deep blue or black, and transforming the cloth itself from merikani to *kaniki*, a dark cloth that was regarded as a feminine

Fig. 2.3. *Female vibarua employed as construction workers wearing kaniki, merikani, and early kanga designs. Reprinted from Vizetelly,* From Cyprus to Zanzibar *(1901).*

form of dress. Merchants from British India had a difficult time break-
ing into the market for merikani, as the cloth manufactured in India
was gray and regarded as dingy and second-rate by local consumers.
But once these manufacturers began dying their cloth with indigo they
quickly captured the local kaniki market.[7] By the end of the century,
local merchants also began producing block-printed designs on merikani cloth, which became known as *kanga za mera*, and these too became incredibly fashionable, particularly among urban female slaves
who could afford them. Thus, even in the nineteenth century, cloth
was read as an indicator of gender, wealth, and status and slaves also
sought to dress up to the degree that they were able.

Because over 95 percent of those who lived in Zanzibar, including slaves, were Muslims, the covering men and women wore on their
heads was also a very important marker of class and status. Slaveholders in East Africa prided themselves on converting their slaves to Islam.[8] The importance of maintaining an immediately perceptible
distinction between slaves and owners, however, overrode the Islamic prescription for believers to cover their heads. Male Muslim
slaves were forbidden from wearing head coverings. As Mtoro bin
Mwinyi Bakari explained of Bagamoyo, a part of the sultan's domin-
ion located on the mainland coast opposite Zanzibar, "A slave was
known by his dress, for never in his life did he wear a cap." He went
on to say, "Female slaves accompanying free women do not wear a
veil or a headcloth."[9] Evidence from Zanzibar suggests that such prohibitions applied on the isles as well and that perhaps as a further
marker of their low social status Zanzibar's slaves also kept their
heads shaved bare (see figs. 2.2, 2.4).[10] The absence of shoes was yet
another immediately visible sign that identified a man or woman as a
member of the servile class, as slaves were also forbidden from wearing shoes in the presence of the freeborn.

At the other end of the social hierarchy were members of aristocratic Omani households who wore the most elaborate of head-
dresses. Omani men were distinguished by a kilemba, composed of
several yards of very expensive cloth, imported from Oman, elaborately wrapped around the head (fig. 2.1). According to contemporary
observers, a man of status never left his home without a kilemba, as

Fig. 2.4. *A suria of Seyyid Said wearing a barakoa and shela, accompanied by a young Nyasa slave attendant, wearing merikani. Reprinted from Guillain,* Documents sur l'Afrique orientale *(1856), vol. 3.*

the kilemba marked him as an Arab man of status and wealth. Female members of Omani households were never seen in public unless they were completely veiled.[11] In nineteenth-century Zanzibar, the veil of such women involved several elements, including a richly embroidered head covering and a silk or brocade scarf that stretched down the back to the knees, called an *ukaya* (figs. 2.5, 2.6). When going out in public women from Omani households also covered their heads and clothes with a dark cloth, known as a *shela*, usually worn as demonstrated in figure 2.4. A few women of the elite, particularly those with paternal connections to the ruling classes in Mombasa or Lamu, draped the black cover over their heads like a tent when walking in public, or had a large, black, tentlike structure carried by slaves under which they walked through the streets. This covering was known in Mombasa as the *ramba* and in Lamu as the *shiraa*, but it was rarely seen in the isles.[12]

Women of the highest classes also wore a silk mask ornately embroidered with gold and silver thread, known as a *barakoa* (the Zanzibar version of the Omani *burqa*), which covered their faces from forehead to mouth, leaving only two holes for the eyes (figs. 2.4, 2.5). The more elaborate the mask the higher the woman's rank and status in society, as well as within a given family. The lavish embroidery on the barakoa of Sultan Seyyid Said's daughter, Seyyida Salme (later known as Emily Ruete), shown in figure 2.5, compared to the unadorned barakoa of a slave concubine (suria) in Seyyid Said's harem illustrates this quite clearly (fig. 2.4).[13] Although Seyyida Salme's mother was also a suria, Salme's rank, status, and future wealth were determined largely by paternity.[14] As a freeborn child with inheritance rights in her father's vast estate, she was adorned much more elaborately than older but unfree members of her father's family.

Once accepted into the harems of the al-Busaidi ruling clan, slave concubines were considered junior members of the family and were expected to conform to patterns of behavior indicative of aristocratic Arab status, including veiling and purdah. As Hilal bin Amour, born

in 1889, explained, *"Masuria* [slave concubines] were the women of Arab men and they dressed just like Arab women. The only difference was that they were not referred to as 'lady' or 'wife.'"[15] Recalling her childhood in the first sultan of Zanzibar's household, Emily Ruete (a.k.a. Seyyida Salme) wrote that masuria were required to change their clothing and adopt patterns of dress that marked them as members of the aristocracy. "People of all races lived in these two houses ... but we were permitted to appear in Arab fashion alone. Any

Fig. 2.5. *Seyyida Salme Said (later known as Emily Ruete), wearing marinda pants and a barakoa. Courtesy of Zanzibar National Archives.*

newly-arrived Circassian or Abyssinian [concubine] had to exchange her ample robes and fantastic attire within three days for the Arab costume provided for her."[16] The important power of dress to signify inclusion within a particular family, class, or ethnic group was thus recognized not only by the poorest members of Zanzibar society, but by its wealthiest members as well. By forcing newly acquired slave concubines to abandon the fashions of their homes, the male Omani elite were literally attempting to strip them of their former identities.[17] The new clothing provided for slave concubines marked their bodies as the property of Omani patriarchs.

Other elements of nineteenth-century Arab women's dress included a long shirt which fell below the knees and tight-fitting pants with frills around the bottoms, known as *marinda* (fig. 2.5). Lavish amounts of gold and silver anklets, bracelets, chains, and earrings were additional markers of a woman's wealth, as the photo of Aziza, the niece of Seyyid Suleiman (the governor of Zanzibar during the reign of Seyyid Said and one of the island's largest holders of human and landed property), graphically illustrates (fig. 2.6). The male parallel of the Arab woman's jewelry was found in the *jambia*, an ornamental dagger worn stuck in the waist cloth, that wealthy Arab men considered the most prized element of their costume and which often had a handle made of gold, silver, jewels, and ivory.[18] Wealthy Omani men also distinguished themselves by the ornateness of the gold and silver embroidery on their floor-length jackets, known as *joho*, and the silk cloths that they tied around their waists (figs. 2.1, 2.7).

According to observers of nineteenth-century Zanzibar, male Swahili residents of the island typically wore a *kanzu*, or white calico gown reaching to the ankles. As freeborn Muslims, they also covered

Fig. 2.6. *Aziza, the niece of Governor Seyyid Suleiman. Reprinted from Guillain,* Documents sur l'Afrique orientale *(1856), vol. 3.*

Fig. 2.7. *A Zanzibari Arab wearing a kilemba, joho, and jambia. Reprinted from Pearce,* Zanzibar *(1920).*

their heads, either with an embroidered cap known as a *kofia* (fig. 2.8) or with a red fez, known in Zanzibar as a *tarbush*.[19] If he was poor, a Swahili man's clothing would be simpler, and perhaps not necessarily white, but care would be taken to insure that his legs and chest were covered and that his head was covered with some type of cap.[20]

Depending on her financial resources, a Swahili woman either dressed in the simple dark cotton cloth of the poor, known as *kaniki* (fig. 2.3), or a piece of imported colored cotton cloth, called *kitambi* (fig. 2.9). According to observers, it was rare to see non-Arab freeborn women veiled in the nine-teenth century.[21] Swahili women, however, did often cover their shoulders, arms, and bodies with an additional piece of cloth that stretched to the ankles when walking in public. Such a cloth was occasionally accompanied by a cap of similar material (figs. 2.9, 2.10). In the mid-nineteenth century, if the Swahili woman's outer

Fig. 2.8. *A Swahili man of Zanzibar wearing a kofia. Reprinted from Guillain,* Documents sur l'Afrique orientale *(1856), vol. 3.*

cloth was dyed dark blue or black it was known as an ukaya. The cloth worn under the ukaya often varied little from that worn by female slaves. It was the wearing of this ukaya which therefore allowed a

Fig. 2.9. (Top) *A Swahili family from Mombasa. Reprinted from Guillain,*
Documents sur l'Afrique orientale *(1856), vol. 3.*
Fig. 2.10. *A Swahili woman of Zanzibar wearing an ukaya. Reprinted from*
Guillain, Documents sur l'Afrique orientale *(1856), vol. 3.*

casual observer to distinguish a poor freeborn woman from a slave
woman in mid-century coastal society.[22]

In nineteenth-century Zanzibar clothing served as an important
and visually immediate signifier of class and status. As is the case

with many of the world's cultures, the clothing of wealthy members of society was far more ornate than that of the working or servile classes. Islam, as the religion of the ruling Omani aristocracy as well as the majority of coastal inhabitants, also contributed additional symbolic markers of status. Free believers, both male and female, were encouraged to cover their heads, while slaves, even if they had converted to Islam, were forbidden from wearing a cap or veil, suggesting that the class interests of the dominant members of society overrode religious recommendations. The bodies of the elite were also elaborately adorned and almost entirely covered, while those of the poor or servile were concealed only to the extent that an individual's social and financial position allowed.

Dressing Up: New Identities and New Clothes

Immediately after abolition, many former slaves began to assert their social and economic autonomy—some by bargaining for reduced labor obligations to their owners, others by establishing themselves as independent peasants, and still others by moving to town.[23] These men and women also increasingly began to identify themselves as Swahili, a coastal freeborn ethnic community. Swahili reputations for being open and accepting of foreigners and guests, as well as socially and culturally eclectic, added to the ease with which "outsiders" could establish their own identities as Swahili.[24] The material and social positions of individual Swahili also varied greatly from town to town along the coast, as well as within each town from household to household, thus minimizing the material acquisitions necessary for "passing" (figs. 2.8, 2.9).[25] From 1890 to 1915, tens of thousands of men and women whose parents would have identified themselves as members of mainland ethnic communities from which slaves were drawn struggled to establish their own identities as Swahili, or free, Muslim members of coastal society.[26] Adopting Swahili-style clothing was one means of giving bodily form to these new identities.

Within three years of abolition, the Swahili *kanzu*, which covered a man from neck to ankle and wrist, had become the most com-

mon form of male clothing in the isles. While nearly all island men
who identified as free Muslims wore a cap and a kanzu, variations in
price and quality served to differentiate wearers by wealth. Local tailors and merchants began sewing kanzus, crafted of merikani cloth,
to meet the rapidly growing local demand of "Swahili" men. These
locally produced kanzus were the cheapest available, selling for one
and a half rupees, or roughly the equivalent of three day's wages.[27]
Men of means frequently sought to set themselves apart from their
poorer brethren, however, by purchasing hand-sewn kanzus that
were embroidered with silk thread and that sold for prices between
three and five times that of the simpler machine-made version. Head
coverings were also in wide demand after abolition. As one analyst of
British trade prospects in the isles suggested, perhaps overenthusias-
tically, ". . . it is the ambition of every black man out here to be able
to sport an embroidered cap [kofia] such as is worn by the aristocratic
Arab." However, the price of these kofias, which were hand sewn and
embroidered with silk thread to match the more expensive kanzus,
sold for more than a typical urban laborer's monthly wage. Felt caps
(tarbush), imported from Austria-Hungary and sold for less than half
a rupee, therefore became the rage among the poorest "Swahili" men.
Beginning around 1900, Asian merchants and manufacturers again began
to cater to this vast potential market, producing simple, machine-
sewn kofias, which sold for somewhere between one-half rupee to one
rupee, depending on the design sewn onto the cap.[28] These machine-
worked caps, produced in Mombasa, gradually replaced the once
fashionable tarbush by the 1910s. By the time of World War I, most
men in Zanzibar dressed in a kanzu and kofia during their leisure
hours, and many during their working hours as well.[29]

The dynamic position of the "Swahili" on the cutting edge of social and cultural innovation also allowed and encouraged them to ex-
periment with the adoption of new fashion materials from across the
globe. Like their wage-earning counterparts on the Zambian Copperbelt and elsewhere on the continent, young Swahili men innovated
on their costumes through the incorporation of imports. In the late
1920s, the tarbush or fez made a fashion comeback among trend-
setting urban youth. In Egypt this style of cap was adopted by young

Egyptian men engaged in "modern" economic and political pursuits.[30] Inspired by the success of Egyptian nationalism and the growing dominance of Egypt as the capital of commercial music and film culture in the Arab world, young men in Zanzibar seized on the tarbush as a fashion symbol of their own cosmopolitanism and "modernity." Elements of European clothing were similarly appropriated during this period and combined "after much anxious thought" and careful planning into innovative costumes.[31] That Europeans found local uses of Western clothing either "haphazard" or patently "offensive" was no deterrent to Swahili men, who took great pride in the creative ways that they could use European clothing items to accessorize a kanzu or transform their fashions altogether.[32] W. H. Ingrams, a colonial official in Zanzibar, was one European who commented explicitly on what he perceived as the increasingly "extravagant inclinations" of "detribalized" Swahili men:

> Recently one has seen objects [Swahili men] clad in fezes with coloured shirts and bow ties, blue serge suits, wearing shoes and socks, wearing a monocle, and smoking cigarettes in long, gold-tipped cigarette-holders. Such caricatures are not pleasing sights to see, and even worse perhaps are the gentlemen who have taken to soft hats and heavy boots. Wristwatches are also in favor.[33]

Ingram's negative evaluation of Swahili men's appropriation of European material culture stemmed in part from his misguided perception that island men were simply mimicking, in rather poor taste, their European superiors. What Ingrams failed to realize was that Swahili appropriations of Western clothing was not a mere imitation of European style. These were new fashions with important local meanings that spoke not to Europeans but to members of an island audience.[34] Captain Craster, a European who noted the careful attention that his own "boys" put into coordinating such outfits, was slightly more sympathetic to local uses of Western clothing. In a section of his memoirs entitled "Our Boys and Their Vanities," he noted the meticulous care with which young men crafted their outfits—deliberately selecting certain caps, pants, and shoes from the local resale market. When he questioned one young man, who had been recently sporting a blue yachting cap, why he had gone back to wearing a red tarbush, the young man explained that the yachting cap looked quite smart with white pants, but that he had recently sold his white trousers. The yachting cap simply did not "go" with a kanzu or his other pants, and he therefore preferred to put the yachting cap away for a while.[35] Sailors employed by the British Royal Navy, who frequently played football and hockey matches against island teams, were a regular source of European clothing and new concepts of fashion for young island men. English words such as *smati* (smart, sharp), *furstklasi* (first-class, excellent), and *fanci* (fancy) also entered into the Kiswahili vocabulary during this era as adjectives used to describe both men's and women's fashions.

Travel and personal relationships with people from outside local society have long been well regarded in Swahili society, as numerous proverbs praising the benefits of travel suggest. The "smart" costumes crafted by young men from items purchased on the local resale market or traded from sailors and shiphands who docked in Zanzibar marked their wearers as men with connections to the wider world.[36]

Men's youthful experiments with fashion were, nonetheless, subject to both debate and critique by other members of society. Many island elders were just as shocked by the sight of young men sporting bow ties, monocles, and gold-tipped cigarette holders as Ingrams, but what they often regarded as even more insidious was the fact that young men were spending cash, which previously would have been shared with other members of the family, increasingly on themselves.[37] The growing individualism of young men who preferred to invest in fashionable clothing, rather than saving to buy plaster or a new door for the family home, was met with a certain degree of trepidation by elders, who found themselves increasingly losing control over both the labor and income of young men in the early twentieth century.[38] Island elders, for instance, encouraged young men to invest their wages in ways that would enhance the status of the entire family, such as building or making improvements on an urban home, buying a fishing boat, or purchasing a farm in the countryside. However, young urban men with access to money earned independent of fathers or patrons often preferred to expend "their" wages in ways that emphasized their individuality and personal autonomy.

The tone of some of these debates about changes in clothing and the values they represented is captured in the following stanzas of a taarab song performed by Siti binti Saad's band. In the 1920s and 1930s, clerks, junior-level members of the colonial service, and even well-paid working-class men began wearing jackets and trousers as symbols of their links to the European-dominated political economy. Many Arab Zanzibaris who worked as low-level bureaucrats within the local colonial administration also began sporting suit coats over their kanzus as emblems of their authority. In this song, some of the discourses circulating in Ng'ambo regarding these men are recorded. In the first stanza of the song, Mwalim Shaaban, who later in life adopted a jacket himself, puts forth the argument that Western fashions, like jackets and trousers, should be viewed as symbols of pride and progress, rather than being condemned. The second stanza of the song, however, gives voice to the adversaries of coats and trousers who objected not only to the fashions themselves, but what they perceived as the hedonistic individualism guiding many of the men who sported jackets and trousers.

> Jackets and trousers are not taboo [*haramu*]
> Especially when worn by a gentleman going to work
> Such men should inspire gazes of desire.
>   Jackets and trousers are not taboo.
>
> When I first saw him it simply did not occur to me
> First he knows no shame and second he is a fraud
> He has destroyed us all, everyone in the neighborhood.
>   Jackets and trousers are not taboo.

Islanders expressed ambivalence about local adoptions of Western fashions because they saw these clothing trends as being linked to the concomitant choice to embrace "Western" values. Of particular concern to people in Ng'ambo was the use of new forms of power by low-level colonial civil servants "to destroy everyone in the neighborhood"—a theme developed in subsequent chapters. As this song suggests, a jacket- and trouser-wearing man may have hoped to inspire "gazes of desire," but in fact many saw this particular apparel combination as indicative of a selfish charlatan. European clothing may have marked a man as "modern" but it simultaneously cast him somewhat outside the boundaries of the local Muslim community, perhaps helping to explain why the rage for European fashions was relatively short-lived, with the exception of jackets, which remained popular among civil servants throughout the colonial era.

During the early years of the twentieth century "Swahili" women also transformed their dress, abandoning items such as the dark kaniki or cheap merikani, those badges of poverty and servility, in favor of the brightly colored kangas (colorful, printed cotton cloths sold in pairs) imported from abroad (fig. 2.11).[39] Although the price of the cheapest kanga was five times the price of a kaniki, by as early as 1900 the former were greatly preferred. The kanga, a new piece good of printed cotton, first began to appear in Zanzibar at reasonably affordable prices during this period, when many former slaves were redefining their ethnic identities and beginning to call themselves Swahili.[40] Abandoning the clothing associated with slave status and adopting new clothing fashions was thus a highly symbolic act for women seeking to publicly pronounce their new status as free women. During the early years of the twentieth century the makers and sellers of kanga were making a fortune off of women in Zanzibar who were said by many to be busily transforming their identities from those of slaves into "slaves of fashion."[41]

According to Jeannette Handby and Elisabeth Linnebuhr, the precursor to the kanga, known as *leso* (from the Portuguese term for handkerchief), was literally invented by women

Fig. 2.11. *Swahili women wearing kangas and grinding grain. Reprinted from Younghusband,* Glimpses of East Africa *(1910).*

in Zanzibar in the late 1870s. Women purchased handkerchief material, sold in strips of three handkerchiefs loomed into a single piece, and then sewed several strips together to form cloths two feet by three feet. These self-created cloths were both unique and significantly cheaper than other forms of cotton piece goods available on the local market.[42] By the 1890s, local merchants and manufacturers began responding to women's demands for cheaper and more variable patterns by block printing on merikani cloth. The earliest designs apparently carried repeating black-spotted motifs, thus inspiring the name *kanga*, after the black-and-white spotted guinea fowl frequently seen in the isles. Kanga za mera followed shortly thereafter and involved block printing of more elaborate designs in red and black on merikani cloth. The first reference to imported kangas appeared in British trade reports in 1897—the year of the abolition decree. Although advocates for British commercial expansion in the isles saw kangas as a new and vast market opportunity, they frequently warned potential investors that "nothing but an intimate knowledge of the local market can determine what designs are most likely to meet the popular taste."[43] Turn-of-the-century island women were quite particular about the designs and colors that they found appealing; they also preferred the sharpness of images created through block printing to those of machine-loomed work. The German, Dutch, and French firms that dominated kanga manufacturing at the turn of the century produced samples of a potential product, which they then sent to Zanzibar for approval or modification before they embarked on a block printing of several thousand pieces, which if found unappealing would never sell. Local Asian merchants, under advice from island women, also created designs that they forwarded on to Europe for production. At the suggestion of island women, kangas also began to carry aphorisms and proverbs, known in Kiswahili as *majina* (names), sometime in the 1910s, and these generally witty sayings quickly came to be regarded as yet another design element that could either enhance a kanga's market potential or cause it to be an utter flop.[44]

The reputation of island women as highly fashion-conscious buyers engaged in endless displays of conspicuous consumption dates from this era. "Zanzibar is the Paris of East Africa," wrote one official in 1900, "and the Zanzibar belles are admittedly the glass of fashion. To keep up their reputation for smart dressing involves the frequent purchase of new *kangas*, of which, I understand, a Zanzibar girl will possess as many as two to three dozen sets at one time."[45] Turn-of-the-century shopkeepers who dealt in kangas reveled in the never-ending marketing opportunities presented by the continuously changing color, pattern, name, and design combinations. Island women preferred cloths that were relatively distinctive and would therefore pay substantially more for a "limited edition" Dutch block print than for the typical English loomed kanga, which arrived in the isles in batches of several thousand.[46] The quick sales and high profits that accompanied the arrival of a popular new design were frequently countered, however, by financial loss when a merchant received a bale of kangas that women found unappealing and the merchant simply could not sell. Even an attractive batch of kangas fell quickly out of fashion. "It must not be supposed that a woman with any proper respect for herself or for her family will be seen in these patterns in three months' time," warned one turn-of-the-century trade official.[47] In order to protect themselves from the calamity of having a large stock of kangas that were going out of style, Asian shopkeepers customarily ordered a limited printing of a particular design, which they hoped to be able to sell within a few weeks of arrival in Zanzibar. In 1900, a newly arrived "smart" kanga design would sell for four to five rupees in the first week of arrival, rapidly dropping in price to a low of one rupee within two months. After that time the only hope a merchant had for disposing of his stock was to ship it off to an associate in Pemba, who, in turn, would ship his unsold stock off to another shopkeeper on the mainland.[48] Women in turn-of-the-century Zanzibar took great pride in establishing the fashion trends of East Africa. Women's husbands, however, frequently complained that the source of women's pride was the source of their own financial and domestic sorrow.[49] Under Islamic law, a man is required to provide his wife with new clothes on a "regular" basis. Keeping her happy and in fashion proved to be a much more daunting task after the invention of kangas. Even in times of drought, when the bottom dropped out of the East African market for the merikani and kaniki worn by slaves and the poor, the demand for kangas in the isles remained remarkably strong.[50]

By the first decade of the twentieth century the formerly common kaniki was associated almost exclusively with women of poor, rural, and slave status. Arafa Salum Ahmed, a town resident born in 1900 and whose family owned slaves, made the connections between clothing, class, status, and urbanity quite explicitly. When asked who wore kaniki she responded,

> Slaves and Swahili people in the countryside [wore kaniki] because of the work they did . . . I *never* wore a kaniki! Even our favored household slaves here in town or those in the houses of the sultan did not wear kaniki. Those were the clothes of rural slaves. We gave our household slaves kanga as demonstrations of their status within our household and to distinguish them from common slaves.[51]

The majority of Zanzibar's nineteenth-century urban slave population did not hold positions as favored domestics in the homes of the elite, rather most of them worked outdoors at the docks, customs shed, or in public works and construction. These "common" urban slaves, particularly those owned by poorer masters, were among the majority of those who went to court to apply for their "freedom papers." Sixty-four percent of the slaves in Zanzibar island who sought emancipation through the courts were city dwellers and over half of them were women.[52] While most slave women employed outside elite households wore the kaniki at the turn of the century (see fig. 2.3), these women were also at the core of those who adopted the kanga during the coming decade as emblems of their growing financial and personal autonomy.[53]

Only one locally born respondent to my 1995 clothing survey, a former slave woman who was born in the countryside of Zanzibar, admitted to wearing a kaniki on a daily basis in the 1920s and 1930s. Nearly all her urban contemporaries asserted that the kaniki "was not something worn in town." As one woman said when asked if she wore a kaniki, *"Si mshamba mie!"* The literal translation of this phrase is "I am not from the country," but the term *mshamba* (a person from the country) carries a great deal more meaning, generally implying boorish, countrified, and unpolished manners. Urban women born in the 1910s or later universally identified wearers of kaniki as belonging to one of three categories of people: slaves, people from the mainland, or country bumpkins. By World War I, all fashionable urban women with any disposable income wore kangas. Reflecting comments made by several other women, Maryam Mohamed argued, "Everyone in town preferred to wear a kanga, the kanga was the *epitome* of urban style in those days!"[54] When I asked another of Maryam's contemporaries, Fatuma Abdalla, about women's preference for kanga or kaniki she said, "It really depended on your financial and social ability (*uwezo wako*). But here in town the kanga ruled!"[55] *Uwezo* is often used by Kiswahili speakers to differentiate the haves from the have nots, and as Garth Myers has demonstrated, uwezo was a critical determinant not only of clothing style, but of living patterns and housing fabrication as well.[56] Social and economic ability, uwezo, was publicly displayed through consumption. Although several Swahili women admitted to wearing kaniki while doing household chores as a means of protecting their "real" clothes, they were insistent that no woman with uwezo would dare to step outside her home in a kaniki. That would be the death knell of her status as a fashionable, upwardly mobile urbanite. Other women who self-identified as members of the urban poor and who continued to work in jobs associated with servility long after the abolition of slavery were much more willing, however, to admit to wearing kaniki into the 1910s and 1920s. They suggested that kaniki were preferred for work because they were durable and did not show dirt very easily. Even these women, however, considered kangas as their "dress clothes." They said it was fine to wear kaniki while hauling rock, farm produce, or water, but whenever they went "out about town," to meet a "companion" or to participate in any number of urban leisure activities, they always changed into kangas first.[57]

In the years following World War I, kanikis also came to be identified with women of mainland origin, who were generally regarded by islanders as far from en vogue. Women who immigrated to Zanzibar from mainland Tanganyika during the 1920s and 1930s often continued to wear kaniki after their arrival in the isles. During the course of interviews, however, they unanimously confessed that after spending time in "fashion-conscious" urban Zanzibar they too felt pressed to adopt the kanga, at least when going "out." The speed with which they abandoned their kaniki in favor of the kanga depended both on their relative desire to integrate themselves in local society and on their ability to earn the requisite disposable income for the purchase of a pair or two of kangas.

Island women generally spoke of their adoption of the kanga as a public display of their urbanity, style, and uwezo, yet mainlanders discussed such displays of conspicuous consumption with a great deal more derision. A descendant of former slaves who claimed in the years between the wars to have purchased a new pair of kangas every Saturday as an expression of her uwezo explained that the only time she ever wore kaniki outside her home was when she went to visit relatives on the mainland outside Dar es Salaam. "They didn't wear kangas there. If I wore a different kanga every day, like I did here in town, people would say, 'Kanga, kanga, kanga. She must be a vain, pretentious woman from Zanzibar.'"[58] Mainlanders' association of kangas with women who "put on airs" were even popularized through *beni (ngoma)* songs, such as the following, recorded outside Nairobi after World War I: "When she puts on a kanga the foolish girl starts to act so smart. / Better the kaniki, dark as rain clouds."[59] Of course, most participants in beni ngoma groups at this time were East African men, who probably objected to kangas not only because the women who wore them "acted so smart," but also because if their own wives and girlfriends developed a taste for kangas it would be much more difficult to keep them "dressed" than if they stuck to the plain old black kaniki. In the early twentieth century wearing a kanga, and particularly having a variety of kangas from which to choose each day, identified the wearer as an urban woman, most likely from Zanzibar, with a relative degree of wealth, a flare for modern fashion, and at least a bit of affectation.

Like their male counterparts, Swahili women used the consumption of imported, trendy clothing to express their economic autonomy and "modern" twentieth-century identities. Kangas sporting central motifs of electric lights, clocks, bicycles, trains, automobiles, steamships, and other symbols of technological innovation and mobility were particularly popular among these new Swahili women in the early decades of the twentieth century. Appreciations for style, patterns, and color, which found expression among elderly women of mainland origin through tattooing and bodily scarification, were echoed by their Swahili daughters and Zanzibari granddaughters, who saw the frequency with which color and design could be *changed* as a major part of the appeal of kangas. In the Paris of the Indian Ocean, young Swahili men and women were on the cutting edge of defining urban fashion as they simultaneously redefined themselves as free, twentieth-century individuals.

Islam, Veiling, and Respectability

The adoption of Arab clothing, as suggested in Pemba peremba, was also a strategy employed by former slaves, many of whom also claimed Arab ethnicities in lieu of Swahili, as they asserted their independence during the first three decades of the twentieth century.[60] Commenting on the widespread adoption of "Arab" fashions, including the veil, by women of servile heritage, Adija Salum Bakari explained,

> During the days of slavery one was not allowed to wear certain clothes, these were the clothes of the Arabs. But, after slavery was done away with and the British grabbed political power, the Swahili and others started to wear these clothes. Now you felt like you had become one of the *mabibi* [wealthy Arab mistresses, ladies]. In the earlier days you couldn't wear such clothes, only the wealthy Arabs wore them. You could never dress like a mistress. Now, however, you could dress like a lady. . . . No one could stop you.[61]

The association of veiling and purdah with status, property, and propriety was widespread in precolonial Muslim Africa. Research across the continent indicates that the adoption of the veil and increased seclusion on the part of slave women was common within families that aspired to move up the social hierarchy in the post-abolition period.[62] In coastal East Africa as well, the adoption of various forms of the veil by servile women was an indication of their growing empowerment. Explaining the difference between contemporary slaves in a portion of the sultan's dominions along the East African coast and those of the past, Mtoro bin Mwinyi Bakari, first published in 1903, asserted that slaves no longer did the work that they used to do; they were disobedient as well as disrespectful. In Mtoro's opinion this "revolution" in slave behavior, when "slaves began to give themselves airs," could be traced to the actions of several slave owners who broke rank with other members of the urban ruling class and gave their female slaves ukaya, veils previously reserved for the free.[63] Reflecting the sentiments of the dominant class, Mtoro observed a distinct correlation between lines of dress that demarcated class and status, and respect for the hierarchies embodied in the dress themselves.

The fashions of veiling popular in the isles changed significantly over time, although they continued to vary depending on wealth and residence. While prescriptions for veiling in public were followed by only the most elite of women in nineteenth-century Zanzibar, by the first decade of the twentieth century nearly all free women in the isles were at least covering their heads and shoulders with a kanga when in public, as illustrated in figure 2.12. Covering the head with a kanga remained the most common form of veiling practiced by women in the countryside through the 1950s. Variability along class lines remained, however, as very wealthy rural women often followed the veiling fashions of town more closely than their poorer rural neighbors, while the poorest urban women often remained content with the simplicity and relative affordability of the kanga over the more elaborate and expensive veils that became fashionable in town.

Around the turn of the century a new form of veil, the *buibui*, also began to appear in Zanzibar (figs. 2.13, 2.14).[64] It was first worn exclusively by the urban elite: wealthy Omani, Comorian, and Arab women of "mixed blood," but was later adopted by women of all ethnic and class backgrounds in the isles. Explaining the rapid spread of the buibui in the years immediately following World War I, several informants suggested that the buibui was "the latest thing to hit town" or that it became the fashion that "everyone who was anyone" was wearing.[65]

Fig. 2.12. *Women wearing kangas and men wearing kanzus and kofias in Zanzibar, c. 1910. Courtesy of Zanzibar National Archives.*

European observers resident in the isles made similar assertions, suggesting that by the 1920s all Zanzibari women of "quality" as well as those who "aspired" to move beyond the lower classes were wearing the buibui.[66] Just as "Swahili" women in the 1900s seized the ever-changing patterns of the kanga as a sign of their transforming identities, young "Zanzibari" women born in the first postemancipation generation adopted the buibui. Women born during and after World War I equated the adoption of the buibui with their families' growing respectability, adherence to Islam, sense of belonging within the island community, and wealth.[67] By the late 1920s, as the number of islanders identifying as members of "indigenous" ethnic categories swelled and those of the Swahili plummeted, complete veiling with the black buibui, as illustrated in figure 2.14, became nearly universal in town.

The buibui was comprised of a long piece of dark silk or cotton cloth sewn in a circle and then tied around the head with a string, as illustrated most clearly in figure 2.13. The buibui also had a sheer veil, known as an ukaya, that could be draped in front of the face, as

Fig. 2.13. *Zanzibari women wearing buibuis, illustrating two veiling fashions. The long cloth hanging from the top of the head down the back is known as an ukaya and can be worn in many ways. Illustration by Helen Liu.*

demonstrated by the woman on the right in figure 2.13 or by the women in figure 2.14. Alternatively, the ukaya could be left hanging down the back of the head, as worn by the woman on the left in figure 2.13. Although figure 2.14 suggests that the face cloth was opaque, in reality it was made of sheer silk or thinly woven cotton, which easily allowed a woman to see where she was going. The style of wearing the buibui illustrated in figure 2.14 was known as *ghubighubi*, from the Kiswahili *ghubika*, to cover from head to foot. According to respondents, ghubighubi was *the* way in which the buibui was worn between the time it first became fashionable, after World War I, until the late 1950s or early 1960s. The ghubighubi fashion was eventually replaced by the fashions illustrated in figure 2.13, the one on the left being known as wazi, or open, and the one on the right as kizoro, after the character in the Zorro films that were popular at the local cinemas. Although some women began to abandon the ghubighubi style in the 1950s, survey respondents were in consensus that after the postindependence revolution, in 1964, women were no longer *allowed* to cover themselves in such a way. Some women suggested that government prohibitions on ghubighubi were the result of socialist policies intended to bring women out of purdah and make them the equals of men, while others interpreted the banning of the ghubighubi style as yet another of the Afro-Shirazi Party's misguided attacks on "Arab" cultural forms. Other women argued that the new president, Abeid Karume, banned ghubighubi out of fear that an enemy intent on assassinating him could hide a weapon, as well as his or her own iden-

Fig. 2.14. *Zanzibari women wearing buibuis in the ghubighubi style and marinda pants. Courtesy of Zanzibar National Archives.*

tity, under the cover of a buibui worn in such a way. Regardless of the reason, after 1964 the ghubighubi fashion was no longer worn by women in the isles.

For the women who came of age following the First World War, covering themselves from head to foot with a buibui was a public demonstration of their respectworthiness as well as their growing understanding of Islamic prescriptions for modesty in dress and behavior. To paraphrase the responses most frequently given to the question,

"Why did women begin to wear the buibui instead of a kanga or
ukaya?" respondents suggested, "A buibui covered you completely,
rather than simply covering your head, and was therefore a sign of respect for yourself, your parents, and Islam." Others suggested, "For religious reasons it was best if you covered your body, especially in front
of men"; "Covering yourself in public demonstrated your modesty";
or "The buibui symbolized that you were a woman of dignity and
rank, and worthy of respect."[68] Although few of the mothers of women
born in the 1910s wore the buibui, they gave buibuis to their daughters
as evidence that their children were "becoming more educated about
Islam"[69] and that "owners could no longer stop [them] from asserting
[their] respectability."[70]

During this same period the number of adherents to Sufism,
particularly the Qadiriyya brotherhood, expanded dramatically in
Zanzibar. New forms of Islamic ritual and practice centered around
tariqa spread widely as former slaves made new claims to the importance of religious practice and piety as the basis for spiritual standing and equality.[71] Unlike the Ibadhi and Shafi'i schools, which
dominated Zanzibar during the nineteenth century, status within
the Sufi brotherhoods was based on religious devotion rather than
heritage or having studied with the most prestigious scholars. The
egalitarian nature of tariqa doctrine and practice in East Africa was
reflected in the relatively large number of individuals from marginal
backgrounds who rose to leadership positions within the brotherhoods as well as the open participation of women in many Sufi religious rituals.[72] The spread of veiling among women of the urban
working poor proclaimed their equality before God as well as their
right to act as respectable adherents of the Prophet's call for modesty among both women and men. The buibui also symbolized
women's growing identities as Muslim Zanzibaris; it was worn by
all young women regardless of class or ethnic background.[73] When
asked to explain why so many young women of her generation
adopted the buibui while those of her mother's generation did not,
one woman explained, "Because we had the opportunity to read and
study we understood the meaning of the Qur'an. God will forgive
them, our elders did not have such opportunities."[74] As the tariqa

brotherhoods, many of which had their roots in the isles, spread throughout East Africa it appears as though the buibui followed in their wake.[75]

While the buibui reflected a growing ideology of spiritual equality among East African Muslims, it nonetheless allowed Zanzibari women the freedom to express and debate hierarchies rooted in a more material basis. The range of imported fabrics that were fashioned into buibuis during this period was extensive and each had a name, often reflecting the particular qualities of the cloth. Women of property displayed their wealth by purchasing fine black silks from which their buibuis were made. The majority of the islands' women, however, typically wore buibuis crafted from imported cottons, though here again the quality of the cotton, its rarity on the local market, or the fineness of the silk or gauze used for the ukaya worn in front of the face were viewed as important displays of consumerism and class.[76] Women often saved over considerable periods of time in order to purchase a higher-grade fabric for their buibuis, as one's public presentation of self-worth was literally wrapped in the choice of buibui cloth.[77] While buibui fabrics were widely read as public statements of uwezo, a number of women suggested that buibuis could also be used to conceal poverty. A buibui crafted from a fine grade of cloth could allow a relatively poor woman to present a public persona of middle-class wealth and respectability. As Salma Halfa told me, "If you put on your buibui no one will know what kind of clothes you have on underneath. Maybe your clothes are ripped or badly worn, but once you put on your buibui you appear clean and beautiful."[78]

A number of respondents also said that the relative anonymity of a buibui allowed women the freedom to engage in activities that ran counter to the very images of respectability they and their families were seeking to advance. A buibui could easily be used to disguise a wearer's identity, particularly at night. Under the cover of a veil worn in the ghubighubi fashion a woman could rendezvous with a lover, enter a house known for selling alcohol, or go to a party uninvited and feel relatively secure that word of her activities would not get back to her parents or husband.[79] Additional precautions were sometimes taken by women who regularly engaged in such activities, such as purchasing a special pair of cheap shoes that could be discretely switched mid-journey for one's regular shoes. As one woman said of the freedom the buibui brought, "If you respected yourself and your parents, but let's say you had a boyfriend they did not know about or you wanted to go drink *gongo* [alcohol distilled from papaya]. You could cover yourself ghubighubi and no one could tell who you were, because all the women in town were wearing buibuis in a similar fashion."

Like the adoption of the kanga by the preceding generation, the wearing of the buibui during its early years was associated with uwezo, social and economic ability.[80] If wearing the buibui acted as a public expression of uwezo, however, it appears as though nearly every young woman who came of age in the 1920s and 1930s in urban Zanzibar had such aspirations. Although few of the mothers or grandmothers of survey respondents adopted the buibui—"each generation has its fashions," explained Fatuma Abdalla[81]—96 percent of the women interviewed who were born in Zanzibar after World War I wore the ghubighubi style in their youth. As "Swahili" mothers gave birth to the first post-abolition generation they not only identified their children as indigenous islanders on their birth certificates, they also gave their daughters buibuis when they matured as visible, public expressions of their children's identities as free, good Muslim Zanzibaris.[82]

A family's relative sense of belonging within the urban citizenry was, nonetheless, reflected in the age at which their daughters first began to wear the buibui.[83] Women from wealthy, Arab, or high-status family backgrounds were typically given their first buibui by their mothers when they were between the ages of seven and ten. Women born in Ng'ambo whose parents were of the laboring classes generally received their first buibui at puberty, or roughly age fourteen. Women born in the countryside typically did not begin to wear a buibui until after they were married, if they wore one at all. When women in the countryside did begin to wear the buibui in large numbers, beginning after World War II, they were often given their first buibui by their husbands as part of their marriage trousseau. The relative "strictness" of a woman's parents resulted in exceptions to these general patterns, however, as a few girls born to working-class parents in Ng'ambo were also given their first buibui well before puberty. Many female migrants from the mainland never adopted the buibui at all, although, as several who did explained, if they wanted to fit in to urban society and be respected they wore buibuis, just like women from Zanzibar. Wearing a buibui was an immediately visible sign that an urban woman, no matter where she came from, identified herself and wanted to be perceived by others as a member of local society.

Women's remembrances of how they felt about wearing their first buibui varied considerably, although most considered the buibui a sign of their growing maturity. Several women who began wearing a buibui at an early age said they felt confined and found their previous freedom to run and jump replaced with continuous tripping when they first began to veil. More typically, however, women said that they felt "fashionable," "respectable," or "like a woman" once they began to go out in a buibui. As Shemsa Mohammed explained,

> A girl started wearing a buibui when still quite young [between seven and ten years of age] because that was the style in those days. At the same time, you gained a certain respectability if you wore a buibui. As a child you were sewn a buibui when you were still small. It would have a very big hem underneath that you would let down as you grew. Each time the hem got let down you felt like you were growing into a woman, like you too were becoming a woman like your mother.[84]

Other women made similar connections between the buibui and adulthood, although for those old enough to personally remember slavery the assertion was that a woman who donned a buibui was making a political statement about her own status as a social adult, rather than her perpetual status as a legal minor under slavery. Adija Salum Bakari, who was born during World War I, vividly recalled the different associations of adulthood that she and her mother made with the buibui.

> Women of the Arab aristocracy were the first to wear the buibui. Slaves were forbidden from wearing the buibui; only the Arab ladies were

allowed to wear it. I remember my mother telling me how she and her friends went out and bought cloth and began wearing buibuis after the end of slavery and how she felt like an adult, like a real lady after she put on her buibui. . . . When I reached puberty my mother had a buibui made for me. I saw myself as beautiful. Suddenly, I felt the happiness of being a woman, a grown, adult woman.[85]

Adija's remarks clearly illustrate the powerful implications that veiling with a buibui had for transforming a woman's own self-perception, as well as others' perceptions of her. Women like Adija, who came of age during the late 1920s or 1930s, often equated their own adoption of the buibui with signs of physical maturation, whereas women of the preceding generation, like Adija's mother, who came of age around the turn of the century, perceived the increasing prevalence of veiling as symbolic of their own development as autonomous social adults.

The adoption of a buibui worn in the ghubighubi style greatly enhanced a women's self-perception as a respectable, urban Muslim lady, yet there is also evidence to suggest that the veil did not always succeed in masking a wearer's simultaneous identity as a woman of marginal status. One of the perennial questions raised by many historians of taarab music in Zanzibar has been, Why did Siti binti Saad cover her face with a black veil when she performed in public?[86] While the answer now seems obvious, Because all women of her generation wore the buibui in such a way, it was a dissatisfaction with the typical answer (because she was ugly) that led me to research the history of the buibui in the first place. Discourses on Siti's allegedly "hideous" features are widespread in Zanzibar. Many people, including those who greatly admire her music, have suggested that the reason she covered her face during performance was out of embarrassment for her looks. When confronted with a picture of Siti (fig. 2.15), many respondents were genuinely surprised by how attractive she was, but they nonetheless generally remained adamant that the descriptions they had heard of her physical appearance uniformly emphasized her ugliness.

This discrepancy between people's personal reaction to Siti's photo and their understanding, based on hearsay, of what she looked like serves to illustrate that although donning a buibui allowed a woman to feel beautiful, contemporary standards of beauty remained based on "Arab" physical and cultural norms. One of the first extensive accounts of Siti's band and their music, published in 1966, was authored by Ali Ahmed Jahadhmy, a child of patricians from the neighboring island of Lamu who grew up in Zanzibar, where he circulated among the intellectual and political elite of Stone Town. Although Jahadhmy described the first performance where he heard Siti sing, at a local cinema hall, in glowing poetic phrases, his de-

Fig. 2.15. *Siti binti Saad*

scription of her physical features was decidedly less positive:

> The theatre was full, all the island's leading citizens were there because it was a benefit concert and, more important, it was said that Siti binti Saad would sing. Oh, I remember the way the beautiful sound pierced my chest and slowly crept over my entire body! Siti binti Saad, what kind of a voice is this? You are an angel! . . . Her voice had no earthly comparison. . . .
>
> But the thing that I did not know that first night when I heard Siti was that the power of her beauty to draw one near was not equal to that of her voice; when I saw her she was wearing a buibui and she had a satin veil covering her face; I was fooled by her beautiful disguise. . . . But the person who said, "all that glitters is not gold" foretold what I came to realize the second time I came to see Siti face to face. I understood what drew her to cover her face when she sang. . . . Covering her face . . . was a way to draw people near rather than making them run away.[87]

Jahadhmy then proceeds to describe Siti's physical appearance, stressing the prominence of her African features. He criticizes Siti's looks because "her face was not beautiful . . . she did not have soft straight hair or eyes like saucers, her eyebrows were not thick, her nose was not long and thin."[88]

Jahadhmy's suggestion that the presence of African features was enough to make a patrician man like himself turn tail and run from a woman—no matter how stunning her other qualities —indicates that despite their own assertions of equality it would take more than a veil to earn African women from servile backgrounds acceptance among the male Arab elite. Nonetheless, Jahadhmy's comments also reflect the perceptions of many women who wore their veils in the ghubighubi fashion: that the cover of a buibui allowed them to project an image of beauty and respectability that was generally accepted, even if only while the buibui was on. Under the cover of a buibui a woman could veil her class or ethnic heritage long enough to gain recognition for accomplishments that might otherwise have been completely ignored simply because of her African or servile origins.

Gender, Politics, and Cultural Change

During the first three decades of the twentieth century formerly strict divisions between the clothing of the female elite of Arab households and those of the urban poor began to give way as "Swahili" women increasingly began to adopt certain forms of dress associated with women of the aristocracy, while women of the elite also abandoned other elements of their nineteenth-century costume, such as the barakoa in favor of the buibui. Changes in the clothing styles of male members of the islands' communities were far less extensive, however. By the turn of the century the kanzu and the kofia became the most common items of clothing for men living in Zanzibar. Unlike Swahili women, however, Swahili men neither incorporated elements of male Omani dress into their costume nor created new fashions, like the buibui, which were simultaneously adopted by Arab men. While former slaves of both genders redefined their social identities over time, women and men articulated these changes in different ways. Among the elite as well, there were gendered differences in expression of social position. The costume of the male members of the Arab ruling class remained largely static over the course of more than a century, as revealed by a comparison of figure 2.1 from the 1850s, figure 2.7 from the 1920s, and pictures of the sultans who ruled in the 1960s. Explaining the reasons behind gendered innovations in dress is difficult, even for Zanzibaris, yet the relative mutability or fastness of fashion possibly reflects the gendered ways in which ethnicity was experienced as well as the gendered means by which access to property and power were achieved in the isles.[89]

Gendered understandings of ethnicity as a fluid and mutable category had deep social and historical roots in the isles. The very fact that one's "official" ethnicity was reckoned patrilineally in Zanzibar would presumably suggest that men invested ethnicity with a much greater sense of permanence than women. A male child who grew up identifying as a Manyema would typically have children who were also identified at birth as Manyema; the children of a male Arab were similarly defined as Arab. A female Manyema, however, could give birth to a child who was Manyema, Swahili, Zaramo, Shihiri, or Arab, or to a number of children, each of whom had a different ethnicity, all of which were different from her own. Interethnic relationships resulting in the birth of children were common in nineteenth- and twentieth-century Zanzibar. The most prominent example of this was of course Seyyid Said, Zanzibar's first sultan. Although some of the mothers of his one hundred children came from as far away as contemporary Ethiopia and central Asia, the children, like their father, were identified as Omani Arabs and they became the core of the islands' "Arab" ruling class.[90] Women of all classes and ethnic backgrounds also frequently had children with more than one father over the course of their lives, thus further increasing the likelihood that when they imagined their own biological families it would be in multiethnic terms.[91] The experience of a single woman giving birth to a number of children who "belonged" to a range of ethnic categories would have conceivably empowered Zanzibaris to recognize the importance of social process, rather than mere biology, in determining such identities. Such a recognition may have been stronger among the poor and socially marginal, as women of wealth and status were strongly discouraged from having children with men "below their rank,"[92] while children of the male elite presumably had little reason to refuse the privileges they inherited at birth.

The procreative powers of island women provided them with the opportunity to transform not only the ethnic identity of their children but their children's class position as well. In the nineteenth century, children born of free fathers and masuria were considered free, legitimate, and the social equals of children born by their father with a free woman. Islamic law combined with local practice to guarantee all children, regardless of their mother's status, equal rights of inheritance in their father's estate. By having a child with a man of wealth and property a poor or slave woman could provide her child with access to important economic and social resources. Evidence is abundant of women from marginal backgrounds giving birth to children with propertied men, thus granting the children a share in the estate and gaining economic and social usufruct for themselves.[93] As one Swahili woman reflected on her own marriage at the age of fifteen to a man of seventy who owned a stone home in town as well as several clove plantations in the countryside, "If I had children with him they would inherit his property."[94] Although the choice of marriage partners, particularly for young women, was often determined by fathers or owners and only later in the life cycle by women themselves, the power of women's fecundity to effect social mobility was widely recognized throughout island society. The first marriage of many women interviewed was arranged with the precise intent of helping them, their children, and by association their entire extended family to move up the social and economic ladder.

There is a strong correlation in the census data between control of property and identity as a member of one of Zanzibar's indigenous ethnic communities. Perhaps the fact that women's procreative powers provided them with a gendered means for gaining access to property helps to explain why there were 22 percent more women than men identifying themselves as natives of Unguja island by the time of the 1924 census.[95] A variety of evidence seems to suggest that women who found it in their interest to do so claimed the class and ethnic status of their husbands or children. While such options were also theoretically available to men, in actual practice it was rare for a man to marry a woman who ranked above him in the social hierarchy or claim paternity of her children.[96] Women's procreative powers gave them potential, although limited, access to wealth and property that men had to acquire through other means.

The differential access that men and women had to formal structures of political power was also deeply connected to their understandings of ethnicity as a social category. Men's access to political franchise in colonial Zanzibar was generated, articulated, and organized through "ethnic associations" defined by the state in very static and bounded terms. The only means by which a man could gain access to the formal channels of political power during the colonial period was by joining the Arab Association, the Indian National Association, or the Ismailian, Goan, Hindu, Parsee, Bohoran, Shirazi, or African associations.[97] By the 1930s and 1940s, many men who were disenfranchised solely on the basis of ethnicity (i.e., they were identified by the state as Africa), including Comorians and Shirazi, began to demand reclassification as Arab, or at least "non-Native" so that they too could have access to the formal structures and benefits of state politics.[98] Collective associations based on "ethnicity" were upheld to men as *the* model of successful political advancement. Until World War II, when the African and Shirazi associations began to compete for members, however, only men were allowed formal membership in these ethnic-political associations. This does not mean that women were not also involved in efforts to effect perceptions of individual and communal standing. As Shirazi and Comorian men elected association officers, distributed membership cards, and lobbied members of the Legislative Council to reclassify their members as Arabs, women donned the buibui and increasingly began practicing purdah. During World War II, when being identified as Arab took on renewed political importance because of the politics of rationing and efforts on the part of "Africans" to gain seats in legislative affairs, growing numbers of urban women withdrew from mixed-sex public spaces.[99] Taarab bands and performances, which had previously been mixed, became gender segregated. New taarab bands whose membership was exclusively female were also created during World War II by young urban women seeking opportunities for "respectable" leisure activities.[100] Women's wedding celebrations and dances were moved indoors or behind screens and football crowds became almost all male at this time. Public political debates and actions also became increasingly segregated by gender, as men in Ng'ambo began to fight for inclusion within colonial political institutions that were defined as male preserves.

The importance of gender and ethnicity as basis for political power in colonial Zanzibar exacerbated the tenacity with which "Omani" Arab men clung to the ethnic identities they were given at birth, as well as the clothing which marked them as inheritors of such privilege. The kilemba, joho, and jambia of the nineteenth-century male costume remained widely popular among the enfranchised elite until the time of the revolution, in 1964. On the other hand, a prominent visual representation of women's status on the margins of Arab privilege, particularly after the establishment of colonial rule, was the near abandonment of the barakoa in the early years of the twentieth century. While all women of the aristocracy wore barakoa in the nineteenth century, informants born in the 1920s or later typically identified the two wives of Sultan Khalifa, who ruled the isles from 1911 to 1960, as the only women ever seen in a barakoa.[101] "Barakoa were only worn by royalty, those with the power to rule," said Mgeni Ali Hassan.[102] Several other women elaborated on this connection, explaining that Bibi Matuka, the first wife of Sultan Khalifa, proudly wore the barakoa long after it had gone out of fashion among other women of the Arab elite because it symbolized her paternal connection to the dynasty of Seyyid Said. In the context of discussions surrounding the barakoa, numerous women mentioned that Bibi Matuka's husband, Sultan Khalifa, was only distantly related to the royal family and certainly not next in line to "inherit" the throne, but that through his marriage to Bibi Matuka, the sister of the previous sultan, daughter of the sultan who preceded him, and great-granddaughter of the founder of the royal family, Seyyid Said, Khalifa's claims to the throne were "legitimated."[103] There was a distinct association in the minds of these Zanzibari women between the barakoa and women's access to state power under the Omanis. Although the number of women who were able to wield political power in the precolonial period was limited, there was nonetheless a long history of female rulers along the Swahili coast and certainly a widely recognized acceptance of women's ability to exercise authority behind the scenes.[104] As women became increasingly disenfranchised during the colonial era the barakoa gradually disappeared. Maulid Rehani made the point most succinctly: "As the power of the English increased the number of women wearing the barakoa decreased. Every form of rule has its signs."[105]

Not all women within aristocratic families were powerful, however, and the doubly marginal status of many female members of aristocratic households, as both women and slaves, combined with contestations over patriarchal control of their bodies and persons might provide additional clues for understanding why nineteenth-century elite female attire was nearly abandoned in the twentieth century while that of the male aristocracy was not. Referring to the abilities of poor women to travel freely in public any time of the day or receive guests outside of their immediate families without the encumbrance of a barakoa, Emily Ruete remarked, "I must say that ladies of higher rank often envy their poorer sisters on account of their advantages. . . ."[106] Evidence regarding other aspects of aristocratic women's personal, social, and cultural lives suggests that struggles around patriarchal definitions of appropriate female behavior were fairly endemic within elite households. European observers regularly remarked on the "unruly," "demanding," and "contentious" behavior of women in aristocratic households, especially slave concubines (masuria).[107] Rebelling against patriarchal limits on social and sexual freedom was not unique to concubines, however, as Ruete's own affair with a German merchant and subsequent premarital pregnancy attest. Throughout her memoirs Ruete cites numerous examples of women escaping the walls that were intended to confine them, including her own father's Persian wife, Shesade, who hunted and rode horseback, unveiled, in broad daylight and was apparently equally public about her extramarital affairs.[108] This widely known taarab song from the early twentieth century, describing the escape of a woman in purdah to a rendezvous with her lover, suggests that the escapades of Shesade and Ruete were not unique.

It is surprising that which is guarded well and with honor.

The guarded always escapes and goes to the robber.
The habitual thief's eyes opened wide, and the guarded said,
'Thief, steal me quickly, I should go back and be guarded.'[109]

If some nineteenth-century elite women found purdah confining it is perhaps not surprising that their daughters sought to modify its more cumbersome or malleable components in the early twentieth century. The careful guarding of young women's social and sexual honor remained important to propertied families; however, fashion was an aspect of personal life over which young women exercised increasing autonomy. In the Paris of the Indian Ocean, young Arab women were just as desperate to keep up with fashion as their Swahili cousins. By the 1920s, being seen in a barakoa was decidedly passé. "The style of life had changed and the time of the barakoa had passed," said several Arabs whose grandmothers or great-grandmothers had worn a barakoa at the turn of the century. The anonymous cover of a buibui worn in the ghubighubi fashion also may have been simply a more practical style of dress for elite Arab women hoping to steal away to secret meetings with their lovers.

The power of patronage to affect social and political standing was

also gendered in ways that impacted clothing. Barred from participation in the legislative, administrative, and advisory bodies that became the center of Arab male privilege during the colonial era, elite women continued to cultivate social power in ways that were more reflective of nineteenth-century patterns. While many enfranchised men sought to cut themselves off from increasingly unrewarding obligations to cli-

Fig. 2.16. *Swahili woman of Zanzibar wearing a kilemba, kanga, and marinda pants. Reprinted from Younghusband,* Glimpses of East Africa *(1910).*

Fig. 2.17. *Seyyida Salme Said (later known as Emily Ruete). Courtesy of Zanzibar National Archives.*

ents, maintaining their positions as patrons was critical for Arab women hoping to retain some semblance of social and political power. As Strobel argued for Mombasa, elite women in Zanzibar also participated in and sponsored cultural activities, particularly dance associations, that helped to maintain their standing in urban society.

Mkinda, a new form of female initiation created by women in urban Zanzibar between 1896 and 1902, was one form of cultural expression that allowed elite women to retain their status as patrons while simultaneously permitting women from servile backgrounds to break down visual boundaries that marked their inferior status. It was in the context of participating in the dances associated with mkinda—*kunguiya* and particularly *ndege*—that Swahili women first appropriated "Arab" clothing on a mass scale, including marinda pants and kilembas, as illustrated in figures 2.16, 2.17, and 2.18. When shown the picture of the woman in figure 2.16, elderly island women overwhelmingly identified her as wearing *mtindo wa kiparisi* (the fashion of little Paris) or *nguo za kiarabu* (Arab dress). "The Arabs were the ones who really wore those outfits," said Rahma Himid, "but we Swahili who succeeded in acquiring things for ourselves [*waliojipata*] wore them too."[110] Several other women said, "The Arabs wore marinda pants and kilembas and we Swahili copied them when we wanted to wear fancy dress," particularly during ndege processions.[111]

Participation in the dances associated with female initiation ceremonies, widely known in East Africa under the generic title *unyago*,

Fig. 2.18. *Amina Seif Othman (BiAmina Mapande),* nyakanga *(leader) of* mkinda *initiation, during a performance of* ndege. *Photo by the author, 1995.*

was taboo for elite women in the nineteenth century. Unyago ceremonies served to mark the physical and social transformation of young East African girls into women. These ceremonies began at the point of menstruation when a girl was introduced to an elderly female teacher, commonly known as a *kungwi*, who taught her about the physical changes taking place in her body and how to care for her personal hygiene during menstruation. When a number of girls in a given area reached puberty their mothers and instructors would prepare a collective initiation ceremony which, depending on the cultural group, lasted between seven days and several months. Through a series of lectures, dances, songs, and demonstrations girls were taught about male and female physiology; the physical aspects of sexuality, desire, and orgasm; fertility enhancement and prevention; pregnancy, birth, and child care; and how to live peacefully with elders, husbands, and in-laws.[112] At the completion of instruction public dances were held to celebrate the young women's reincorporation into society as adults. While some women of the Arab elite began to have certain aspects of these teachings provided to their daughters in the nineteenth century, participation in the public dances that announced a woman's sexual availability for procreation was restricted to women of slave and lower-class backgrounds. As Bakia binti Juma explained,

The Waswahili played [unyago], but you never saw an Arab playing. They would have their daughters taught about matters of unyago inside by her *somo* [private instructor], but you would never see her at an initiation ceremony because she is mwungwana [freeborn, of high social standing].[113]

Elite women interviewed by Strobel in Mombasa similarly suggested that initiation dances "were for slaves, for lower-class people."[114]

By contrast, women of all class and ethnic backgrounds in urban Zanzibar participated in the dances associated with mkinda. While mkinda drew on the teachings of earlier forms of unyago it was regarded as a more "respectable" form of initiation, primarily because of the widespread participation of free, wealthy, and elite women in its performance.[115] Women of the royal family, including Rusoona binti Tamim, the slave concubine of Seyyid Ali, who abdicated the throne in 1911, and Bibi Matuka, who continued to wear the barakoa and whose husband, Seyyid Khalifa, followed Ali to power, even became leading members of the dance clubs associated with mkinda. Slave concubines had their daughters initiated into mkinda in large numbers in the early years of the twentieth century. As one Swahili friend of Rusoona said, "They [masuria] were free now and their masters or husbands [mabwana yao] couldn't stop them."[116] The differential position of Rusoona and Bibi Matuka within the royal family was, however, reflected in the relative degrees of their involvement in mkinda. Rusoona and her daughter ZemZem became high-ranking instructors in Vuga, the association dominated by women of Swahili descent. On the other hand, Bibi Matuka served only as a financial patron of Vuga's competitive rival, Malindi. Rusoona, widely regarded by colonial officials in Zanzibar as a rebellious slave concubine, danced in public; Bibi Matuka, who was praised as the epitome of a good Arab wife, did not. "Bibi Matuka supported the group financially, but she didn't dance because she was in purdah . . . ," explained Kiboga Bakari. In Bibi Matuka's group, known as Malindi, "We Swahili were made to dance the public dances of mkinda: kunguiya and ndege for [the women of the aristocracy]," said Amina Seif Othman.[117] As Strobel argued for Mombasa, different women used the stages provided by dance associations for different and sometimes contradictory purposes. In some respects dance helped to undermine social inequalities, while in other regards it served to affirm class and status differences within urban society.

The wealth and status of the membership of the two competing associations, Vuga and Malindi, also impacted their ability to successfully win the annual competitions. Vuga, which had the majority of its members drawn from Ng'ambo's Swahili population, regularly won the competition for the dancing of kunguiya. They could turn out many more dancers than Malindi and draw a larger crowd of observers to the dance. Yet Malindi typically won the competitions over the dancing of the second dance associated with mkinda, ndege, as the winners of this competition were determined not only by the number of dancers, but more importantly by the elaborateness of the dancers' costumes. The performance of ndege was unlike traditional unyago celebrations and much more reminiscent of nineteenth-century processions in which the titled members of coastal society paraded through town in celebrations that marked individuals' rank within the urban citizenry. In the course of ndege processions, initiates and their mentors paraded through streets lined with crowds of observers (fig. 2.18). Dancers wore marinda pants and kilembas and each dancer carried an umbrella or parasol that matched her outfit. These umbrellas were considered one of the most important symbolic elements of male ruling-class attire in nineteenth-century Swahili towns.[118] Women also adorned themselves with large quantities of gold jewelry; gold bracelets went up the arm as far as possible, and gold coins and trinkets were sewn into an elaborately crafted coiffure. Many women claimed that initiates' heads were often completely covered with gold. Obviously, having connections to members of the aristocracy came in handy on such occasions. Vaults of heirloom bracelets, necklaces, earrings, and recently smithed gold chains were opened during the annual performances of ndege and used to adorn the daughters of friends and family as well as would-be Swahili and Zanzibari clients. The marinda pants and kilembas worn during ndege processions were sometimes, though rarely, given by female members of the nineteenth-century Arab elite to their personal slave attendants as signs of intimacy and affection. Ndege allowed elite patrons and their clients to carry these practices into the twentieth century and, more important, into the public realm.[119] In addition to being the clothes of Arabs, "marinda pants required several yards of expensive cloth and the costs associated with tailoring and embroidery were exorbitant," said Nunu Salum. For these reasons it was important for young Swahili women to maintain close ties with female patrons willing to assist them in dressing up. It was in the course of these annual ndege processions that many Swahili women were first given the ability to dress in "Arab" fashion. "Oh, they really dressed us up!" said Amina Mapande, recalling her own experience of being adorned in silk and gold by her wealthy patrons in Malindi.

A woman's degree of integration into the patron-client networks of urban society was reflected in her membership in either Vuga or Malindi. Amina Mapande again recalled:

> Our mothers danced in Vuga; this was in fact our club, the club of the Waswahili. . . . Women of the royal family, those with money, lived in Stone Town and belonged to Malindi. Eventually I went to dance for them. . . . People from the mainland, those who didn't have patrons, danced for Vuga, whose clubhouse was located in Kisiwandui. But my father married another wife, a favored domestic slave [mzalia] of the Arabs, and she got me into Malindi.[120]

Dancing for Malindi gave young women and girls the opportunity to be adorned in costumes that were much more elaborate than their counterparts in Vuga. The gold jewelry, finely embroidered marinda pants, and silk parasols that were lavished on the young women of Malindi brought notice and pride to both clients and their patrons. From 1900 through the 1930s, when these dances were at their most popular, Swahili and Zanzibari women earned respect and adoration through their participation in these pageants, in which they adorned themselves with symbols of previously exclusive Arab privilege. Like the women who adopted the buibui, dressing up in "fancy," "Arab" clothes allowed them to transform their public image as well as their own sense of identity. When the parades were over, the young women returned their borrowed gold, but their marinda pants, kilembas, and the sense of self-worth and assurance they earned

through participating in kunguiya and ndege were things no one
could take away. Financing mkinda celebrations, loaning jewelry,
and buying clothes and parasols for clients also brought female patrons public recognition and reaffirmed their uwezo in ways that few
other activities continued to allow an Arab woman to do.[121] Elite patrons in Malindi also regularly helped to negotiate marriage arrangements for their Swahili clients, often to men of wealth or status,
thereby further assisting their clients to climb the ranks of island society. By the early twentieth century, providing their clients with
gold, parasols, marinda, and relatively wealthy husbands was as important to maintaining Arab women's power as depriving their slaves
or clients of such adornments had been in the past.

Conclusion

Throughout history men and women have consciously manipulated
their material world in order to physically fabricate their identities as
well as to differentiate themselves from others. In nineteenth- and early-
twentieth-century Zanzibar as well, consumption served to display
subjectivity. Customary practices combined with material inequalities
to visually distinguish members of the islands' nineteenth-century aristocracy from the majority slave population. Veils, kilembas, bara-
koas, and johos immediately identified a wearer as a member of the
elite while simultaneously "naturalizing" this position. In a region
where most residents were Muslims, the relative nakedness of many
slaves served as "proof" of their barbarity. Covering their heads and
bodies was one of the first public demonstrations that formerly servile
men and women made of their freedom in the post-abolition era. In
adopting clothing styles formerly reserved for members of the freeborn
or elite, newly emancipated slaves asserted their right to be seen and
treated as cultured adults worthy of respect. That Swahili women incorporated elements of Arab dress into their new twentieth-century
costumes while men looked to Europe to inspire their new fashions
perhaps reflected their gendered perceptions of where the greatest
hope for empowerment lay. As Randall Pouwels has suggested, the

cash earned from wage labor "served as a social lubricant for the lower strata of town society," yet the majority of these newly created wage opportunities were gendered male. Women's options for access to property, power, and status, although limited in both cases, were often greater under the old patrician order than the new colonial one. The importance of gender and ethnicity as the basis for political power in colonial Zanzibar exacerbated the tenacity with which Arab men clung to the ethnic identities they were given at birth, as well as the clothing which marked them as inheritors of such privilege. For Arab women, however, cultural barriers intended to separate them from the majority of island women no longer served to suggest the promise of privilege. While Arab men increasingly abandoned their clients during the twentieth century, women often found that their only hope for status, respect, and political power within the urban community rested on their continued cultivation of personal clients. These gendered differences in the cultivation and maintenance of power were reflected not only culturally, but materially as well. Members of the male aristocracy, including several of the sultans themselves, were often ardent supporters of the commercialization of urban land in late-nineteenth- and early-twentieth-century Ng'ambo and the concomitant severing of patron-client ties that were literally grounded in the land itself. The most vocal and persistent Arab opponents of these processes were Bibi Khole and Bibi Jokha, the daughters of the nineteenth-century patriarch Seyyid Hamoud bin Ahmed al-Busaidi. These two women fought until their deaths, shortly after World War I, and long after the majority of male patricians had abrogated such obligations, to protect the historical right of the family's poor clients and freed slaves to live in Ng'ambo rent free.

Chapter 3

"The Land Is Ours! Why Should We Pay Rent?"

Land, Law, and Housing in Colonial Ng'ambo

Between the 1890s and the 1920s access to land in Ng'ambo was gradually removed from the arena of face-to-face negotiations between patrons and clients and placed squarely within the impersonal arena of commercial, contractual, and judicial relationships. This process began in the 1870s, as South Asian and Arab businessmen sought to commercialize urban land relations as one means of amassing capital for other business concerns. With the establishment of the protectorate, in 1890, the commercialization of land proceeded with increasing rapidity, as landholders seeking to profit from their properties gained support from a British administration anxious to impose capitalist relations of production within the isles. The greatest potential losers in this process were, of course, the poor, particularly the poor of Ng'ambo, whose access to and control over urban housing was increasingly threatened by these transformations.

The tensions caused by the commercialization of land relations grew over the course of several decades, ultimately erupting in direct and violent conflict between Ng'ambo home owners, landowners, and the colonial administration, in 1928. At the center of these conflicts were ever-increasing ground rents—a curious colonial creation that allowed an "owner," usually the state or a private Arab or South Asian landlord, to claim a monthly payment of rent from an individual whose home or business had previously been built on land now "owned" by someone else.

Although Ng'ambo residents were unable to completely interrupt the dynamics of commercialization, the outcome of the 1928 rent strike illustrates that collectively the urban poor exercised considerable power in shaping the limits of capitalist transformations in land. Outlining the changing nature of urban land tenure, the processes by which land was commercialized, and the ways in which Ng'ambo residents, private landlords, and the British administration sought to shape these processes are the central concerns addressed in this chapter.

Although Ng'ambo residents were consistently opposed to ground rents, the terms in which they voiced their opposition changed over time, revealing gradual transformations in their individual and collective identities. In the 1890s, when ground rents were first demanded, the majority of Ng'ambo tenants were either manumitted slaves or free clients of the islands' wealthiest Omani clans. Arguing from their positions as slaves and clients, these men and women protested against their patrons' abrogation of their historical "obligation" to provide clients with rent-free land for housing. By World War I, few urban residents openly self-identified as slaves and even many free clients became reluctant to identify as the underlings of former patrons as the economic and political reasons for doing so gave way. Increasingly, Ng'ambo residents came to identify not as so-and-so's client, but as a class of the poor (sisi maskini), whose interests were in direct opposition to those of Ng'ambo landholders and the colonial administration, which supported landlords' interests. The growing salience of this class identity intensified in the 1920s, spurred in part by the growing demands of landlords for ever-increasing rents. By the late 1920s, the majority of Ng'ambo residents identified themselves not only as a class willing to mobilize to protect key economic and political goals, but, as the census data indicates, also as "indigenous" islanders. These identities were also expressed during the ground rent strike of

1928. Repeatedly, during the course of meetings and mass public marches, Zanzibari protesters asserted, "The land belongs to the natives!" and "The land is ours! Why should we pay rent?" Like their cousins in the country who identified as Hadimu, Tumbatu, and Pemba when census enumerators and members of the Department of Agriculture came around, the women and men of Ng'ambo asserted both identities as Zanzibaris and as citizens with rights to, and security in, property ownership.

This chapter also highlights the growing, day-to-day impact that British administrative power had on people's lives, over the course of four decades, as well as the willingness of the urban poor to directly engage the state in debates to define the shape of twentieth-century society. While Ng'ambo residents were certainly annoyed by turn-of-the-century attempts by landlords to lay claim to the dirt lying under their homes, their annoyance grew into outrage, in the 1920s, when colonial courts began to order evictions, imprisonment, and the demolition of homes belonging to tenants whose rent was past due. When the administration began to back private landlords' demands for ground rent with the clout of its courts and jails, the relative strength of landlords and tenants in this tussle over the control of urban land shifted dramatically in favor of capitalist landlords. The decision of Ng'ambo's two largest private landholders to raise their rents 300 to 400 percent, first in 1927 and then again in January 1928, combined with the administration's decision to serve eviction notices on several hundred of their past-due tenants, pushed many Ng'ambo home owners to the brink of disaster. This combination of rapidly increasing ground rent rates and the administration's willingness to use its power to enforce landlords' demands provided the spark that ignited long-smoldering discontent in Ng'ambo.

In response to these developments, residents organized an area-wide rent strike against what they perceived as thievish, greedy landlords and an uncompassionate state. Beginning during the Islamic holy month of Ramadhan, in February and March 1928, nearly all of Ng'ambo's estimated eight thousand home owners and ground tenants joined the call to strike. For nearly a year, rental clerks found their efforts at collection futile as well as increasingly dangerous. In the neighborhoods, residents repeatedly impeded the sale of property confiscated from past-due tenants. And, on at least three separate occasions, crowds of several hundred men and women broke friends and neighbors out of court or jail, after they had been convicted for refusal to pay their ground rent. By the end of the strike the women and men of Ng'ambo were demanding not only the abolition of ground rent, but also that land be nationalized and private ownership be abolished.[1]

Competing discourses of law and justice were weapons that all sides wielded in this fight to shape the economic contours of life in the city. Legal pluralism provided ample material for debate; "customary" law, English common law, some aspects of British Indian law, and Ibadhi, Sunni, and British interpretations of Islamic law all operated within the protectorate simultaneously. Claimants on all sides were adept at drawing on whichever legal "code" best fit their particular needs. While private landlords and their allies within the colonial administration generally placed emphasis on the legal *rights* of individuals, particularly landlords' rights to profit from private property ownership, the poor tended to emphasize the *duties* and obligations of society, and especially of the wealthy and the state, to guarantee everyone's basic access to subsistence, including housing. Throughout this period, Ng'ambo residents drew on discourses rooted in popular interpretations of Islam and the creative refashioning of "tradition" to add moral weight to their fight to protect their homes and rights to live in the city rent free. The British certainly held the upper hand in terms of writing laws which favored their aims, yet the events of 1928 illustrate that even after nearly forty years of rule they still had not managed to convince the majority of Ng'ambo tenants that their law had anything to do with justice.

From Kiungani to Ng'ambo

The changing nature of the social and political relationships that existed between the ruling class and former slaves was given its most explicit expression in the terms used to name the section of Zanzibar Town where the majority of urban poor lived. In the nineteenth century, this area was

Fig. 3.1. *A street in Ng'ambo, c. 1900. Courtesy of Zanzibar National Archives.*

commonly referred to as Kiungani, a name derived from the Swahili root *-unga*, to join together, connect, or unite. Kiungani was often translated by Europeans as "suburb," but to islanders the term reflected an ideology of interdependence that linked the wealthy and the poor through the give and take between patron and client. Urban land relationships were not commercial; they were subsumed within larger personal negotiations over patron-client ties. The political obligations and social identities of clients were literally grounded in the land on which they lived; if you lived on land controlled by a particular patron then you were his or her client.

Patriarchy and patronage were central to the language of politics in Zanzibar, as well as in the distant homes from which Omani aristocrats and African slaves originated. Senior patriarchs, "big men," or heads of the "family" in all three locales provided juniors with access to land, trading connections, physical protection, and a host of other material and social goods. In return, juniors provided the labor and political support that allowed patriarchs to extend their control over additional resources for the group. The larger one's "family" the more options one had for support in time of need, and both individuals and extended families negotiated their ties in order to maximize their access to others. Human relationships provided economic, social, and emotional security, and kinship often provided the central idioms through which these relationships were organized. Patriarchs and juniors were mutually dependent and this interdependence was often couched in discourses of family, although the material and social interests of "fathers," "sons," "mothers," and "daughters" were routinely at odds. Families were large and extended and they included not only biological relations, but also others who had been adopted by one means or another.

Omani men who migrated to Zanzibar in the early to mid-nineteenth century needed to establish themselves as the heads of a large and extended network if they hoped to achieve positions of economic or political power in the isles, yet because the bulk of their biological kin remained in Oman, and the free population of Zanzibar was relatively small and largely uninterested in serving as the underlings of the Omanis, control over large numbers of slaves became critical to success. Profits derived from the sale and labor of slaves allowed many of these men to become extremely wealthy, yet certain classes of slaves also served important social and political functions. *Masuria*, or slave concubines, produced legitimate heirs for Omani men, allowing them to establish themselves as the head of a large biological family. Several of Zanzibar's more powerful sultans had upward of fifty concubines. Because the children born to masuria were considered free, legitimate children of the fathers, elite men were able to produce many more children than if they had limited their reproductive strategies to the biological capacities of a free wife or wives. Trusted male slaves were armed and called upon for political and military support as the need arose. *Wazalia*, a category of second- or third-generation coastal slaves born in the house of an owner, were often spoken of as junior or adopted family members and many exercised considerably autonomy and power.[2] Wazalia were often appointed as plantation and household supervisors. They participated in the running of their owners' business concerns and shared in the profits. Female wazalia managed their owners' domestic routines, raised and reared their children, and sometimes educated, directed, and reprimanded free junior members of the household as well.[3] Many wazalia, both male and female, were given extensive freedom to travel, socialize, and engage in business independent of their owners. They had start-up money for independent businesses given to them by their owners and it was not uncommon for favored wazalia to have significant amounts of money or property willed to them at their owners' death.[4] Slavery in Zanzibar was far from benign, but in a context in which the Omanis controlled so much wealth and power and relied so extensively on patronage to hold the system together, it was often better, as one observer noted, "to be the trusted slave of a rich master than a free non-entity."[5]

I am not attempting to argue that slavery in Zanzibar was neither oppressive or coercive, but it is important to recognize the relative autonomy of many urban slaves vis-à-vis their rural counterparts. As James Christie noted in the 1870s, "The town negroes look down upon their country cousins with a good deal of contempt, and consider themselves a superior class."[6] In many regards, urban slaves were a superior class. Although urban slaves accounted for only 10 to 15 percent of the entire slave population, they had a number of options available to them, particularly if they belonged to a wealthy owner, that were not available to rural plantation slaves. For instance, manumission rates for urban slaves were much higher than for those of plantation slaves. Manumission was considered a pious act under Islamic law, and owners who manumitted their slaves received blessings for the act in the afterlife. Many owners in the isles, particularly those concerned with enhancing their images as devout Muslims and generous patrons, chose to free their slaves upon their death. "That manumission was a common and socially rewarded act reflects not just Islamic ideals," notes Frederick Cooper, "but the social and political necessity of living up to them. Manumission—as well as the modest degree of mobility allowed within slave status—helped prevent the formation of a homogenous slave class,"[7] in a region where slaves vastly outnumbered the free population. By holding out the hope of manumission, particularly to wazalia, patrons gave their slaves a very real stake in the system and a reason for playing by the rules. At his death, Zanzibar's first sultan, Seyyid Said, freed thousands of urban slaves, including slave concubines, soldiers, domestics, and messengers, yet his plantation slaves remained in bondage. To quote from Cooper again, God's blessings were "very much desired, but so too was a large clove harvest."[8] The sultan's son, Seyyid Barghash, also included in his will a provision to free all his urban slaves, who numbered more than three thousand, as well as the slaves in his army and the concubines in his harem. Upon their deaths, other members of the royal family, including Seyyid Khalid and Seyyida ZemZem, each of whom owned some five or six hundred slaves, also freed their slaves.[9]

The workloads of urban slaves, particularly those of the wealthiest masters, were substantially less than those of rural slaves and sizable numbers of urban slaves were also allowed to hire themselves out, something that was largely unheard of in the countryside. Household slaves, the majority of whom were wazalia, not only cooked and cared for the domestic needs of biological and fictive kin, they also enhanced the prestige of a family.[10] Household size was a key diagnostic of patrician power in nineteenth-century Zanzibar and slaves who allegedly did little other than "gossip and lounge about" were important tools that allowed a patrician to enhance his or her status, if not actual wealth.[11] Being able to house, feed, and clothe slaves who produced no wealth was an important indicator of social and economic ability (uwezo). As Seyyida Salme, the daughter of Zanzibar's first sultan, Seyyid Said suggested, "keeping slaves for mere show . . . [was] a custom with people of rank and wealth."[12] The price paid for slaves of various classes bears this out, as plantation slaves, who produced the largest amounts of wealth for their owners, sold for £5 to £8 (in the late nineteenth century) while domestic servants, who did little to enhance their owners' wealth but a lot to boost their prestige, sold for £12 to £25.[13] Although the vast majority of island slaves served productive purposes, either on plantations or packing and transporting goods in the urban commercial sector, there were significant numbers of male and female slaves, particularly in town, whose function was largely social and political. Large numbers of urban slaves, most of whom were wazalia, were also hired out for wages. These slaves, known in Kiswahili as vibarua (sing. kibarua), were paid wages for their labor, a portion of which went to their masters.[14] The "standard" arrangement in Zanzibar was that 50 percent of the wages earned by a kibarua slave were retained by the owner and 50 percent

by the slave, although this fluctuated considerably depending both
on the negotiating skills of the slave and the economic need of the
master. As Rashid bin Hassani said of his own experience working as
a kibarua, "it depended upon our owners how much we got, but the
generous ones took half and gave us the other half. . . ."[15] When
Rashid first began his career as a kibarua, working as an unskilled
construction laborer, his mistress appropriated nearly all his wage, although later, after he married one of his mistress's favored wazalia he
was allowed to keep his entire wage for himself and his family.[16]
Vibarua worked as skilled slave craftspersons, including carpenters,
boatbuilders, smiths, bricklayers, boat hands, and as unskilled dockhands, construction laborers, and porters for European and South
Asian trading companies, whose owners were legally prohibited by
British law from owning slaves. Vibarua slaves, who were both men
and women, were often able to amass considerable capital, and it was
not unheard of for vibarua to own slaves of their own.[17]

By the 1870s, it was estimated that nearly half the urban population of Zanzibar was comprised of manumitted slaves, primarily from
the slave categories of masuria, wazalia, and vibarua.[18] These women
and men formed an elite strata among island slaves and because of
their privileged status they had a firm sense of their personal rights
and their patrons' "duties." A lifetime of exposure to patrician discourses of benevolence and generosity taught them how to use these
ideologies to their own advantage. As Cooper persuasively demonstrated more than two decades ago, paternalism was an interactive
process, a "subtle equilibrium." "What to the slave-owners appeared
as generosity, appeared to the slaves as an obligation."[19] These slaves
were among the first to mobilize against the demands for ground rent
in Ng'ambo. They were also the most persistent in demanding that
the colonial administration and the sultan do all that was necessary to
guarantee their rent-free access to urban housing.

The majority of manumitted slaves lived in Kiungani, where they
were given land to build a home by their former owners. This land in
Kiungani was taken over by Seyyid Said when he established his rule
over Zanzibar in the 1830s. He set aside vast sections of Kiungani for
settlement by his own manumitted slaves and free clients as a way of

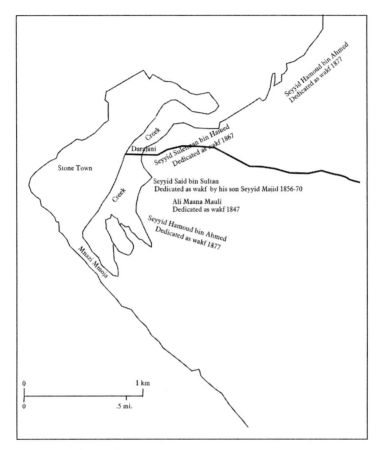

Map 3.1. *Nineteenth-Century Land Control and Major Wakf Properties*

grounding their ties to him and the al-Busaidi clan. Other sections of land in Kiungani were distributed by Seyyid Said to his wealthy and prestigious political supporters, including his two closest advisors, Seyyid Suleiman bin Hamed al-Busaidi and Seyyid Hamoud bin Ahmed al-Busaidi, who in turn made grants of land for homes and farms to their slaves and clients. Seyyid Said, Seyyid Suleiman, Seyyid Hamoud, and many other wealthy patrons also established extensive permanent endowments of property in Kiungani. These endowments are known under Islamic law as *waqf*, commonly spelled in Zanzibar as *wakf*. Once endowed, wakf property legally belonged to God. It was inalienable, indivisible, and perpetually dedicated "until God inherits the earth together with its occupants." Rents or produce generated by wakf property could be used to endow a mosque, pay for the reading of the Qur'an at the grave of a deceased loved one, or be divided among legal heirs or other beneficiaries. Elite patrons also established wakf for their manumitted slaves and, from the 1840s through the 1870s, vast sections of Kiungani lands "together with everything pertaining to them such as trees, buildings, roads, rights and easements" were "eternally dedicated as wakf for the benefit of [a particular patron's] freed slaves and their posterity."

Wakf dedications contained explicit instructions on how the property was to be used. In some instances, produce from trees on wakf property was to be sold and the income generated from it divided between named slave beneficiaries, such as the wakf of Seyyid Hamoud at Jang'ombe, dedicated "for the benefit of his freed slaves, namely, Zafran the mother of his two sons Ali and Seif, and his concubine Birileh Habshia. After they are given their freedom Zafran shall take two-thirds of the income derived . . . and Bireleh [sic] shall take the remaining third."[20] In other cases, patrons like Seyyid Hamoud established wakf for specific slaves to live on, such as that dedicated "for the benefit of his freed slaves Salama and binti Tajiri, the widows of his freed slave Barut, and Isa the freed slave of his freed slave the said Barut." In Kiungani large tracts of land were also dedicated as wakf for the rent-free occupation of hundreds of unnamed, and most likely unknown, "freed slaves . . . and their posterity, who may use the income thereof and live on them [wakf lands], but none of them nor any other person shall have the right to dispose of them by sale or any other means."[21] By establishing pious endowments for the use of poor clients and manumitted slaves aristocrats were accruing blessings in the afterlife, as the endowment of property for the benefit of the poor was considered a form of *sadaqa* (alms)—a gift to God. Of equal importance, wakf dedications also allowed patrons to make their control over both land and people a visible feature of urban geography.

In the first half of the 1800s, after Zanzibar became a territory conquered by Seyyid Said, land in the isles was legally defined as belonging to God, in whose interests it was allegedly administered by the sultan. The sultan, in turn, granted use rights to others. Although land as such could not be owned, one could own and sell any trees, buildings, or other improvements one made upon the land. Gradually, in the second half of the century, after Seyyid Said's death, these laws began to change and land began to take on qualities of private, commercial ownership. The 1860s and 1870s were difficult years for plantation-owning aristocrats in Zanzibar, who saw their financial solvency undermined by a number of factors, including the division of estates among numerous heirs, a declining world market for cloves, and a hurricane that decimated many island plantations. Faced with growing debt, many landholders began to mortgage or sell their properties. According to one observer, by the 1860s the majority of property previously controlled by Omani aristocrats in the isles was either mortgaged or already in the possession of South Asian merchant financiers.[22] Because of the declining profitability of clove plantations, as well as British laws that forbade British Indian subjects from owning slaves, Asian financiers were reluctant to foreclose on mortgages of rural property, including clove plantations. However, urban land was showing signs of increasing commercial viability and it was this land that Asian businessmen increasingly sought to secure. Debt even impacted the royal family, "giving rise to the rueful proverb to the effect that ill-gotten wealth does not survive the third generation."[23] In the 1860s and 1870s, the male children of Seyyid Said mortgaged large sections of their Kiungani holdings in order to get the necessary capital to repay debt. As a consequence, powerful Asian merchants, including Tharia Topan—one of the "farmers" of customs and an important financier of business ventures of the royal family—came to own much of the land.[24] Building on these early acquisitions, by the 1920s, Tharia's son Muhammedhussein Tharia Topan had become the single largest private landholder and by far the most important landlord in Ng'ambo.

As the land in Kiungani changed hands the status of those who had built their homes and businesses in Kiungani was gradually transformed from that of clients into tenants. In 1873, Amer bin Said al-Harthy, a wealthy agent of American and British merchants in

East Africa, sold a parcel of land in Kiungani to an Asian businessman, Remtulla bin Hema, for $1,200 in silver. Amer had been given
the land by the sultan and had redistributed parcels of the land to his
own free and slave clients. Shortly after the sale, Remtulla attempted
to collect rents from business and home owners resident on the land,
which sent Amer's clients running to Amer for protection. Pressured
by his clients, Amer attempted to persuade Remtulla to respect the
"rights" of Amer's clients to live on the property rent free. But, as
"owner" of the land, Remtulla felt that he had no obligation to abide
by agreements made between Amer and his clients. Had Remtulla
been willing to grant these women and men rights to rent-free occupation of "his" land he would in effect have made them his clients.
Remtulla apparently had greater use for the cash paid by tenants than
the blessings and headaches associated with scores of poor clients.
His demands for rent continued despite the objections of Amer.
Upon his death, Remtulla willed the property to his sons, Gulamhussein and Mohammed, who continued to expand the family's holdings. By the 1920s, the Remtulla brothers were two of the largest and
least-liked landlords in Ng'ambo.

Despite or perhaps because of growing debt in the 1860s and
1870s, many wealthy aristocrats continued to dedicate large tracts of
urban property as wakf. Wakf property was legally protected from
sale or foreclosure for debt. By dedicating their property as wakf,
members of the aristocracy were thus able to preserve a portion of the
family estate. Wakf property could be rented out and the income generated from the rents could be dedicated for the support of heirs. Income derived from wakf rental property could also be used to fulfill
important social or religious goals, such as endowing a mosque,
financing annual or semiannual religious festivals, or feeding and
clothing the poor.[25] By dedicating property for such pious purposes,
nineteenth-century patrons were able to ensure that even as their
heirs' and descendants' personal wealth declined, the family name
was preserved and their position as charitable patrons recalled on a
regular basis. Wakf property dedicated for the permanent, rent-free
occupation of slaves and poor clients served similar purposes. Seyyid
Hamoud's extensive wakf dedications from this era, as well as those

that his daughters endowed during the early colonial era, served to ensure that members of the family were regarded as pious, prestigious patrons well into the twentieth century.[26]

With the establishment of the protectorate, in 1890, the protections wakf dedications offered to both the wealthy and the poor were increasingly undermined. At the turn of the century, it was estimated that nearly half of island property had been dedicated as wakf.[27] Tying up property in perpetuity directly conflicted with the "modernizing," capitalist ideals that were so popular among colonial powers at the turn of the twentieth century. From Zanzibar to Egypt, Algiers, and other Muslim regions that came under colonial control, there was a general move to either establish colonial administrative control over wakf property, or preferably overturn wakf and return the property to the realm of private ownership. To aid the Zanzibar Protectorate's administration in the furtherance of these goals, the British established the Wakf Commission, in 1905. Commission members, including local Islamic scholars, were appointed by the British resident, the highest ranking administrative authority in the isles. The British administration maintained an official majority on the Wakf Commission.[28] The Wakf Commission, under the advice of the sultan and the British resident, also assumed the power to codify and execute wakf law in the isles. As a result, Islamic law (shari'a) pertaining to wakf was generally "modified" to "make it easier" for the administration to deal with wakf property.

The new laws governing wakf property were indeed, as described by Pouwels for the Kenyan Coast, "an eclectic patchwork of provisions taken from various schools of Islamic law,"[29] sewn together in the interests of colonial practicality. There were several key differences between the Shafi'i school of law, adhered to by the majority of island poor, and the Ibadhi school, followed by most Omani dedicators. Ibadhi law relating to wakf normally fit the administration's interests better than Shafi'i and by and large it was adopted as the operative law in the isles, although it too suffered numerous "modifications." One of the more important differences between Ibadhi and Shafi'i law was that the former allowed for the sale and exchange of wakf property, under particular circumstances. On the other hand, according to Shafi'i law, the rule was "once a *wakf* always a *wakf*."[30] Not surprisingly, the Wakf Commission adopted the Ibadhi position on this particular issue, and over time large numbers of wakf properties in Zanzibar were sold, transferred, or exchanged, though almost always over the vociferous objections of dedicators, beneficiaries, and sometimes even Ibadhi members of the Wakf Commission. During the 1910s, Muslim and non-Muslim members of the commission repeatedly came into conflict regarding the overly zealous efforts of British members of the Wakf Commission to privatize wakf property, particularly that which produced little revenue for the Crown. Sunni and Ibadhi *kadhi* (Islamic judges) joined together to protest these efforts, arguing that although certain interpretations of shari'a allowed for the transfer or exchange of wakf property under particular circumstances, "it is absolutely forbidden" to sell dedicated wakf property in the manner proposed by the commission.[31] The British majority on the Wakf Commission also attempted to modify provisions in wakf dedications, which also raised objections from the Muslim members of the commission on occasion. Ali bin Mohammed, the Ibadhi appointee to the commission, argued that "as far as *sheria* is concerned . . . [a] wakf deed . . . can never be altered."[32] His Sunni (Shafi'i) counterpart, Ahmed bin Abubakar, also stated that wakf dedications "can in no way be altered." Nonetheless, realizing that the British would probably do as they pleased anyhow, he added a caveat that exempted Muslim members of the commission from responsibility for such transactions, stating that "the Sultan has placed legal limits on shari'a as administered in Zanzibar. Thus legal questions are decided not in accordance with shari'a as interpreted by kadhis, but by the local administration."[33]

There were two particularly significant "limits" or "modifications" made to wakf law in Zanzibar during the early years of the commission's existence. The first was passed by a decree of the sultan, under advice from the British resident, in 1910. It gave the Wakf Commission power to nullify a wakf dedication, thereby "freeing" the property, if any portion of a wakf was improperly administered for twelve consecutive years. In the same year that this "statute of limitations" to wakf administration was passed a large Kiungani wakf, dedicated by Seyyid Suleiman bin Hamed, in 1867, for the "eternal" benefit of destitute free persons and liberated slaves, was sold by public auction. It was the sale of this particular wakf that initiated the conflicts between the Zanzibari and British members of the commission, as cited above.

If a wakf could not be privatized then the next best thing, according to the administration, was to have the property and any income it generated come under the direct control of the Wakf Commission. Members of the administration realized that income generated by wakf property could prove substantial to the Crown. Properties under the control of the commission also came to play a significant role in the implementation of town planning schemes, urban "development," and "slum" clearance.[34] To aid the administration in securing authority over wakf properties a second decree, which allowed the Wakf Commission to seize administrative control of wakf property from an "incompetent" manager, was passed. Typically, wakf property was administered by the senior member of the dedicator's family or other trusted procurator, known as a *mutawalli*. The mutawalli was responsible for managing the property and distributing any income generated by the wakf as outlined in the dedication. In the 1910s, the Wakf Commission began to question the "competence" of many mutawalli as one means of vesting managerial control of wakf property in the commission. Charges of incompetence were most often leveled against female and poor wakf managers, so that by the 1920s the vast majority of wakf properties were either under the administrative control of the commission itself or very prominent and politically connected Arab men.

One important example of the Wakf Commission's use of this decree can be seen in the commission's struggles to wrest control of Seyyid Hamoud's wakf from his daughters. By the time of World War I, one of the wakfs of Seyyid Hamoud bin Ahmed, containing some 1,100 Ng'ambo homes immediately adjacent to the creek, was the largest contiguous urban wakf remaining.[35] The land had been set aside by Seyyid Hamoud, back in the mid-1800s, for his slaves, poor dependents, and heirs, and had been administered since Hamoud's death by his two daughters, Bibi Khole and Bibi Jokha binti

Hamoud. The British administration had covetously eyed this property since at least the 1890s, and, in 1915, the Wakf Commission began to make a concerted effort to seize control of the wakf from Bibi Khole and Bibi Jokha binti Hamoud. Arguing that Bibi Khole and Bibi Jokha's refusal to impose tenancy agreements and ground rent on residents on their father's wakf would "ultimately result in the loss of this valuable property," the commission attempted to take the property away from Hamoud's daughters. Bibi Khole presented her case both to the sultan and the British resident, stating "I have not the slightest fear of anyone turning around in the future and presuming to acquire rights in my land. They are all poor, law abiding Swahili citizens of Zanzibar and I shall be obliged if you will assure the Wakf Commissioners that they need have no anxiety on this behalf."[36] Despite Khole's assurances, for the next three years the commission continued to pressure the women to impose contracts, in the form of ground rent, on those living on the land. The sisters were also approached privately, on numerous occasions, by friends of the Wakf Commission, in attempts to persuade them to impose ground rent but, from the perspective of the British, the sisters remained "obdurate" in their refusal to do so. Khole and Johka insisted that the men and women who lived on their land were not tenants but clients: "poor Swahilis" and "freed slaves of the family." Drawing on social custom and Islamic law, Khole and Jokha asserted that their clients had an inalienable right, as established in their father's wakf dedications, to reside on the land rent free. Bibi Khole and Bibi Jokha had a lot of social and economic capital invested in this property. At stake for them was not only their control over a large piece of urban real estate, but their very status as pious, responsible, and respectworthy patrons, capable of protecting thousands of family clients.

After three years of struggle, in 1918, the Wakf Commission took unilateral action and had the wakf vested in itself, arguing that the women's refusal to demand rents from the family's clients clearly demonstrated their "incompetence as property managers."[37] To add insult to injury, the commission did not even bother to personally inform the women of the action it had taken. It was only while reading the *Official Gazette* that Bibi Khole learned that the property had been confiscated. Bibi Khole and Bibi Jokha were legitimately outraged and appealed to both the sultan and the British resident to intervene on their behalf. The secretary of the commission justified the action the commission had taken to the British resident by arguing that the women "didn't know how to manage the property," again citing as evidence their refusal to impose ground rents on their clients. Seven months later, however, the administrator general forced the wakf commissioners to return control over the wakf to the sisters. The administrator general informed the commission that it had no legal right to enforce the signing of agreements between mutawalli and their tenants, nor to enforce the collection of rents against the wishes of beneficiaries.[38] Bibi Khole and Bibi Jokha had their property returned to them late in 1918, but preliminary discussions of "Town Planning and Improvement" caused the Wakf Commission to seize the land, yet again, in 1920.

By 1920, the sisters were left with fewer members of the administration who were sympathetic to their "outmoded" aims of protecting Ng'ambo residents from the "modernizing" impacts of ground rent. To continue the battle to preserve family control of the land and her position as a patron of the poor, Bibi Jokha was forced to hire A. R. Stephens, Barrister at Law. Once again, the case was found in Jokha's favor, but by the time it was settled both Jokha and Khole had passed away. Control over the wakf was assumed by the next senior member of the family, Seyyid Hamoud's granddaughter, Bibi Shawana. Yet shortly thereafter the Wakf Commission again moved to seize the property from family control. Shawana fought the Wakf Commission, unsuccessfully, for the next three years, taking her case all the way to the Court of Appeals for Eastern Africa. Rather than attempting to establish Shawana's "incompetence," the commission opted for a legal strategy that rested on a reinterpretation of the original deed of dedication. The point of contestation regarded the interpretive definition of "*auladihi min sublihi*," or "children from one's backbone," and whether as a grandchild Shawana had any legal claim to the wakf.[39] Here again, the Wakf Commission sought to "modify" Islamic law as administered in the isles by conflating juristic interpretations regarding descendants' rights to receive distributions from income generated by a wakf with their right to act as mutawalli. Unless a deed specifically mentioned otherwise, Ibadhi jurists in Zanzibar typically interpreted a dedication for the benefit of descendants to refer only to the first generation of children. After the extinction of this first generation, although grandchildren could continue to manage the property, any income generated by the property was supposed to be used to support pious or charitable causes. Shafi'i law, on the other hand, generally interpreted the phrase "children from one's backbone" much more broadly, extending the legal definition of descendants capable of receiving monetary disbursements from wakf property two or three generations and sometimes in perpetuity.[40] In the 1920s, the Wakf Commission adopted the Ibadhi interpretation of this phrase as law in Zanzibar, thus prohibiting grandchildren of dedicators from receiving disbursals from a wakf estate, and giving control over income generated by such a wakf to the Wakf Commission. During the course of their struggles with Shawana, the Wakf Commission also extended this interpretation to apply to the legal right to administer wakf property.

Upon the death of Jokha, in 1922, Shawana assumed administrative control of the wakf. Although no rent was charged to family clients in Ng'ambo, there were also eleven large homes in Stone Town that were part of this same wakf, whose sizeable rental income was dedicated to supporting heirs. When Shawana lost her legal battle against the Wakf Commission, she not only lost control of the property in Ng'ambo, she also lost her right to support from the rental income generated by the Stone Town homes. Shawana, like the grandchildren of many nineteenth-century patriarchs, relied heavily on the rental income derived from her grandfather's estate to maintain herself, and this ruling left her utterly destitute. The sultan was forced to give her a home in Ng'ambo in which to live, rent free, but he could not afford to support her. The sultan appealed, on Shawana's behalf, to the wakf commissioners, arguing that "many Arab gentlemen feel great shame that the granddaughter of such an illustrious Arab should be in want." The sultan also argued that, as the grandchild of the dedicator, Shawana should be first in line among the poor to whom income from the wakf was disbursed. Apparently in retribution for her "audacious" behavior of taking the commission before the Court of Appeals for East Africa, the wakf commissioners declined to support the sultan's plea, and the granddaughter of one of the wealthiest men in nineteenth-century Zanzibar was left to live out the remainder of her life in destitution.[41]

By the end of World War I, Bibi Khole and Bibi Jokha were among the last remaining wealthy nineteenth-century aristocrats who continued to honor their positions as patrons to hundreds of poor clients. Ideologies of patron obligation remained strong among the urban poor, but as early as the 1880s and 1890s many clients were having increasing difficulty convincing the elite, especially the male elite, of their "duties." As the social and material gap between the elite and the poor widened, the term used to refer to the area where the majority of urban poor lived gradually changed from Kiungani to Ng'ambo, or literally "the other side." This "othering" of Ng'ambo and its residents intensified with dramatic speed during the early years of the protectorate. British civil servants perceived Ng'ambo not as an extention of Stone Town, nor even as a part of town, but as "a separate town," or, as the official tourist guide to Zanzibar described it in 1932, "a different world."[42] Between 1890 and 1928, the notions of reciprocity and patron-client give and take that had previously helped the poor and wealthy to find common ground in Kiungani were gradually undermined. As the political economy of the isles was transformed during the early colonial era, rent-free housing for clients was gradually replaced by demands for ground rent from tenants. In the process of these transformations, many of the social and political bridges that had helped to link the wealthy and the poor living on opposite sides of the creek in the nineteenth century were gradually swept away.

Hut Tax, Ground Rent, and Resistance to World War I

The imposition of rents or tax, in one form or another, on all African men was a cornerstone of British colonial policy. After the abolition of slavery in Zanzibar, in 1897, the British administration began a

concerted effort to impose either a hut tax or ground rent on all who
lived on land for which they held no documented title. Free peasants
and others living outside government-controlled land were required
to pay a hut tax of Rs 2.2 per annum, while slaves and squatters resident on government plantations or other "Crown lands" were required to pay a similar fee in the form of ground rent.[43] As Director of
Agriculture Lyne explained, by imposing the hut tax, "we shall compel the people to pick cloves in order to find money for paying their
taxes. This sounds logical, but we frequently find the logic of western
thinking curiously wrong in dealing with eastern peoples."[44] In the
case of Zanzibar, the logic of the administration could not have been
more flawed.

Confrontations with the new colonial administration over the issues of hut tax and ground rent involving free peasants and freed
slaves began almost immediately after the taxes were first imposed, in
1898. The real goal of the administration in imposing the hut tax was
to insure a sufficient labor supply for the harvesting of cloves, a fact
which they made transparent by offering a tax refund to those who
worked in the harvest while imposing a doubling of the standard tax
on those who refused to participate.[45] The problem, from the perspective of free peasants as well as recently freed slaves anxiously claiming
status as free Swahili, was that picking cloves was historically the
work of slaves. Suggestions that free women and men perform the
work of slaves was, according to sympathetic administrators, patently
offensive to "native notions of justice." When combined with intimi-
dation, threats of prosecution, and attempts to physically force people
from their homes, the government's actions were widely perceived by
rural residents as tantamount to "extortion" or worse, a reimposition
of slavery.[46]

The collection of hut tax and ground rent quickly became the
bane of existence for employees working in offices responsible for its
collection. Administrative efforts to force people onto plantations to
pick cloves often resulted in complete boycotts of clove plantations.
Women and men living in areas where forced labor policies were im-
plemented not only refused to pick, but also to weed or trade with
plantation owners who were supposed to benefit from the administra-

tion's efforts. Attempts at tax collection also frequently led to what top officials euphemistically referred to as "tensions" and those closer to the scene frequently described as "riots" between local government officials and rural residents.[47] As a result of organized opposition on the part of peasants, slaves, and squatters, neither the hut tax nor ground rent succeeded in either generating labor or raising revenues. Despite intensive effort to force laborers into the trees, in 1902, five years after the abolition of slavery, the government estimated that nearly half the clove crop on private plantations and over one-third of the crop on government plantations was left on the trees to rot, due to a lack of picking labor.[48] The administration fared little better in the collection of taxes. By 1911, when the revenue from the hut tax was balanced against the costs of prosecuting over half the population who refused to pay, the state was losing rather than gaining money.[49]

The British administration had an equally difficult time dealing with slaves, now known as squatters, who lived on plantations formerly owned by the sultan, which were taken over by the Crown Lands Department, along with all "unoccupied land" in the isles, in 1902. The administration rarely received more than 10 percent of the rents it requested from squatters who lived on Crown lands, including clove plantations.[50] Former slaves argued that they had never been obliged to pay ground rent to the sultans and that the state's coercive attempts at forced labor left them with "much bitterness in their hearts," a bitterness which they quelled by refusing to pick or weed the government's trees. In 1910 the administration attempted to scare squatters into either working the harvest or paying their rents by taking a number of squatters to court, but this too backfired. Squatters pointed to established trees, mature annual crops, and existing homes and in many cases successfully convinced the courts that the land did not belong to the Crown at all, but was in fact their "private property."[51]

When the administration tried more forceful tactics to convince rural residents to either work the clove harvest or pay a tax or rent, their "labor problems" repeatedly blossomed into political ones. In 1903, when the administration pressured local government administrators to physically force people from their homes and out into the plantations to pick, over one thousand Hadimu, Tumbatu, and Swahili residents from the northern area of Unguja island, in the region of Mkokotoni, marched some twenty miles to the sultan's palace. They demanded a meeting with the sultan and an end to coercive efforts to force them into performing what they defined as "the labor of slaves." In 1910, when the administration attempted to evict several hundred squatters who refused to either pick cloves or pay ground rent for land they occupied on some of the larger Crown plantations, the sultan was again confronted by angry crowds of squatters. These women and men demanded that he put a stop to efforts to evict them from "his" plantations. When the administration persisted with their eviction attempts, the director of agriculture was summoned to yet another mass meeting and duly warned by the crowd that if he continued to take action against any individual on any plantation he would face a strike of both free and slave pickers from across the island.[52] In light of the bumper crop of cloves then coming into bloom, several members of the administration convinced the Department of Agriculture "not to run the risk of unsettling the people."[53] The director of agriculture was ordered not only to stop collection, but also to return the taxes he had already collected.

Much to the surprise of some members of the administration, once the state abandoned its coercive policies more peasants and squatters came forward to work the 1911 harvest than had been seen in all the years of the preceding decade combined.[54] The actions of rural residents ultimately convinced the administration that only through "wise and tactful treatment," and certainly not by force, could the people of the isles be induced to cooperate with the state. Encouraged by the turnout of laborers for the clove harvest of 1911, and reluctant to revisit the mass protests of the preceding year, in 1912 the hut tax was abolished and efforts at collecting ground rents on rural Crown lands were abandoned.

The population of Zanzibar learned a number of important lessons from these early struggles with the colonial administration. One was that the new government itself was divided over policy and that these divisions weakened the administration's ability to deal forcefully with resisters. Members of the Department of Agriculture and the Crown Solicitor's Office advocated for rent and tax collection, coupled with eviction, in order to force laborers into the trees at harvest time as well as prove the "might" of the Crown. Staff at the collection offices and members of the courts opposed such policies, however, recognizing that they usually resulted in "driving people from the trees," inciting "riots," and greatly increasing their own stress levels and workloads. A second lesson learned was that the administration could in fact be beaten and forced to retreat from its stated goals. After more than a decade of continuous political trouble combined with financial loss, the state abandoned its attempts to impose taxes and rents in the rural areas.

A third important lesson learned during this decade of struggle with the administration was about the power and strength of unified collective action. Little evidence remains regarding the organization of these early actions. The state had little understanding of the internal social dynamics of these movements and, no doubt, the men and women involved had little interest in revealing these facts and thereby leaving themselves open to prosecution. The rural populations of Zanzibar were extremely diverse in terms of origins, language, and economic and social position. Despite these divisions, however, they were linked through intricate cross-cutting webs of familial, cultural, and market relations. In the process of struggling against ground rents and hut taxes they succeeded in mobilizing these networks of daily life and turning them to their political advantage. These lessons and insights became part of the islands' collective social memory and were repeatedly invoked in the decades to come, as thousands of rural residents moved to town and once again found themselves being confronted with demands for hut tax and ground rent.[55]

Transformations in Urban Land Tenure and the Early Years of Ground Rent in Ng'ambo

Beginning in the 1890s, the British administration began to encourage holders of land in Ng'ambo to collect ground rents from tenants. The British perceived the majority of Ng'ambo residents to be even lazier than their rural counterparts, and believed that imposing a ground rent on them would induce them to seek waged labor. After the abolition of slavery, in 1897, the administration also feared that the urban population would swell, and hoped that the imposition of ground rents would help deter slaves from moving to the city. They believed that ground rent would also serve to establish the principle of private property ownership in town and undermine any existing perception that urban land was something of a commons, where anyone could build a home on wakf land and live rent free. By the 1910s, nearly all Ng'ambo residents were being subjected to demands for ground rent, regardless of whether they lived on land claimed by the Crown, private landlords, or the Wakf Commission.

British attempts to undermine the rights of clients to live rent free on land dedicated as wakf began almost as soon as they established the protectorate, in 1890. In support of the their goals, the British had a great friend in Sultan Seyyid Hamed Thuweni (1893–96), who was brought to power through the efforts of the British counsel general. Seyyid Hamed Thuweni was the first sultan to largely accept his position as a mere figurehead of power under the tutelage of the British Crown.[56] Under the advice of the counsel general, Seyyid Hamed Thuweni distanced himself from his family's historical obligation to support al-Busaidi dependents. He relinquished control of family accounts to the British, who in turn began limiting the monthly "allowance" available to members of the extended family and, whenever possible, removing members of the extended family and their dependents from the list of eligible beneficiaries. Sultan Hamed also turned control of Ng'ambo wakf lands, dedicated by previous sultans, over to the British administration and followed British advice to impose ground rents on the freed slaves and clients living on al-Busaidi wakfs in Ng'ambo.[57] Seyyid Hamed Thuweni apparently perceived himself as somewhat of a progressive, arguing in relation to religious laws, including those related to wakf, "The wise men who made the Law, Christ and Mohammed, lived a very long time ago and made the Law according to their lights, but they did not know many things that we know now, and the world has moved on further since their Law was made."[58] One of the things Christ, Muhammad, and the early dedicators of wakf property in Zanzibar were apparently oblivious to was the fact that the thousands of residents living on al-Busaidi wakf land in Ng'ambo represented a potentially lucrative source of income for the Crown.

Early on in his reign, Seyyid Hamed also confiscated the wakf lands of the Seyyid Suleiman bin Hamed al-Busaidi, the regent of Zanzibar and principal advisor to Sultans Seyyid Said and Seyyid Majid, from Hamed's descendants.[59] This wakf, in the area known as Darajani (at or near the bridge) had been dedicated by the regent during the reign of Seyyid Majid (1856–70) for occupation by clients of the family. Seyyid Suleiman rented spaces on one portion of the wakf to shopkeepers, dedicating the income derived from these spaces to the support of his heirs. A second portion of this same wakf, on the north side of the main road leading from the Darajani bridge out of town, was set aside as an "eternal and permanent dedication" for the rent-free occupation of Seyyid Suleiman's manumitted slaves and poor clients. After Seyyid Suleiman died, in 1872, his daughter, Seyyida Shariffa Suleiman, known as "a great friend of all the poor," and her fourth husband, Hamed bin Suleiman, became the mutawalli (administrators) of the wakf. Shariffa's husband, Hamed, was an official at the palace, but he came into numerous conflicts with Sultan Seyyid Hamed Thuweni, who eventually placed him under house arrest and confiscated all his property, including the wakf of Seyyid Suleiman.[60] Once again, the sultan turned the land over to British administration and began demanding a monthly payment from poor residents living on the wakf. In doing so, the sultan was willfully violating the wakf dedication, as well as the social tenets of Islamic patriarchy in Zanzibar, which beseeched the wealthy, and particularly the reigning al-Busaidi, to protect the right of the poor to housing. Between the 1850s and the 1890s the basis of royal power had changed significantly. Unlike those who had dedicated the land as wakf, Seyyid Hamed was far more reliant on British guns for his power than he was on the prestige derived for supporting a large retinue of poor clients. Nonetheless, the Sultan's actions were severely chastised by a wide range of island residents, including those who lived on these wakfs. As one observer noted, "For this action [imposing rents on residents living on wakf

Fig. 3.2. *Swahili women at a well. Reprinted from Younghusband,* Glimpses of East Africa *(1910).*

dedicated to the poor] all those living on it [Seyyid Suleiman's wakf] joined tongues not only in invoking Heaven to pour down Its imprecation and cursing on His Highness in this world, but also to make His Highness' abode in the hottest part of *Jehannum* [Hell] in the world to come."[61] These curses of the poor and invocations of the Lord's justice were apparently answered shortly thereafter, as Seyyid Hamed became suddenly ill one morning in 1896 and died by noon of the same day.[62]

Between 1890 and 1902 private landlords, including Tharia Topan and Remtulla Hemani, also began collecting ground rents from those who had built their homes on land for which they now claimed ownership.[63] Ground rents represented a potentially sizable source of income to landlords. Of equal importance, however, was the fact that in the absence of titles and boundary markers the ability to collect ground rent served as prima facie evidence of land ownership in early colonial courts.[64] In fact, when the government temporarily stopped collecting rents from residents on the wakf land of Seyyid Suleiman, at Darajani, and the wakf of Seyyid Majid, in Zizi la Ng'ombe, in 1908, Mohammed Remtulla moved in, convincing residents that the land was really his, which is why the government had given up its efforts at collection in the area. Mohammed Remtulla

Fig. 3.3. *Ng'ambo, c. 1920. Courtesy of Zanzibar National Archives.*

then used this history of rent collecting to "prove" his "title" of ownership against the Crown Lands Department in court. This strategy of using the collection of rents to prove, and thus secure, a title was so successful that, in the 1910s, Mohammed Remtulla used it to acquire portions of the Mauli wakf in the neighborhood of Mwembetanga as well.[65] Through similar means portions of a number of wakfs in Ng'ambo became the "private property" of aspiring Asian and Arab landlords. In the 1900s and 1910s, collecting rents became one of the principal means of creating legal records and "titles" of "ownership" where none previously existed.

With the establishment of the Wakf Commission in 1905, the residents on commission-controlled wakf land also began to face demands for the payment of ground rent. Seeing that private landlords, like the Remtullas, were using their ability to collect ground rents to acquire ownership of wakf land, certain members of the commission advocated the introduction of ground rents as one means of protecting their own "titles" to urban wakf property. The potential income that could be derived from the homes standing on wakf land in Ng'ambo was another major incentive for imposing ground rents. Although imposed in fits and starts, by the end of the first decade of the twentieth century nearly all the residents of Ng'ambo, regardless of

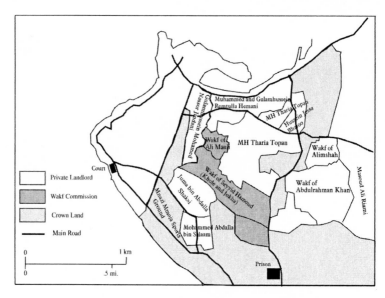

Map 3.2. *Control of Land in Ng'ambo, c. 1928*

where they had built, were being subjected to demands for the payment of ground rent.[66]

The fact that landlords across Ng'ambo now demanded rent did not mean, however, that tenants agreed to pay. In fact, many residents flatly refused to pay. Collectors described many tenants as "habitually insolent" and rent clerks were frequently confronted by tenants who openly told them that their goal was to give them "as much trouble as possible" or that they would "have no objection to living in a Kilimani jail, [so long as it was] at the expense of the government."[67] Conditions at the Zanzibar prison at this time were regarded as being "easy and comfortable," allegedly earning the prison the nickname "The Kilimani Club."[68] Tenants, who were apparently less than fearful of prison conditions, allegedly taunted rental clerks with requests for a rent-free week of vacation at "the Club." Other residents voiced objections that were more grounded in African customs regarding usufruct or local Islamic law pertaining to land, asserting that the dirt lying under their homes simply could not be owned. The men and women who had built their homes on wakf land dedicated for their permanent rent-free occupation were among the most adamant in their refusal to pay ground rents to either private landlords or the Wakf Commission. The women and men of Ng'ambo employed numerous strategies to avoid the payment of rent. For instance, multiple parties often claimed to "own" a single piece of land and rent collectors employed by the Wakf Commission, the Crown Lands Department, and private landlords continuously complained of tenants who told them that a competing collector had already been paid.[69] As home owners were the individuals legally responsible for paying the rent, rental clerks were also consistently frustrated by home owners who traveled at collection time or "just stepped out" as they arrived.[70] In the 1900s and early 1910s, landlords had no legal right to take tenants to court to force payment, and Ng'ambo residents used the law, or lack thereof, to their own advantage.

From 1890 to 1910 the state supported attempts to impose ground rents in Ng'ambo, but it had not yet created the legal apparatus necessary to ensure their payment. In 1912 the government attempted to deal with this problem by proposing legislation that gave landlords the legal right to collect ground rent, and thus a basis for taking tenants to court if they refused to pay.[71] Private landlords and the Crown began taking tenants to court in an effort to secure payment, yet fully half to three-fourths of Ng'ambo tenants continued to refuse to pay their rent. Ng'ambo residents were fully aware of the success that their country cousins had in securing the abolition of the hut tax and ground rent through their recent marches and protests, and presumably saw no reason why they should pay ground rent when the administration had just given in and abolished it in the countryside.

Up through the 1910s, the efforts of Asian landlords and the British Colonial Administration to collect ground rents in Ng'ambo remained largely a failure. Tenants in Ng'ambo, like those in the countryside, simply refused to cooperate. Men and women from across Ng'ambo repeatedly argued that they had been granted the land for their homes by the late Seyyids, and that under these agreements both they and their descendants had a right to live rent free. Many of the poor used wakf dedications as moral weights in support of their position. When that did not work, they used evasion and out-right deceit to avoid making their payments. Although ground rent laws existed on paper, their imposition was thwarted by the resistance of those who lived in Ng'ambo. Through World War I, landlords were content, if not entirely happy, with collecting rents from whom-ever they could get to pay. Despite their efforts at universal collection, by default they adopted a policy of catch as catch can. With the end of the war, however, colonial courts became more supportive of private landlords, who also became increasingly diligent and coercive about receiving the rent they demanded. Taking resistors to court, evicting nonpaying tenants, and even tearing down the homes of those who refused to be evicted became increasingly common tactics used by ground landlords in the 1920s.[72]

Growing Tensions over Ground Rent

After the war, in addition to increasing harassment of tenants who re-fused or were slow to pay, many landlords also began to dramatically increase the amount of rent they charged. By 1918, rents throughout town had been raised an average of 50 percent and by 1922 it was not unusual to find rent rates at 100 to 400 percent of their prewar rates.[73] Landlords did not discriminate in their raising of rents. Asians and Arabs who rented flats and rooms in Stone Town found their rents raised as much, and in some cases more, than those of African ground tenants in Ng'ambo. Recognizing the threat that such exorbitant in-creases posed to tenants, the government began, in 1918, to pass leg-islation that encouraged landlords to fix room rental at rates charged before the war. Despite this legislation, however, in the early 1920s the government was regularly receiving letters and petitions from tenants demanding that the government put teeth into its rent con-trol legislation in order to protect them from rapacious landlords.

The South Asians who dominated the landlord class, both in Stone Town and Ng'ambo, developed a reputation during the period immediately after World War I as greedy businessmen of the lowest order. Such perceptions were not racially based, as Asians too complained of their landlords attempting to "squeeze every drop of blood from poor tenants by threatening to drag them to court if their greediness is not complied with."[74] The South Asian population in Zanzibar was extremely heterogeneous, divided not only by region of origin, caste, language, and religion but also by economic class.[75] Poor Asians were often marginalized within communal associations, but the dramatic increases in rent being demanded in the late 1910s and early 1920s pushed them to use such institutions to organize against the wealthier members of their communities, who were often their landlords. In 1921 the poor and middle-class members of the Indian National Association pushed the organization's leadership to organize an effort to get the South Asian landlord class to quell the rapid increase in rents, as well as their efforts to evict hundreds of Asian tenants from their apartments in Stone Town. When these informal, personalized efforts proved futile, the Indian National Association presented to the administration a petition, signed by over five hundred members, demanding that the government institute rent control and protect poor tenants from the ravages of wealthy landlords.[76] The Bohoras, another subgroup within the Asian community, also used their communal organizations to solicit support for resolutions calling on the administration to limit the rent increases allowable to landlords and to institute some penalty for landlords who increased their rents above the legal limits.[77] Indian and Arab civil servants circulated yet another petition, signed by more than two hundred men, requesting that the government intervene and protect tenants who were being threatened with evictions because of their inability to pay the two- and three-fold increases in rents being demanded by Stone Town landlords.

As a result of such pressure, the administration passed the Increase of Rent Restriction Decree of 1922, which set rent rates at not more than 80 percent of that charged in 1914. Although this represented a substantial increase in rents over the prewar rate, it effectively reduced the majority of rents in Stone Town by at least half. Under this legislation, landlords were allowed annual increases of up to 10 percent, but only if they could prove that such increases were being used for structural or sanitary improvements on the premises.[78] This legislation also effectively saved thousands of Stone Town tenants from the immanent

Fig. 3.4. *A street in Ng'ambo and a woman wearing a kaniki. Reprinted from Younghusband,* Glimpses of East Africa *(1910).*

threat of eviction, as pending eviction cases were denied hearings by the courts.

After the war, ground landlords in Ng'ambo also became increasingly persistent about collecting the rents they demanded from tenants. Those who did not pay found themselves subject to harassment by collectors and an increasing number of Ng'ambo home owners also found themselves in court facing eviction orders. In several extreme instances, landlords took the law into their own hands, tearing down homes and businesses of past-due tenants. Mohammed Remtulla Hemani (see map 3.2) and his brother Gulamhussein Remtulla Hemani were two notorious Ng'ambo landlords who, on more than one occasion, destroyed the home of a tenant who was behind in ground rent payments. The Remtulla's actions were extreme, but representative of the increasing daily harassment that urban tenants were subjected to by their landlords during the 1920s.

After the war, Ng'ambo residents, like their Stone Town counterparts, also organized meetings, circulated petitions, and conveyed letters to the administration calling for rent control. The extant letters and petitions were authored by Ng'ambo residents who identified themselves as poor and humble, but morally upright citizens who were inter-

ested in protecting not only their own property, but that of the Wakf
Commission and the Crown from encroachment by "land-grabbing"
landlords. These early letters were framed in moralistic terms, invoking
respect for religious trusts as well as shock at the actions of certain Muslim landlords, like the Remtullas, who, it was argued, held a lust for
money and property above a commitment to fellow human beings. Such
desires for profit at all costs were regarded by many as being in direct
contradiction to the teachings of the Prophet Muhammad, himself a
businessman, but one who decried usury and economic exploitation.

In the early and mid-1920s, residents on wakf lands that had become "private property" were the most vocal tenants calling for administrative aid in their battle against landlords. These tenants not
only complained about ever-increasing rents, but also about the
privatization of wakf land. The poor of Ng'ambo fully understood the
important role played by successive administrations in "modifying"
Islamic law pertaining to wakf, yet they challenged the British resident, as the administrative head of the isles, to protect wakf property.
The signatories to these letters argued that the British resident had a
legal obligation to ensure that wakf property was administered according to the dedication, as well as a moral responsibility to protect
the rights of the poor to their homes. One letter, sent by residents on
the wakf of Seyyid Suleiman bin Hamed, argued the ground on which
their homes stood was dedicated as wakf more than fifty years ago, for
the benefit of the poor

> to build their huts and live on it free of charge. The deed under which
> this wakf is made was duly executed and testified by the late Sultan
> Seyyid Majid bin Said, by Seyyid Hamoud bin Ahmed and by other wit-
> nesses. The said ground was recognized as the wakf of poormen for
> many years, and now we see the Wakfship of that ground nullified under
> the very eyes of the British Resident and the wakf deed . . . set aside. . . .
> Seif bin Hamed, the Arab who has misappropriated this Wakf ground, is
> now selling the land and has employed certain brokers to offer higher
> bids for every piece of land sold, so that it is impossible for us to buy the
> ground on which our huts are built. Mostly . . . Indians buy the ground.
> We poor men cannot buy it and the result is that we will be turned away
> from our homes. We appeal to you Sir to come forward and help us.[79]

The poor women and men who sent this letter attempted to persuade the British resident to respect local law and custom and protect the wakf dedications of nineteenth-century patriarchs.

Just before the war, a prominent sheikh in the employ of the royal family, Saleh Ali, raised a similar appeal before the British resident. Sheikh Saleh found a copy of the original deed of dedication, dated 1867, for this wakf in the library of the sultan, and presented it to the British resident as legal evidence that the property had been dedicated "along with all its appurtenances such as land, trees, boundaries and rights," for the poor as an "eternal and permanent dedication." The sheikh argued that according to the dedication, the wakf land was "inalienable, unpresentable and uninheritable. It should be considered as a permanent dedication 'until the time when God will inherit the Earth and those on it.' "[80] The British resident failed to heed the sheikh's call, asserting instead that because portions of the wakf had been mortgaged or sold outright (or both) by the heirs of Seyyid Suleiman, beginning in the 1890s, the twelve-year "statute of limitations" imposed by the Wakf Commission applied, and the entire wakf was therefore null and void.

By the mid-1920s the majority of this wakf had been acquired as the "private property" of Mohammed Remtulla Hemani. Mohammed Remtulla was the Varas of the Khoja Ithna Asheris—a position of religious authority that he inherited from his father in 1906—as well as the president of the Agha Khan Council in Zanzibar. He was highly regarded by the administration as a business and civic leader, but also widely condemned by Ng'ambo residents, who frequently accused him of embezzling from widows, blackmailing the poor, and stealing both state and private property. Ng'ambo tenants found Mohammed Remtulla's actions as a landlord particularly offensive because of his position as a Muslim religious and communal leader, from whom they apparently expected better.[81] Many appeals were sent to the British resident by tenants on properties controlled by Mohammed Remtulla, including the following, in which fourteen residents called upon the British resident to protect them from unreasonable increases in rent as well as the illegal destruction of their homes and other personal property:

We have the honor to inform you . . . about part of the government [al-Busaidi] ground which was taken by Varas Mohammed Remtulla Hemani. We are now hardly pressed up by the said person by charging us a very heavy rent which no land owner in Zanzibar charges. Mohammed Remtulla is most notorious for embezzling the rights of the poor and widows and has blackmailed the properties of a good many. Through his intrigues he has forced a good many buildings to be pulled down without proper notice or reasonable time and he has never moved with pity and compassion. . . . [We] therefore think it is your duty to champion the rights of persons like ourselves in embarrassed circumstances. . . . [He] would leave no stone unturned to ruin us, being well versed in the art of cheating simpletons coming into contact with him.

These petitioners went on to complain that Mohammed Remtulla wrote rent receipts in Gujarati, which few Ng'ambo residents could read, thus allowing Remtulla "to do every sort of fraud he likes in accounts." The principal author of the petition had himself been summoned to court in 1925 and ordered to pay all past-due rent, which he did. But in 1926 he was once again brought before the court after Remtulla produced receipts in Gujarati suggesting that he was still nearly two years delinquent in his ground rent payments. It was this action by Remtulla that prompted the author and other tenants in similar circumstances to petition the British resident. After thoroughly condemning the landlord, the petitioners played on discourses of state beneficence, reminding the British resident of his "*duty* to champion the rights of [poor] persons" and concluding, "We have no doubt that the Government will see its way to help us in these miserable circumstances before we perish."[82]

Another strategy employed by people living on "privatized" wakf land was to encourage the administration to reclaim the land and place it under the control of the Wakf Commission. Although tenants on property controlled by the commission were also liable for ground rents, their rent rates were substantially less than those charged by private landlords.[83] Like their Stone Town counterparts, these men and women used their religious and social organizations to facilitate the circulation of petitions among poor tenants. One example of such petitions was sent to the British resident by three hundred people living on the former wakf land of the al-Busaidi royal family in the neighborhood of

Zizi la Ng'ombe. This land was dedicated as wakf for the rent-free occupation of al-Busaidi slaves and poor clients during the reign of Seyyid Majid (1856–70), but had been "privatized" by the Remtullas in the 1910s. Like the preceding letter, the authors of this petition highlight the exorbitant rents being demanded by the Remtulla brothers and attempt to convince the British resident of his obligation to enforce rent control. Better yet, they argue, the land should be restored as wakf and placed under the control of the Wakf Commission.

> We the undersigned poor of Ng'ambo beg most respectfully to approach before Your Excellency with this humble petition. . . . We are all harassed by one Khoja Mohammed Rhemtulla Hemani, who has wrongfully acquired government [al-Busaidi] land and claims it to be his. Some of us for the last 40 years have never paid any rent and the rest were made to pay from 1 anna and now [are charged] Rs 3 [48 annas, or a forty-eightfold increase]. If the government doesn't think the land belongs to the government then we ask Your Excellency to interfere in the matter and reduce the ground rent, as if [you] make enquiries Your Excellency will find that other ground owners charge only annas 8 [half a rupee]. If we poor are made to pay Rs 3 for ground rent for a hut only then what about our living?[84]

The authors of these letters argued that the state had a legal duty to protect wakf dedications from ground landlords who had "embezzled," "misappropriated," and "wrongfully acquired" wakf land. They also attempted to convince the British resident to accept the personal obligation, historically expected of citizens from the head of state, to protect the rights of the poor to housing. However, the colonial administration flatly denied that it had any such obligation. The final line in the file that contained many of these appeals was, "This makes for interesting reading; and that is all." The official response of the British resident was to encourage tenants who felt they had a case to take their appeals to court, but few of the poor Ng'ambo tenants who wrote these letters in the 1920s had either the financial means or the faith in the justice system required to do so.

Examining court records from the early 1920s reveals that it was typically landlords who brought tenants to court, rather than vice versa, and that invariably the private property rights of landlords were upheld by the courts over any alleged duties claimed by tenants. The early 1920s were heady years for private landlords, who rarely found their claims, either of ownership or for rent, denied in Zanzibar's courts. Encouraged by a judiciary that clearly sided with their goals, landlords expanded their property claims to include the most marginal pieces of urban land. In one case, Abdulla Mbaruk, the proprietor of a *boriti* (mangrove poles used for construction) business found himself facing threats of eviction and confiscation of his business assets for three years of past-due ground rent on the area he used for the storage of boriti poles. The land in question was completely washed over by the sea for eight to ten days every month. When brought to court, Abdulla questioned how land covered by the sea could be considered private property?[85] The court, however, ruled in favor of Abdulla's landlord, Mohammed Remtulla. Abdulla was ordered to either pay the three years' rent being demanded by Remtulla or find himself imprisoned in the city jail.

Ng'ambo tenants were not the only ones who found themselves in court fighting against the capitalist zeal of landlords in the 1920s. The administration itself was also frequently brought to trial and surprisingly it often fared little better in local courts than poor home owners. For instance, the Lands Office and Public Works Department lost a series of disputes with Mohammedhussein Tharia Topan, the largest private landlord in Ng'ambo. When the Public Works Department began providing electricity and piped water to Ng'ambo, Topan objected, arguing that the erection of light poles and the passage of water pipes through his property, much of which had also been wakf, compromised the number of huts he could claim ground rent from. Topan won his case in court and the administration was required to pay ground rent for the land on which light poles were erected and for areas through which water pipes were passed.[86] In 1927, Topan also asserted his private property "rights" to close the widest road in Ng'ambo, which just happened to pass through his land. The director of public works and the inspector of police brought a case against Topan for his actions, because closing the road effectively prevented police vehicles from gaining access to certain Ng'ambo neighborhoods. Although the case was brought by the administration, the attorney general ruled that even though the road had been open for some thirty or forty years, Topan had every right as "owner" to close it. In a gesture of "good will," Topan later agreed to reopen the road, provided it was officially named in honor of his deceased mother, Lady Janbai, and paved by the state.[87]

Despite persistent petitions from Ng'ambo residents, as well as their own encounters with ground landlords, the administration was slow to respond with efforts to curb the zeal of Ng'ambo landlords for ever-increasing ground rent. Members of the administration had little contact with those who lived in Ng'ambo, and any sympathies certain members of the administration may have felt for the plight of the poor were tempered by the belief that the payment of rents would help to induce a work ethic among a population generally perceived as lethargic. Between 1924 and 1927, numerous letters and petitions were laid before the British resident asking that he personally intervene on behalf of the tenants of Ng'ambo and protect them from ground landlords. Yet these letter-writing and petition campaigns were largely ineffective in spurring the administration to address the mounting conflicts between Ng'ambo home owners and ground landlords. In the late 1920s, many residents therefore began taking more direct action against landlords, assaulting clerks who came to collect the rent, and gradually organizing others to join in a rent strike.

The Ground Rent Strike of 1928

At the heart of the 1928 ground rent strike was a widespread belief, shared by many of the men and women of Ng'ambo, that one of their basic rights as citizens of Zanzibar was the right to urban home ownership. Evolving identities as Zanzibaris emboldened Ng'ambo tenants to fight for this right, even if it brought them into direct and open conflict with the state. Recalling the success of the preceding generation in stemming the imposition of hut taxes and ground rents in the countryside, the men and women of Ng'ambo determined that collective organizing and mass resistance were perhaps the most effective weapons they had remaining to deal with the impending threats to their homes and livelihoods.[88] Prior to 1927, individual tenants resisted landlords, but within their own homes and on a month-to-month basis. After that date, tenants came to coordinate their opposition to ground rents as they became increasingly conscious of their position as members of a tenant class at war not only with landlords but with the colonial administration that backed landlords' demands. At the height of the 1928 rent strike, the commissioner of police was threatened one day while being pulled through town on his rickshaw. He was allegedly accosted by a "native" who shouted at him, "You, you will die, you brother of the Asians!" The commissioner was shocked by this unusually aggressive behavior and confused as to why he was being referred to as the brother of the Asians. As the administration began stepping up its enforcement of eviction notices on past-due tenants, however, it became increasingly clear in Ng'ambo that without the support of colonial courts and jails landlords had no power.

Tenants living on former wakf property now claimed by Muhammedhussein Tharia Topan and the Remtulla brothers were some of the first tenants to openly begin fighting their landlords' claims for ground rent. As of 1926, roughly one-third of the tenants on these former wakf lands were refusing to pay ground rent.[89] In 1927, when Topan and the Remtullas increased their rents several hundred percent, a growing number of their tenants joined the call to strike. Topan and the Remtullas again raised their *kiwanja* (plot) rates 300 to 400 percent, in January 1928, and then added a little salt to the wound, notifying more than five hundred home owners of their intent to evict them for failure to pay their ground rent.[90] Topan and the Remtullas were the most powerful private landlords in Ng'ambo. They controlled nearly half the area's property and were continually expanding their control of urban land. Ng'ambo tenants' moral disdain for Topan and the Remtullas was coupled with a fear that other landlords would soon be making similar moves to increase rents if Topan and the Remtullas were successful. In 1927 the strike began to spread beyond the boundaries of privatized wakf land. By the end of the year, approximately half of Ng'ambo's ground tenants were openly refusing to pay their rent. As eviction notices were served with increasing frequency on Ng'ambo tenants, more and more home owners began to heed the call to strike. By March 1928, the ground rent strike had become universal and none of the landlords in Ng'ambo, including the Wakf Commission, were able to collect any rent whatsoever.[91]

Intensive growth in the urban population, in the years following the war, lead to a severe housing shortage in Ng'ambo, which landlords hoped to capitalize on by raising their rents. As Topan argued to members of the administration who questioned his rate of increase, he was only following the "natural law" of supply and demand.[92] The continuously growing demand for urban housing meant that both women and men were able to rent out rooms of their homes to friends, family, and acquaintances (*jamaa*) who recently moved to town and were in need of accommodation. Renting out rooms of their home allowed men and women to earn a respectable income, while simultaneously establishing themselves as patrons capable of helping newcomers find their way about town. Urban women, whose access to waged employment was undermined during the early colonial era, found their homes to be a particularly important economic asset. In the 1920s, an individual who rented out two rooms of a three bedroom Ng'ambo home, at the going rate, could easily recoup the cost of building the home in less than five years.[93] The profits derived from room rental could then be invested in the building of a second home, or used to meet other needs. By raising the ground rents charged to homeowners, ground landlords were hoping to accrue some of this profit themselves. However, the exorbitant increases in ground rents and threats of eviction of the late 1920s threw the accumulationist strategies of homeowners into question. In fact, it was widely speculated by Ng'ambo residents that the administration supported ground landlords' demands precisely because landlords and the state wanted to see relatively well-to-do home owners transformed from property owners with a social and economic stake in the town into renters, who could be removed at will.

From 1926 through early 1928 the vast majority of organizing for the rent strike was carried on informally utilizing the networks of daily life within the neighborhoods. As people sat on *baraza* (stone

Map 3.3. *Housing in Urban Zanzibar, c. 1939*

seats built against the outer walls of a house) at night, gathered for
taarab or ngoma performances or football matches, cooked and ate
with family and friends during the day, or gathered after prayer at
neighborhood mosques, they inevitably discussed the rent strike and
worked to persuade others to join.[94]

Although the issues at the heart of the rent strike were not framed
by Ng'ambo residents solely in religious terms, the networks of daily
life fashioned through participation in Islamic ritual provided opportunities to create an enhanced sense of community solidarity as well as
the space and time to discuss issues of justice, equity, and power. It is
perhaps not coincidental that participation in the rent strike became
nearly universal for the first time during the Islamic holy month of Ramadhan, a time of sustained personal and collective will as Muslims
across the globe fast from sunup to sunset.[95] In addition to the usual
five daily prayers, many Muslims use the occasion of Ramadhan to
deepen and renew their appreciation for the teachings of the Prophet
Muhammad, a man whose childhood experience as a poor orphan
influenced his calls for generosity and compassion toward the poor.

Although the days of Ramadhan can be quite solemn as individuals struggle to overcome their physical desires for food and drink, the evenings and nights are the most festive times of the year. Female friends, family, and neighbors gather together and spend a good part of their entire day preparing special foods with which to break the fast. As the sun sets, extended family, neighbors, and friends gather together after prayer to enjoy the women's preparations. From sundown until well past midnight people visit from home to home, sharing food and news, which in 1928 undoubtedly included information on the rent strike.

The month of Ramadhan provided Ng'ambo residents with the occasion to evaluate society against a higher "golden rule" as well as numerous social occasions to share their observations with friends and neighbors. Participants in the rent strike were further encouraged to persevere in their efforts through public readings by local religious leaders of *Al-Badr,* a religious book commemorating soldiers of the Prophet Muhammad who, although outnumbered by more than three to one, defeated an attacking army sent by wealthy Meccan merchants to seize the Muslims' property and expel them from their homes. The battle of Badr also occurred during the month of Ramadhan in 624.[96] Ng'ambo tenants drew collective strength from the parallels they perceived between the struggles of the Prophet Muhammad's followers against thriving businessmen, supported by a non-Muslim and hostile state, and their own struggles against similar forces in Zanzibar.

Although there was little concrete evidence implicating the Islamic brotherhoods *(tariqa)* in directly organizing or supporting the strike, the police repeatedly identified Sheikh Zahor Mohammed, a leading member of the Qadiriyya brotherhood, as "*the* most cunning and dangerous ringleader" involved in the events of 1928. Sheikh Zahor never spoke publicly at the organizational meetings associated with the strike, but the messages he delivered while leading prayers often centered on issues of social and economic justice. His biting critiques of class inequality and his lucid analysis of the impacts of colonialism lead the senior commissioner and other members of the Zanzibar administration to repeatedly brand him as "a person of evil influence" who "never desisted from instigating and inciting the natives to resist the government."[97] The Sheikh spent many years at the turn of the century organizing the Qadiriyya brotherhood and spreading *zikiri* in Tanganyika. He and his brother, Sheikh Sufi Muhammed, were widely known and respected among recent African converts to Islam, from the coast to Tabora and Ujiji, in western Tanganyika. Yet the teachings that brought him praise and converts from among the poor frequently brought him into conflict with conservative religious and secular authorities.[98] Sheikh Zahor was forcibly returned to Zanzibar in 1908, after being exiled from the mainland by the Germans for his alleged involvement in an anti-imperial movement, frequently referred to as the Mecca Letter Affair.[99]

The protectorate's administration, in typical colonial fashion, attempted to blame the entire 1928 strike on the "misguided" actions of incorrigible tenants who were "intimidated" into joining by "ringleaders" like Sheikh Zahor. At the end of the strike, in 1929, sixteen men were prosecuted as ringleaders and deported to the island of Pemba for two years. Several of the more "cunning and dangerous" were sentenced to prison terms in addition to their internal exile.[100] Interviews with elderly Zanzibaris who either personally witnessed the 1928 strike or recalled stories of their elders who participated in it confirm the organizing roles played by at least three of these so-called ringleaders, including Sheikh Zahor, who lived on the former al-Busaidi wakf in Zizi la Ng'ombe. Faraji Mpira, a tenant of Topan who lived in the neighborhood of Raha Leo, and who occasionally acted as the bodyguard of the taarab singer Siti binti Saad, was another man recalled by local elders as playing a prominent role by speaking about the strike in public, as did Juma Surura of Kwahani. Several elderly Zanzibaris recalled Faraji Mpira from their youth and they described him to me as being "as tall as a tree and as wide as a lorry" and "a slave of the Arabs" who was known throughout Ng'ambo as "trouble."[101] One might reasonably question, however, whether a man known as trouble would have the persuasive abilities to convince seven to eight thousand ground tenants to strike against their landlords. A number of the sixteen men who were deported were clearly identified by members of the secret police (CID), who infiltrated crowds, as leading orators at the mass meetings that were held to discuss the strike. However, oral and archival evidence clearly indicates that the movement had widespread grassroots support throughout Ng'ambo and was in fact being organized between neighbors long before these men emerged as visible and identifiable "ringleaders." As one witness of the rent strike said when speaking about Faraji Mpira, "He was a major leader of opposition to the government and was always fighting against government policies. Some people followed him. When it came to the rent strike though, *everyone* followed him because this was something *we were already doing* and something which *everyone* believed in!"[102] The police arrested and deported as ringleaders men who were most immediately visible, often as a result of their willingness to speak at public meetings. As the above comments suggest, however, the women and men of Ng'ambo were already engaged in the strike and actively organizing its spread long before the public meetings of 1928. In fact, some three-fourths of the tenants living on land owned by Topan, the only landlord for whom extensive records are available, were already engaged in a rent strike by this date.[103] The men identified as ringleaders certainly played a role in the strike, but it was the tenants themselves who began it.

In arresting only men as ringleaders the colonial administration displayed not only a lack of understanding for how the strike was organized within the neighborhoods, but also a disregard for the significant role played by Ng'ambo women as community and political leaders.[104] Police records indicate that women played a major role in organizing and executing opposition to the payment of ground rent. Women were at the core of door-to-door organizing activities during the early period of the strike and regularly comprised one-third to one-half of those who attended the public meetings called to discuss strategies regarding the strike.[105] A list of hut owners taken to court by Topan for arrears confirms the crucial role played by women in initiating and expanding the strike, as 85 percent of Topan's female tenants were refusing to pay their rent long before the mass meetings and marches of 1928.[106] In addition, during one of the more crucial and volatile demonstrations, in which crowds of demonstrators repeatedly clashed with police over the course of an entire day, women outnumbered men by a ratio of three to one.

The women who participated in the Ng'ambo ground rent strike were not acting out of fear of "ringleaders" but rather out of fear that the skyrocketing rent demands of landlords would cause them to lose not only their homes but also their economic and social autonomy.

Owning their own homes and collecting rent from rooms that they let to others afforded urban women opportunities to live independent of husbands and male kin, something which was decidedly more difficult for their rural sisters. Many former female slaves moved to the city and built their own homes precisely because such options for autonomy were greater in town.[107] While there are no complete records of home ownership in Ng'ambo for this period, deeds of purchase and sale and lists of ground tenants suggest that women owned an average of 30 percent of the homes on land controlled by Topan and the Remtullas.[108] On land controlled by the Wakf Commission, women accounted for an even larger percentage of home owners, averaging 40 percent.[109] Compared with the high incidence of female home ownership in Ng'ambo, by the 1920s women comprised far less than 10 percent of landowners in rural Zanzibar.[110] The number of women involved in the strike was thus roughly proportional to their position as home owners. There is no evidence to suggest that women joined the strike out of fear of "thugs," but a great deal of evidence indicating that through their involvement in the strike they hoped to protect themselves and their families from the impending prospect of homelessness. We can assume that male home owners were motivated by similar concerns.

Beginning in August 1928, the organizing activities of the women and men of Ng'ambo began to move beyond neighborhood-based social and religious networks, about which the administration knew very little, to more vocal and visible public demonstrations. As the area's three principal landlords—the Remtullas, Topan, and the administration—intensified their attempts to intimidate tenants into paying their rent by ordering numerous evictions, Ng'ambo residents also intensified their public displays of contempt for landlords and the courts that enforced landlords' demands. Regular public meetings, attended by crowds of fifty to three hundred men and women, were held in a variety of Ng'ambo neighborhoods. Larger Ng'ambo-wide demonstrations, attracting crowds of seven hundred to one thousand, were also common during August and September 1928.[111]

At these meetings participants encouraged each other to persist in their refusal to pay rent and reaffirmed their commitment to protest en masse if any one of them was called to court or threatened with eviction.[112] On 8 August 1928 the protesters made good on their promise for the first time. Rehani Ferajalla, a Ng'ambo tenant, was called to court that day for contempt of a court order to pay his ground rent. Rehani was accompanied to the courthouse by several hundred friends, neighbors, and supporters, and as the judge sentenced him to prison these men and women broke into the court and secured Rehani's release. The crowd then proceeded to the nearby Mnazi Moja football grounds, where they were joined by hundreds of other resisters. According to one police estimate, by 11:30 A.M. more than seven hundred men and women had gathered at the football grounds, where they debated what action to take. Rehani addressed the crowd and, after thanking them for their support, encouraged them "not to pay rent to the Indians."[113] According to the testimony of police detectives mingling in the crowd, other speakers, including Faraji Mpira, encouraged the crowd of men and women to arm themselves in preparation for battle with the forces of state. Faraji also allegedly advocated an "assault" on any landlord or clerk brave enough to attempt collecting.[114]

This mass meeting was not the last; approximately one month after freeing Rehani from court, Ng'ambo residents came together for another meeting, on Sunday, 9 September, which again drew over seven hundred participants. The meeting was held at the Polo Grounds, a location chosen not only because it could hold such a large crowd, but also because it symbolized the issues which were at the core of the strike. Zanzibaris were prohibited from using the grounds and the premises were surrounded by signs which read, Members Only! which one elderly man translated for me as "twenty-five white men and their horses."[115] Faraji Mpira was again one of the leading speakers at this meeting. He drew attention to the inequity of a political system that allowed foreign (British) interests to determine where and under what conditions Zanzibaris could play as well as live. He also argued against the very principal of ground rent, asserting, "Nobody has any right to get rent for land!" In reference to the wakf lands that had been privatized, as well as early-nineteenth-century law and custom, which recognized only usufruct, Faraji reminded the assembled crowd, "The land belongs to God and not to any man!" One man in the crowd challenged Faraji, "Why if the land belongs to God are our huts sold and ourselves imprisoned by order of the court?" to which Faraji replied that "this was soon to be a thing of the past and in the future no one could sell their huts, imprison them or do them any harm."[116] According to police reports, Faraji was a persuasive public speaker who repeatedly encouraged the assembled crowds to organize and fight to protect their homes.

Faraji was one of the most popular speakers at these events. His speeches proclaiming, "Zanzibar belongs to the Natives!" and "The land is ours from the beginning! Why should we pay rent?" regularly drew massive applause from the crowd.[117] In the course of public speeches Faraji repeatedly called for the nationalization of land and the abolition of ground rent. He also allegedly advocated the expulsion of the British from the isles, because of their persistent efforts to undermine the interests of "indigenous" Zanzibaris, like himself. Faraji was actually a former slave of Manyema descent but, like thousands of others who grew up in the isles, by the late 1920s he identified as a Zanzibari. Faraji's contemporaries were well aware of his heritage, yet no one ever publicly questioned his self-proclaimed identity as a native Zanzibari, nor his willingness to fight to protect the rights of other "indigenous" islanders to urban home ownership.[118]

The courts and the jails were the principal sites of the state's support for landlords and as such they became the primary focus of the people's anger and contempt during the rent strike. On three separate occasions, in August and September, several hundred men and women attacked the court and jail in order to secure the release of someone who had been convicted of nonpayment of ground rent or failure to abide by an eviction notice. These actions were not characterized by disorder, violence, or looting, but rather by restraint and quiet resolve. The crowds never moved on anything other than the court or the jail and once they had succeeded in liberating the prisoner, they dispersed. Another instance when a boisterous Ng'ambo crowd intervened at the court occurred on Friday, 28 September, when Rehani Maktub was convicted by the resident magistrate for failure to vacate his house after being evicted. As the judge pronounced Rehani's sentence—ten days in jail—a crowd of several hundred friends and neighbors who had been observing the trial through the courthouse windows moved into the court and secured his release.[119] This was the second time in less than two months that such a crowd had intervened at the court. Members of the administration were rightfully embarrassed, and the police were ordered to find Rehani and put him in jail. Rehani turned himself in, thirty-six hours later, and was taken by the police to prison. Once again, however, a crowd of over four hundred men and women appeared at the prison gates demanding his release. Paul Sheldon, the senior commissioner attempted to negotiate with the crowd, promising to remit Rehani's sentence if, according to the acting commissioner of police, the crowd would also agree to "behave themselves."[120] While the senior commissioner perceived himself as negotiating a return to order, the commissioner of police suggested that Sheldon's concession to the crowd only furthered the resolve of the strikers.[121] With Rehani leading the boisterous crowd, the group marched off from the prison on a tour of Ng'ambo, singing and chanting of their most recent victory and their dreams of ultimately defeating both landlords and the colonial state in the war over ground rent.

Demonstrations by angry crowds at the court and jail were a common feature of popular protest in colonial Zanzibar. To the poor and powerless the courts and the jails were not symbols of justice, but of injustice where inequalities and repression were daily reinforced. When asked why Zanzibaris felt they had a right to break people out of court or attack the jail, one elderly man who remembered the rent strike of 1928 explained it like this:

> There was a tendency in Zanzibar towards bias and favoritism. If two people were caught for the same crime and the evidence implicated both, the rich, whose parents could buy them out, got off, while the poor went to jail. The poor would then join together. They would say, "This isn't justice! It isn't fair that only the poor go to jail or get taken to court!"

This man argued that classism and racism accounted for the willingness of administrative officers to protect Stone Town tenants from the rapacious demands of landlords, in the 1920s, while ignoring similar pleas from tenants in Ng'ambo. He also questioned why courts commonly ordered the eviction of past-due Ng'ambo tenants, but took pity on civil servants living in Stone Town who were also negligent in paying their rent. He continued,

> When this would happen hundreds would join together and place themselves in the middle. Otherwise the poor didn't get justice. . . . If they were persecuting or oppressing someone then four hundred people would enter into the middle. They would say, "This is discrimination! This is not justice!" and they would protect those who were being charged.[122]

He concluded, "The only way for the poor to get justice was if they came together and organized."

Another elderly man who was involved in attacks on the court and jail explained the events in a similar fashion:

> We were all united in our opposition to the government. We had all agreed amongst ourselves to stick together. We said, "Take us all to jail and not just the ten or twelve you have taken to court. We all refused your policies and we all want to go to jail!" So we went to Kilimani jail and asked to be put in prison. . . . We were organized and unified.[123]

Invoking a Swahili proverb he continued, "A single finger cannot kill a louse," implying that only through coordinated action could a (civic) body rid itself of the pests which were annoying it.

Inspired by popular notions of justice and a growing sense of unity, Ng'ambo residents were also emboldened by their belief that individual police officers and many prison warders were on their side. At the August meeting held at the football grounds after freeing Rehani Farajalla from court, Faraji Mpira reportedly told the crowd that, "they did not need to be afraid of the *askaris* [police] because the askaris were their own people living among them."[124] Faraji's assessment, unlikely to have been formally negotiated with the police, was more than likely based on the fact that many members of the police force were also members of the Ng'ambo community. Somewhere between one-third and one-half of the policemen at this time were

"Zanzibaris" and many of them owned homes and lived in Ng'ambo. Although members of the police were ordered on several occasions, in the 1920s, to move to the police barracks at Ziwani, precisely because the administration wanted to distance them from the "crowd" among whom they lived, the majority of Zanzibaris in the force refused. These men "hated the regiment [*sic*] of camp life" and found the constant supervision of their lives in camp oppressive. They also drew on discourses of local "custom and tradition" that supported polygyny to argue that the cramped quarters at Ziwani were inadequate for their multiple wives and numerous children.[125] In the 1910s and 1920s, Zanzibari police officers were often considered by their British superiors to be far more troublesome and prone to questioning authority than other members of the service, leading eventually to a policy of hiring the majority of island police from other areas in British East Africa. Interviews with one former member of the colonial police service, while not necessarily representative of overall police sentiment, suggests that at least he and several of his colleagues were completely sympathetic to the actions of the strikers.[126] As Ng'ambo home owners, they too were threatened by ever-increasing rents and feared eviction from their homes as much as any other tenant. When ordered to take action against friends and neighbors from Ng'ambo, he and others were less than diligent in executing the orders.

Pushed by the persistent actions of Ng'ambo tenants, in late 1927 and early 1928, the administration began to debate several versions of a decree intended to protect tenants from arbitrary and dramatic increases in ground rent. The initial version of the Ground Rent Restriction Decree was an utter failure in resolving tensions between landlords and tenants. Topan spearheaded landlord opposition to the decree, arguing that the proposed ground rent rates effectively required landlords to "give our land on charity to the native tenants of Zanzibar." He also claimed that government interference in the matter only "provided a channel of encouragement to a few miscreants," and that owners and renters were perfectly able to come to a "mutual agreement" on their own. Shortly after the initial decree was proposed, Topan symbolically thumbed his nose at the administration, quadrupling the ground rent charged on the majority of his Ng'ambo property.[127] Despite the objections of landlords like Topan, however, by November 1928, three months of mass meetings and breakouts from court and jail had convinced the administration that a revised decree that came down much more firmly in favor of protection for tenants was needed. Admitting that the previous version of the decree had been "very difficult" to administer and had "not resulted in the settling of differences between landlords and tenants,"[128] the authors of the revised decree brought all of Ng'ambo under government-enforced rent control. Landowners and a few members of the administration, including the land officer, tried to push for the adoption of a scale of rents similar to those currently being charged. The chief secretary, however, vetoed their proposal, arguing that leaving rents at their current rates "would not be wise at this time."[129]

The amended decree fixed rent rates, based upon plot size, and effectively reduced the ground rent of most Ng'ambo tenants by 300 to 600 percent.[130] The standard ground rent paid by the majority of Ng'ambo tenants was set at 4 annas (one-fourth of a rupee) per month, which was roughly the equivalent of the rates that the state had been charging on Crown lands back in 1904. This rate was also only half that proposed as "reasonable" by the wakf tenants who petitioned the British resident prior to the strike. Under this legislation, landlords were free to negotiate higher rents with their tenants, but they could not sue for arrears for any amount in excess of the standard. A moratorium was also placed on court cases for arrears. Landlords were not allowed to bring suits against tenants for periods preceding the enactment of the amended decree and bygones were thus legally declared bygones.[131] The decree also included several clauses that made it illegal to go to people's homes and attempt to persuade them to abstain from paying their rent, to gather in groups of twelve or more persons with the goal of encouraging resistance to rent, or to speak before an unlawful assembly, as defined by the decree.

The strikers of 1928 failed to secure the complete elimination of ground rents, but the rates that were established were so minimal that nearly every Ng'ambo resident could afford them.[132] The Ground Rent Restriction Decree was reenacted every three years up to the time of independence, in 1963, when ground rents were finally abolished and the calls of Ng'ambo tenants for the nationalization of land were finally answered by the postrevolutionary Afro-Shirazi government. Up to the eve of independence, landlords, under the leadership of Topan, continued to complain that they were being "kept down-trodden under the shoes of native hut owners" and "slaughtered on the altar of native hut owners like humble and miserable sheep," but to no avail.[133] Ground rents were never officially increased beyond the rate established in 1928. The women and men involved in the ground rent strike may have lost the battle against capitalist attempts to declare Ng'ambo land private property, but they won the war to protect their own security to live in a rent-controlled city.

The provisions of the revised Ground Rent Restriction Decree that forbade court action against past-due tenants effectively restored a superficial calm to town, but in January 1929, protesters once again took to the streets, this time taking their demands for the complete elimination of ground rent to the sultan himself. Throughout November and December, Ng'ambo residents had continued to meet in groups, well in excess of the legal limit of twelve persons, to debate their acceptance of the administration's offer to impose ground rent control. There were those who found the rates established by the decree acceptable, yet there were many others who continued to scorn the very notion of ground rent.[134] Several hundred of the women and men in the latter category brought their case before the sultan, Seyyid Khalifa, on 11 January 1929. Until this time the sultan had remained outside of the conflict, yet protesters apparently felt that he too needed to take a public stand on the issue. In the nineteenth century, individuals who were unhappy with the decisions of judicial or administrative officers were free to bring an appeal before the sultan, who served as final arbiter in all disputes. Even during the early colonial era there was a common perception that, when all else failed, the sultan could be called upon, and possibly persuaded, to intervene on behalf of the poor. The present sultan, Seyyid Khalifa, came to power in 1911, that fortuitous year when picking boycotts combined with repeated marches on the sultan's palace by slaves, peasants, and squatters ultimately succeeded in convincing the colonial administration to abandon ground rents and hut taxes in the rural areas.

Just a few months earlier, in October 1928, the prisoners from the city jail broke out of prison so that they could bring their concerns before the sultan. The prisoners began by taking control of the jail on the evening of 29 October and demanding a meeting with the senior commissioner, Mr. Sheldon, to discuss their concerns. Sheldon came, but although the details of these negotiations remain unclear, it appears that the prisoners were dissatisfied with his response. The following morning they called him to a second meeting, and when he failed to appear, ninety men broke out of prison and marched through town to the sultan's palace. The sultan agreed to meet with two representatives from the crowd to hear their complaints, but ordered the remaining men to march themselves back to prison, which they apparently did once their representatives were accorded a meeting with the sultan.[135] Apparently taking their cue from the recent actions of the prisoners, in January Ng'ambo tenants who remained dissatisfied with the administration's offer to substantially lower ground rents brought a final appeal before the sultan.

As Zanzibaris, the women and men who convened at the sultan's palace in January 1929 were legally defined as "subjects of the Sultan," and it seems that they were calling on him to re-assert his control as the official head of state, re-establish respect for Islamic notions of patriarchal "obligation" and compassion toward the poor, protect wakf dedications, and abolish ground rent completely. Apparently, this latest attempt by a Ng'ambo crowd to bypass the administration and engage in direct conversation with the sultan was perceived by at least some British officials as a direct attack on their control of the protectorate. For reasons that are left unexplained by the archival records, *none* of the evidence regarding the ground rent strike, the mass public meetings that took place as part of the strike, or the successful efforts of Ng'ambo residents to remove their friends and neighbors from the courts was ever compiled by the authorities until after the January march on the sultan. While one can only speculate on why there was no mention of the rent strike in the administration's written records from 1928, it is clear that the decisive action taken against protestors at the sultan's palace in January was intended to convince critics in the Colonial Office in England that the local administration in Zanzibar was making concerted efforts to act more decisively with local troublemakers. As the crowd marched on the sultan's palace in January, the administration was in the process of being thoroughly scrutinized by an official commission of enquiry into the October jailbreak. While fault was found at various levels for the October mishap, when the official report was completed, the subtext was that the administration had learned from its earlier mistakes and acted much more effectively against the crowds in January. The acting director of prisons, in particular, was chastised for his leniency in October, but it was argued that he did "much to retrieve his reputation by the way in which he dealt with the demonstrations against the Ground Rent Restriction Decree. . . ."[136] In the latter case, the police intervened repeatedly, effectively preventing the crowd from ever convening a meeting with the sultan. The police arrested twelve men in the crowd identified as "ringleaders," and several detachments of police were also sent to the homes of four additional "provocateurs" to secure their arrest. This time there was no remittal of sentences and no negotiation with the crowd. Each of the sixteen men arrested, including Faraji Mpira and Sheikh Zahor, were either sentenced to time in jail, deported to Pemba, or both.[137]

The January march on the sultan's palace should be understood not only as a continuation of the protest against ground rent, but also as a collective attempt by members of the Ng'ambo community to restore certain elements of precolonial political practice to civil society in colonial Zanzibar. These practices included respect for the political opinions voiced by members of a large and angry crowd and recognition of the rights of women as citizens of the isles. On the morning of 11 January 1929, a crowd of three hundred people, most of whom were women, had gathered at the Sultan's town palace, Beit al-Ajaib, by 8:30 A.M. The crowd continued to voice its opinion that land in the isles belonged to Zanzibaris and that no one had a right to claim ground rent from Ng'ambo residents. Faraji Mpira was once again the leading speaker, and with him at the fore the crowd repeatedly chanted, "The land is ours from the beginning! Why should we pay rent?"[138] After some time, word began to circulate amongst the crowd that the sultan was not at Beit al-Ajaib, but at his country residence in Kibweni. The crowd therefore began a six-mile march from Stone Town through Ng'ambo and out to the Kibweni palace. By the time the crowd reached the Kibweni palace some three hours later, they had been joined by several hundred additional protesters. Despite the fact that Faraji and most of the men identified by the British as the "ringleaders" were arrested by the police as the crowd made its way from town out to Kibweni, the crowd, three-fourths of whom were women, remained insistent in their calls for a meeting with the sultan.[139] The police spent hours unsuccessfully attempting to disperse the crowd, but to no avail. Eventually the police attempted to bribe the crowd to leave by offering protestors free rides back into town on PWD lorries. Several men in the crowd apparently moved to take the police up on their offer, but they were forcibly removed from the lorries by women who taunted them and cursed them for their cowardly behavior. The official police report of the incident at Kibweni stated:

> The men were perfectly reasonable and in fact seemed quite ready to return but the women were extremely excited and refused to listen to any form of persuasion. . . .We made several other attempts to induce the crowd to return, but in each case we were frustrated by the hysterical obstinacy of the women.[140]

These police reports share a number of interesting parallels with the official reports by British officers involved in the 1929 Igbo women's war in Nigeria as well as other anti-colonial tax protests in British Africa.[141] The "hysterical obstinacy" of African women who refused to back down from the colonial state was remarked on repeatedly by administrative officials across the continent. These vocal expressions of collective pressure have been explained in much of the literature as emanating from African women's historical participation in political life, a tradition that was being rapidly undermined in the 1920s by colonial rule, but which African women continued to exercise in times of collective crisis through mass action. Traditions of female involvement in community politics and even of female rule were common along the Swahili coast and among many of the people of the mainland from whom Ng'ambo residents descended. Although these traditions were in some cases threatened by Omani rule and directly undermined by the British, they remained very much alive in the collective social memory of Ng'ambo in the 1920s.[142] In many African cultures, including those represented in Zanzibar, the use of mass public demonstrations by women whose economic survival was being threatened was also sanctioned when other avenues of redress had been exhausted. British administrators characteristically interpreted the African women's actions as "hysterical," "obstinate," and "out of control," but within their communities, protests of this nature would have been viewed as legitimate and effective testimony of widespread popular disdain for specific economic and political policies. As the following chapter will further illustrate, women objected not only to ground rent, but also to British efforts to undermine their legal, economic, and political standing as island citizens. Although the women never succeeded in meeting with the sultan on 11 January 1929, they continued to voice their concerns about economic and political issues through other means.

The January demonstrations before the sultan marked the last time the people of Ng'ambo took mass action to demand the abolition of ground rent, but this did not really bring an end to the strike. The residents of Ng'ambo no longer took to the streets, but they did not necessarily start paying their rent. A register of court cases prepared by the Wakf Commission shows that between 1929 and 1930 the commission was forced to take court action against 335, or some 40 percent, of its Ng'ambo tenants who continued to refuse to pay.[143] In 1934 the administrator general, who was also the secretary of the Wakf Commission, wrote a letter in support of renewing the contract of Mr. Vaghji Praji, a wealthy merchant and broker who leased the right to collect ground rents on land controlled by the Wakf Commission, in exchange for half of the rents collected. The administrator general praised Praji's methods of collection: "He refrained from harassing tenants, contenting himself with whatever rent he could collect without undue rigor."[144] In a subsequent letter to the commissioners the administrator general admitted, however, that at the end of Mr. Praji's lease it would be "very likely" that each of their eight hundred tenants would need to be sued for arrears.[145] Apparently, in the years following the ground rent strike, the administration measured its success not in terms of the amount of ground rent collected, but in terms of keeping Ng'ambo demonstrators out of the streets and away from the courts and palace.

Still reeling from the effects of the ground rent strike, the Zanzibar administration was forced into another conflict with the residents of Ng'ambo in 1933, when the Colonial Office pressured the local administration to impose a hut tax in Ng'ambo.[146] As most local administrators could predict, their attempts at collecting the hut tax were an utter failure. In the first year the tax was imposed, less than 40 percent of expected revenues were collected.[147] By 1935, the state was forced to initiate court action against 4,339 hut owners who refused to pay, or more than half the home owners in Ng'ambo.[148] This resort to legal proceedings caused tensions not only with Ng'ambo residents, but also within the administration itself, as members of the judiciary were in an uproar over the substantial increase in their workloads that resulted from trying to bring over half of Ng'ambo's population to court. In 1937, "owing to the difficulty of collecting the tax" and perceptions that, in the words of the municipal officer, it was "not politic" to take another four thousand residents to court, the hut tax in Ng'ambo was officially abolished and replaced by a levy on imported foods. Although the administration succeeded in raising the necessary revenue by taxing imported food, it was forced to hide the tax within a slightly elevated cost of food and, more significantly, to move the burden of paying the tax to the Protectorate population as a whole, rather than only urban home owners.[149]

The unanimity of action displayed by Ng'ambo residents during the ground rent strike and subsequent actions against the hut tax illustrates the power and strength of the community that had been built in Ng'ambo by the late 1920s. Although the men and women of Ng'ambo came from a melange of cultural backgrounds, by the late 1920s they had succeeded in fashioning a collective sense of self as Zanzibaris. As citizens of Zanzibar, they demanded respect for their right to own property, including urban homes, and were far more successful than most others in colonial Africa at resisting the imposition of hut taxes and ground rents. The evidence gathered from police investigations is disappointingly vague regarding the means by which this unity or shared sense of identity had been created. Marches, mass meetings, and protests were highly visible but also atypical venues utilized by the women and men of Ng'ambo for the debate of political ideas and social ideals. In the following chapters we will see how popular pastimes, including taarab performances and football practices, created much more characteristic opportunities for the daily conversation and interaction that allowed the women and men of Ng'ambo to craft a sense of community. In the course of popular pastimes they also actively debated the values that they wanted to build twentieth-century island society around.

Chapter 4

The Music of Siti binti Saad
*Creating Community, Crafting Identity, and
Negotiating Power through Taarab*

In March of 1928, as the Ng'ambo ground rent strike moved into
high gear, Siti binti Saad and her taarab band traveled to Bombay for
their first recording session. Although the band was absent during
the height of the strike, their music played a critical, if indirect, role
in bringing the strike to fruition, as the band's music helped to craft
the community and mold the class consciousness that were at the root
of the strike. The events of 1928 did not emerge out of a discursive
vacuum; people talked and argued about the issues that were at the
core of the strike on a daily basis and Siti's performances were one
among the numerous forums in which such debates took place. In addition, Siti binti Saad and her band used their skills as performers to
give poetic form to the often trenchant critiques of economic and political power that circulated in Ng'ambo during the period between
the two world wars. Their songs assessed the inequalities that permeated urban society and literally created a record of the thoughts and
visions expressed by their friends and neighbors in Ng'ambo about
alternative ways to structure personal and social relations. An analysis of these songs demonstrates the growing salience of class identity
among Ng'ambo residents during the 1920s and 1930s, as well as an

astute awareness on the part of Ng'ambo residents of the ways that colonialism was reproducing and enhancing political and economic inequality within island society.

The band's music also provides rich evidence of the transformations in female identity that were being negotiated in the post-abolition era. Amid the host of changes taking place in island society during the 1910s and 1920s, women struggled to create new definitions of femininity, definitions that enhanced their personal autonomy while simultaneously preserving those aspects of nineteenth-century law and custom which they found empowering. These efforts occasionally caused strife between women, their families, and their lovers, and as these songs reveal, often brought women into direct conflict with colonial institutions intent on reifying patriarchal control. Siti's songs lament the fact that colonial law not only favored the wealthy, but that it also further institutionalized gender inequality. As Islamic law was reinterpreted, in early-twentieth-century island society, it became increasingly difficult for women to get a divorce or maintain control of their property. Women who brought cases of rape and domestic abuse before the courts were also frequently dissatisfied with the judgments offered by *kadhi*s (Islamic judges) and British magistrates. The band's songs reveal the personal stories of individual women as they contested these processes and provide rare insight into the emotional impact such struggles had on both women's and men's lives. The band's music did not privilege the public as the preeminent domain of power in women's lives, but exposed and explored critiques of domestic and sexual subordination as well. Through these lyrics we hear the stories of individual women as they reframed discourses of power and sexuality and in the process asserted new definitions of self and femininity in the post-abolition era.

An examination of Siti binti Saad's life history and her musical style provides concrete illustrations of some of the ways in which formerly servile members of island society worked to undermine the ideological and practical divisions that existed between slave and free-person, Arab and African and to create a somewhat cohesive cultural identity as Zanzibaris. Siti's success as a national songstress did not merely echo articulations of belonging heard elsewhere in twentieth-century society; her music was critical in helping to constitute and give cultural form to this emerging Zanzibari identity. Her ascendance as a performing and recording artist was based, in large part, on her unique ability to craft a musical style that recognized and revered the unique contributions that all cultural groups contributed to island society.

Taarab and the Creation of a Zanzibari Identity

The genre of music that Siti popularized was a revolutionized version of taarab—a form of nineteenth-century courtly praise music performed in Arabic for Zanzibar's sultans. Taarab was created in Zanzibar during the reign of Seyyid Barghash (1870–88), a sultan widely known for his opulent and luxurious court life.[1] Barghash spent more than ten years in exile, traveling to India, Arabia, and Europe before he was recalled to take the throne.[2] During his time abroad Seyyid Barghash developed an appreciation for the forms of courtly entertainment and patronage of the arts indulged in by fellow members of the ruling elite across the oceans. When he returned to Zanzibar he devoted considerable resources to the development of royal architecture[3] as well as his own unique brand of courtly music, which became known as taarab.

The musical instruments of taarab were largely of Middle Eastern origin, including the *nai* (end-blown flute), *qanun* (trapezoidal plucked zither), *tari* (tambourine), *udi* (mandolin), *dumbak* (a goblet drum), and fiddle, while the sound reflected the cosmopolitan mix of Indian Oceana that came together in Zanzibar and made the islands famous. The language and performance culture of taarab were intended to celebrate and reaffirm the power and exclusivity of Zanzibar's Omani ruling class, as well as their ties to Arabian trading networks and the center of Arab mass culture, Egypt. Taarab songs were composed and performed in Arabic and consisted largely of songs praising the sultan or other members of the royal family. Taarab also was performed exclusively within the palace; individuals outside of the court were allowed to hear taarab only at the invitation of the royal family. The stories of musicians hiding along the edge of the palace walls in order to sneak a listen (apparently risking great punishment if discovered by the sultan), which abound in manuscript collections and oral traditions of the earliest public clubs, speak volumes to the symbolic power of taarab as a musical means of reifying the cultural boundaries separating the Omani ruling elite from the remainder of the islands' population.[4]

Between 1895 and 1910, however, taarab gradually began to move into the public sphere as young men from wealthy and politically connected families in Stone Town appropriated taarab's symbolic power and turned it to their own ends.[5] Reflecting the growing political power of members of the Arab elite born outside the royal family, by the turn of the century these budding young musicians became increasingly confident that they no longer had to hide their musical endeavors from the sultan.[6] These were also years in which the power of the British over the throne was becoming increasingly visible and new musical metaphors of power, including a brass marching band under the control of the British military, began to dominate official entertainment. In 1905 the first nonroyal taarab band, Nadi Ikhwan Safaa, was formed, followed in 1910 by a second band, Nadi Shuub.

Growing out of earlier traditions of competitive ngoma, Ikhwan Safaa and Nadi Shuub became competitive rivals. They rivaled each other not only musically, but in the sponsoring of elaborate picnics and feasts where they vied to provide the greatest amount of food for the largest number of guests. The two groups also competed for invitations to perform their music at the celebrations of the island's leading families. Playing for the al-Barwani, one of the wealthiest landed clans in Zanzibar, became a special area of competition, as two members of the al-Barwani extended family belonged to each of the competing clubs. Each Barwani celebration therefore became the site of intense competition, where the bands would play against each other, struggling to see who could draw the largest crowd and maintain the spectators' attention for the longest period of time.[7] Unlike many competitive ngoma which came before and after them, however, these two bands did not compete in the exchange of dialogic poetry, or competitive verse exchange, rather they prided themselves on their ability to perform precise copies of Egyptian tunes, available on gramophone discs, or taarab songs poached from the sultan's band.[8] Ikhwan Safaa and Nadi Shuub not only took their names from Arabic, they also sang exclusively in Arabic, but the fact that few of their members were fluent in Arabic impeded their ability to compose original songs.[9] The language and performance style of their music attempted to reify the relationship between their club members, the aristocracy for whom they performed and ideologies of ustaarabu, "civilization" rooted in Arab cultural norms. The performances of Ikhwan Safaa and Naadi Shuub brought taarab into the public domain, but "the public" was still largely limited to those with connections to the landed gentry or mercantile elite. Until Siti binti Saad began to popularize taarab and bring it into the neighborhoods of Ng'ambo, sometime after World War I, it remained a cultural symbol of the wealth, power, and exclusiveness of the landed, slave-owning aristocracy.

Siti and her band are credited by many historians of taarab as being the first musicians to perform taarab in Ng'ambo. What is perhaps more accurate is that they were the first performers from Ng'ambo recognized by the elite as taarab musicians.[10] The precursors of Nadi Ikhwan Safaa, the first taarab band to perform for an audience outside of the sultan's palace, were in fact ngoma groups based among *kuli* (slave porterage) gangs at the port. This earlier music was not regarded as taarab because it was performed by slave and working-class men of Hadhrami and African descent who sang in Kiswahili and performed at the docks. The dhow crews that frequented Zanzibar's wharf were also widely known for their lively nightly performances, which incorporated some of the instruments, rhythms, and melodies of taarab, but they were nonetheless still regarded as "something other." Like Ikhwan Safaa and Naadi Shuub, Siti's band performed songs in Arabic, including original compositions as well as copies of material of the famed Egyptian songstress Umm Kulthum. Yet the bulk of the band's material, and that for which they were most acclaimed, was composed in Kiswahili—the indigenous language of Zanzibar. The fact that the band performed in both languages allowed them to speak to residents on both sides of the creek. However, it was their ability to compose and sing rhymed and metered poetry in Arabic that brought them recognition among the elite as "real" taarab musicians and not "just" another working-class ngoma troupe that incorporated Arabic instruments and rhythms into their repertoire.[11] Yet the choice of Siti and her band to perform primarily in Kiswahili enhanced taarab's ability to communicate with a much wider island audience than the music of Ikhwan Safaa or Naadi Shuub. The band's decision to sing in Kiswahili also helped to transform taarab from an Arab cultural form into one that became quintessentially Zanzibari.[12]

Like many Zanzibaris of her day, Siti binti Saad incorporated elements of both African and Arab sensibility into her life. As an artist she also creatively refashioned a number of already existing cultural and musical practices into a form that made taarab attractive to a cross-section of island society. Through her incorporation of stylistic elements drawn from the musical and performance cultures of the islands' Arab, African, and South Asian residents, Siti crafted a musical space that widened the boundaries of "belonging."[13] The variety of contexts in which she sang, including free public concerts held on the open ngoma grounds in Ng'ambo, wedding celebrations for East Africa's wealthiest merchants and landowners, open houses in Ng'ambo with food and entertainment during Ramadhan, private shows for the sultan and British resident, and fund-raising concerts at the cinema also helped to articulate these growing transformations in consciousness within the public domain of performance. Her musical style was able to cross over into a range of previously distinctive performance spaces; it mediated and minimized existing distinctions between the leisure pursuits of wealthy "Arab" patricians who patronized and produced "civilized" culture (*utamaduni/ustaarabu*) and the popular "uncultured pastimes" of the majority populations.[14] As Christopher Waterman has argued, musical styles not only mirror but also shape other historical processes.[15] The musical style of Siti's band, which incorporated Arabic instruments including the oud (lute), *nai* (flute), and fiddle along with African drum rhythms, the Kiswahili language, and South Asian melodies, gave musical form to the emerging Zanzibari identity of the interwar era.

Islam also provided much common ground for island residents, and this carried over into musical appreciation as well. Although the African majority and the Arab elite belonged to different sects in the nineteenth century and adhered to somewhat different devotional practices, they shared a great deal, including reverence for the same sacred texts.[16] Appreciation for the skills of a solo vocalist who could traverse an octave and a range of tones within a single phrase, while adding ornaments and cadences that helped to enhance a text's meaning, were musical elements based in the creative recitation of the Qur'an which were widely shared among all Muslims.[17] The centrality of lyrics to musical performance and an appreciation for skilled oratory was another common feature in African praise poetry, Swahili verse, and Arabic music that created common ground among Siti's diverse audiences. Virginia Danielson's description of the qualities appreciated by Umm Kulthum's Egyptian audiences applied as well to those in East Africa, where "[v]erbal cleverness, in oratory, poetry, song or ordinary speech separates the witty from the dull neighbor, the effective from the ineffective argument, the artistic from the banal performance."[18] Siti's use of rhyme, meter, and metaphor earned her respect in a culture in which talking is considered an art form.

Ethnomusicologists have frequently noted that musics are rarely stable in contexts of social change and that in the process of urbanization, in particular, new musical styles are often created to articulate the dreams and disillusionments of recent immigrants to the city.[19] As David Coplan argues in the context of South African urbanization, "In situations of change, identity is dynamic, and people manipulate its symbols in order to define who they are, who they are not, and who they wish to be."[20] The new form of taarab created by Siti binti Saad and her band was one cultural symbol that gave musical expression to the desire of Zanzibar's burgeoning urban population to be recognized as full citizens of island society.

Background on the Band and the Role of Religion in Their Rise to Fame

Siti binti Saad and the other members of her band—Mwalim Shaaban Umbaye, Mbaruku Effandi Talsam, Subeti bin Ambari, and Budda bin Swedi—all lived in Ng'ambo, but their origins reflected the diversity of the Ng'ambo community at large. Siti, Subeti, and Budda were all born in Unguja, while Mwaalim Shaaban and Mbaruku were immigrants from the mainland. Mwaalim Shaaban, the band's principal poet, was born in Malawi in 1900 and was Mnyasa by birth. He was brought to Zanzibar at the age of four, where he was raised by his father's brother, who worked as a clerk in the office of the Bububu railway. Mbaruku Effandi Talsam, born in 1892, was the son of a suria (slave concubine) owned by a wealthy Arab trader, Abdulkarim Talsam Mabasheikh, from Mombasa, Kenya.[21] Mbaruku's family invested their money not only in trade throughout the Indian Ocean but also in a variety of competitive ngoma popular on the island of Mombasa, including the parading *(gwaride)* beni band Skochi, in which one of Mbaruku's uncles was "King."[22] Mbaruku became blind at the age of ten after contracting smallpox, yet he followed in the family's musical tradition, mastering the flute, fiddle, and several other stringed instruments including the oud. Mbaruku worked and studied music in Lamu as well as Mombasa, but in 1920, at the age of twenty-eight, he moved to Zanzibar in hopes of joining the band of Siti binti Saad, a band whose reputation had already begun to spread throughout the coast.

As children born into fairly privileged economic circumstances, both Mbaruku and Mwalim Shaaban attended Qur'anic school during their youth. As late as 1948, according to Edward Batson's *Social Survey of Zanzibar,* only 19 percent of Zanzibar's population had attended Qur'anic school and fewer that half of them had completed the basic course of study *(kuhitimu).*[23] Here children memorized the thirty-three chapters of the Holy Book and gained a formal knowledge of Islam, which helped to elevate their stature within the Muslim community. Through the early 1900s, Kiswahili was written in Arabic script and those who attended Qur'anic school also gained literacy skills that were largely unavailable through other means.[24] Although attending Qur'anic school and becoming literate in Arabic was only the first step in a lifelong process of becoming an Islamic scholar, regardless of how far a student continued on with his or her education, the basics imparted at Qur'anic school opened up many doors that remained closed to those who had not attended school.

The vocal skills they learned through recitation of the Qur'an helped both Shaaban and Mbaruku to establish themselves as Islamic musicians. Before turning his attention to the performance of taarab music, Shaaban developed a reputation as a performer of Islamic sacred music, Qur'anic recitations, and *qasida* (religious poetry performed at either sacred or secular events). Shaaban also worked as an instructor at Qur'anic schools in both Zanzibar and Dar es Salaam, thus earning the title Mwaalim (learned man, teacher), as well as a living.[25] Although Mnyasa by birth, Shaaban's religious training and personal commitment to enhancing the understanding of Islam among island youth brought him respect and facilitated his full incorporation into Zanzibar society.

Although Shaaban was a known and respected Qur'anic teacher, not all the band's members were completely observant followers of the articles of the faith. Like nearly all island residents, the band members were professed Muslims, but like many of their contemporaries they were also less than dogmatic about their adherence to certain rules, particularly those restricting the consumption of alcohol. Siti, Subeti, and Mbaruku reputedly indulged in *mtindi wa mitindi* (yogurt of yogurts)—one of many local euphemisms for *gongo*, a high-powered locally distilled spirit made from papaya—as a lubricant for their creative powers.[26] Although most island residents would have agreed that this was not a "good" thing for a Muslim to be doing, judgment of an individual's moral standing were largely left by Zanzibaris to the Creator. As J. A. K. Leslie argued of Muslim Dar es Salaam, the principal town opposite Zanzibar on the mainland, which was also largely populated by recent immigrants from a host of cultural backgrounds, "A man's private life is his own business (though paradoxically it is the subject of endless gossip)."[27]

The immense variety of linguistic, cultural, and social backgrounds found in Ng'ambo, and in many Swahili towns along the littoral, generally encouraged tolerance of difference and discouraged interference in the affairs of others. Coastal religious culture recognized that "people are created with dissimilar natures and are likewise imperfect. It is up to every person to behave as . . . tactfully, politely, hospitably, morally and amicably as possible . . . rather than to demand such things of others. To blame, criticize or sanction those who fall short . . . is to be tactless. . . . It is [for God], not for me, to sanction."[28] Within Zanzibar and other heterogeneous coastal towns, if someone identified themselves as a Muslim, they were a Muslim, even if they drank or rarely prayed.[29]

Having neither the time nor the money to devote themselves to the study of Islam's written heritage, many East Africans lived Islam as a social religion—laying greater emphasis on issues of neighborliness, tolerance of difference, and building consensus within the community *(ijma)* than on interpretations of law and text.[30] There were those like Shaaban who fasted during Ramadhan and taught at Qur'anic school, and others like Subeti and Mbaruku who in lieu of evening prayers went out and had a drink. While behaviors like the latter were rarely held up for children to emulate, so long as a community member's behavior did not interfere with others, it was left between them and God. In the event that an individual's drunkenness became openly offensive and infringed on neighbors, however, it became a matter of general concern to the community. The famous and still widely popular tune "Muhogo wa Jang'ombe" was performed by the band with the precise intent of chastising one errant neighbor of Shaaban's who regularly returned home falling-down drunk after excursions to Jang'ombe, a neighborhood widely reputed for its production of alcohol, and then making a sport of offending area women with his lewd behavior. One stanza from the song, in which cassava is used as a euphemism for gongo, the offender is reminded that he is alone in his indulgence and, more important, that inebriation does not excuse him from the need to give respect to women in general and in particular to those who have earned it by virtue of their age, knowledge, reproductive power, or dedication as "mothers" of the community. "Cassava of Jang'ombe, I haven't yet licked the spoon / Do not curse the midwife or that which gives us life." Drinking alcohol, so long as it was done quietly, was fine, but not when it became openly offensive or threatened the safety of neighbors. Prescriptions for tolerance and brotherhood contained in the Qur'an allowed individuals to overlook a neighbor's drinking habits, but not his harassment of local women, which threatened the very core of social community. Songs like "Cassava of Jang'ombe," which chastised aberrant behavior or actions that placed individual satisfaction above the good of the community at large were a hallmark of the band's music.

Unlike Mwalim Shaaban and Mbaruku, Siti binti Saad did not have the advantages of attending Qur'anic school during her youth. Binti Saad (daughter of Saad) was born in the countryside a few miles outside Zanzibar Town in the mid-1880s. Her given name, Mtumwa, translates literally as slave or servant and reflects the subordinate status into which she was born.[31] As a child, Mtumwa binti Saad shared the life of many village youth, playing in the fields and streams of the countryside, helping with domestic and agricultural chores from an early age, and gradually learning from her mother and other village women the skills of a potter, which would help her earn an independent income as an adult. Like many women of her day, Mtumwa married while still in her early teens. This first marriage did not last long and shortly after the birth of her only child, Mariam (more commonly known as Kijakazi—a diminutive of female slave), Mtumwa and her daughter returned to her parent's home, where they lived for the next ten years.[32] But binti Saad's mind was elsewhere, according to biographers. "She hungered for change and new experiences."[33] In addition to farming, raising her daughter, and making pots, Mtumwa also began collecting pottery from other village women, which she carried into town and sold in the streets and neighborhoods of Ng'ambo. Through her regular trips to town she became acquainted with the people and possibilities of urban life, and in 1911, as Mohammed Khatib puts it, she decided to leave "her dusty life in the countryside and to enter into the city."[34] One of many thousands, binti Saad joined Zanzibar's version of "the Great Migration" from the countryside to the city—searching for economic opportunity as well as new possibilities for social and personal autonomy in the post-abolition era.

While marketing her pottery throughout town, Mtumwa binti Saad earned a reputation as an engaging and entertaining singer of folk songs and riddles, which she performed both to pass the time and to call attention to her goods. Word of her wit and the power of her voice reached the attention of several performers of Islamic ritual music who convinced her, shortly after her move to town, to begin training to become a performer herself. Then in her late twenties or early thirties, Mtumwa binti Saad began to learn the Qur'an and the rules of recitation *(tajwid)*, which emphasizes correct pronunciation, breathing techniques that allow phrases to remain intact, and the importance of tone and timbre to the conveyance of textual meaning.[35] The vocal training, introduction to Arabic, and knowledge of the Qur'an binti Saad received from her tutors was instrumental in her transformation from a quaint singer of colloquial tunes into a highly sought after performer of Islamic ritual music.

During the 1910s, the chanting of the Qur'an as well as the performance of religious poetry known as maulid or qasida were becoming increasingly popular forms of public and private entertainment among all sectors of the islands' population. Although maulid and qasida as practiced throughout East Africa today regularly include female as well as male performers accompanied by drums or tambourines, this was not always the case. In the 1890s, Sheikh Habib Salih (d. 1935), one reformer widely credited for his efforts to introduce African musical and ritual practices into Islamic worship along the coast, was literally drummed out of the neighboring island town of Lamu by the religious establishment for these efforts. Sheikh Habib was accused of heresy for his attempts be more inclusive of the island's African community by incorporating drumming, Kiswahili, and women into ritual performance.[36] Although scorned by the orthodox religious establishment, Habib's innovations became extremely popular among the poor in Lamu and spread quickly throughout the East African coast, including Zanzibar.

In the nineteenth century, maulid celebrations in commemoration of the birth of the Prophet Muhammad were also not very common. When they were performed at all, they were generally small, private, and fairly austere recitations of religious poetry in Arabic. Building on the innovations introduced by Habib, however, by the time binti Saad began performing maulid, in the 1910s, the public performance of poems sung in Kiswahili and accompanied by tambourines and drums had become widely popular.[37] *Maulid Barzanji,* an abridged Kiswahili version of an Arabic maulid celebrating the birth of the Prophet Mohammed, became commonly recited in private homes during this period. The Zanzibar government also institutionalized the performance of this maulid as a mass national celebration held on the city's sports grounds, beginning after World War I—thus providing further acknowledgment of the importance of both Kiswahili and popular Islam as symbols of national identity. Island residents began performing maulid not only in celebration of the Prophet's birth, but also in celebration of their own children's births and weddings, to pray for the soul of a deceased loved one or to give thanks for a bountiful clove crop. By the 1910s, maulid were also regularly accompanied by feasting and in many cases took on the air of competitive ngoma. The popularity of maulid continued to grow until, by the early 1930s, an average of eight hundred maulid were performed in town annually.[38] Binti Saad's natural talents as a singer and her training in the Qur'an allowed her to ride this wave of new devotional practice and to become one of the most sought after performers of the day. The growing popularity of more performative and musical maulid coincided with a general shift away from a literate and orthodox Islamic tradition to one that more openly embraced devout, yet poor and nonliterate, men and women within Sufi brotherhoods and zikiri rituals.[39]

Innovations in religious practice introduced at the turn of the century thus opened up new possibilities for individuals—including women like Mtumwa, who were from poor, servile, and Kiswahili-speaking backgrounds—to earn respect for their knowledge and performance of religious ritual. No less significant, such opportunities also provided new opportunities for earning a living. By the mid-1910s, Mtumwa's skills were in high demand, not only in Ng'ambo but in the countryside and within Stone Town as well. As one of binti Saad's supporters suggested, "From being a nonety [sic] with a slave name, Siti captivated wealthy Zanzibaris and they became her slaves. No occasion was deemed successful, be it a wedding or the celebration of a birth, among Zanzibar's elite, without Siti's performance."[40] The quality of her voice, her range of tones, resonance, nasality, and intonation, is said to have moved her listeners to another plane of existence.[41] In fact, according to the legends that surround her life, it was in the course of one particularly dynamic performance that the title Siti, from the Arabic term for "Lady," was bestowed upon Mtumwa by a member of the islands' gentry out of reverence for her allegedly impeccable pronunciation of Arabic and performance of ritual text. It was thus as a result of her training in the Qur'an that Mtumwa the slave was able to transform herself into Siti the lady.[42]

The Creative Context of Siti's Songs

Although Siti binti Saad's taarab music was popular among all classes of Zanzibaris, her music spoke most directly to the working-class men and women of Ng'ambo among whom she lived. Long before she rose to fame as an international recording star she earned the respect and adoration of her neighbors for her ability to transform the latest news and local gossip, as well as individual and collective struggles, into song.[43] Much of this material went unpublished, yet a great deal of it remains etched in the memories of elderly men and women who frequently credit themselves as coauthors of Siti's work.[44] The band's nightly practices were held at Siti's home in Ng'ambo and island residents were encouraged to attend. As Siti and the other members of her band composed the poems that became the lyrics to her songs, the audience would join in and openly praise the power of particular phrases or suggest reworking others. Siti's home became one of the central gathering places in Ng'ambo in the 1920s and 1930s, drawing men and women from across the town. Attending a practice or performance in Siti's home was often the highlight of a trip to town for people from the countryside or for friends and relatives visiting from the mainland.[45] The nightly practices in Siti's home were so well attended that a stranger would have thought them to be an official performance. The crowds grew during the holy month of Ramadhan, when the band provided not only entertainment but refreshments for the guests as well. The band in turn fed off the response their music generated in their audiences. Creation was not an individual act, but a public and collective one.

The most important way the audience influenced the band's music, however, was by providing stories that served as the basis for songs. People came together at Siti's home in Ng'ambo to socialize and enjoy the music, but also to exchange news and to analyze local and world events. Siti prided herself on her ability to compose extemporaneously and her contemporaries were regularly amazed by her ability to transform their talk into a poetic song.[46] Siti used her performances not only to entertain her audiences but also as a means of circulating and editorializing upon the news of the day or the week. Siti's taarab songs became akin to a Ng'ambo news sheet and word of her performances enjoyed widespread circulation. Even if there had been a printed newspaper neither Siti nor most of her contemporaries would have been able to read it, yet her music and the news it contained were accessible to all who could speak Kiswahili. The historical importance of Siti's music as a venue for communicating the issues and concerns of the day was so significant that when the Tanzania Media Women's Association (TAMWA) began to publish the nation's first feminist popular journal in 1988, they chose to name the journal *Sauti ya Siti* (Voice of Siti) in commemoration of Siti's work as a journalist in an oral genre.[47]

Like current cultural practices of "reading" the paper in East Africa,[48] the news and editorials that were circulated by Siti and her band were also subject to interpretation and vociferous debate. In fact, many of Siti's contemporaries contend that her intentional desire to spark debate around a range of class, gender, and political issues accounts, at least in part, for the unforgettable place the artist and her songs occupy in the collective memory of the era.[49] Siti's songs were not background music that one could listen to without bothering to hear, but poetic expressions that necessitated and forced engagement.

Unlike *Sauti ya Siti*, whose audience is comprised primarily of women, Siti's work was equally popular among both genders. Although island women were increasingly adopting the veil in the 1920s and 1930s, men and women continued to interact in mixed-gender public spaces, from protests against ground rent and mass public meetings at the sports grounds to taarab and ngoma performances. During Siti's day, civil society in Zanzibar had not yet succumbed to the "liberalizing" effects of tutorials in Western political theory; the public sphere included women and directly addressed the links between the public and private in civil life.[50] Only with the onset of World War II did twentieth-century leisure, politics, and the public sphere become increasingly gender segregated.

Through the process of meeting, talking, and debating, the women and men who gathered at Siti's home for practices, discussed her music after performances, or sang the band's songs while doing their daily chores actively helped to constitute bonds of community, evaluate reputations, and formulate discourses of social and political values. Private and public scandals—from abusive husbands to corrupt public officials—generated endless urban gossip as well as the material for many of the band's songs. As Luise White has argued, "The very act of talking about others—or oneself—disciplines; the very practice of sorting out the epistemologies that shock and scandalize creates and catalogues ideas about deviance and virtue which are enforced with each telling."[51] The band's songs not only related "facts" about particular cases, but in the very act of telling made evaluations of those facts as well.

The majority of those who lived in Ng'ambo between the two world wars may have been excluded from formal participation in the political institutions of colonial Zanzibar, but they were actively involved in formulating the debates which constituted civil society. Taking part in the vibrant music culture of Ng'ambo was just one of the many ways they did so. Songs that chastised and made fun of wrongdoers embarrassed the subject of scandal and publicly articulated the community's lack of respect for individuals engaged in such behavior. The songs of Siti binti Saad often summarized popular opinion while simultaneously spurring public debate of the religious, social, and cultural principles that contributed to the constitution of community.[52] Singing and gossiping about the deeds and misdeeds of others helped to define norms and affirm values among those who told and those who listened, and thus the participants set themselves apart from the few in urban Zanzibar who did neither.

As social documents the lyrics of the songs performed and recorded by Siti and her band provide unique insights into the world of interwar urban Zanzibar. By listening to the lyrics to these songs and the stories that surround them we can hear snippets of the daily conversations and heated debates that preoccupied residents of Ng'ambo. The focus here will be on songs that illuminate urban class and gender relationships, both because these issues are at the core of this study and because they constitute a significant part of the band's repertoire. Songs dealing specifically with class and political relationships in colonial Zanzibar constitute slightly more than 20 percent of the band's material that I have managed to collect and translate.[53] It seems probable that such material figured even more prominently in the band's live and unrecorded performances, as it is these songs in particular which are most vividly recalled by elderly Zanzibaris. A large portion of the band's material also addressed issues of love, sex, and domestic arrangements, although here again the band's take on these issues was decidedly political. When asked to recall their favorite songs from the era, elders who lived in Ng'ambo during this era invariably began to recite lines from Siti's songs which critiqued political abuse or economic injustice or which called for eradication of persistent gender inequalities. A textual and historical analysis of these songs comprises the core of the remainder of this chapter.

Continuity and Change in the Constellations of Colonial Power

Siti binti Saad and her band performed for the sultan and other members of the coastal elite but, like the praise poets across the continent, they did not simply flatter the powerful; rather they used the opportunity to critique the exercise of power and remind the strong of their obligations toward the weak.[54] The abuse of power by wealthy and politically connected members of urban society was a reoccurring theme in music performed by Siti binti Saad and her band. Although the might of the elite was certainly nothing new to twentieth-century Zanzibar, the imposition of colonial rule did alter the channels through which power was exercised. No longer directly dependent on the support of clients for their positions, members of the ruling class became increasingly immune to the pressures for reform exerted from those below. Emboldened by the enhanced authority granted by virtue of their appointed positions—often for life—within the colonial system, many civil servants also learned to manipulate these new bureaucratic tools to their own advantage. In the songs of Siti binti Saad the inability of the poor to constrain the power of colonial civil servants is a common lament, as is the perception that class inequalities were being increasingly institutionalized through the efforts of the colonial administration. Politicians of all kinds, be they members of the aristocracy or appointed bureaucrats, were perceived as increasingly distant from and unconcerned about the plight of the common people. Although the majority of those in Ng'ambo were excluded from participation in the formal discussions of policy-making bodies, these songs reveal their daily participation in public political debate. The band and those who helped create and evaluate their songs not only complained about the abuse of power, they chastised and in the process perhaps curbed it as well.

To many of Siti's literate contemporaries, the band's invitations to perform for the aristocracy—where they frequently earned more in a single evening than the typical laborer earned in a year—epitomized the economic potential of the era. Subtexts within the dominant folklore eulogizing Siti as an icon of the possibilities available in turn-of-the-century urban Zanzibar suggest, however, that Siti's nonliterate contemporaries also understood that monetary success for the poor was not always followed by concomitant elevations in respect. Just as the tales of Mtumwa being presented with the title of Siti were often accompanied by reference to the pejorative songs that circulated about her origins, recollections of the band's invitations into the inner rooms of the palace also frequently include stories of ridicule at the hands of the aristocracy. One of the most popular tales of this nature refers to an incident in the palace of the sultan, when after a performance before the royal family and their guests Siti and her band were presented with a lavish banquet of food and drink.[55] Rather than being allowed to enjoy the food presented to them like cultured human beings, however, they were allegedly ordered by Sultan Seyyid Khalifa to act like animals, throwing the food at each other and smearing themselves with the treats. According to urban legend, the band complied with the sultan's demands, to the great amusement of his aristocratic guests.

Although the band members felt that they had little immediate recourse, Mwalim Shaaban composed the following song, known as "Kigalawa" (a small dugout canoe with outriggers used by local fishermen), which they performed at the palace during their next visit. Shaaban's lyrics intentionally hid the author's meaning from the sultan, yet the band made it generally known throughout town why they had composed the song. In an explanation accompanying a published version of the vague and complicated lyrics to this song, Mwalim Shaaban indicated that his intent was to allude to the fact that the poor and powerless, although dependent on the wealthy for their livelihoods, were nonetheless human beings deserving of dignified treatment.[56] The lyrics made no direct reference to the incident at the palace, and many stanzas were incomprehensible. The royal audience was thus encouraged to dismiss the larger intent of the band and to sit back and enjoy the instrumentation of the song. A few of the more straightforward lines from the song go as follows:

> A small dugout canoe is the same as any other boat.
> A small dugout canoe is the same as any other boat.
> In the sea they always go with their outriggers of support.
> Why should I remove the cloth which is hiding these
>   matters?

> Surprisingly the little canoe has things inside.
> Surprisingly the little canoe has things inside.
> I will not scratch like a chicken for this little bit of work, it is
>   not theirs.
> I will not scratch like a chicken for this little bit of work, it is
>   not theirs.

Tales like that of "Kigalawa" reveal as much about popular understandings of Zanzibar history during the interwar period as they do about the band itself. Whether the alleged incident occurred or not, it appeared to be a reasonable possibility to those who heard the story. The tale behind "Kigalawa" became an accepted part of local discourses of power between the aristocracy and the islands' common people during the twentieth century. Members of the royal family were far more dependent on amicable relations with the British for their power and status than they were on their relations with clients in Ng'ambo. The sultan's alleged ordering of Siti to act like a monkey in public became a trope for political power within the protectorate; a trope highlighted in many postrevolutionary histories of taarab for its ability to symbolize the contempt common people perceived to be emanating from the increasingly closed circle of Arab, British, and Asian political authorities living in Stone Town.[57] The availability of new economic and cultural options—including taarab performance—provided opportunities for the poor for economic advancement, yet such possibilities remained highly contentious social acts. Institutionalized power may have extended beyond the royal family, but it did not expand to include the majority of those living in Ng'ambo, as "Kigalawa" and many of the band's other songs suggest. Simply gaining entrance to the inner rooms of the palace did not necessarily mean that one would be treated with dignity and respect.

However, stories surrounding the song "Kigalawa" reveal that other aspects of the social relationships between the powerful and the servile established in the preceding century remained intact well into the twentieth century. The poor were still frequently dependent for their livelihoods on the financial largess of the wealthy. Although Shaaban asserted, "I will not scratch like a chicken for this little bit of work," the band continued to play for the sultan and his wife, Bibi Matuka, nearly every week. Presumably the cash they received for their performances and the praise they received from contemporaries for their sheer ability to meet with the sultan was worth the cost of occasional denigration. As with many relationships based on dominance and subordination, the band also never directly confronted Sultan Seyyid Khalifa about his transgressions. Instead they sought redress in ways that were much more typical of precolonial coastal patterns; they sang of their equality and publicly reaffirmed their personal dignity through performance. They spoke and spoke loudly of the inhumane way in which they had been treated and in doing so they damaged the sultan's reputation far more than they damaged their own. They denounced the sultan not to his face, but behind his back, where their concerns would resonate with those who would listen, bringing shame on the island's supreme patriarch while simultaneously guarding the band from retribution. If confronted by the sultan about the rumors circulating regarding the meaning of the song, the band could simply suggest that their words had been misinterpreted. Denying the rumors would in no way compromise the satisfaction they gained from having the sultan know that his reputation had been damaged, whether or not it was their intent.

The power of gossip to affirm or destroy a patron's standing in society was well understood. Gossip, or the threat of it, was a tool clients had used for generations to direct the behavior of patrons. Nineteenth-century slaves and clients could rarely afford to take the risks of confronting a superior directly, but in a society in which family and personal power depended so extensively on the politics of patronage, grumblings of discontent could undermine one's standing as a just and benevolent patrician.[58] Slaves also voiced these critiques through work songs that ridiculed abusive masters or celebrated the triumph of the weak over the strong.[59] Siti and her band evoked this tradition of gossip, rumor, and song, enhancing its efficacy by divulging the secrets of the powerful through catchy rhymes and tunes which people could not help but repeat.

One particularly successful example of Siti binti Saad's use of song in such a way was the song "Wala hapana hasara" (There is no loss), which celebrated a corrupt official's fall from colonial grace and his banishment to the town's rock quarry. The tune was so catchy and the topic so timely that the words and melody reputedly spread throughout town like a wildfire that burned incessantly for weeks. The lyrics documented the case of Bwana Mselem, a wealthy Arab landowner and corrupt colonial official of Zanzibar Town who was widely despised by those in Ng'ambo for his habit of using his office to cheat the poor. Like the landlords, the Remtullas, Mselem was accused by those in Ng'ambo of keeping two sets of books and of using his power over the written word to defraud the nonliterate of their property. Disdain for Bwana Mselem grew to a feverish pitch in 1928, when it was discovered that he was one of the state's principal informants against those involved in the ground rent strike.

It was widely understood by Ng'ambo residents that Mselem

used the power of his office for his personal enrichment both by cheating the poor of personal property and demanding bribes. The colonial authorities who appointed Mselem to his post were either oblivious of or unconcerned about his actions. Ultimately, however, Mselem was caught by his British superiors after embezzling money from the office accounts to finance his daughter's wedding. As a powerful Arab clerk, Mselem felt obliged to display his wealth and authority on the occasion of his daughter's wedding. Like the celebrations of other patricians of the era, the party Mselem threw lasted more than a week. The food and entertainment were lavish. In fact, Mselem allegedly ordered every band and ngoma in Zanzibar to perform at the wedding, or face denial of their future applications for the required permit to play in town, which he controlled. Mselem not only used the authority of his appointed post to bring forth the entertainers, he also used his office accounts to pay the debts he incurred for the celebration. He was eventually caught, convicted, and sentenced to hard labor in the town's rock quarry, as well as being subjected to great embarrassment by the following song composed by Siti in honor of his demise. This song became so popular that a kanga, "Jiwe la Mselem" (Mselem's rock), was also printed to further celebrate Mselem's castigation. The kanga was white, yellow, and brown and bore a picture of Bwana Mselem carrying a rock on his head. It allegedly became one of the most popular kanga designs of the era, selling well not only in Zanzibar but throughout the Swahili coast, where many communities were suffering similar abuses at the hands of appointed Arab clerks.[60]

Wala hapana hasara

Wala hapana nasaba mimi uladi fulani
Neno kama dharuba launguza kifuani
Jina lake wewe baba na jiwe liko kichwani.
    Na jiwe liko kichwani . . .

Wacheni yenu dhuluma kunyang'anya masikini
Hasa wasiyosema wajinga wa ujingani
Kalamu yao daima ni wino wa kidoleni.
    Ni wino wa kidoleni . . .

Haifai udokozi kuiba serekalini
Mabuku yao ya wazi moja moja la saini
Neno la mwaka juzi hungiya pekesheni.
      Huingiya pekesheni ...

Jamaa msihadaike hayo yangu yashikeni
Tanbihi muiweke isiwatoke rohoni
Kwa kidogo mtosheke haki yenu makarani.
      Haki yenu makrani ...

∎

There Is No Loss

There is no pedigree; I am the child of so-and-so,
A word like a sudden blow which burns in the chest.
The name is yours, my man, and the rock is on your head.
      And the rock is on your head ...

You men should stop oppressing and stealing from the poor,
Especially those who are said to be the stupidest of the
    stupid.
Forever their pen is ink upon the thumb.
      Is ink upon the thumb ...

It is not right to pinch, to embezzle from the government.
Their books are all open with each and every signature.
A word from years ago can always be investigated.
      Can always be investigated ...

You men should not be deceived; this is mine, I should take it.
A memento should be created so it does not leave their
    hearts.
You clerks should be satisfied with what you are entitled to.
      With what you are entitled to ...

The use of literacy to defraud the nonliterate—or the "stupidest of the stupid," who were required to place their thumbprints in lieu of a signature on documents they could not read—was a common complaint of the poor in interwar Zanzibar. Paper documents increasingly came to replace personal agreements as the basis for numerous legal and commercial transactions. However, as late as 1948 only some fifteen thousand individuals (5 percent of the protectorate's population), five-sixths of whom were male, had attended either government or mission schools, where they would have learned at

least the rudiments of literacy in roman script.[61] The vast majority of
the islands' population was obviously at great disadvantage when it
came to negotiating and interpreting written documents. By the
1920s and 1930s increasing numbers of previously verbal agreements,
including property exchanges, rent payments, marriage agreements,
and pawnshop receipts, were being written down and affixed with a
thumbprint. The nonliterate frequently found themselves in court
contesting interpretation of a written contract whose oral translation
was significantly different than the written form.[62]

Judging by the frequency with which the greed of civil servants
and the use of political office to further personal gain served as topics
of the band's songs, one would conclude that such abuses were not
unique to Bwana Mselem. A verse from another of the band's songs,
"Do Not Place Greed before All Else," warned,

> Tamaa wee tamaa si kitu chema
> Mara huja pinduka, tamaa si kitu chema
> Ni heri kuiepuka mali mengi hasama
> Ukiwa huna aa, aa pakuyapata
> Akupendae daima mwisho wee kumwepuka
> Kwepuka, kwepuka, kwepuka, mwisho wee aa kwepuka
> Tamaa siweke mbele, utumaini kwa kifu, utumaini kwa kifu
>
> ∎
>
> Greed, ohhh greed, is not a good thing.
> It may be sudden, but you will always be overturned; greed is
>   not a good thing.
> It is a blessing to avoid it, excessive wealth can be an enemy.
> If you do not have any, aa, aa, where will you get it?
> The one who loves you forever, in the end you will avoid them.
> Avoid it, avoid it, avoid it, in the end, aa, aa, avoid it.
> Do not put greed before all else, you should desire to be
>   satisfied, you should desire to be satisfied.

The band's warning that greed was not a good thing and that in
the end it would cause certain downfall is the subject of another of
Siti's widely popular songs. Like Mselem, Mohamed Said was caught
stealing money from the accounts he oversaw. More familiar with judicial procedure than most Zanzibaris, Mohamed Said hired two lawyers from Nairobi, the judicial capital of British East Africa, to mount
his defense. In this song Siti and her audience laugh at the defen-

dant's futile attempts to use the rule of law in his favor, and salute the
fact that yet another of the government's gluttonous officials found
himself locked up in jail.

Ela kafa ndugu zangu

Ela kafa ndugu zangu wa shamba hata mjini
Mwenye kazi ya Mzungu mailiki wa duniyani
Roho mzipige rungu cha mtu msitamani.
Msitamani . . .

Msicheze na Hakimu ahukumuye mezani
Bure mtajidhulumu kwa akali kitu duni
Na hayo mwayafahamu jiti la ncha jichoni.
Jiti la ncha jichononi . . .

Wala haifai wakili aliyesoma Landani
Bure ataila mali upelekwe gerezani
Aikaze suruwali akimbiliye nyumbani.
Akimbiliye nyumbani . . .

Msishikwe na tamaa kama ipo rufaani
Hiyo niya ya hadaa mjitiye mitegoni
Halipo la manufaa ikishapita saini.
Ikisha pita saini . . .

∎

A Warning to You My Brothers

A warning to you my brothers, from the country to the city,
You who work for the white man, the ruler of the world,
Beat down your greed with billy clubs, do not desire what
    belongs to someone else.
Do not desire what belongs to someone else . . .

Do not play with the judge, the one with authority over the
    scales [of justice].
You will defraud yourself for nothing, on account of
    something worthless.
These matters, you should understand them, the point of a
    stick in your eye.
The point of a stick in your eye . . .

Nor is it of any use to have a lawyer who studied in London.
He will eat your wealth for nothing; you should be sent to jail.
He will hoist up his trousers around his waist and he will run
    for home.
And he will run for home . . .

> You should not live in hopes that there will be an appeal of
>   the case.
> The aim of these is merely to deceive you, you will place
>   yourself in a trap.
> There is nothing that can be of use; the judgment has
>   already been signed.
>   The judgment has already been signed . . .

Although many of those in Ng'ambo perceived themselves as unable to effectively use tools of colonial power to challenge the dominance of appointed Arab clerks like Bwana Mselem or Mohamed Said, they certainly celebrated those rare instances when the courts convicted the wealthy who had committed crimes. The poor also used the tools at their disposal, including rumor and song, regardless of prosecution, to popularize perceptions that what these men did was wrong. Each time the song was repeated, be it by Siti, a woman washing clothes, or a fisherman hauling in a catch, alternatives to the dominant colonial discourse of the just and selfless service of bureaucrats were advanced. Common people in Zanzibar were fully aware of the ways in which political power was abused to the detriment of the disenfranchised, yet with lines such as, "You men should stop oppressing and stealing from the poor," they voiced a demand that the situation be changed. Mselem was chastised by the government only after he was caught stealing from the state, but in the song the band makes clear that stealing is wrong and that embezzlement should be punished, regardless of whether the property is taken from the government or "the stupidest of the stupid." The tradition of government officials enriching themselves with public funds has deep historical roots in the isles. But rather than choosing to ignore such practices the band made them public political issues, arguing, "You men should not be deceived; this is mine I should take it. . . . You clerks should be satisfied with what you are entitled to."

Through their music the band not only raised political consciousness, they also helped to raise the spirits of those who were frequently on the losing side of the law. Various forms of popular culture, from kangas like "Mselem's Rock" to songs and jokes, allowed the poor and allegedly powerless to chastise and poke fun at "those who ruled the world." Like the wily trickster Abunuwas, a famous character in Swahili folktales, Ng'ambo residents used their wit and sense of humor to compensate in their struggles against those who were stronger. The band drew an explicit connection between the underlying message of their music and the folktales of Abunuwas. Mwalim Shaaban even set a few of the Abunuwas tales to verse and music, including one in which a rapacious guard of the sultan is tricked by Abunuwas into receiving fifty blows with a whip rather than the bribe he desired. Although the poor and nonliterate did not always succeed in winning their battles against the strong, they popularized, celebrated, and sang of the precious victories that did come their way.

Gender and the Colonial Courts

Instances in which the decisions of the courts coincided with local conceptions of justice were relatively rare in colonial Zanzibar. Court cases figured as a prominent topic of the band's music, but songs like those about Mselem and Mohamed Said, which heralded the magistrates' decisions, were as unusual as the rare convictions of the wealthy and powerful. Far more common were songs that offered scathing critics of the system and alternative interpretations of justice. The 1910s and the 1920s were important decades for the formulation and institutionalization of colonial law in the isles. As the breakouts at the central court in 1928 suggest, however, the people of Ng'ambo did not passively accept the legitimacy of colonial definitions of law and order. Alternative discourses of justice circulated widely in Ng'ambo and the band's music provided an important forum for articulating and propagating these alternative understandings. The practices and performances held at Siti's home provided almost daily occasions for community-based discussions about justice and colonial law. The actions taken during the rent strike also make it perfectly clear that the men and women of Ng'ambo were not afraid to turn their talk into action.[63] Legal decisions surrounding ground rent and evictions were not the only issues that Ng'ambo residents took objection to. Of equal, but related, concern was a perceived class bias in favor of the wealthy. As one man stated, "It was usually only the poor who went to jail. The wealthy could always bribe their way out,"[64] a refrain that was repeated in many of the band's songs. A great deal of the band's material also comments on the persistent use of the law to further institutionalize gender inequality. While poor men and women certainly engaged in battles among themselves over gender, power, and property, the reception of the band's music and its place in the memory Ng'ambo residents of both genders suggest that there was fairly widespread agreement that the legal changes introduced under colonialism typically served to further the power of the islands' wealthiest men at the expense of everyone else. Such perceptions were not unique to Zanzibar. During the colonial era, women and the poor became increasingly alienated from religious, customary, and civil courts throughout the British African colonies.[65]

The song "The Police Have Stopped," composed by Mbaruku, is one such song which critiques the class and gender preferences accorded wealthy men within the colonial court system. In the song, Mbaruku documents the story of a woman who was murdered by her husband, a wealthy and well-known businessman who provided materials for the booming urban construction trade. Although the accused was caught in the act by a witness, the defendant argued that the witness was really motivated to testify because of his desire to undermine the defendant's business. The question of the integrity of the principal witness, combined with state's failure to produce a murder weapon, prevented the full prosecution of the defendant by the colonial criminal court. The jury in Ng'ambo, however, reached a different verdict and urged that the defendant be sent to jail.

Pilisi wamesita

Pilisi mesita aawe kukutu
Amekukamata ewe mwana kwetu
Mahaba waitwa umeuwa mtu.
        Umeuwa mtu . . .

Ungepitapita umebwaga zani
Hakika matata yanawe mwandani
Mahaba waitwa wende gerezani.
        Wende gerezani . . .

Ungejizuzua upate muradi
Mwenzangu beluwa imeshakubidi
Mahaba yauwa nami ni shahidi.
             Nami ni shahidi . . .

Nataka radidi enyi walimwengu
I wapi hadidi mikononi mwangu
Huyu si shahidi ni hasimu yangu.

∎

The Police Have Stopped

The police have stopped, he should be breathing a sigh of
    relief.
He has caught you, you son from our house.
The evidence is called deficient, but you have killed
    someone.
             You have killed someone . . .

You would pass this over, but you have brought misfortune
    of a terrible, terrible kind.
For certain these troubles have you as their companion.
The evidence is called deficient, but you should go to jail.
             You should go to jail . . .

You would play the fool so that you could make a plan.
My friend this is a terrible thing, it has already compelled
    you.
There is evidence you have killed and I am the witness.
             And I am the witness . . .

I want a big knife, one of this world.
Where is the iron [weapon] in my hands?
This person is not a witness, he is my rival.
             He is my rival . . .

The song "Kijiti," written and performed by Siti, is another song
that openly questions the "justice" of the colonial legal system. This
song relates the story of a woman from Dar es Salaam who came to Zanzibar to visit some friends living in the Ng'ambo neighborhood of
Michenzani. She was invited by some female neighbors for a night on
the town but was later raped, tortured, and murdered by one of the men
in the group, who was named Kijiti. The murderer escaped from the
police and ran to the mainland, while the two women who organized

the party and provided the alcohol for the occasion were found guilty of the woman's death after testifying against Kijiti. In the final lines of the poem Siti invokes God to deliver a more acceptable form of justice.

Kijiti

Tazameni tazameni alivyofanya Kijiti
Kumchukua mgeni kumchezesha foliti
Kendanae maguni kamrejesha maiti.

Tuliondoka nyumbani hatukuaga ruhusa
Na tende yetu kapuni tumechukua kabisa
Magoma yako Chukwani mauti Sharifmsa.

Kijiti alinambia ondoka mama twenende
Laiti ningelijua ningekataa nisende
Kijiti unaniuwa kwa pegi moja ya tende.

Jaji alikasirika kitini alipoketi
Kasema bilalifuli mashahidi wa Kijiti
Tukafunga Sumaili na K binti Subeti.

Mambo haya ni ajabu kila tukiyatizama
Kijiti kauwa mtu na tumboni mna mwana
Kijiti kavuka mto mashahidi wamezama.

Kijiti nakuusia Darisalama usende
Utamkuta kibabu kakuvalia kiwembe
Watu wanakuapiza mola akupe matende.

∎

Kijiti

Look you all, look at what Kijiti has done,
To take a guest and force her to run from his chase.
He went with her to the bush and brought her back as a
    corpse.

We left home, we did not ask for permission.
Our alcohol in the bag, we took it with us.
The dance is in Chukwani, death in Sharifmsa.[66]

Kijiti said to me, "Come on, girl, let's go!"
Oh, if only I had known I would have refused, I wouldn't
    have gone.
Kijiti, you are killing me for a single shot of booze.

The judge was mad in his chair where he sat
And said, "You bloody fools!" to the witnesses of Kijiti.
We put you in jail, Sumaili and K, the daughter of Subeiti.

These things are amazing every time we look at them.
Kijiti killed someone and in her stomach was a baby.
Kijiti crossed the river, the witnesses they have drowned.

Kijiti, I warn you, do not go to Dar es Salaam.
You will meet an old man and he is carrying a razor just for you.
People are cursing you, may God give you elephantiasis.

Women and men in Ng'ambo were appalled by both Kijiti's actions and the judge's decision finding Sumaili and binti Subeiti guilty of the crime.[67] How could the female witnesses be held responsible for the murder merely because they organized a party and brought the liquor? Charging them with violation of liquor laws would have been understandable, but convicting them of the murder of their friend was not. Public opinion, echoed in Siti's song, suggested that the victim was being blamed for the crime, while an incompetent administration and its police let a man who had committed rape and murder get away.

The punishment of Sumaili and binti Subeiti followed a fairly common pattern, in which British magistrates and other members of the administration sought to chastise and punish island women for drinking alcohol, "misbehaving," acting "like public women," and allegedly disgracing their families or the community at large.[68] During such cases, the families and friends of female defendants frequently testified on their behalf, concurring that the women's actions may not have lived up to the highest standards of morality, but arguing nonetheless that such transgressions clearly did not warrant judicial censure or punishment. Certain members of the administration argued, however, that island men were lax in controlling their women and it was therefore the "duty" of the administration to reprimand women for their "immoral misbehavior."[69] Such reprimands were delivered with greatest frequency on women from elite families—especially masuria and their daughters of the al-Busaidi clan—but as the tale of Kijiti suggests, judicial censure of women's behavior knew no class bounds. This and other songs voice the community's opposition to these practices, as well as the court's tendency to blame women for the violence which befell them, particularly if the case involved sexual assault or the consumption of alcohol (or both).[70] "Kijiti" and "Pilisi wamesita" also suggest that although violence against women occurred, and frequently went unpunished by the courts, it was not easily condoned by Ng'ambo residents. The community expected abusive men to be held accountable for their actions and voiced their objections when such expectations went unmet.

Assaults on the bodies of women were generally treated by the courts as representing a less significant threat to public order than attacks on men.[71] In cases of rape or sexual assault women were also frequently blamed by British magistrates for "asking for" the violence which befell them. In one particular case in which a young man was found guilty of intercourse with a prepubescent girl, which she alleged took place without her consent, the judge declared, "If either of the two . . . are shown to be disposed to a life of immorality it is the girl herself." "[She] has an immoral bent. She frequently wanders about at night. The fact that she has an immoral bent makes it more probable that the accused did have intercourse with her." Although the girl suggested that there were numerous witnesses to her abduction by the accused, while on her way home after an ngoma, none of these witnesses were called before the court, again suggesting that rape was not the offense the magistrate was most concerned about. Rather than focusing on rape, the case centered instead on parental, and particularly maternal, neglect. The girl's mother had gone to her farm in the countryside, as many women at this time frequently did, and left her twelve-year-old daughter in town. Because the mother did not place her daughter under the direct custody of another adult, but left her free to choose to sleep at the home of any one of five different relatives, including that of her father, who lived at the Ziwani police barracks, the judge declared her "under no one's custody. She slept where she wanted. If there is no custody, there can be no abduction from custody." Throughout the case the judge consistently displayed greater concern for the fact that she had been "abandoned" by her mother than the fact that she had been forcibly dragged to her assailant's home and raped. The young man was found guilty of intercourse, not of rape, sentenced to ten strokes with a light cane, and released. The victim, however, was placed under court supervision for immorality and her parents were censured by the judge for not maintaining stricter control of their daughter. The decision in this case was not atypical of colonial courts, where British magistrates regularly sought to strengthen the hand of male patriarchs, and ensure that women were always under the "control" of a man.[72] In colonial Zanzibar, men who were brought to court for domestic violence, battery, or sexual assault rarely were awarded sentences that female plaintiffs perceived as just.

During the colonial era, women in Zanzibar also experienced a gradual eradication of their property rights as guaranteed under Islamic law, in ways that further reinforced male dominance.[73] Muslim women in Zanzibar owned and controlled a great deal property. Women owned homes and businesses, acted as moneylenders, held mortgages, and managed their own farms and plantations. Beginning in the 1910s and with increasing frequency by the 1930s, however, British administrators, magistrates, and Islamic judges began a systematic reinterpretation of shari'a as administered in the isles in ways that reinforced male control over both women and property. Wakf property administered by women was particularly subject to attack in the courts. The case of Bibi Khole Hamoud and Bibi Jokha Hamoud, whose wakf property in Ng'ambo became the object of repeated confiscation attempts in the 1910s and 1920s, set the stage for what was to come. During the early 1930s, the Wakf Commission took their attacks on women's rights to control property to new heights, issuing a series of rulings that argued that women's inability to pray during menstruation and after childbirth, combined with the restrictions of purdah, rendered them utterly incapable of being appointed mutawalli (administrators/executors) of wakf property. While the British controlled Wakf Commission succeeded in taking the property of countless numbers of women away, in 1934, two women with the fortitude, legal knowledge, and financial ability to launch an appeal fought the Wakf Commission of Zanzibar all the way to the Court of Appeals for Eastern Africa, in Nairobi. The Court of Appeals ruled in the appellants' favor, finding that gender alone was insufficient grounds for disqualify a woman from being appointed as a wakf trustee. The appeals court's decision rested on the fact that shari'a explicitly stated that women could not be disqualified or declared incompetent to manage property solely on the basis of their gender. The ruling went further to declare that the Wakf Commission's contention that "Arab custom in Zanzibar" prohibited women from being appointed administrators of property was simply unsupported, as there were many women in Zanzibar, many of them in purdah, who were successfully managing vast estates.[74] Nonetheless, these were difficult years for coastal women, who found themselves fighting a fair number of British administrators and magistrates who clung to their misperceptions that "a native woman, being herself property, can own no property."[75]

Declarations defining Muslim women as the property of men were first given the rule of colonial law in 1897, when concubines were specifically denied their right to freedom under the abolition decree. In the first decades of the twentieth century, legal codes in Zanzibar were further refined in ways that made it increasingly difficult for even free women to leave their husbands. Yielding to pressure from various Christian missions in Zanzibar, the administration made it virtually impossible for Christian women to obtain a divorce, even when they had proven beyond a doubt that their husbands were beating, abusing, or cheating them of their property.[76] Muslim women fared little better. While certain kadhis were more sympathetic to women's interests than others, from the 1910s through the 1930s women's rights to sue for divorce were systematically undermined. Ibadhi and Shafi'i law relating to marriage and divorce differ in several respects, yet both schools view marriage as a *contract* between two parties, each of whom has the right to break the contract in the event that the other party has failed to meet one or more of their stipulated contractual responsibilities.[77] A woman suffering from domestic violence, who has been abandoned for more that three months, whose husband either refuses or is incapable of supporting her and her children financially, or whose sexual needs and desires are unfulfilled by her husband is generally recognized as having a right to a divorce.[78] Yet even in cases such as these women were frequently ordered by the courts in colonial Zanzibar to return to their husbands.

One case that illustrates this decline in women's legal status quite vividly is that of Mgeni binti Salim, who appealed a kadhi's decision denying her a divorce to a British civil court of appeals, in 1913. In a letter to the judge Mgeni explained her situation:

> I have been married to my husband for nearly three years and during the entire time he does not support me, I support him. Then he asked me to buy his shamba [farm] and I refused. He then came with my brother Mohammed [Mgeni's guardian after the death of her parents] . . . and the Arabic lawyer and they jointly made me buy the shamba . . . for Rs 460. I had someone else translate the deed for me and it said that it was a deed of mortgage and not a deed of sale. When I asked my husband why he lied to me he took out a knife and said that if I asked again he would kill me and inherit all my estate [worth Rs 10,000 (£666)].[79]

Mgeni sued for divorce on the grounds that her husband had neglected his obligation to support her, had intentionally defrauded her of Rs 460, and that he was physically abusive. Not only did he threaten to kill her, on more than one occasion, but he also forced her to have sexual intercourse against her will. Mgeni initially brought her case before the court of an Islamic judge, Sheikh Tahir. Although Ibadhi law allows the court to dissolve a marriage in cases of cruelty and abuse, rather than granting the divorce, Sheikh Tahir ordered Mgeni to return to her husband's home and grant him his "conjugal rights." Mgeni, obviously displeased with the sheikh's decision, began a very lengthy series of appeals. In her first attempt, she argued that Sheikh Tahir did not allow her to present her grievances, nor did he call any of her supporting witnesses. She was also displeased with her lawyer, trained in Islamic law, whom she felt openly sided with her husband. Finding little help within the Islamic court system, Mgeni hired a European lawyer to bring an appeal. Once again, however, she was disappointed. Rather than suing for divorce, he instead sued for maintenance. "My lawyer knows full well that I told him to sue for divorce," stated Mgeni, "I then told him to file for rehearing but nothing was done. . . . I am a woman sixteen years old and know nothing about the court. I beg Your Honor to help me receive justice."

Mgeni's plea to the British magistrate to help protect both her person and her property illustrates several patterns common in court cases of the 1910s and 1920s. Young women of property, but without kin in a position to protect them, were often married off at the age of twelve or thirteen to elderly friends of their legal male guardians. As Mgeni argued before the High Court, "[I]t is also the bad habit with poor Arab men to try and marry a woman of a little means and then take her estate. I have seen my husband trying to do this with me. For this reason I did not want to live with my husband any longer." Numerous court cases and archival records support Mgeni's contention regarding the "bad habit" of poor Arab men marrying women, particularly young women, in an effort to get control of their property. While the consent of the bride to a marriage is a legal requirement under Islamic law, in reality few young girls—especially those whose parents had died or whose mothers were masuria of marginal status and thus unable to defend them—were in a position to resist the suggestions of their male guardians. By the age of sixteen or eighteen, however, many of these women were apparently coming to the realization that their husbands and guardians were more interested in their property than the young woman's personal welfare. In what must have been a final attempt to save themselves from destitution, as well as mental and physical abuse, many East African women turned to the British courts "for justice."[80]

Mgeni provided four witnesses during the course of her appeal who testified that her husband either neglected his responsibility to support her or physically abused her (or both). Nonetheless, the British magistrate on the case found, "The wife's evidence in this case is obviously grossly exaggerated, the husband denies in on oath, and I find that the wife has not proved her case and I dismiss her suit for divorce." The two kadhis who sat on the bench along with the British magistrate concurred,[81] saying that the husband "is able to maintain his wife" and they therefore saw no way of granting a divorce. They did, however, require the husband to take an oath promising to support Mgeni with Rs 15 per month, provided she returned to live with him and grant him his "conjugal rights."

Cases like those of Mgeni were numerous in the first decades of the century, and not surprisingly became the topic of songs by Siti binti Saad's band, which editorialized on the general lack of protection for women's interests within either of the existing legal systems. In the song entitled "Kadhi, Give Me Judgment," Mwalim Shaaban discussed the case of a female neighbor who was facing circumstances similar to those of Mgeni. Shaaban's friend, also facing physical abuse as well as destitution, was similarly ordered by the kadhi to return to her husband. Mwalim Shaaban's stated intent in composing this song was to assert women's right to live free of domestic abuse as well as to remind Islamic judges of their obligation to protect all individuals equally, regardless of their gender or financial status. The fourth stanza of the song echoes a common refrain in both the band's music and oral histories from the era: If you have no money, you have no happiness and you certainly have less standing within the judicial system.[82] In the final line, Shaaban warns listeners that both God and other spirits will also be rendering a judgment on human actions here on earth. He also reminds his audience that the decisions of these later judges will not be swayed either by bribery or the status of the perpetrator. A man who forced his wife to "restore conjugal rights" against her will might be upheld by the Zanzibar courts, but such a man risked offending supernatural powers who might see fit to impose a sentence of insanity or an afterlife in hell on such an offender.[83]

Kadhi nihukumu

Kadhi nihukumu na wangu haribu
Amenihasimu pasi na sibabu
Menilisha sumu hakuja nitibu
  Kadhi nihukumu . . .

Risala ondoka nenda kwa hamamu
Nenda kwa haraka kampe salamu
Nimesalitika sipati laumu.
  Kadhi nihukumu . . .

Nawapa hakika wenzangu akili
Nimeatilika daima silali
Yaliyonifikia malimwengu hii ni ajali.
  Kadhi nihukumu . . .

Mahaba ya sasa siyaendekeze
Kama huna pesa hukai huchezi

Utababaika roho upoteze.
             Kadhi nihukumu . . .

∎

Kadhi, Give Me Judgment

Kadhi, give me judgment on my injuries.
He has pushed and pulled me and without any reason.
He has fed me poison and did not come to give me treatment.
             Kadhi, give me judgment . . .

Messenger, leave, go quickly to the public baths.
Go quickly and give him this message:
I have been treated harshly, I cannot get reproach.
             Kadhi, give me judgment . . .

I give you assurances, my intelligent companions,
I have been severely injured; I will never sleep again.
These things which have befallen me in this world, this is
       the hour of death.
             Kadhi, give me judgment . . .

I cannot make this current love go right.
If you have no money you have no contentment.
You will go crazy, you shall lose your soul.
             Kadhi, give me judgment . . .

The final line of "Kadhi, Give Me Judgment," which beseeches otherworldly powers to intervene and inflict punishment on the guilty, reflects a common pattern in many of the band's songs. Island residents, then and now, frequently took solace in the fact that *Mungu ndiye anayejua* (God is indeed the one who knows), assuring themselves that justice would ultimately be done, if not in this world, then in the next.

This does not mean, however, that people did not attempt to persuade supernatural powers to come to their aid in the here and now. The powers of the Qur'an, in the form of *Al-Badr* and medicines written out by a healer *(mganga)* and worn as a charm of protection *(hirizi)* or consumed through a specially prepared drink were often used to invoke divine protection from evil.[84] Spirits of ancestors *(mizimu)* or those that are part of the Swahili spirit complex, known alternately in Zanzibar as *jinni, pepo,* or *mashetani,* can also possess an individual, either to offer their protection or to render divine punishment for evil deeds already done.[85] The concluding lines of "Kijiti," "Kadhi, Give

Me Judgment," and many of the band's other songs end with an invocation of otherworldly powers to deliver punishment to offenders or protection for the weak in a world overrun with greed and lack of respect for the poor. Economically and socially marginal members of Zanzibar society compensated for their compromised positions before the courts by attempting to resolve as many of their problems as possible through nonjudicial means. Women facing neglect or abuse from their husbands were far more likely to seek the aid and intervention of their families and friends than that of judicial authorities. On occasions when such attempts were unsuccessful, they also regularly sought redress by resorting to the power of rumor and reputation to curb and restrain. Siti was herself obviously a master of this art form and she invoked the power of her songs to reprimand her own antagonists on more than one occasion. Unmarried women from socially marginal backgrounds were frequently subjected to unwanted sexual advances as well harassment from men who apparently presumed that a woman's poverty rendered her exclamations of "NO!" meaningless. Siti was no exception.[86] In several of her songs, including "Nauliwani" (Why am I being eaten?), Siti used the power of her voice to publicly shame and rebuke such advances.

"Wewe paka" (You cat) is another song performed by Siti in response to her experience of being sexually harassed. In this case the power differentials of gender were compounded by those of class and status, as the offending man was apparently a wealthy and well-connected patrician from Stone Town. Despite Siti's repeated rebukes of his advances, the offender followed Siti about town and subjected her to both physical and verbal abuse. He also attempted to use his political connections to have her thrown in jail on a trumped-up charge.[87] Throughout the song, Siti laments the fact that as a poor woman she was legally powerless to stop this man's attacks, although she ends both the first and fourth verses suggesting the type of punishment that might be warranted. In the third verse she offers a moving articulation of the despair and powerlessness overwhelming the poor: "I understand what poverty and insignificance are like. / It is the solitary condition of the poor in the world. / In my condition there is nothing I can do." She ends the verse by calling upon God to "please watch over me." Ultimately, the combined power of Siti's song and her prayers to God succeeded in galvanizing the requisite support for restraining her attacker. He was never beaten, fined, or sent to jail, as Siti suggested he should be, but he was so roundly censured by the community that Siti was once again free to walk about town without fear of being harassed.

Wewe paka

Wewe paka kwani waniudhiyani
Wewe paka unaudhi majirani
Utapigwa ukalipiwe faini.
          Ukalipiwe faini. . .

Mimi paka sasa napigiwani
Mimi paka sili cha mtu sinani
Nnajuta kuingiya vibandani.
          Nnajuta kuingiya vibandani . . .

Naona unyonge kitu gani
Ni upweke masikini duniyani
Hali sina la kufanya ela Mola Mannani.
          Mola Mannani . . .

Langu tiba imeingiwa na huzuni
Matilaba nimeyapata zamani
Ukizinga utarejea ngamani.
          Utarejea ngamani . . .

∎

You Cat

You cat, why, why do you harass me?
You cat, you are harassing the neighbors
You will be beaten, you should be made to pay.
          You should be made to pay . . .

Cat, why am I being beaten now?
I cat do not eat the food of others, I am nothing, nothing at all
I regret going into the poor homes of Ng'ambo
          I regret going into the poor homes of Ng'ambo . . .

I understand what poverty and insignificance are
It is the solitary condition of the poor in the world
In my condition there is nothing I can do, God please watch
    over me.
          God please watch over me . . .

My medicine has been mixed with grief and sorrow

I realized your intentions long ago
If you besiege and harass women, you should go to jail.
You should go to jail . . .

The gender discrimination faced by women within the colonial legal system may not have galvanized the kind of mass action against the courts that evictions did, but these songs provide evidence of a local awareness of, and resistance to, attempts to further the institutional marginalization of women. Be they calls for the imprisonment of men who assaulted women, or pleas for the recognition of a woman's right to sue for divorce, these songs suggest that community standards of justice were evaluated against a different moral standard than that used by colonial magistrates. The fact that many of the songs that spoke out against violence against women, be it physical or institutional, were written by the male members of the band indicates that these concerns were not perceived as being solely "women's issues." In an era in which the struggles by the poor to overcome economic and social inequality were paramount, there appears to have been a general recognition among both men and women in Ng'ambo of the importance of advancing gender equity as well. Popular discourses of justice advocated not only for the poor, but for the empowerment of women too.

"When you wanted me I stayed with you /
Now you do not want me I have no need for you":
Love, Sex, and Rejection between the Wars

In addition to offering critiques of institutional and class-based inequalities in island society, the music of Siti binti Saad's band also directly addressed issues of power intertwined within intimate personal male-female relationships. The band's music did not privilege the public as the preeminent domain of power in women's lives, but exposed and explored critiques of domestic and sexual subordination as well. Although these songs discuss a wide range of gender-based disparities, the images they convey of women are not those of helpless victims, but rather of individuals who know what they want and who are capable of not only articulating their desires, but actualizing them as well. The very real women on whose lives these songs are modeled went beyond merely "complaining" about husbands who spent their money elsewhere, neglected their children, or took up with other women; these songs provide us with a unique set of historical documents that illuminate the numerous strategies women used to redress gender inequalities in their own lives and in society at large.

Asserting control over their own sexuality was a key component of women's struggles for autonomy in the post-abolition era. In the nineteenth century, elite men's privileged sexual access to black women was both a tool and a symbol of their institutional and coercive power over others. Yet in popular songs like "You Cat," cited above, Siti and her band celebrated African women's right to reject unwanted sexual advances, and in the process helped to popularize critiques of Arab male class and sexual dominance. The women of Ng'ambo did not entirely repudiate the prospect of sexual and emotional relationships with the elite, but we get the sense from these songs that they were becoming increasingly forthright about demanding that the fulfillment of their own needs and desires was a condition for the continuation of cross-class relationships. In their relationships with men of similar class and status backgrounds the women of Ng'ambo who are portrayed in these songs were also strong and self-directed. Nearly 60 percent of the songs authored by the male members of Siti's band, for which I have transcriptions, explored aspects of their own romantic entanglements. One reoccurring theme is the grief and loss they experienced after being left by a lover whose needs they either could not or would not fulfill. The women of early-twentieth-century Zanzibar not only rejected masters' control over their sexuality and personal autonomy, but that of husbands and lovers as well. Through these lyrics we hear the stories of African women engaged in reframing discourses of power and sexuality and in the process asserting a new, autonomous sense of self.

The 1920s and 1930s were important decades all across the African continent as young urban men and women negotiated new standards and practices of courtship, marriage, and sexuality that were distinct from those of their rural parents.[88] The urban milieu offered new opportunities for personal freedom and romantic experimenta-

tion, as well as an often confounding array of new hazards and problems. Advice columns proliferated in African newspapers during the
interwar era, as members of the emerging African bourgeoisie attempted to debate and establish standards of sexual propriety for
urban youth. The urban working class and poor engaged in similar
debates, although the medium was often new forms of urban music
including palm-wine, *maringa, marabi,* beni, and taarab.[89] Through
their songs, Siti's band explored the very real and day-to-day emotional and financial problems that entangled the love lives of urban
youth and offered both warnings and advice on how to deal with such
problems. By 1928, Siti and the other members of her band ranged in
age from their mid-twenties to their mid-forties. While still relatively
young, they all had been involved in domestic relationships that had
ended in separation. Their songs spoke to the issues and concerns of
men and women at a similar place in their life cycles—still young and
hopeful of the possibility of finding a satisfying relationship, but
sufficiently jaded by personal experience to know that living happily
ever after was an improbable outcome. Like their songs of class and
politics, their songs of "love" expressed an overriding realism. They
portrayed the lived physical reality of average women and men, rather
than the saccharine sweet romantic idealism that would come to dominate post–World War II taarab songs.[90]

One of Siti's most popular songs, and one that continues to be
performed in Zanzibar to this day by the women's taarab band Sahib
el-Arry, speaks to issues of parental responsibility and the domestic division of labor for child rearing. Although the close and affectionate
relationship Siti had with her own daughter was well known within
the community, in this song, entitled "Uchungu wa mwana" (The
pain of a child), Siti, herself a single mother, literally wails over the fact
that the most painful, bitter, and demanding aspects of child rearing
were often faced by the mother alone. Although island women are
often supported by extensive networks of kin and friends in the rearing of their children, the refrain from this song is still commonly
voiced by island women, "The bitterness—ehhhe—of a child—
ehhhe—the one who knows is Fatuma, the mother." Mwajuma Ali,
who occasionally performs this song for Sahib al-Arry, said during an

interview that the painful whines and wailing interspersed throughout the song evoke the physical and emotional distress faced by
women whose partners neglect the responsibilities that follow from
begetting a child. As someone who has helped raise the children of
more than one overstressed mother and errant father, she also said that
in performing this song she hopes to encourage both women and men
to rethink gender norms which overburden women with responsibility for their children, while simultaneously neglecting to admonish
men who walk out on their emotional and financial obligations to both
their partners and their children.[91] While many island men take a very
active role in child rearing and can regularly be seen playing with, caring for, and teaching their children, the continuing popularity of
"Uchungu wa mwana" suggests that many island women feel that gender parity in the raising and rearing of children has yet to be realized.

"My Husband Doesn't Sleep at My House" (*Mume wangu halali
kwangu*) was composed by Budda bin Mwendo with a similar intent
of reminding delinquent husbands of their duties toward their wives
and children. Islamic law allows a man to marry up to four wives, *if* he
is capable of providing and caring for all of them equally. In reality
this is frequently impossible, a fact which most islanders of both genders historically have admitted quite freely. Domestic quarrels over
favoritism, or the unequal distribution of attention, time, and money
often ensue among parties involved in polygynous relationships.
Such tensions are exacerbated when the husband is poor and does not
even have the financial means to support one wife and her children
adequately. In this song, Budda relates the story of one of his neighbors whose husband took a second wife and subsequently began ignoring both the sexual and financial needs of his first wife. The song
is composed in the first person, making the sense of anguish and
abandonment experienced by the forgotten wife both personal and
immediate. However, the song does not portray the woman who is its
subject as an object deserving of pity. Budda's friend, on whom the
song was modeled, did not languish in despair, and in his rendition of
her plight Budda depicts her as a woman of action. In each stanza, the
wronged woman states her complaints against her husband matter-
of-factly, as well as what she has done to resolve the problems.

Mume wangu halali kwangu

Mume wangu halali kwangu
Akilala hunipa mgongo kama mwanangu
Nimechoka ugonjwa wa maisha nakwenda zangu.

Mwambiye bibi usiku mkubwa kwa jioni aje
Nakuuliza upande wa kaniki kaupataje.

Nalisafiri na bwana akanitupa malezi
Kapigwa jua la kutwa nami njaa siiwezi
Natangatanga na njia nikashindwa upagazi.

Nyororo nyororo ndio maamura
Chaka la watoro limeingiya vura
Kula aliye kasoro hujifanya bora.

My Husband Doesn't Sleep at My House

My husband doesn't sleep at my house.
If he does sleep with me he turns his back to me like my
    child.
I am tired of this sickness of life, I am leaving.

Tell the late-night woman she should come in the evening
    [to prepare your food].
I ask you, How did she get that new piece of kaniki cloth?

I traveled with the man and he threw the chore of raising
    [the children] all on me.
I was left out in the sun all day, and hunger I can not endure.
I waver and totter on the road, I was beaten by the load.

Poor and helpless is indeed how I am.
The forest used by refugees has become infested with spirits.
Eat the one who is underprivileged, you always see yourself
    as so important.

This song clearly laments the position of poor women who were
financially dependent on errant husbands. Images of food, hunger,
and neglect reappear stanza after stanza. However, the song also illustrates several means by which women sought redress; the most obvious being a woman's ability to publicize her husband's wrongdoings
by talking to neighbors, friends, and family and thereby exerting social pressure that would hopefully encourage him to mend his ways.
Gossip was utilized to reform not only "public" behaviors but "private" misdoings as well. In fact, both "The Pain of a Child" and "My

Husband Doesn't Sleep at My House" suggest that the Western bourgeois dichotomy between public and private did not exist in early-twentieth-century island society. In Zanzibar, and throughout much of the rest of the continent, institutionalized and ritually sanctioned means for bringing "public" pressure to bear in the resolution of "private" problems existed in the form of spirit possession. Women in particular were often afflicted by spirit-induced illnesses, in which a spirit would possess an individual and then speak to the community on her behalf, detailing the symptoms of her illness as well as the ultimate cause of her misfortune.[92] Other individuals afflicted by similar spirits, as well as the ill woman's family and friends, would then become involved in an elaborate series of healing rituals designed to appease the offended spirit by addressing the root cause of her illness. Issues that typically are defined in the West as the most private of individual problems, such as infertility, incest, sexually transmitted diseases, or domestic abuse, are often addressed in African spirit possession cults as symptomatic of larger structural, institutional, and public problems, such as poverty, patriarchy, and migrant labor, which can only be addressed through public discussion and collective resolve.

In the final line of the third stanza the woman declares, "I waver and totter. . . . I was beaten by the load." The word *upagazi* can be translated in two ways, either of which will work in this situation. The more literal translation is the work of a porter, or someone who is paid to carry heavy loads. This was a frequent form of employment for slave and poor rural men in coastal East Africa during the nineteenth century. A literal interpretation of this line would suggest that the domestic burdens that Budda's neighbor is carrying are too heavy for her to endure. A second usage of *upagazi* refers to witchcraft or the state of being possessed by a spirit. This could be interpreted either that the second wife has caste a spell on the husband, causing him to neglect his obligations to the first wife, or that the first wife has become possessed by a spirit who is seeking to redress these domestic troubles by bringing them to public attention. This latter interpretation is reinforced by the final stanza of the poem, which also alludes to the prevalence of spirit possession among women in Ng'ambo, and their healing ceremonies which are often conducted in secluded places. Spirit possession was and remains a common and socially acceptable way for women to seek redress for domestic problems. This song suggests that in the course of a spirit possession ritual the spirits afflicting Budda's neighbor called upon the husband to either meet his obligations for support or divorce his neglected wife. Such prescriptions for divorce were frequently offered by spirits as a means of allowing an afflicted woman to pursue other sexual and economic options, without burdening her with the additional financial and emotional costs of bringing her case to court, where in all likelihood it would be dismissed by an unsympathetic judge.[93] Like the songs addressed earlier in this chapter, here we are once again presented with the popular image of the powers of the supernatural intervening on behalf of the downtrodden as they seek a resolution to their plight. This woman was not content to wait until the afterlife for justice, however, or to passively rely on the supernatural to resolve her grievances. In each stanza of the song she takes some form of action to improve her situation. Rather than resorting to despondence or resigning herself to fate, in the very first stanza the subject of the song declares, "I am sick of this life, I am leaving."

The economic alternatives available to women in early-twentieth-century urban Zanzibar were limited, yet the music of Siti's band reveals women who were by no means frozen by their fears of poverty. The very real women whose lives formed the basis of these songs were women who, no matter how poor, demanded a certain level of commitment and respect from their partners. While they could not always command such esteem, they left relationships when such regard was not forthcoming. In post-abolition urban Zanzibar, female poverty was by no means synonymous with emotional or sexual servility. Demands for respect from domestic partners and lovers was as central to emerging identities as free and independent female adults as was physical autonomy from former owners.

Another song which addressed these issues of respect, autonomy, and paternity obligations was written by Mwalim Shaaban, and it was again based on the experience of one of his female neighbors and close personal friends. The woman whose story is related in this song had been involved with a wealthy man from Stone Town, she became pregnant and pressed her lover to marry her, but he refused. The woman's lover apparently expected to continue with the affair, but she said no, asserting that her dignity and her child were much stronger pillars to build a future upon than an uncommitted lover and his money. Again, the problem of this woman's financial dependence on her male partner is made poignantly clear, but so is her reluctance to sell her self-respect—as well as that of her coming child—for economic support. She may have lived in a small mud hut in Ng'ambo, and he in a multistory home in Stone Town, but his superior economic and social position was insufficient to compel her to remain in a relationship in which her marginality, and that of her child, had become painfully obvious. As in the previous song, the woman depicted here does not lament her helplessness. Although she is frank about the power differentials between her and her partner, each stanza is focused on a pragmatic resolution to her plight. Taking control of her destiny she addresses her lover, "My dear, worthless friend do not try and deceive me. . . . This affair has gone on long enough. When you wanted me I stayed with you, now you do not want me I have no need for you. When my father comes I will tell him the one with the bed has been scorned."

This song also raises the issue of the precarious impact of "freedom" on the lives of poor African women and their children. While slave concubines in nineteenth-century Zanzibar had legal rights to support for children born with free men, "kept" women in the twentieth century were guaranteed neither support, inheritance, nor legitimacy for children born of such affairs. While some men certainly continued to regard such children as legitimate heirs protected by Muslim law and custom, contesting heirs often found legal support for the exclusion of such children within colonial courts. In one such case, a woman gave a slave girl named Panya to her son as a concubine, in 1907, and they subsequently had a child. When the child attempted to gain its inheritance upon the death of its father, however, the chief justice ruled that the Slave Trade Prohibition Decree of 1890, which prohibited the sale and purchase of slaves, made the transfer of Panya illegal. Panya's son was declared by the courts to be illegitimate and denied any legal claim to inheritance that he may have had under Islamic law as previously administered in Zanzibar.[94] During this period many children born of free fathers and mothers who were concubines came to be known by a new Kiswahili term, *besar*. Besar were "illegitimate" children and had no legal right to inheritance. Unlike their nineteenth-century counterparts, they were also far from being considered the social equals of children fathered by the same man with a free, legal wife.[95] As the song "My Dear, Worthless Friend" suggests, women hoped that emotional and financial support would be forthcoming from the fathers of their children, regardless of the couple's marital status, but the new legal codes and changing social customs left them few grounds on which to base demands for compensation. Leaving such a "dear, worthless lover," reclaiming her dignity and publicizing her partner's irresponsible, if not illegal, behavior was sometimes the best a woman could do.

Sahib mwandeni

Sahibu mwandeni usifanye hila
Mwenyewe sitaki kwenda mahala
Kisa kimeshinda cha Alifleila.
　　　Sahibu mwandeni . . .

Nyumba ya udongo ghorofa ya mawe
Uliponitaka nalikaa nawe
Sasa hunitaki sina haja nawe.
　　　Sahibu mwandeni . . .

Watoto mnara mnara wa njiwa
Akija baba takuja mwambiya
Kile kitandacho kimebuliwa.
　　　Watoto mnara . . .

∎

My Dear, Worthless Friend

My dear, worthless friend do not try to deceive me.
I myself I do not wish to go anywhere.
This affair has gone on long enough.
　　　My dear, worthless friend . . .

A house of mud, stories of stone,
When you wanted me I stayed with you.
Now you do not want me, I have no need for you.
　　　My dear, worthless friend . . .

Children brighten a woman's darkness and guide her way.[96]
When my father comes I will tell him
The one with the bed has been scorned.
                    Children brighten a woman's darkness . . .

As documents that discuss the daily lives of those who inhabited
Ng'ambo in the 1920s and 1930s these songs reveal intimate details
about gender relations and perceptions of gender norms that are unavailable from other sources. Looking at the most general types of colonial documents reveals that there were limited means by which
urban women could gain regular access to much-needed cash.[97] Examining the lyrics and the stories behind these songs illustrates, however, the ways in which such bare economic facts impacted the
personal and emotional relationships that were at the center of both
men's and women's lives. Conflicts over resources were a central feature of household gender struggles. These struggles over resources
caused pain and disappointment to both parties in a relationship and
became frequent topics addressed in the band's songs. Their music
addressed not only women's financial dependence on men, but also
the ways in which both parties sometimes left a relationship feeling
used and unfulfilled.

The majority of the band's songs discussed such issues from the
perspective of a woman whose partner was neglecting his financial
obligations or, alternatively, attempting to literally buy a woman's af-
fections with money. The song "My Silk Lover" *(Mpenzi hariri)*, written by Mwalim Shaaban, is one of the few pieces which explores the
problems of financial dependence from a man's perspective. In it
Shaaban chastises the wife of one of his friends for what he perceives
as her greed and lack of commitment. Like many of Shaaban's songs,
this one encouraged lovers, whether married or not, to be honest and
responsible in their treatment of their partners. Here he chastises his
friend's wife for changing the metal of her husband's worth from gold
into iron, through continuous demands for money—demands to
which her husband readily acceded because of his blind and unques-
tioning infatuation. After exhausting her husband's financial re-
serves, the woman then deserted her husband in favor of one of his
wealthier friends. In each stanza the audience is presented with both

the painful feelings of abandonment experienced by Shaaban's friend, as well as the warning, "a person who eats for two comes to no good end." Shaaban's intent was to make the connection between one person's rapacity and another's pain poignantly clear. The band's music chastised the all-too-prevalent personal characteristics of greed and selfish desires for wealth, regardless of whether such characteristics were displayed by civil servants or "silk lovers." A few stanzas from the song go like this:

Mpenzi hariri

Mpenzi hariri unanisukuma
Unanibadili dhahabu kwa chuma
Mla kwa miwili hana mwisho mwema.
      Mpenzi hariri . . .

Mali nainabu zikimemetuka
Fedha na dhahabu zikitawanyika
Aloniharibu ni wewe kumbuka.
      Mpenzi hariri . . .

Kwako taabani ujuwe yakini
Usije fitini sahibu makini
Silali sioni daima njiayani.
      Mpenzi hariri . . .

∎

My Silk Lover

My silk lover, you are pushing me,
You are changing me from gold into iron.
A person who eats for two comes to no good end.
      My silk lover . . .

Wealth, if you have it, sparkles like the stars,
Silver and gold, if they are frittered away.
Remember the one who ruined me was you.
      My silk lover . . .

You should know that when it comes to you I am a mess.
You should not bring conflict between two good friends.
I don't sleep, I cannot see, I am forever wandering about
    aimlessly.
      My silk lover . . .

"My Silk Lover" and many other songs with a similar theme suggest that women's use of their sexuality as a means for gaining access to men's money was an open and accepted, if not always appreciated, fact in early-twentieth-century Zanzibar. Much more common within the band's repertoire than tales of women changing their partners from "gold into iron," however, were songs which chastised men for their attempts to literally buy the favors of female companions. Mwalim Shaaban in particular was critical of such practices and in many of the songs he wrote he upbraided men who used their wealth in this way and then complained when their partners left them for another. In one stanza of a song composed by Shaaban to warn men of the dangers of using their wealth in such a way, he tells his audience, "Use your head, think about getting a wife whom you marry formally. / The other you may desire to grab, but she will always break your heart, / And in the end she will lead you on, laughing and ruining your reputation." Shaaban used his songs to instruct island men, arguing that when men treat women's sexuality as a commodity that can be bought with gifts and financial favors, they should not be surprised to find the "object" of their desires in the hands of the highest bidder.

Songs like "My Husband Doesn't Sleep at My House" and "My Dear, Worthless Friend" also encouraged female members of the band's audience to reexamine their willingness to rely financially on men—be they relatively poor husbands who could only afford a kaniki or lovers who spent lavishly on silk and gold. In another song written by Mwalim Shaaban he suggests, "If you want a relationship that will last forever, one that is fulfilling and complete, / Do not allow desires for wealth or sexual mischief to get into your blood. / Love the one who holds you dear and respects your faithfulness." The band's love songs reveal a certain level of personal contradiction. Men and women living in early-twentieth-century Zanzibar seem to have hoped that their amorous partnerships would be based on commitments that went beyond the financial, but they lived in a society in which elements of nineteenth-century sexual culture—a culture that encouraged men to buy women as objects of conspicuous consumption while simultaneously promoting women's use of their sexual powers for material advance—continued.

In one song composed and performed by Siti, "Kikombe cha zari" (A cup painted with gold leaf) Siti counters the sentiments expressed in Shaaban's "My Silk Lover" and openly and almost tauntingly discusses women's use of men for their money. Here Siti uses a fancy porcelain teacup, intricately painted with gold leaf designs, to symbolize a woman. Referring to the Zanzibari habit of taking tea with milk and a lot of sugar, she calls on her man to bring these essential ingredients, suggesting that without his support she would have to drink her tea "dry," like the poor. In the final two lines she proudly declares, with absolutely no sign of remorse, that there is more than one lover adding sugar to her tea. The symbolism here obviously extends beyond the material, with *sugar* serving as a double entendre for lovemaking in many cultures, including that of the Swahili. Many of Shaaban's lyrics reflect a growing "romantic" patriarchal disposition. Although Shaaban was frequently involved with more than one woman at a time, in many of his songs he laments that his lovers are not satisfied with him alone.[98] Shaaban and other male band members wrote and performed many songs in which they spoke, and occasionally boasted, of their multiple sexual relationships. "A Cup Painted with Gold Leaf" is unique in this respect among Siti's extant material. Nonetheless, this song indicates a public recognition and implicit acceptance of women's use of the resources they had available to get at resources that were out of reach.

Kikombe cha zari
Kizuri kwa chai
Utie maziwa
Na nyingi sukari
Ukiondoka wewe
Mwengine tayari.

A cup painted with gold leaf
Is good for tea.
You should add milk
And a lot of sugar.
When you leave
Another is ready.

Women of Siti's generation exercised their autonomy, including that of their own sexuality, to create financial and emotional opportunities for themselves. If a woman's position within the urban economy prevented her from affording milk and sweetener for her tea, then out of necessity she would find herself a sugar daddy. Post-abolition urban women were autonomous and the control they exercised over their sexuality was an important aspect of their understanding of personal empowerment. Numerous songs written by male members of the band discuss their own experiences of romantic and sexual involvement with women from Ng'ambo and Zanzibar's countryside. While none of these songs presents an image of a woman as defiantly sexualized as that of "Kikombe cha zari," band members, who were themselves regularly involved with more than one lover at a time, sing of frequent confrontations with lovers who asserted, What's good for the gander is good for the goose as well. Many of the band's songs address instances in which band members or their male friends were abandoned by women whose needs—be they physical, emotional, or financial—were no longer being met. Song notes and interviews indicate that these songs were not composed with the intention of "reforming" women's behavior, but rather as realistic reflections of the gender politics of the era, in which women refused to be bound like slaves to their men.

These songs demonstrate that for many women in Ng'ambo, assertions of respectability were not necessarily based in a denial or repression of black female sexuality, but rather—like the music of many female African-American classic blues performers of the same period—in a celebration of women's sexuality under conditions of their own choosing.[99] As Hazel Carby has suggested, during this era many poor and working-class black women found it important to reclaim female sexuality from an objectification of male desire to a representation of female desire and control.[100] In the 1920s and 1930s, working-class women of African descent on both continents proclaimed their freedom to choose their partners as well as to love them and leave them as their needs and desires changed. Poor women in Zanzibar were no longer bound to endure unfulfilling relationships like those described in "My Dear, Worthless Friend," or "My Husband Doesn't Sleep at My House." As these songs reveal, women in this era faced numerous emotional and financial problems stemming from their love affairs, yet they were also socially autonomous actors who could choose with whom and under what conditions they would become involved in amorous relationships. The large body of songs which spoke of women's multiple affairs suggests a public acknowledgment that while Islamic law sanctioned a man's involvement with up to four wives and as many concubines as he could support, local custom recognized that necessity or desire could spur women to make similar choices.[101] Exercising choice and asserting their own sexuality was a critical component of the larger struggles for self-direction and respect mounted by women of the post-abolition generation.[102]

Conclusion

The judicial powerlessness of the underclass, the persistent abuse of power by those appointed to political office, and the general disregard for the needs of women and the poor by the institutions of the colonial state were dominant themes in the music and the daily lives of Siti binti Saad and her band. Listening to the lyrics of these songs we can hear the laments of Siti's contemporaries that social justice and equality did not necessarily flow from abolition. While advances had certainly been made in many areas, institutional power in Zanzibar society remained heavily concentrated in the hands of a few very wealthy men, the majority of whom lived in Stone Town. The men and women of Ng'ambo were critically conscious of these facts as well as the means by which the institutions of the colonial state—the civil service, Wakf Commission, schools, courts, Legislative Council, town planning department, and police—reinforced and reified this control. Clearly, however, such power was not hegemonic. The British and their domestic allies certainly controlled the institutions of domination, but these songs reveal their very limited ability to constrain debate regarding the reasonable, feasible, and just. The women and men of Ng'ambo discussed the ways that colonialism was transforming relations of power as well as the human practices which gave them form on a daily basis. And at night they gathered at Siti's home to hear how the band transformed these critiques into song. Though institutionally feeble, the men and women of Ng'ambo used "the weapons of the weak" to affect social change.[103] The nature of economic and political domination may have been moving away from personalized, face-to-face negotiation between patrons and clients, but in this fairly small community in which reputation remained central, gossip and God retained an immense amount of power.

Siti and her band used their presence as performers not only to entertain, but to raise the social and political consciousness of their publics as well. Many of Siti's songs were intentionally designed to elicit debate or to publicize debates that were already circulating in town. The band's music became a popular forum contesting violence against women and the poor, as well as an important means of vocalizing dissatisfaction with the state's reluctance to punish perpetrators. These songs and the subsequent debates they engendered enhanced people's critical consciousness. The band's music foregrounded individual cases of injustice, yet in the process they also transformed them from isolated incidents, easily swept under the rug, into frames of a much larger picture of systemic class and gender oppression. In addition, the band's songs provided a public space in which alternative discourses of power and social justice could be voiced; nearly every song offered both a critique of existing relationships as well as a suggestion for improvement.

Siti's music was immensely popular not only because it voiced the critical consciousness of her contemporaries but also because it comforted them as well. While listening to these songs, audience members gained assurance that at least the problems they were facing were not theirs alone, that their poverty was not a result of personal failure, but of systemic economic injustice. In addition, songs like "Kijiti," which had the power to bring tears to people's eyes, helped to initiate catharsis and begin the often painful process of personal and communal healing. While the sound and lyrics of their music were often sorrowful, the band used *natiki* (mime) to make fun of the gestures and habits of the elite and to lighten the tone of the performance.[104] Mimicking the judge who swore, "You bloody fools!" or lawyers hoisting up their trousers around protruding bellies did not diminish the critical intent of the songs, but it did allow for a brief moment of comic relief during an otherwise solemn performance. The laughter and friends that were part and parcel of an evening's performance allowed audience members to temporarily forget their cares and to rejuvenate the courage they needed to carry on. While there were certainly aspects of Zanzibar society which could be improved, the band and the audience consistently reminded each other of the need to rejoice and enjoy the many good things that life had to offer—not the least of which were the nightly practices in Siti's home and the free Thursday and Friday night performances in Ng'ambo.

Chapter 5

Colonial Politics, Masculinity, and Football

As C. L. R. James demonstrated in *Beyond a Boundary*, cricket, field hockey, and football (soccer) can easily be read as allegories on life in the British colonial empire. The organization of team sports epitomized colonial attempts to inculcate hierarchy, discipline, and respect for authority within the minds and spirits of the colonized. Yet these values were not passively internalized. Football, like taarab and other popular pastimes in colonial Zanzibar, became a central terrain for the development of alternative discourses of power and society. As James said of his training in the West Indies, "Cricket had plunged me into politics long before I was aware of it. When I did turn to politics I did not have too much to learn."[1] Island men utilized football to challenge the "public transcript" of British domination; they trounced their "overlords" before thousands of spectators, openly defied European referees, and adapted the networks of club football to meet class, communal, and nationalist goals.[2] Although the British wrote and administered the rules of play, colonial officials spent much of their time playing a defensive game, reacting to the initiatives taken by island men, for whom playing, watching, and organizing football became a central preoccupation of urban life.³ Like taarab, football was a "foreign" cultural form, but one that island men shaped and adapted to meet their own needs. Many aspects of football competitions in Zanzibar resonated with the aesthetics of competitive ngoma, and sports rivalries gave concrete cultural expression to the class, neighborhood, and political divisions of urban society. Team sports also allowed men opportunities to earn respect, achieve positions of authority, and enhance their self-esteem in ways that were few and far between in colonial Africa. Examining the historical development of football in the isles allows us to appreciate both colonialism as an interactive process and the central importance of leisure and sport in the lives of the men who lived in Zanzibar between the two world wars.

Sport in Zanzibar, as elsewhere in the empire, often carried undertones of conflict and at times became overtly political, yet football represented much more than a political battlefield to the players and spectators engaged in the game. Football was fun. Football provided urban men with a period of two to four hours every day when they could play, laugh, tease, and joke in the company of friends and neighbors. On several occasions, during the course of interviews, recollections of departed friends or the passing of youthful football careers brought tears to men's eyes. The friendships and connections that

Fig. 5.1. *Malindi Sports Club, 1950, with the Rankine Cup. Courtesy of Mwalim Rajab and Malindi Sports Club.*

men established through sport often endured for a lifetime. On the field, island youth developed and expressed the styles and skills that defined them as individuals. Some were quick and clever, and unstoppable once they had the ball. Others were slower and more deliberate and took greater pride in making passes or creating space than scoring a goal. Whatever their skill level or style, football provided urban men with a regular, ritualized time and space for developing themselves, testing others, and playing together as a team. Football also became entangled in evolving definitions of masculinity like no other leisure pursuit of the interwar era. During interviews, many elderly Zanzibaris stressed that it was here that they grew to become men. Men's passage through the stages of a sports career came to mark their place in their life cycle and their relative status within the community like age-sets or initiations did within the communities of some of their fathers and grandfathers. As players and supporters of football clubs, boys and men became integrated into dense urban networks through which they made friends, found jobs, and secured access to housing. Football also provided urban men with the space to contest the status of personal and collective rivals. Football clubs and clubhouses marked the boundaries of urban space and transformed open fields, baraza, and streets into places where collective identities and male solidarities could be crafted and explored. Practice time and match times set the tempo for men's late afternoons and evenings, while the schedule of league and cup competitions came to define the seasons of urban life as much as the rains and the clove harvest did in the countryside. By the early 1920s, football had become a central component of the urban experience. It was pivotal to the development and transformation of individual, neighborhood, and communal identities.

The Early Years of Football in Zanzibar

Football, field hockey, and cricket were first introduced into the islands of Zanzibar in the late 1870s by workers employed by the British-based Eastern Telegraph Company (ETC) who came to the isles to lay the cable linking Zanzibar to Aden and England.[4] The twenty Europeans and eight Asians who comprised the permanent crew of ETC on Zanzibar regularly divided themselves into teams and passed their evening hours playing one of these three games. During this same decade, the Universities' Mission to Central Africa (UMCA) opened its St. Andrew's College, just outside Zanzibar Town. St. Andrew's was intended as a training post for African teachers and clergy, who were then sent throughout East and Central Africa to open churches and schools and spread Christianity. Football and cricket were widely incorporated into the curriculum at St. Andrew's and graduates of the college have been credited with spreading these games in East Africa.[5]

During the industrial revolution in England, industrialists, members of Parliament, and moral reformers came together to transform popular recreation and leisure pursuits in an attempt to "civilize" and "stabilize" the working class and urban poor. Leisure activities such as drinking, gambling, racing, and cockfighting were increasingly subjected to state control, while moral reformers attempted to modify the recreational tastes of British men in order to make them more "suitable" to the "modern," capitalist era. In the nineteenth century, football was appropriated by the middle and upper classes and gradually transformed into a more "rational" form of recreation.[6] The guiding philosophy of the rational recreation movement was that the new values necessary for industrial life could be subconsciously developed within the working classes by reforming leisure, including sport. Football and cricket had long been played by rural working men, but football matches typically involved innumerable players in a village, who drank, played, ate, drank, and then played some more in the course of a game. Now, however, contests no longer lasted until men were either too drunk or too sore to play; they went on for a specific period of clock-measured time. Games that were organized around a clock and divided into halves and quarters were believed by the advocates of rational recreation to instill respect for clock-measured time, to teach men to "make the most" of their time, as well as the necessary discipline of being on time. The codification of game rules was also believed to instill the type of discipline necessary for factory work, while the policing of games by a referee was intended to instill respect for authority in all areas of life. Exercise, or what widely came to be known as "muscular Christianity," was said to contain and safely expel pent-up sexual energy, which might otherwise be turned to antisocial or un-Christian ends. Even the establishment of organized teams was said by philosophers of the era to be of value to society, teaching young men the need to suppress their personal goals and desires for the greater good of the team, factory, and nation.

These philosophies of rational recreation and muscular Christianity were transported across the globe during the colonial era. During the early twentieth century, colonizers across the African continent began laying increasing emphasis on the development of sport within the colonies, in hopes of molding a "disciplined" working class from the mixed assortment of individuals living in urban Africa.[7] Colonial administrators in Zanzibar saw the expansion of team sports as an important means of ridding the islands' men of what the British perceived as their "sloth" and "lack of initiative."[8] As the publishers of Zanzibar's *Official Gazette* commented, "the health of young Zanzibar cannot fail to benefit by increased inducement to enjoy vigorous exercise during the afternoon leisure instead of loafing in the stuffy bazaars."[9] Sport, it was hoped, would transform the "lazy" African into a disciplined man working hard in the interests of the empire.

Members of the mission community and colonial service played an important role in the formation of some of the earliest teams in the isles. Three of the earliest African teams to organize in Zanzibar were the St. Andrew's (Kiungani) College Boys, the UMCA school, and the team of the government school. Until the end of the colonial era, participation in sport remained a central component of the "educational experience" of urban, island men. Juma Aley, who later captained the Zanzibar national cricket team for ten years, recalled how sport was used to instill respect for law and authority among the students at the Boy's Secondary School, where he attended as a child and later taught as an adult:

> Sports did a great deal of good not only from a physical angle, but in inculcating discipline which had many great and lasting impacts on character training. The referee's word is final and the umpire's decision is final went into the head of every [student]. . . . There were no appeals of

the referees decision and you could not play unless you were prepared to follow the rules! Back then, young men learned to obey authority.[10]

The UMCA incorporated the "lessons" of sport into the curriculum not only at its primary and secondary schools, but also at the "Boys Club" that it ran for urban youth. The aim of the club was to catch homeless and uncared-for youth at an early age, "before they began a life of crime and developed into hardened old criminals," and to teach them about the dignity of labor, the value of authority, and the manners of good citizens. Boys who attended the club were given neither food or clothing, as this would run counter to the goal of teaching them the value of waged labor, but were helped in finding jobs around town, primarily as runners and porters at the bus stand. Boys were also required to participate in the "healthy recreation" offered by the club, such as football, boxing, and table tennis, which club organizers believed would "instill in them the club spirit . . . and a sense of good citizenship."[11] Through these schools and clubs young men were also unconsciously groomed to accept their relative "place" within the colony. Young Arab and Asian men who were being prepared for positions of authority or supervision within the administration were encouraged to develop a taste for the refinements of cricket, those deemed more suited for jobs as junior-level clerks were directed toward field hockey, while football and boxing were the sports considered most "appropriate" for the African working class.

Watching students at the various schools or British employees of the empire play these games became an increasingly popular urban pastime in and of itself and gradually the young men of Zanzibar Town began to take up football themselves. During the 1910s, football took off with lightning speed. As Khamis Fereji said,

Football started in *uzunguni* [Europe] but everyone here learned how to play. For a football we would buy a tennis ball; they were cheap in those days—for a few cents we could buy a ball. And then we would run off and play anywhere there was a little space. We played with each other in the narrow streets *(vichochoroni)* . . . or we would go over near the port. Before they had built the Public Works it was a big football ground. In the evening the men would come down and rest, enjoy the breeze, or fish and we kids would play football. This was the very beginnings of football, us kids playing in the narrow streets with our tennis balls.[12]

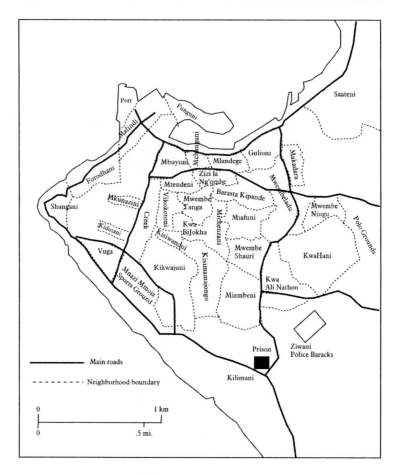

Map 5.1. *Selected Urban Neighborhoods, c. 1940*

Children continued to play football anywhere and everywhere they could find a little space, but by the time of World War I, teen-aged boys began organizing their own teams to compete against the teams of UMCA and the boys' school. These contests were held on the public recreation grounds known as Mnazi Mmoja.

The aspirations of the first post-emancipation generation were reflected in the naming of two of the most popular clubs of the era, New Kings and New Generation, and like many of the popular pastimes of the 1910s and 1920s, including the ngoma *changani* and the women's initiation dance (kunguiya), New Kings and New Generation were built around patron-client ties. Both New Kings and New Generation incorporated players from both sides of the creek and actively encouraged men from the entire range of urban Zanzibar's class and ethnic spectrum to play and compete together. New Kings was organized by two Arab brothers, Mohammed Said and Massoud Said, who lived in the Stone Town neighborhood of Shangani, but it was captained by Hamidi Feruz, a young Swahili man who lived in the Ng'ambo neighborhood of Kikwajuni. As Hamidi Feruz explained, "Most of our players came from the areas of Shangani and Kikwajuni because we were neighbors." Being neighbors in this case did not necessarily imply physical proximity but the kind of social proximity that was fostered through patronage, dance, religious, and leisure networks. Hamidi knew the Said brothers through other social networks. The brothers greatly admired Hamidi's skill as a center-half and asked him to captain their team. Another Swahili footballer, Abdulrahman Othman, recalled being recruited to New Kings by the team's center forward, an Arab schoolteacher known as Mwalim Jidawi.[13] Two other teams from this era, Vuga and Kidutani, were named after particular Stone Town neighborhoods, but like the women's initiation group, Malindi, they too incorporated players from both sides of the creek. The most important factor in the minds of the men who organized the clubs that emerged during World War I was not the class or ethnic status of their players, but their skills as footballers. Football became the premier pastime of this new, post-abolition generation, and now even a Swahili man could become the new king, directing the play of men whose parents or grandparents may have owned his parents in the past.

Although the form of football was new to the isles, the principles of organization and competition resonated with existing forms of recreation that were widely popular in nineteenth- and twentieth-century urban Zanzibar, expressed most prominently through ngoma (drum, dance, and poetry competitions). Like ngoma groups, football clubs were often organized in paired rivalries, and although each team played all the other teams, matches that pitched rivals against each other (such as New Kings vs. New Generation, Kidutani vs.

Vuga, or Caddies vs. Comorians) were often the most intense.[14] Like ngoma, football also provided individuals from poor and socially marginal backgrounds with opportunities for achieving status, titles, and positions of authority, both within a team as well as in the larger urban society. For instance, Hamidi Feruz, a Manyema by birth, not only captained New Kings, he also became widely known and respected among men in town because of his skillful ability to move the ball and direct the game from his position at center-half. His control over the ball and impressive talent at cutting through players on the opposing team, as he drove the ball toward the goal, also earned him the nickname Mapanga, after the big, sharp machetes wielded by island men. By the time he was twenty, Mapanga had become a household name. He was also highly regarded among European football fans in the isles, and glowing reports of his latest football feats were not uncommonly reported in the *Official Gazette*, the closest thing to a national newspaper at this time. According to many participants, football became the male equivalent of women's dance associations, competitive clubs in which every participant stood a chance of emerging as a star known throughout the town.[15] In a world in which good old African know-how could open many doors, football allowed men with little financial capital to attract patrons, clients, and followers in a way they only could have dreamed of before.

According to men who grew up in town during these years, by the 1920s "everyone" was playing football.[16] The publishers of Zanzibar's *Official Gazette* were utterly amazed at the speed with which football had taken off during the war. The small, unobtrusive sports column that focused on write-ups of European golf and cricket matches in the late 1910s grew to several pages dominated by coverage of football by 1921. In the *Gazette* of 7 February 1920, the editors declared, "the enthusiasm for football among the natives shows no sign of diminishing. New teams are continuously forming and we have difficulty accommodating all the teams on the playing field."[17] During the second half of the decade enthusiasm for football continued to grow—three additional football pitches were added in an open space adjacent to the makeshift ground at Mnazi Moja and the editors of the *Official Gazette* were proclaiming football "the national game."[18]

Island men were attracted to football not because it imbued them with a respect for British authority or a sense of their position within the empire, but because it resonated with aspects of competitive coastal culture and indigenous leisure pursuits. Members of Zanzibar's colonial administration had very little respect for one of the most popular existing forms of leisure in the isles: gathering in courtyards and on barazas (stone seats built along the front of Swahili homes) to dissect and disseminate the latest local gossip. British perceptions of these activities as "loafing" illustrates that definitions of what constitutes constructive use of leisure are culturally bound. For many island residents, this practice of gathering in their neighborhoods to socialize and disseminate news was and still is a highly enjoyable and valued leisure activity as well as an essential element of community membership.[19] It was from such gatherings that the topics of many songs performed by Siti binti Saad and her band emerged. As increasing numbers of Zanzibari men began to play football, they adapted football to meet their own local needs, combining the "rigors" of football with preexisting leisure pursuits and turning football grounds, practices, and clubhouses into some of the principle sites where men would meet to exchange and debate local and international news.[20] Playing or watching football and gossiping on a baraza were not mutually exclusive leisure activities. Men gossiped about local politics while attending football practices and matches between 4:00 and 6:00 P.M. and then continued their discussions on the baraza, late into the evening, adding analysis of the latest match and debates about referees to their other topics of conversation.

Like certain ngoma, part of the fun of competitive sport was that it gave men like Hamidi Mapanga opportunities to display their individual talents, while also providing the poor and disenfranchised with a ritualized space to challenge the power of the elite or temporarily upset the existing social order.[21] On the football field, the casual laborers, boatmen, and domestic servants who comprised New Generation could challenge and even beat the young men who were training to become African missionaries at UMCA or colonial clerks at the government school. During the war, the men who worked as caddies on the European golf course formed their own team, United Service, which was more commonly known simply as Caddies. Although these men were not so affectionately referred to as "wretched little golf totos [children]" by many of the Europeans for whom they worked on the golf course,[22] Caddies players challenged colonial discourses of African infantilization by trouncing the team of European men, Mnazi Mmoja, on the football field in full view of thousands of spectators.[23] Outmaneuvering European players, especially members of the colonial service, enhanced island men's sense of manhood and symbolically undermined colonial hierarchies that placed Europeans at the top of the racial scale. For reasons that remain unclear, Europeans, including low-level members of the civil establishment, regularly participated in sports matches against island men, a practice that was largely unheard of elsewhere on the continent.[24] Zanzibaris also took great satisfaction from their frequent wins over sailors from HMS ships, which regularly called at Zanzibar's port and always included sports contests as part of their shore leave.[25] Clubs supported by the Omani aristocracy and educated civil servants of the Comorian Association, the Young Arabs and the Comorians, respectively, were similarly defeated on a regular basis, in the 1910s and 1920s, by New Kings, New Generation, and Caddies—teams comprised largely of men from poor, slave, and working-class backgrounds. However, the low economic or social status of many teams' members was irrelevant on the football field, where they regularly trounced teams whose members comprised the precolonial and colonial ruling classes. As C. L. R. James said of sports in the West Indies: "here on the . . . field if nowhere else, all men in the island are equal."[26]

Between the two world wars, football became an exceptionally popular pastime not only for players, but for spectators as well. The size of the crowd was one criterion used to determine who won certain ngoma competitions, and this tradition of incorporating spectators as a central part of the competition was continued in sport. Like the crowds who came to watch dance and music contests, observers of football matches played a decisive role in proclaiming victory for one team over another, particularly in the years before matches were refereed or in the street matches played by young men. Regardless of a referee's presence or the final score of the match, it was the spectators on the sidelines who determined the "winners" through their endless analysis of players, strategy, and style.[27] Good moves often made a bigger impression on fans than the actual score. And unlike British theories of the game which emphasized teamwork, passing, and the execution of plays, fans in the isles held a definite preference for the beauty of fast, bold, and unconventional moves by individual players, an emphasis that remains a defining feature of the island style to this day. Gathering at neighborhood meeting spots, known as baraza, to debate the relative worth of players and the nuances of their individual styles became an exciting nightly pastime in and of itself. Talking about strategy, style, teams, players, and matches was also a pastime that could be thoroughly enjoyed even by those too old or immobile to play.

The excitement generated by football, combined with the fact that matches were played on an open ground and admission was therefore free—until 1949, when the first enclosed stadium was built in the old rock quarry—meant that competitions were extremely well attended. Khamis Fereji told me, "when there was a big match Mnazi Moja was packed with people! Football was free, you didn't have to pay like you do now." "Many people came to watch the matches," said Hamidi Feruz, "many, many people. It was free. You didn't have to pay admission, so everyone used to come and watch, everyone!" Reports in the *Official Gazette* confirm that, by the mid-1920s, matches at Mnazi Moja were regularly drawing crowds of three to four thousand spectators. Crowds of as many as ten thousand were common for particularly heated matches, such as the 1927 season final between New Kings and the Comorians, or a 1928 match that pitted the team sponsored by the educated elite of the Comorian Association against the poor and working-class Comorians who dominated Caddies.[28] Attending football competitions along with thousands of other fans was one of the defining characteristics of urban living during the 1920s, and one of the highlights of a trip to town for visitors from the countryside.

The enthusiasm of players and fans was brought to a new height, in the mid 1920s, when annual trophy tournaments began to take place. In 1924, Mr. Ibrahimji Darugar, a local Asian businessman, donated the first competition cup for football, the Darugar Cup. Competition was on an elimination basis and in the first year ten teams vied for the new trophy. The final cup match, which pitted Caddies against the European team known as Mnazi Moja,[29] drew thousands of spectators. At the end of regulation time the score was 0-0, so the match went into overtime, yet still there was no score. These were the years before penalty kicks decided tied matches, so a few days later, some four thousand excited spectators returned to witness the rematch and cheer the Caddies on. Although the European team ended up defeating Caddies by a score of 1-0, the final score was less important to the African working-class crowd than the skillful way Caddies outplayed Mnazi Moja and the sheer fact that they were able to take on the men whose bags they carried on the golf course and hold their own.[30] Caddies demonstrated their ability to beat the British at their own game later in the year, when they met again in a contest for another trophy, the Samachar Cup, which had been donated by another local Asian businessman. The nerves of the spectators were drawn taut as the match once again ended in a draw. This time, however, in the rematch Caddies beat the Europeans 1-0, amid "great cheers" from the crowd.[31]

The jubilation of fans whose team had won often erupted into spontaneous parades as supporters gleefully escorted their team back home or proudly circled around town displaying their trophy. After particularly important matches the clubhouse often became the center of a celebration that drew scores of men, women, and children into the festivities. Beni bands—a form of African ngoma modeled on military marching bands, but which parodied Europeans, with their uniforms, side-drums, bugles, and trombones—often accompanied teams from the field back home, adding to the air of jubilation.[32] Beginning in 1926, annual competitions during the August bank holidays were held among football, cricket, and hockey teams from Zanzibar and the Tanganyikan capital, Dar es Salaam. Fares on the government steamers were cut in half so that fans and well-wishers could accompany their favorite players and teams. According to men who remember these years, work in the town came to a virtual standstill when the ships returned, as "everyone" converged on the port to greet the teams as they came off the boat with their newly won trophies. The streets again were filled with the sounds of revelers and ngoma and beni

Fig 5.2. *Miembeni Sports Club, 1952, with the Jinnah Cup and the Rankine Cup. Courtesy of Abdulrahman Othman. (Back row, left to right) Salum, Mohammed Ali, Mtoro Suleiman, Mtumwa Diwani, Mansur Ali, Kitwana Khamis, Said Seif, Omar Juma; (middle row) Ali Makame, Keya Maulidi, Mohammed Ali, Abdulrahman Othman, Songoro Faradi, Suleiman Mohammed; (front row) Abdallah Almasi; Juma Simba.*

bands as thousands of spectators proudly escorted the teams back to their clubhouses, where they spent the remainder of the day and half the night listening to tales of the matches in Dar es Salaam and soaking up news from the mainland.[33]

Enthusiasm for football among both players and fans grew at an astonishing rate during the decade between World War I and the mid-1920s. What "dressing up" and dancing ndege did to enhance women's sense of autonomy, respectworthiness, and belonging within the urban citizenry, football clubs and competitions did for men. Urban men were drawn together in this new game, a game in which individual physical and mental skills were far more important determinants of status and potential than pedigree or property. Building on the traditions of competitive ngoma, football players and spectators took a European game and transformed it into a highly popular form of recreation that resonated with the rivalry and revelry that were and remain a central part of Zanzibar society.[34]

The Politics of Sport in Colonial Zanzibar

By the mid-1920s, several leading members of the English community in Zanzibar began to advocate for European supervision of football. Until 1926, when Mr. Jenks of the Eastern Telegraph Company was appointed supervisor of sports, control over the organization of football matches and competitions was in the hands of the players and coaches who formed the teams. Impressed with the talent he saw exhibited by Zanzibari players and overwhelmed by the sheer enthusiasm with which boys and young men had taken to the sport, Jenks convinced the administration of the need for government oversight of competitive team sports. In 1926, Jenks organized the first league competitions for football, in which nine teams entered. Two years later, in February 1928, the Sports Association of Zanzibar was officially inaugurated.[35] Some members of the European community advocated expansion of administrative support for sport simply because they themselves were avid sportsmen and they wanted to see such activities expanded in the colony. Others, however, like their counterparts from Brazzaville to Mombasa and Johannesburg, were becoming increasingly concerned about the independence of team sport, which they feared African men might begin to utilize for "covert nationalist activities."[36] By the mid-1920s, colonial officials across the African continent were initiating efforts to assert European control over the form, content, and structure of team sports in hopes that they might quell the emergence of nationalist sentiments and reinforce respect for European colonial authority.

In the eyes of senior island administrators, the governing of sports was no game. The oversight of leagues and the control of competitions and grounds were taken as seriously as the running of any other part of the colony. The administrative structures governing sport paralleled those of the protectorate as a whole. Through the composition of the Sports Control Board, the highest administrative body for sports in the isles, the administration attempted to reproduce and "naturalize" the political hierarchy in colonial Zanzibar. Seif Rashid, who played for various first-division football teams for twenty-three years and who was obviously aware of these parallels, explained the organization of the Sports Control Board (SCB) to me:

> The British Resident [the highest ranking colonial official] was in charge of everything. Under him was the Chief Secretary, who was the administrator of the government and controlled things like passports and governance. It was these very same men who were in charge of the Sports Control Board. . . . They nominated and selected the members of the board. Europeans were always in charge.[37]

The appointment of members to the board was no trivial matter. As with all governing bodies on the island, from the Legislative Council to the Wakf Commission, Europeans guaranteed themselves an official voting majority on the SCB. Administration of the board was undertaken by a committee of eight, five of whom were appointed by the British resident and three of whom were elected by the twenty-two clubs who joined the association in 1928.[38] Records from the SCB indicate that appointees were selected by the British resident based on the belief that they would generally vote as the administration suggested they should. Although local men were also appointed to the board, they were very carefully selected. Endless memos went back and forth between the British resident and chief secretary over each and every appointment.[39] As with the Legislative Council and Wakf Commission, a certain amount of dissent from appointees was permissible, provided it stayed within acceptable bounds. However, any appointee who overstepped these bounds found their appointment terminated at the earliest possible chance. The British maintained an official majority on the SCB until the eve of independence, a practice for which they were increasingly criticized after World War II. As one editorial in the local press commented in 1956, "Now that there will be free election in Zanzibar isn't it time people could chose their own representatives to the Sports Control Board?"[40]

Zanzibari appointments to the Sports Control Board read like a who's who of island society. Like the Legislative Council, preference was given to wealthy and educated men of Arab, Asian, and (occasionally) Comorian descent. While the Tanganyika Football League had an African assistant secretary from its very beginning, not a single African was ever appointed to the SCB in Zanzibar by the administration, although several African delegates to the football subcommittee were elected by the clubs.[41] Participation in the governing of sports was seen as basic training for groups and individuals who would one day take control of the colonies, and in Zanzibar the administration steadfastly refused to entertain the idea that Africans would ever play a decisive role in governance. Footballers were generally regarded as unfit for leadership roles. Although working-class African men living in Ng'ambo comprised the majority of football players and fans, their presence was largely absent in the official bodies that governed sport. Members of the local elite who played the "refined" game of cricket were usually among those chosen for appointment to the SCB. Because Arabs were perceived by the administration as the "rightful" heirs of political power in the isles, when the Arab Sports Club—the sporting arm of the Arab Association— petitioned for a permanent Arab appointment to the board, in 1932, their request was quickly met.[42] As a fitting metaphor for his future role as sultan and symbolic head of the protectorate and Legislative Council, Prince Abdulla Khalifa, the son of Sultan Khalifa, was appointed by the British resident as permanent vice president of the Sports Control Board.[43] A European, although not necessarily a high-ranking one, was always president of the SCB.

Through their domination of the Sports Control Board the colonial administration in Zanzibar was able to secure control over the institutionalized structures of sport. The symbolic reproduction of these structures of domination and subordination were attempted as well, as during the annual Zanzibar Cup competition, when the season's trophies were awarded, and through the selection of referees. However, controlling appointments to a governing board was one thing, influencing the interpretation of elusive symbols was quite another.[44]

The Zanzibar Cup originated in 1926, after Mr. Jenks opened a fund and began soliciting donations from local Asian, Arab, and European businessmen for the purchase of a trophy. Controlled by the administration, the Zanzibar Cup was intended as the principle competition cup for football, awarded at the end of the year after the winners of the other cups had been decided. In 1926, nine teams from Zanzibar Town entered the competition for the cup. On the occasion of the first Zanzibar Cup competitions, a permanent grandstand was erected at the edge of an otherwise open field at Mnazi Mmoja—the first such "improvement" on the football pitches undertaken by the administration. Seats in the grandstand were sold to leading business and political figures, who were seated in a semicircle behind His Highness, Sultan Khalifa, and the British resident. In anticipation of a large crowd of African spectators, the field was roped off and a hundred police were stationed along the perimeter of the field in a show of state power and control of "the game."[45] Halftime entertainment during the final match was provided by the sultan's band, a military-style brass band under the control of the commissioner of police, which specialized in such numbers as "March Forth to Battle," "March of the Liberators," and "Romance underneath the Stars."[46] Read as a theater of power, the show was complete when His Highness the Sultan awarded the inaugural Zanzibar Cup to the only European team in the league, Mnazi Moja, which defeated New Kings by a score of 1-0.

Although the administration invested considerable time and money in choreographing Zanzibar Cup events, the side show which focused on local actors was of far more interest to Ng'ambo fans than the official performance. That the crowd was far more interested in the "fast clever footwork" of the players than the parade of leading businessmen into the grandstand was attested to by the fact that although the game did not start until 4:40 P.M., "before three o'clock native spectators, armed with adequate 'sunshades,' had taken up all the best positions along the touch line."[47] While the pomp of military uniforms and the sounds of brass bands certainly held an attraction for the inhabitants of Ng'ambo, according to the director of the band himself, the native crowds found the official performances of the sultan's band a positive bore.[48] The sounds of the official band were often drowned by the music of various beni and ngoma bands, which marched teams and fans from the clubhouses located throughout the town down to the field, where they continued to parade and circle and draw even more attention away from the grandstand and His Highness' band.[49] At the completion of the competitions for the Zanzibar Cup a rush was made toward the grandstand, where all the trophies for the entire year were presented to the winning teams by the sultan. The awards were completed with three rousing cheers, interpreted by British observers as being for the sultan, but more than likely directed by the crowd at that year's winning players and teams. According to Juma Aley, it was the awarding of the season's trophies and the parades about town after the games that made the Zanzibar Cup final "the biggest occasion of the year."[50] Sharing in the victory of their teams was an important draw for fans, whose attendance at the Zanzibar Cup final more than doubled, from four thousand in 1926 to ten thousand by 1928.[51]

The symbolic role of the referee was another aspect of the game that was similarly read in very different ways by the European administration and Zanzibari footballers. The administration of game rules by an impartial referee was, according to nineteenth-century theories of sport, assumed to instill respect for authority among subordinate populations.[52] As an emblem of their alleged ability to mediate fairly between otherwise biased interests, only Europeans, and occasionally Goans, were allowed to act as referees during the early years of league football. Only after World War II, as the administration gradually began to move toward self-rule in the isles, were other members of the Sports Control Board allowed to hold positions as referees.[53] Again, however, working-class men from Ng'ambo were barred from acting as referees until the dawn of independence. Rather than making their class and racial prejudices overwhelmingly obvious, the British used the command of particular skills, including literacy and fluency in English, as prerequisites for appointment to the SCB. Because most Ng'ambo footballers were denied the opportunity to attend school, where they could have learned to read, write, and speak English, they were barred from serving on the SCB and were thus ineligible to serve as referees.

Records from Zanzibar suggest that although local administrators controlled the selection of referees, they were continually frustrated by their inability to impart unconditional respect for these men's decisions among the local population. The president of the

Sports Control Board attempted to convince island men that "the acceptance without protest or demure of a decision, which in his opinion is a wrong one, is the mark of a true sportsman,"[54] but to no avail. The president of the SCB continued, "It is this sportsmanlike spirit that is the great gift which the worthy playing of a game can bestow upon its votaries and it is this spirit which we must foster and encourage. As Kipling says, 'The game is more than the player of the game.'" Undoubtedly, island footballers would have disagreed with Kipling on more than just this point. The latter half of the 1920s, when Europeans first attempted to assert their authority over football and wrest control from independent island teams, were years of particularly visible conflict over referees and their decisions. Certain referees were perceived as biased and teams voiced their opposition to those referees by boycotting the matches they umpired. Key league and cup matches had to be postponed on numerous occasions in the late 1920s and early 1930s as a result of the SCB's inability to find a referee acceptable to both teams. Public challenges to British authority were at a height in 1928, and ground rent protesters were not the only citizens who took their appeals to the streets. Players and fans also followed referees to their homes and offices on several occasions, in an effort to register the depths of their dissatisfaction with particular decisions, causing the SCB to publicly remind players and fans, in 1928, that "the word of the referee is final. Any attack on a referee, even if off the field and away from the game, is considered as if it was during the game and players will be dealt with accordingly."[55] Attempts to imbue islanders with respect for "impartial" European judges and referees or the hegemony of British interpretations of "the rules" were obviously less than successful. Boycotts of matches and challenges to the decisions of referees remained a hallmark of Zanzibari football throughout the colonial era.

Such attempts by Zanzibari football players and fans to engage the SCB in a discussion on impartiality and fairness were misinterpreted by members of the administration, who believed that a basic lack of understanding for the rules of play lay at the root of Zanzibari challenges to European authority both on and off the field. In the 1930s, the SCB began offering regular seminars on the rules of play, which not surprisingly were poorly attended. In the 1940s, they also translated the rules and regulations into Kiswahili and distributed the publication free to clubs in an effort to increase understanding of the rules as well as respect for the rulings of referees among local footballers.[56] These rule books and translations were themselves contested, however. Urban footballers objected not only to the contention that they lacked an understanding of the game, but also to European attempts to "save" Kiswahili from bastardization by translating terms like *penalty kick* into the cumbersome *adhabu ya eneo* rather than simply adopting the widely used Swahilized version: *penalti*.[57] The SCB preferred to hide behind the façade that conflicts between players and referees came as a result of ignorance on the part of local players, but in light of discourses circulated through taarab songs and protests at the court, it is probably more accurate to conclude, as local footballers did, that these conflicts stemmed not from a lack of understanding of "the rules" but rather objections to the prejudicial way in which the rules were applied.[58]

Although the efforts of the SCB to contain the spirit of independence that permeated urban football were of limited success, through their control of waged work the administration was ultimately able to exercise some power over the leisure activities of Ng'ambo men. In the late 1920s, work-related teams, such as the Public Works Department (PWD), Medical Department, and police began to sponsor football teams. Initially, PWD and Police posed little challenge to New Kings, Caddies, or Comorians, who retained control of the three championship cups throughout the 1920s. But the PWD, the police, and the Medical Department represented three of the most important sectors of employment for Ng'ambo men and, by the 1930s, SCB rules that required men to play for their work teams began to undermine the power and vitality of independent teams. The European men who controlled the department teams of course wanted their team to be the best, and to this end many of the best footballers in Ng'ambo were "encouraged" to join the department teams, especially PWD and Police, where men were often given jobs because of their skill as footballers.[59] Omar Said (Kidevu), the center-forward for Caddies and one of the faster dribblers and most prolific scorers in Zanzibar's early football history, was himself given a job in the PWD as a driver during this time.[60] Abdulrahman Othman, another of Zanzibar's most famous early players, told me he had to leave the team he really cared for in order to play for Police, where he worked as a tailor. When I asked him why, he said, "I had no choice. If you worked for a department they could take any player they wanted. The department teams took all the best players! Really they did! They even gave people jobs because they were good footballers."[61]

One man particularly noted for his role in sport and his ability to confer both jobs and drivers licenses on good African footballers was Mr. Wheatley, a British mechanic in the PWD.[62] Discussions with elderly men who played during these years suggest that Wheatley's recruiting methods were not always regarded as fair or sportsmanlike, particularly by members of the teams who played against PWD. Those who played for Wheatley and the PWD team denounce these accusations, however, saying that their competitors were simply looking for an excuse to justify their persistent trouncing at the hands of PWD. Nonetheless, by the early 1930s, three of the most prominent teams in Zanzibar's early football history—New Kings, New Generation, and Caddies—began a precipitous decline down to Division II, ultimately disappearing from the rankings altogether.[63] Because of Wheatley's skillful recruiting and coaching abilities, PWD quickly rose to the top. In 1931, PWD beat out Police in the finals for the Zanzibar Cup—securing a cup for the first time. For the next twenty years, PWD remained one of the most formidable teams on the island, often taking the league championship, along with at least one other cup.[64] While Wheatley's players appreciated the fact that their football abilities could earn them both jobs and driving skills, many of the men who played for department teams still resented the fact that they were "required" to play for a team managed by a European, especially when they had to miss the matches of their own independent teams in order to attend work-related games.[65]

What attracted these men to football was not merely the game itself, but the way in which individual, neighborhood, and community identities could be generated and expressed through sport. Working for the PWD was a way for these men to earn a living, but their larger social identities were built around their friends, neighborhoods, and leisure communities, not their jobs. What this meant was that men would often miss practice or show up late for PWD, Police, and Health Department matches so that they could attend the games of their own teams, which were simply more important to them.[66] The Europeans who controlled the work teams repeatedly condemned players for what they perceived as "laziness" and "lack of commitment."[67] As insightful authors of studies of resistance to work discipline have noted, however, the persistence of lateness and absenteeism should be read as a sign of struggle over time and work, and in this case leisure, rather than accepted as a testament of "laziness."[68] The men who played for government-controlled teams simply did not experience the same degree of satisfaction playing for PWD or Police as they did while playing for New Kings, Caddies, and New Generation.[69] The fact that they also risked losing their jobs if their performance as footballers became "too lazy" served to further define the time they spent with government teams as work time rather than leisure time.[70] The joy of participating in sports competitions was not generated simply by playing football, but by the camaraderie and rivalry that came from playing with and for the team of one's choice.

Ethnicity, Nationalism, Masculinity, and Community: The Multiple Meanings of Football in Island Life

During the 1930s, clubs organized by ethnic associations also began to play an increasingly prominent role in sports. Government policies that looked to groups like the Arab, Comorian, Bohora, Goan, and Hindoo associations for advice on administrative appointments and colonial policy encouraged Zanzibaris to ally themselves with such organizations if they wanted to make their voices heard through formalized channels. The leaders of such organizations also sought to strengthen their position as spokesmen for their respective communities and, as early as the 1920s, they began sponsoring cricket, hockey, and football teams as a way of enhancing their visibility and support within their communities and encouraging potential mem-

Fig 5.3. *African Sports Club, 1952. Courtesy of Abdulrahman Othman.*

bers to identify themselves as belonging to a particular group. As the politics of ethnic affiliation began to intensify after the formation of the Legislative Council, in 1926, formerly mixed teams, such as Caddies, New Generation, and New Kings, began losing their best players not only to PWD and Police, but to competing ethnic associations as well. Hamidi Feruz, the captain of New Kings, explained:

> In New Kings there were Arabs, Comorians, and Hadhrami. They were also members of Caddies. But then they all started to leave and to join the teams which were organized by their respective ethnic groups. So that left our teams weak. Everyone was trying to make their team sound. Football was really intense in those days! And we were spread all over. So we decided to form our team: African Sports. We broke up New Generation, New Kings, and Caddies and we made these three teams into one.[71]

The aim of the men who founded African Sports, in the early 1930s, was to rebuild a team that was capable of taking the league championship and to reassert the power of football clubs that operated free of European oversight and patronage. Quickly, however, several African footballers with a growing desire to participate in colonial affairs began to turn African Sports toward a more political goal. Like the leaders of the other ethnic associations they used their sports club as a means of building a sense of ethnic unity among their members and asserting the importance of their communal group within the structures of colonial governance. The folklore surrounding the importance of the formation of African Sports to the development of African nationalism in Zanzibar is rich and extensive.[72] Many of the official publications of the Afro-Shirazi Party (the party which represented "indigenous" islanders and immigrants from the mainland in the islands' independence elections and which governed the isles from 1964 to 1977) stress the importance of football in uniting Africans in the isles and instilling them with a sense of pride in their heritage. According to at least one of these publications, prior to the formation of African Sports the term *African* was one of derision and a label that no one in the isles applied to themselves.[73] Written after the 1964 revolution, these publications also tend to glorify the power of African unity epitomized by a winning sports team. According to one such publication, before the founding of African Sports, Africans were not only politically disorganized, but "humble and weak." This same publication alleged, however, that within three years of the founding of African Sports, the African Association was born and quickly grew to include a grossly exaggerated membership of fifty-six thousand island residents.[74] R. K. Mwanjisi, who authored the official biography of the postrevolutionary leader Abeid Karume, also argued that African nationalism was conceived on the football field. "Great things begin from small," asserts Mwanjisi. "The beginning of politics in Unguja and Pemba and of Abeid becoming known for his leadership skills was in football." Mwanjisi continues,

> At this time the people of Unguja and Pemba started to open their eyes and to see the meaning of foreign rule and the nature of its oppression. So it came that the citizens were given hope and brought themselves together, it doesn't matter if it was through sports, in order to free themselves from their bitterness.[75]

Players for African Sports also recalled the ways in which Karume and others utilized the networks of the club to further the organization of a political association run along the lines of the Arab Association or the Comorian Association, but which worked to further the interests of the island's working class. Abdulrahman Othman, a former player for New Kings and member of African Sports, explained the link between African Sports and the African Association in terms remarkably similar to those of the official Afro-Shirazi Party publications: "It was Karume's plan. He saw that if he brought Africans together, if he pulled us from our isolation and brought us together in a group it would give us strength. It was his plan to bring us together there [in African Sports], and then we went along, along, along until we formed [the African Association and then] the Afro-Shirazi Party."[76]

Hamidi Feruz, captain of both New Kings and African Sports and a political ally of Karume's, also recalled the ways in which Karume utilized leisure activities, including football, to draw crowds for political discussions, but he pointedly disagreed with the "official" version of the story of African Sports, arguing that football was the real focus of the team's founders: "Mzee Abeid [Karume] was a member [of New Generation], but at the time when we decided to merge the three teams he was out of the country. He was in Europe working as a sailor and when he returned he saw what we had done. When he came back he added his foot to the team; and his head, well, his head was already swimming with ideas about politics."[77] According to these two men, their enthusiasm for African Sports and that of most of the original players came not from nationalist desires as such, but out of a desire to reestablish a winning, independent team. Playing for African Sports provided hope for Ng'ambo players who had become tired of playing for losing teams like Caddies, New Kings, and New Generation, or teams like PWD and Police that were controlled by Europeans.[78] Although African Sports certainly played a role in organizing Ng'ambo men for the bitter games of ethnic associationalism that led up to national independence, this was far from being the most important or most memorable aspect of the team. Far more important than its role in begetting African nationalism was the part played by African Sports in maintaining a link between the glories of the earliest independent clubs and the exhilarating neighborhood clubs that emerged after World War II.

In 1942 the colonial administration banned ethnically affiliated football clubs from participating in the urban "reserve" football league and from competing for the two most important football cups: the Kettles-Roy and Zeigler Cup and the Rankine Cup, named after the British resident, Richard Rankine, who served from 1930 to 1937. Men who were most suspicious about the administration's motives in banning ethnic clubs described the policy as a direct attack on the growing associational power of the African Association, and as yet another example of the administration's divide-and-rule tactics. As one anonymous sports enthusiast remarked, "The policy of the British was based on the principle of divide and rule. They encouraged people to organize themselves and their teams along ethnic lines as a means of further dividing them politically. But when the Africans, who were easily the majority, started to come together through African Sports, it made them very nervous. Their whole plan started to fall apart." Whether or not men believed that the intent of the administration was to undermine African Sports, and thus the African Association, Zanzibaris of all political and ethnic stripes agreed that during World War II ethnic antagonisms and animosities grew to a pitch previously unheard of in the isles. The ethnic complexity of many Zanzibaris was reduced to an oversimplified dichotomy between Arabs and Africans by the administration's rationing policies, and during the war African Sports and Arab Sports emerged as the competitive rivals whose matches drew the biggest crowds and elicited the greatest tensions in town. As the anonymous authors of a confidential report on the history and future of sports in the isles argued, "It will be recalled that political discourse during this era centered on dividing people based on heritage, skin color, and race. . . . These divisions were also prevalent in sports, including football, where the most important associations [The African Association and the Arab Association] brought their conflicts onto the field. . . . In fact, clubs under the auspices of ethnic associations often acted more like political parties than sports clubs." Banning racial clubs was seen by some as a means of lessening ethnic tensions and by others as a concerted attempt to thwart the development of African nationalism, yet all agreed that after the formation of the new Area League the "real action" in football was focused on the neighborhood clubs, which played in this new league.

Fig. 5.4. *Arab Sports Club, 1949, with the Kettles-Roy and Zeigler Cup and the Jinnah Cup. Courtesy of Mwalim Rajab and Malindi Sports Club.*

The reason many men interpreted the creation of the Area League as symptomatic of British efforts to "divide and rule" was because the new reserve league effectively divided the men of Ng'ambo, where the African Association was strongest, among a host of neighborhood-based teams, while keeping the players of Arab Sports united in the only Stone Town team. In 1942, when the new league was started, there were four teams that inaugurated the Area League. There were three teams from Ng'ambo, Vikokotoni, Kikwajuni, and Mwembeladu, and one team from Stone Town, Malindi.[79] The net result was that the men who had played together for African Sports were now divided among a number of neighborhood teams while the majority of men who played for Arab Sports remained united behind Malindi. "They were the same players, only the name was changed because ethnic teams were not allowed [in the reserve league]," said one man who played for both Arab Sports and Malindi.[80] A second "open" league allowed for teams affiliated with ethnic associations to compete against teams sponsored by work departments, but Arab Sports was the only ethnic club that remained truly competitive after 1942.[81] The Arabs took the "open" league in 1942, 1946, and 1947, and won the Zanzibar Cup as well in 1946 and 1947. The teams fielded by African Sports and

Fig. 5.5. *Kikwajuni Sports Club, 1943, with the Kettles-Roy and Zeigler Cup. Courtesy of Abdulrahman Othman. (Back row, left to right) Msubah, Keya Maulidi, Juma Ali, Ibrahim Makundo, Salum Ali, Othman Haji; (middle row) Ahmed Hussein, Saddat Ali, Rajab Abubakar, Omar Said, Juma Rajab, Ali Khasim; (front row) Salim Juma, Adbulrahman*

Comorian Sports were hurt not only because their players did not have the same opportunities to practice and play together as the men who played for Arab Sports and Malindi did, but also by the fact that men who worked for the PWD or Police were still required to give first priority to their work team, rather than the team fielded by an ethnic association, in the open league. There was no such work-related football team drawing away the collective strength of the young men who played for Arab Sports. Although PWD remained the team to beat in the open league, taking the league championship as well as the Zanzibar Cup in 1943, 1944, and 1945, beating the Arabs while playing for PWD simply did not bring players the satisfaction that losing to the Arabs while playing for African Sports or New Generation did.

Regardless of the political intent of the administration in creating the area teams, island men quickly turned these teams into intensely meaningful centers of individual and neighborhood life. Moietal rivalries had long been a central axis of competition in Swahili towns, and the area teams offered a new venue for expressing both older and emerging neighborhood rivalries. Area teams paired off and established competitive foes like earlier dance and football clubs. Competitions between the neighborhood teams of Malindi and Vikokotoni were intense and expressed some of the ethnic and political tensions that previously surfaced in matches between the Arab and Comorian Sports clubs. One anonymous man suggested:

> Malindi and Vikokotoni were big, big rivals! I don't know why, but I can tell you this secret. You know in Malindi there are a lot of Arabs, but Vikokotoni was the place where there were a lot of Comorians. Indirectly, indirectly there were racial issues that were there: Comorians versus Arabs, although it was now Vikokotoni and Malindi so it was neutralized a little, but it was there. . . . Some of those players from Vikokotoni used to say, "You are a Comorian. What are you doing playing for those Shahiris [immigrants from Yemen] and Arabs?" But I didn't care. I played for my team. I'd say, "You guys are going to be beat! This is my area, man. I was born in Funguni [a subsection of Malindi], man, in Malindi, so that is my love! I don't play for Arabia, I play for Malindi! I play for [coach] Jidawi!"

Mohammed Salum, who played for Vikokotoni for twenty years, also spoke of the Vikokotoni-Malindi rivalry. "Our big rival was Malindi. We never wanted to be beaten by Malindi and they never wanted to be beaten by us. . . . They were coached by their teacher, Jidawi, but we were unstoppable with crosses and headers!"[82] He also spoke of the other major pair of rivals in the 1940s, Kikwajuni and Miembeni. Kikwajuni was one of the initial teams formed when the area teams were inaugurated, but in 1944, Abdulrahman Othman and several other players broke away from Kikwajuni to form a team in the neighborhood in which they lived: Miembeni. Despite the loss of several key players in 1944, Kikwajuni remained highly competitive, retaining the prestigious Kettles-Roy and Zeigler Cup, which they won for the first time in 1943, in 1944, and 1945. Within a year of their break from Kikwajuni, however, Miembeni was proudly flexing its muscle in public. In 1945, Miembeni won the league championship and took the Rankine Cup home to its clubhouse for the first time. The rivalry between Kikwajuni and Miembeni lasted for decades. "Our competitions were intense," said Abdulrahman Othman, "but it helped us to improve our skills to have rivals like that."[83]

Despite the excitement that was generated by the fans of a winning team, supporters of defeated area teams took their losses gracefully. Hooliganism was not a part of island football culture during these years. There is no evidence in any of the records of fights between competing groups of fans during the games or of violence in town following area league football matches. F. B. Wilson, a senior member of the Department of Agriculture who played for a European team known as Bila Jina (Kiswahili for No Name), said that football was of a relatively high standard, yet it was played within a very friendly atmosphere. Wilson neither witnessed or heard of disturbances at football matches during his fifteen-year tenure in Zanzibar.[84] Men who played for various Zanzibari teams similarly stressed that tensions between teams and fans existed only during the match. As Said Mohamed (nicknamed Said Nyanya—tomato—by the men he played football with because he worked as a vegetable hawker) recalled, "You fought like hell on the field, but after you were finished and you shook hands, that was it. You were friends again—you went to weddings together and funerals together." Khamis Fereji also stressed that the rancor engendered by football existed only during the time of the match. "The animosity was of the ordinary kind," he said, "You can't have football without animosity. People fought, but only while they were playing. After the game, that was it, each player had their 'brother' on the opposing team." Abdulrahman Othman echoed these comments: "We competed, but it was only sports related. Once we left the field we were friends. . . . If we went on picnics we invited 'brothers' from the other clubs. Even though we [Miembeni] broke away from Kikwajuni they still came on picnics with us."[85] Although club rivalries were intense, men who were rivals on the football field were often allies in their support of particular dance groups, prayed at the same mosque, or fished together on the same boat and this helped to temper the enmity created by football.

Area teams also helped to strengthen the sense of unity and pride of those who lived within a neighborhood. Said (Nyanya) Mohamed said that football not only brought the players on the team together, but brought others in the neighborhood together behind the team. While women did not play football and rarely participated in the daily life around the clubhouses of the 1940s, the involvement of their sons, husbands, and brothers in football elicited a vicarious, yet very real, love for their neighborhood team.

> Everybody from the neighborhood was behind the local team and supported the local boys. Not everyone was a member, but they were still strong supporters. People from the neighborhood would help us with money, etc., and we would go around to the shopkeepers and wealthy people in the neighborhood and ask for support. . . . Mothers and sisters would cook for the team before matches, help us organize picnics, and cook for visitors hosted by the team.[86]

When the men who played for the neighborhood team won an important match or came home with a championship cup the neighborhood often erupted in a celebration that included not only the players, but the men, women, and children of the neighborhood who constituted their most dedicated fans.

Many of the area teams drew upon preexisting male neighborhood networks, such as mosques and barazas, to build their early teams. For instance, the Malindi team took its name from the location of the baraza where players met to listen to the radio during World War II. Mwalim Rajab explained:

> In this particular area of Malindi people came together. It was during the war, and you know at that time there were very few radios, and people wanted to hear the news about the war. So this hotel in Dega, the Narrow Street Hotel, played the broadcasts and everyone gathered there to listen to the radio and get the news. Some people supported the British and others were for the Germans, and they all came there to listen to the news and discuss what was going on, like they do today [the Gulf War was going on at this time], and they debated the news. All the young men gathered there. They didn't gather in Shangani [another Stone Town neighborhood that also had men who played for Malindi] because people didn't go there to hear the radio. So they formed the club here. They called it Malindi because it started there [at the hotel]. . . . They didn't have a baraza in Shangani, the most important baraza was in Malindi, so we chose Malindi as the name for our team.[87]

As the area teams took hold, clubhouses built by the teams and their supporters often became the central gathering places for neighborhood men, including those who did not play. Here men gathered to gossip, play checkers and *bao* (makala), or analyze the most recent match. Not all the area teams had clubhouses, but mustering the resources needed to build a clubhouse elicited great pride among those who succeeded in achieving this goal. Malindi, for instance, did not have a clubhouse until the 1980s, but the men of Kikwajuni, Miembeni, and Mwembeladu built clubhouses very early on. Clubhouses were regarded as important physical signs of neighborhood strength, wealth, and autonomy within the geography of the colonial town.[88] The players of Kikwajuni, Miembeni, and Mwembeladu may have primarily been poor and working-class men from Ng'ambo, but together they had the skills and building materials necessary to build a clubhouse where men could meet to discuss the team, gather for celebrations, house visiting teams and other friends from Tanganyika and Kenya, or just relax and socialize in the evening after work or between prayers. The men who built these teams and clubhouses gained immense satisfaction in their accomplishments. As Abdulrahman Othman said of his work with the Miembeni club, "I am proud, very proud, of the time I spent with the club. We built one of the best clubs in Unguja. . . . And we encouraged the development of many young men." These sentiments were echoed by Ali Makame, who began playing for the boys' team in Miembeni at age eleven and continued to play for the Miembeni team for many years, "I can honestly say that during my youth it was Miembeni [sports club] that raised me. . . ."[89]

The neighborhood teams that were founded in the 1940s became the basis for some of the most significant relationships in men's lives. On more than one occasion, men came to tears recalling the friendships they created and nurtured through these teams. I was repeatedly astounded by the ability of the men whom I interviewed to recall the names, as well as the positions, of all of the men with whom they played some fifty or sixty years ago. Yet, as Mohamed Salum said, "You know, the people in the neighborhood club had a love for each other like brothers," a sentiment which many other players from this generation shared.[90] Inside the area clubs many men passed their lives, remaining actively involved even after they quit playing, by coaching younger players, running the clubhouse, raising funds, organizing trips, and acting as surrogate fathers to the boys in the neighborhood. The majority of young men who play for the area teams today continue to look upon the founding elders of the club with great respect, not only for starting the teams, but also for continuing to support and nurture today's players.

Playing football for the neighborhood team was not a passing diversion for young children, but a passionate part of becoming a male adult in postwar Zanzibar. On average the men I interviewed played football for well over twenty years. Boys who began their careers playing with tennis balls in the streets were often playing for the juvenile team in their neighborhood by the time they were eleven, twelve, or thirteen, marking an important social milestone of community recognition for their growing maturity as young adults. Between the age of fifteen and twenty many would then go on to play for the first-division team. Moving from the juvenile to the first-division team within the neighborhood became an increasingly important rite of passage, a form of initiation marking the social transformation of a boy into a man. Hamisi Fereji said, "It wasn't like it is now, when you have to wait until you are eighteen or twenty until you get to come out from the bottom and start to move towards the upper divisions. In the old days, if you were a skillful player, if they saw you had ball skills, you could play with the adults. I started to play with the men when I was only fifteen. You can imagine what that meant to be playing with the men!"[91]

The growing sense of manhood that playing for the first-division team engendered was further enhanced by a player's growing notoriety around town. One of the most important "profits" men said they earned from playing football was becoming "known." Abdulrahman Othman described with great pride how R. S. Wheatley, president of the SCB for many years and the organizer of the PWD team, "looked him up" at the clubhouse many years after Abdulrahman had stopped playing, when Wheatley came for a visit to Zanzibar after his retirement. Except for his skill as a footballer and his work with the Miembeni club, Wheatley and other Europeans would never have known who Abdulrahman was. "I was known by everyone," said Abdulrahman, "if I ever had problems of any kind in the government, the bank or the post office people would recognize me from football and help me out."[92] Many other men also described how notoriety earned through football opened doors in their personal, occupational, or political lives that otherwise would have remained firmly shut. Through football, many young men from this generation transformed themselves not only into men, but men who were "someone."

Football played an increasingly important public and personal role in shaping definitions of manhood during the colonial era, but individual men and clubs were not the only ones engaged in these debates. Members of the administration and ethnic associations also saw in football a means of shaping and transforming definitions of masculinity. From the 1920s through the 1950s, the leadership of the Comorian Association promoted the playing of sports as an alternative to male participation in ngoma. The Comorian Association took great pride in the prowess displayed by their sports clubs,[93] but by the end of World War II they had grown increasingly embarrassed by the continued participation of many Comorian men in urban ngoma that involved men dressing in drag. Eventually they appealed to the administration to aid them in the banning of several ngoma, including *shambe,* which involved men dressing in women's clothes and performing dances which the association's elderly leadership considered "vulgar and obscene."[94] Large crowds were regularly drawn to the performances of this and other ngoma that involved men dressing in women's clothes and dancing "like women," particularly during the monsoon season when these ngoma were performed down near the docks to entertain dhow crews. The district commissioners of Zanzibar readily agreed with the Comorian Association's description of such dances as "obscene" and "filthy."[95] According to the DC urban, dances like shambe were "lewd" not because of the songs or type of dance, "but because of the type of people who dance . . . and the way men dress like women." He argued that shambe's performance caused a congregation of "idiots" in public, a word he later apologized for using, stating that "effeminate" men would have been a better choice. He fully supported the Comorian Association's efforts to ban the ngoma, arguing that such " 'effeminacy' in the open by immoral men" was the cause of "objectionable scenes in public" as well as innumerable private "evils." The district commissioner sided with the "progressive and enlightened members of the Comorian community," and supported their efforts to have such ngoma banned. Yet many of the boatmen, dockhands, caddies, and domestic servants who played or watched football in the evenings also found great enjoyment participating in these ngoma at night.[96] While certain segments of the Zanzibar elite hoped that football could help to redefine masculinity along straighter lines, many of the real men who played found no incompatibility between their various leisure pursuits. Dancing in drag and playing football were equally enjoyable pastimes, and both drew large, appreciative crowds of spectators. After the war, football was certainly the most widely popular form of male recreation, but it by no means precluded men's continued participation in preexisting forms of leisure, including those defined as effeminate by the administration and their domestic allies.

Although the men I interviewed spoke of area-based football first and foremost in terms of the ways it enriched their personal and neighborhood lives, many also mentioned the ways in which area-based clubs enhanced the budding nationalist movement. Area-based teams created ties that not only crossed generations, but which spanned class cleavages. The men who played for Miembeni and Kikwajuni in the 1940s, for instance, represented such diverse occupations as workers for the public works, medical, health, and police departments as well as dockworkers, fishermen, carpenters, tailors, musicians, farmers, and teachers.[97] While the status and pay associated with their jobs varied greatly, during discussions before and after practice men often found that their experience of social, economic, and political conditions in the colony were quite similar.[98] Area teams and clubhouses created spaces for men to come together and discuss not only leisure, but politics as well. Men who continued to play for ethnically affiliated sports clubs, such as African Sports, as well as an area-based team also served as a conduit, some consciously and others unintentionally, of ideas and information between men at the neighborhood level and the leadership of the ethnic and nationalist associations.[99]

Despite the potential of football to augment early nationalist organizations, according to the men I interviewed, area clubs worked much more explicitly to assuage the ethnic antagonisms that came to dominate nationalist discourse. Men who played football together and enjoyed each other's company around the clubhouse developed an appreciation for each other that transcended the simplicity of narrowly defined ethnic identities or political affiliations. Spending extensive amounts of time together, on the field, in the stands, at the baraza, or hanging out around the clubhouse allowed men, in all their diverse forms, to develop an appreciation of the complexities, frailties, and inconstancies of their fellow human beings. Mwalim Rajab explained how the formation of the area clubs helped to thwart the ethnic antagonisms that erupted during World War II:

> Now those people who were previously fighting were together. Because before, if an Arab lived in Ng'ambo he would play for the Arabs and if an African lived in Ng'ambo he would play for Africans. But when these area teams came, an Arab who lived in Ng'ambo and an African who lived in Ng'ambo would play together. . . . It helped a lot. Because now you would find a Comorian playing with an Arab together with an African in one club. . . . You can't hate me while I'm playing with you in the same club. You love me because I'm playing with you. You learn to appreciate me like a brother.[100]

Women who participated in the neighborhood-based taarab clubs that emerged during World War II made similar remarks regarding the ways in which their clubs refocused people's energy and attention away from growing ethnic animosities toward the building of neighborhood and the promotion of neighborliness *(ujirani)*. Independent women's taarab bands, based in particular urban neighborhoods, emerged during World War II, and by the mid-1940s there were ten women's taarab clubs in Zanzibar Town.[101] These clubs became *the* leading form of urban female entertainment and leisure in the post–World War II era. Like the men's football clubs, they were often organized in competitive pairs, like that which pitted the women of Royal Air Force against their rivals, Royal Navy. Unlike the taarab of Siti binti Saad, from whom many of these performers drew musical and personal inspiration, the women's clubs did not provide public concerts in mixed-gender spaces, rather they performed only for the female guests attending the wedding celebrations of club members and their families. These taarab clubs, like earlier dance associations and ngoma groups, were extremely competitive. Each group vied to produce the most hard-hitting lyrics, known in Kiswahili as *mipasho,* directed at their rivals, as well as the most elaborate and well-attended wedding feasts. The competitive nature of women's taarab had many direct parallels with men's football. Uniforms, equipment, clubhouses, and picnics were regarded as important public displays of club and neighborhood power. As Nasra Mohamed Hilal, the leader of one of the earliest groups to form during this era, Sahib el-Arry, suggested, "The men had their football clubs; we women had our taarab."[102] Although leisure became almost entirely segregated by gender during and after the war, paired rivalries and very public competitions remained a defining characteristic of both women's and men's pastimes.

The taarab and football clubs that emerged during the war thrived on competition between neighborhoods, yet they actively enhanced cooperation within them, bringing men and women from a range of class and ethnic backgrounds together to share their leisure hours. There were certainly neighborhoods where large numbers of people from a particular ethnic background lived, but many Ng'ambo neighborhoods were quite heterogeneous. Whether it was women's taarab or men's football clubs, the popular pastimes of the immediate postwar era encouraged people to recognize and celebrate the cultural diversity that made Zanzibar what it was: an island populated by fairly recent immigrants from a multitude of different backgrounds. The power of these clubs and rivalries was not rooted in British efforts to divide and rule, but in neighborhood-based efforts to celebrate and enjoy the diverse strengths people found in their families and communities. The 1940s was widely regarded by the men and women whom I interviewed as a decade of intensive revelry, rivalry, and fun. Fond memories of the 1940s were no doubt enhanced by the fact that, in the decades that followed, taarab and football "all but died" in the words of several informants, as ethnic nationalism expressed through party politics emerged as a newer and decidedly more deadly "national game."

Conclusion

Football clubs and competitions were institutions that both British colonizers and island nationalists attempted to harness in pursuit of their political goals. In both instances, however, they were largely unsuccessful in wresting control of the sport from the men for whom it became a premier popular pastime. Football players and spectators never denied that sport in the colony frequently carried political overtones, but this was rarely what drew them to football or what kept them engaged with it for most of their lives. Far more important to players and fans was the competitive nature of team sport and the way that football resonated with ngoma culture. The organizational basis of football teams and the most popular clubs changed over the decades but, like the changing fashions of ngoma, football continued to provide players and fans with endless opportunities for thrilling and unique performances. Football also gave individual and collective groups of men regular occasions to publicly display their creativity, stamina, and style. Clubs and clubhouses provided the space for young boys to grow into men, and above all else they created the opportunity for island men to establish and develop the friendships that would last them throughout their lives.

Chapter 6
Conclusion

From the perspective of many islanders abolition and emancipation were the principal transformations that took place in island society between 1890 and World War I. The British were certainly responsible for initiating abolition, but slaves themselves were the agents who defined and gave real meaning to this otherwise abstract legal term. The practices and performances of emancipation took a variety of forms, and in many cases they were highly gendered. While all slaves sought to enhance their personal autonomy and improve their economic position, the strategies women and men used to achieve these goals were in some cases rather different.

Acquiring independent property was one of the first steps taken by many former slaves as they began their long walk toward "freedom," in the first decade after abolition. For many, this involved moving to unclaimed land, planting trees, and building new homes as one means of establishing "ownership" of property. Staking a claim as an owner of rural property appears, however, to have been a practice that was easier for men than for women. In town, on the other hand, both genders had roughly the same opportunities to build or acquire a home, and many women seeking to establish themselves as the head of a household chose to move to town. Waged work was difficult for women to find, but the "informal" economy offered plenty of opportunities for former slaves of both genders. In the period between 1890 and 1930s the size of urban Zanzibar doubled, as thousands upon thousands of former slaves left the rural plantations and moved to the city in search of new opportunities for economic, social, and personal autonomy.

Leaving the plantation and moving to town was certainly one way that many women and men asserted their identities as autonomous social adults, but there were many other ways that these identities were proclaimed, both publicly and privately, as well. Almost immediately following abolition, former slaves of both genders began to adopt forms of dress that they had previously been forbidden from wearing. Owners could no longer prevent a slave from covering his or her body or head, or even from wearing shoes, and within a year of the abolition decree the vast majority of former slaves had adopted clothing styles that were considered more "modest" and appropriate for free coastal Muslims. Consumerism, particularly of clothing, was seized by former slaves as one very visible means of demonstrating both social and economic power. Foreign manufacturers and traders struck it rich in Zanzibar at the turn of the century, as demands for kangas, kofias, kanzus, and even yachting caps, bow ties, and boots soared. In the 1920s and 1930s, former slave women also began to wear the black buibui as an additional expression of their social and moral equality with former mistresses. The buibui gave material expression not only to their desire to be seen as Muslim women worthy of respect, but also to their growing identity as Zanzibaris, or citizens of the isles. Clothing that formerly served to distinguish Arab, Swahili, and indigenous women in the isles was all but abandoned by this time in favor of the brightly colored and constantly changing kanga designs and the black buibui. Asserting control over their own sexuality was another very important component of women's attempts to actualize emancipation. The songs performed by Siti binti Saad's band, which were based on the real-life struggles of the band's friends and neighbors, provide numerous vivid illustrations of women denying the unwanted sexual advances of powerful men, or of women leaving husbands and lovers who were no longer meeting their needs.

Advancing identities as respectworthy women did not mean that women had to deny their sexuality. Rather, for women, actualizing emancipation meant that they should be free to choose with whom and under what terms they would get sexually involved. Former slaves utilized a wide variety of new forms of leisure to express their evolving identities as autonomous, respectworthy social adults.

Islamic ritual and performance were also transformed by former slaves, in the years immediately following abolition, in ways that granted slaves a more central position in religious life. Membership in the religious brotherhoods and participation in zikiri rituals expanded dramatically in the late nineteenth and early twentieth centuries. Many former slaves who had been denied the opportunity to formally study the Qur'an also began to pursue such opportunities after abolition. In the decades to come, they also emphasized the importance of attending Qur'anic school to their children. Former slaves, like Siti binti Saad, used the skills and knowledge they gained from Qur'anic school to enhance their social positions and visibility within Islamic society. Siti binti Saad first began her career as a paid musician by reciting the Qur'an and performing religious poetry for others. No doubt there were many others who made use of these new ritual practices to open doors to economic and social opportunity for themselves.

Former slaves also gradually changed their ethnic self-identities as they attempted to secure respect for their rights as citizens of the isles. In the early 1900s, former slaves moved away from ethnic identities associated with slavery and began to identify themselves as freeborn Swahili. By the late 1910s and early 1920s, these identities as Swahili were also gradually abandoned as former slaves began to assert new identities for themselves and their children as indigenous Zanzibaris. Ancestry carried a lot of weight in coastal society, and during the colonial era indigenous ideas combined with those of British authorities to give new meanings to ethnicity. Coastal residents had a long history of negotiating and transforming their ethnic identities through a variety of forms of public performance and they continued to do this throughout the colonial era, despite British attempts to convince them that ethnicity "should" be a biological given. But local women and men were no dummies. When they saw or heard that the colonial administration was attempting to restrict certain rights—including the right to own land, purchase particular kinds of food, or gain access to credit and marketing facilities—to members of particular ethnic communities, they pragmatically claimed membership within such communities as one means of laying claim to those rights.

Census enumerators employed by the British allowed respondents to identify themselves as a member of only one ethnic category, making the choices and changes in claimed identity seem much more sudden and stark than they probably were. Life histories of urban residents suggest that women and men were rarely required to make such severe choices in the course of their daily lives. The vast majority of the men and women with whom I spoke were raised in ethnically heterogeneous households. An individual who identified as an (Omani) Arab for census purposes many have had a Swahili mother, a Manyema grandmother, a Shihiri uncle, and a Comorian brother-in-law. In most cases these individuals availed themselves of the advantages that came from the diversity of their family's heritage. In the early years of the twentieth century, the overwhelming preference was to keep one's options open, to maintain ties with as many different people and groups as possible, rather than limiting oneself unnecessarily to the confines of a particular, circumscribed ethnic category. Rather than choosing to adopt but one "subjectivity," men and women displayed each of their identities, sometimes in different situations, other times simultaneously. Women had their daughters, nieces, and clients initiated into a new form of female initiation, mkinda, that marked participants not as members of a particular ethnic community, but as urban Zanzibaris. A few weeks before or after this, however, many of these same girls were initiated into the Manyema, Yao, and Zigua forms of unyago by their mothers, aunts, and grandmothers. In the realm of daily performance, it was not necessary to be either an urban Zanzibari or a Manyema; you could be both. Women and men may have readily identified as Manyema on the day of a *tukulanga* ngoma performance in Ng'ambo. But, the following day, when an official from the colonial administration visited them at their farm, a situation in which their identity as a Manyema would have undermined their legal claim to landownership, they probably would have identified as Arab, Hadimu, or Shirazi when asked. Identities, including those of ethnicity, could also be situational.

The principal networks, the axes of alignment, for urban life also shifted over time. From 1890 through World War I, ties based in patron-client give-and-take and rooted in nineteenth-century economic and political alliances remained key to urban social and leisure organizations. Kiunga ties rooted in the land extended to social and cultural domains. Until the 1920s, dance clubs and football teams were organized principally through kiunga ties. A particular club may have taken its name from the Stone Town neighborhood where the club's financiers lived, but it drew its participants from both sides of the creek. The mkinda dance club Malindi relied on the jewelry and clothing provided by elite patrons from Stone Town for its pomp, but it was just as dependent on the beautiful young women from Ng'ambo, who knew how to dance before a crowd, to win the annual competition. Football clubs at this time also reflected and gave cultural form to the social and personal ties that bridged the creek. New Kings, New Generation, and Kidutani drew men from a broad range of class and ethnic backgrounds together in their clubs. What was important for club membership was not a man's heritage, but how well he could handle a football, and the accuracy of his shots on the goal.

Participation in these cross-cutting social and cultural networks did not undermine the recognition of difference, but it did help to prevent these differences from becoming essentialized. The poor of Ng'ambo may have had nothing but disdain for Arab clerks, like Msellem, who used their positions within the administration to defraud the poor of their property, but regularly playing football or dancing mkinda with other Arabs kept them from projecting the negative traits of Msellem onto all Arabs. Certainly there were Asians, like the Remtullas, who seemed to care nothing about the demands of Ng'ambo's poor for affordable housing, but there were also other Asians in Zanzibar Town who helped finance the annual maulid celebration or who bought competition cups for the football league. In the 1930s, ethnic associations became increasingly prominent organizers of social and political life, but friendships built through leisure continued to help negotiate the hardening of ethnic animosities. Even though New Kings broke up in 1932, and Mwalim Jidawi moved over to Arab Sports and Abdulrahman Othman began playing for African Sports, the two men remained on very good terms. Abdulrahman described the matches between African Sports and Arab Sports with intense passion, but he retained immense respect for Jidawi, describing him as a skillful footballer, a marvelous coach, an accomplished teacher, and a very nice man. Through the 1930s, and in some cases well beyond this date, sociability mediated the development of stark divisions between urban Zanzibaris along strict class and ethnic lines. By the 1940s and 1950s, however, there were fewer and fewer leisure activities that worked to bridge the growing divide between residents of Stone Town and Ng'ambo. At the same time that leisure became increasingly segregated along class and ethnic lines, there was a concomitant hardening of political and associational animosities.

Popular pastimes and the communal networks that were crafted through leisure also served as important vehicles through which the African urban poor expanded civil society beyond the narrow boundaries drawn by the British administration. The poor of urban Zanzibar used ground rent strikes, jailbreaks, and popular taarab songs to critique the exercise of colonial power and articulate alternative visions of social, economic, and political order. The African poor were completely excluded from the official debates and institutions of political power, but they made their voices and ideas heard through other mediums that they controlled. The fact that Ng'ambo residents "won" the battle over ground rents illustrates their power to shape society and the islands' political economy; it also demonstrates that colonialism was an interactive process, and that the British and their domestic allies did not always succeed in getting what they wanted in the form they wanted it.

Although the early colonial era was certainly a time of intense economic exploitation, it was also a time of promise and fun. The lively and engrossing urban culture that permeated Zanzibar Town was itself a major factor drawing immigrants to the city. By the 1920s and 1930s, men and women could select from a host of urban entertainments. Ng'ambo was swimming with popular dance ngoma, or if one preferred entertainments of a more sacred kind there were maulid, qasida, or zikiri from which to choose. In the evening, a man could join thousands of others at the Mnazi Mmoja recreation grounds to watch a heated football match. As the sun set, he could then retire to a favorite neighborhood baraza or to a coffee shop that played the latest releases of Siti binti Saad's gramophone discs. Dressing up and going out—to taarab performances, ngoma competitions, or the cinema—provided women and men with important opportunities to revel in their newfound social and personal autonomy. Being part of a large and often boisterous crowd, at an anti-ground rent rally, a football match, or a practice at Siti's home, was also a central component of the interwar urban experience. As Phyllis Martin argues in her study of colonial Brazzaville, leisure "turns out to be an unexpected window on the multi-faceted colonial experience."[1] By looking at leisure and urban popular culture we can see and hear the struggles that took place both between and within the broad categories of colonizer and colonized. But more important to the men and women who lived through the era than the politics of leisure were the numerous ways they could use their popular pastimes to humanize the colonial experience and bring fun and enjoyment to their individual and collective lives.

Notes

Chapter 1

1. *Shairi,* often translated simply as poetry or song, is a verse form typically composed of four lines of sixteen syllables each, which rhyme at the end of each line, as well as in the middle. This form is frequently used for debate in Swahili literature. Jan Knappert, "Swahili tarabu songs," *Afrika and Übersee* 60 (1977): 116-55; Kelly Askew, "Performing the Nation: Swahili Musical Performance and the Production of Tanzanian National Culture," (Ph.D. diss., Harvard, 1997), 148-60; Mohammed Abdulaziz, *Muyaka 19th Century Swahili Popular Poetry* (Nairobi: Kenya Literature Bureau, 1979).

2. The band recorded with the Gramophone Company, the Asian and African arm of His Master's Voice (HMV), in 1928, 1929, and again in 1930. Following on the heels of Gramophone's success, Odeon, Pathé, and Columbia also began to produce Swahili language recordings in 1930. EMI, "Review of the Present Vernacular Record Trade" (unpublished manuscript, 1931), 1-5. This report is identified by Graebner as authored by H. Evans, a representative of EMI in Africa. Werner Graebner, "The First Thirty-Five Years of Commercial Recording in East Africa, 1928-1953," paper delivered at the Institute of African Studies, University of Nairobi, 1989; Paul Vernon, "Feast of East," *Folk Roots* (1995): 26-28; Laura Fair, "Music, Memory and Meaning: The Kiswahili Recordings of Siti binti Saad," *Swahili Forum* 5 (1998): 1-16.

3. Shaaban Robert, *Wasifu wa Siti binti Saad* (1958; reprint, Dar es Salaam: Mkuki na Nyota, 1991), 62; Leila Sheikh-Hashim, "Siti's Magnetic Voice," *Sauti ya Siti* 1, 1 (March 1988): 3-4; W. H. Whiteley, A. A. Jahadhmy, S. Matola, and Mwalim Shaaban, *Waimbaji wa juzi* (Dar es Salaam: Chuo cha Uchunguzi wa lugha ya Kiswahili, 1966). Interviews with Mwalim Idd Farhan,

23 December 1991; Fatma binti Baraka (Bibi Kidude), Kiswandui, 30 September 1991; Said Mohamed, Mwera, 25 March 1992; Nasra Mohamed Hilal, Malindi, 28 July 1991.

4. It was really not until after national independence that one could really speak of anything approaching a vibrant Swahili-language recording industry. Graebner, "The First Thirty-Five Years"; Vernon, "Feast of East"; EMI, "Review of the Present Vernacular Record Trade," unpublished manuscript, 1931. The fact that Siti's records were in fact some of the only Swahili records ever produced certainly must have helped maintain her legacy over the generations.

5. A. A. Suleiman, "The Swahili Singing Star Siti binti Saad," *Swahili* 39, 1 (1969): 87–90. This process was furthered by the selection, in 1931, of the Zanzibar dialect of Kiswahili, known as Kiunguja, as the "standard" Kiswahili promoted by the British throughout East Africa. Wilfred Whiteley, *Swahili: The Rise of a National Language* (London: Methuen, 1969), esp. 79–96.

6. A few of these famous poets would of course include Saiyid Abdalla bin Ali (1720–1820), author of *Utendi wa Inkishafi;* Mwana Kupona, author of *Utendi was Mwana Kupona;* Mujaka bin Haji (1776–1840); and Saiyid Mansab (d. 1922), author of *Maulid Barzanji.* See Mohammed Abdulaziz, *Muyaka: Nineteenth-Century Swahili Popular Poetry* (Nairobi: Kenya Literature Bureau, 1979); Lyndon Harries, *Swahili Poetry* (Oxford: Clarendon Press, 1962); W. E. Taylor, *African Aphorisms* (London: Sheldon Press, 1891); Ann Biersteker, "Language, Poetry and Power: A Reconsideration of 'Utendi wa Mwana Kupona,'" in Kenneth Harrow (ed.), *Faces of Islam in African Literature* (Portsmouth, N.H.: Heinemann, 1991), 59–78; Ibrahim Noor Shariff, *Tungo Zetu* (Trenton, N.J.: Red Sea Press, 1988).

7. The band's popularity allowed them to command fees for one such performance that were well in excess of the average salary earned by a typical unskilled island laborer in an entire year. While playing at a wedding for Ali bin Salim, each member of the band earned Shs 225/ for their performance. On another occasion, in 1936, they were invited to play for a leading family in Pangani, where Siti was given Shs 1200 for one night's work. At this time the average monthly wage for an unskilled laborer in Zanzibar was Shs 30/. Shaaban, *Siti binti Saad,* 59; Whiteley et al., *Waimbaji wa juzi,* 5.

8. Carol Eastman, "Women, Slaves, and Foreigners: African Cultural Influence and Group Processes in the Formation of the Northern Swahili Coastal Society," *International Journal of African Historical Studies* 21, 1 (1988): 1–20; A. H. M. El-Zein, *The Sacred Meadows: A Structural Analysis of Religious Symbolism in an East African Town* (Evanston: Northwestern University Press, 1974); John Middleton, *The World of the Swahili* (New Haven: Yale University Press, 1992).

9. Each of Siti's biographers makes reference to these songs, and in the folklore that surrounds her life they often serve as common tropes suggestive of her unique ability to persevere in the face of trouble. My reading is that they are far more symptomatic of the larger struggles over emancipation and autonomy occurring at this time and that part of the reason for her immense

popularity was that her personal struggles resonated with those of many members of her audience. Muhammed Seif Khatib, *Taarab Zanzibar* (Dar es Salaam: Tanzania Publishing House, 1992), 17; Issa Mgana, *Jukwaa la taarab Zanzibar* (Helsinki: Mradi wa Medafrica, 1991), 42–45; Shaaban, *Siti binti Saad*, 29–32; Nasra Mohamed Hilal, *Siti binti Saad* (Dar es Salaam: Tanzanian Media Women's Association, 1990), videocassette.

10. This and all song translations are my own. While I have attempted to keep the translation as literal as possible, in certain instances, such as this line, it has been necessary to stray from the precise translation in order to convey the meaning as understood in Kiswahili.

11. Interviews with Mwalim Idd Farhan, 23 December 1991; Nasra Mohamed Hilal, Malindi, 28 July 1991; Mgana, *Jukwaa*, 42–46.

12. James Scott, *Weapons of the Weak: Everyday Forms of Peasant Resistance* (New Haven: Yale University Press, 1985).

13. Mark Horton, "Closing the Corridor: Archaeological and Architectural Evidence for Emerging Swahili Regional Autonomy," in David Parkin (ed.), *Continuity and Autonomy in Swahili Communities* (London: School of Oriental and African Studies, 1994), 15–21; G. S. P. Freeman-Grenville (ed.), *The East African Coast: Select Documents from the First Century to the Early Nineteenth Century* (Oxford: Clarendon Press, 1962); Derek Nurse and Thomas Spear, *The Swahili: Reconsidering the History and Language of an African Society, 800–1500* (Philadelphia: University of Pennsylvania Press, 1985); F. B. Pearce, *Zanzibar: The Island Metropolis of Eastern Africa* (London: TF Unwin, 1920), 17–71; James de Vere Allen, *Swahili Origins* (London: James Currey, 1993), 55–76, 165–212; Eastman, "Women, Slaves, and Foreigners," 1–20.

14. Abdul Sheriff, *Slaves, Spices, and Ivory in Zanzibar* (Athens: Ohio University Press, 1987), 8–32; C. S. Nicholls, *The Swahili Coast* (New York: Africana Publishing Corporation, 1971), 19–119; Justus Strandes, *The Portuguese Period in East Africa*, trans. J. F. Wallwork, (1899; reprint, Nairobi: East Africana Literature Bureau, 1961); F. J. Berg, "The Coast from the Portuguese Invasion to the Rise of the Zanzibar Sultanate," in B. A. Ogot and J. A. Kieran (eds.), *Zamani: A Survey of East African History* (Nairobi: East African Publishing House, 1968), 119–41.

15. Sheriff, *Slaves*, 127, 130–33.

16. Ibid., 128–37.

17. W. S. W. Ruschenberger, *Narrative of a Voyage around the World in 1835, 1836, and 1837* (1838; reprint, 2 vols., London: Dawsons of Pall Mall, 1970) 1:64; Charles Guillain, *Documents sur l'histoire, la géographie et le commerce de l'Afrique orientale*, 3 vols. (Paris: Libraries de la Société de Géographie, 1856) 2:80; Joseph Osgood, *Notes of Travel; or, Recollections of Majunga, Zanzibar, Muscat, Aden, Mocha, and Other Eastern Ports* (1854; reprint, Freeport, N.Y.: Books for Libraries Press, 1972), 35; C. P. Rigby, *Report on the Zanzibar Dominions* (Bombay: Education Society Press, 1861), 3; Henry Morton Stanley, *How I Found Livingstone* (New York: Scribner, Armstrong and Co., 1872), 11; James Christie, *Cholera Epidemics in East Africa* (London: MacMillan, 1876), 418.

18. Osgood, *Notes of Travel*, 35; Guillain, *Documents*, 2:78; Richard F. Burton, *Zanzibar: City, Island, and Coast*, 2 vols. (London: Tinsley Brothers, 1872), 1:368–72; R. C. Harkema, "De stad Zanzibar in de tweede helft van de negentiende eeuw" [The town of Zanzibar in the latter half of the nineteenth century] (Ph.D. diss., University of Groningen, 1967), 26–40.

19. Guillain, *Documents*, 2:81; Ruschenberger, *Narrative*, 64; Burton, *Zanzibar*, 1:81; Sheriff, *Slaves*, 60, 228–31; Edward Alpers, *Ivory and Slaves in East Central Africa* (Berkeley: University of California Press, 1975).

20. This estimate was made in 1895 by Sir Lloyd Mathews, first minister of the sultan of Zanzibar. Report of Sir Lloyd Mathews, cited in *Report of the Commission on Agriculture* (Zanzibar: Zanzibar Government Printing Office, 1923), 38.

21. Frederick Cooper, *From Slaves to Squatters: Plantation Labor and Agriculture in Zanzibar and Coastal Kenya, 1890–1925* (1980; reprint, Portsmouth, N.H.: Heinemann, 1997), especially 34–46, 72–84, and 295–96, which provides the text of the abolition decree. Concubines were specifically excluded from the original abolition decree, and were only allowed to claim their freedom in 1909, and then only if they agreed to forfeit custody of their children and rights to material support from their master.

22. J. P. Farler, "Notes on Labour in Pemba, 1898," AB 4/38: Clove Labour, 1898–1926.

23. Others who have examined the process of abolition and emancipation from a social, personal, or family perspective include Barbara Cooper, "Reflections on Slavery, Seclusion and Female Labor in the Maradi Region of Niger in the Nineteenth and Twentieth Centuries," *Journal of African History* 35, 1 (1994): 61–78; Pamela Scully, *Liberating the Family* (Portsmouth, N.H.: Heinemann, 1998); Justin Willis and Suzanne Miers, "Becoming a Child of the House: Incorporation, Authority and Resistance in Giryama Society," *Journal of African History* 38 (1997): 479–95; Claire Robertson, "Post-Proclamation Slavery in Accra: A Female Affair?" in Claire Robertson and Martin Klein (eds.), *Women and Slavery in Africa* (Madison: University of Wisconsin Press, 1983), 220–45; and Marcia Wright, "Bwanikwa: Consciousness and Protest among Slave Women in Central Africa, 1886–1911," in Robertson and Klein (eds.), *Women and Slavery*, 246–270. See also Pier Larson, *History and Memory in the Age of Enslavement: Becoming Merina in Highland Madagascar, 1770–1822* (Portsmouth, N.H.: Heinemann, 2000) for an insightful analysis of the impact of the slave trade on natal communities, families, and politics.

24. Karin Barber, "Popular Arts in Africa," *African Studies Review* 30, 3 (1987): 1–78; Karin Barber, "Views of the Field," in K. Barber (ed.) *Readings in African Popular Culture* (Bloomington: Indiana University Press, 1997), 1–12; Johannes Fabian, *Moments of Freedom: Anthropology and Popular Culture* (Charlottesville: University Press of Virginia, 1998), 1–40.

25. As Frederick Cooper remarked in the preface to the reprint of *From Slaves to Squatters*, "The difficulty in studying the end of slavery . . . is that it is far easier to point to what ended than to what began." This book is an attempt to point at some of "what began." F. Cooper, *Slaves to Squatters*, ix.

26. Robert R. Kuczynski, *Demographic Survey of the British Colonial Empire*, 2 vols. (London: Oxford University Press, 1949) 2: 651–52.

27. Such divisions were also a cornerstone of early Swahili scholarship, written largely by anthropologists who tended to seek out their principal informants from among the ranks of patricians. Patrician worldviews fit nicely with the binary oppositions which dominated scholarship of the 1960s, 1970s, and early 1980s. Studies that emphasize interplay between city and country include Nurse and Spear, *Swahili;* James de Vere Allen, "Swahili Culture Reconsidered: Some Historical Implications of the Material Culture of the Northern Kenya Coast in the Eighteenth and Nineteenth Centuries," *Azania* 9 (1974): 105–37; Justin Willis, *Mombasa, the Swahili, and the Making of the Mijikenda* (Oxford: Clarendon Press, 1995); Garth Andrew Myers, "Sticks and Stones: Colonialism and Zanzibari Housing," *Africa* 67, 2 (1997): 252–72; Jonathon Glassman, *Feasts and Riot: Revelry, Rebellion, and Popular Consciousness on the Swahili Coast, 1856–1888* (Portsmouth, N.H.: Heinemann, 1995).

28. Christie, *Cholera*, 312.

29. Frederick Cooper, *Plantation Slavery on the East Coast of Africa* (New Haven: Yale University Press, 1977), 182–252; Jonathon Glassman, "The Bondsman's New Clothes: The Contradictory Consciousness of Slave Resistance on the Swahili Coast," *Journal of African History* 32 (1991): 277–312.

30. Emily Ruete, *Memoirs of an Arabian Princess from Zanzibar* (1888; reprint, New York: Marcus Weiner, 1989), 54, 64–66, 81, 85–90, 146; Miss Allen, "Glimpses of Harem Life," *Central Africa* (1883), 147–49; Edward D. Ropes Jr., *The Zanzibar Letters of Edward D. Ropes Jr., 1882–92*, ed. Norman Bennett (Boston: Boston University African Studies Center, 1973), 11.

31. Margaret Strobel, *Muslim Women in Mombasa, 1890–1975* (New Haven: Yale University Press, 1979); Sarah Mirza and Margaret Strobel, *Three Swahili Women: Life Histories from Mombasa, Kenya* (Bloomington: Indiana University Press, 1989), 17–40, 69–86; interviews with Amina Seif Othman (Bibi Amina Mapande), Michenzani, 19 July 1995; Arafa Salum Ahmed, Malindi, 9 July 1995; response of Latifuu Ali Marzuk to clothing survey, Kisimamajongoo, 16 August 1995.

32. Claire Robertson and Martin Klein, "Women's Importance in African Slave Systems," and Margaret Strobel, "Slavery and Reproductive Labor in Mombasa," both in Claire Robertson and Martin Klein, *Women and Slavery in Africa* (Madison: University of Wisconsin Press, 1983), 3–28 and 111–129.

33. Response of Adija Salum Bakari to clothing survey, Miembeni, 3 July 1995.

34. In the nineteenth century elite women often scorned slave initiation ceremonies or if they did have their daughters taught the lessons of initiation it was in private rather than as part of a public celebration. Laura Fair, "Identity, Difference and Dance: Female Initiation in Zanzibar, 1890–1930," *Frontiers* 17, 3 (1996): 146–72; Strobel, *Muslim Women*, 10–12, 196–203; Mirza and Strobel, *Three Swahili Women*, 70–71, 81, 98.

35. August Nimtz, *Islam and Politics in East Africa: The Sufi Order in Tanzania* (Minneapolis: University of Minnesota Press, 1980), 55–94; Glassman, *Feasts and Riot*, 133–45; Peter Lienhardt, "The Mosque College of Lamu and Its Social Background," *Tanganyikan Notes and Records* 52 (1959): 228–42; C. H. Becker, "Materials for the Understanding of Islam in German East Africa," originally published in 1911, edited and translated by B. G. Martin, *Tanzanian Notes and Records* 68 (1968): 31–61.

36. Fazlur Rahman, *Islam* (Chicago: University of Chicago Press, 1966); J. Spencer Trimingham, *The Sufi Orders in Islam* (Oxford: Clarendon Press, 1971); Becker, "Islam in German East Africa"; Randall Pouwels, *Horn and Crescent: Cultural Change and Traditional Islam on the East African Coast, 800–1900* (Cambridge: Cambridge University Press, 1987), 143–44; Nimtz, *Islam and Politics*, 55–94.

37. Nimtz, *Islam and Politics*, 118–34, 141; Sheikh Abdallah Salih Farsy, *The Shafi'i Ulama of East Africa, c. 1830–1970: A Hagiographic Account*, ed. and trans. Randall Pouwels (Madison: University of Wisconsin African Studies Center, 1989); Pouwels, *Horn and Crescent*, 155–62; J. Spencer Trimingham, *Islam in East Africa* (Oxford: Clarendon Press, 1964), 93–103.

38. The performance of *dhikr* rituals (*zikiri* in Kiswahili), or the "remembrance of God," through the continuous repetition of some of the ninety-nine Beautiful Names of God, derived from the Qur'an, while simultaneously bowing forward and backward, turning from side to side, or spinning in a circle, is common to the devotional practices of the brotherhoods. Zikiri are usually performed collectively, with the members of a given brotherhood gathering regularly to perform the ritual in a member's home, in a mosque, or in the streets of a neighborhood. By the 1910s and 1920s, zikiri rituals occurred almost nightly in the isles, drawing men and women from a cross-section of society together to sing and drum and pray well into the morning. Captain J. E. E. Craster, *Pemba, the Spice Island of Zanzibar* (London: T. Fisher Unwin, 1913), 31–11; Valerie Hoffman, *Sufism, Mystics, and Saints in Modern Egypt* (Columbia: University of South Carolina Press, 1998).

39. Garth Andrew Myers, "Eurocentrism and African Urbanization: The Case of Zanzibar's Other Side," *Antipode* 26, 3 (1994): 195–215.

40. Benedict Anderson, *Imagined Communities: Reflection on the Origin and Spread of Nationalism* (London: Verso, 1983); Charles Ambler, *Kenyan Communities in the Age of Imperialism: The Central Region in the Late Nineteenth Century* (New Haven: Yale University Press, 1988); Bill Bravman, *Making Ethnic Ways: Communities and Their Transformations in Taita, Kenya, 1800–1950* (Portsmouth, N.H.: Heinemann, 1988).

41. Willis, *Mombasa*, 95–113, 174–200; Frederick Cooper, *On the African Waterfront: Urban Disorder and the Transformation of Work in Colonial Mombasa* (New Haven: Yale University Press, 1987).

42. Interview with Salum Baraka Said, Miembeni, 13 July 1992.

43. Interview with Nunu binti Salum (Bibi Raba), Kiswandui, 18 March 1992.

44. AB 39/337: Rules under the Ngoma Regulation Decree, 1929–53.

These nightly soirees provided important opportunities for large numbers of urban men and women to earn a living as musicians, singers, and dancers. According to E. Batson's 1948 social survey, more than 25 percent of urban African and Arab women earned their livings through entertainment. A large number of men were similarly employed, although less than 2 percent of the urban male population relied exclusively on income generated from entertainment to support themselves. Batson, *Social Survey of Zanzibar Protectorate*, 21 vols. (Cape Town: School of Social Sciences and Social Administration at the University of Cape Town, 1960), vol. 13. Jahadhmy also relates that the vibrant nightlife of Zanzibar drew musicians from the mainland to Ng'ambo, where it was said a musician could play music all day and all night and live "in comfort and with respect." In Whiteley et al., *Waimbaji wa juzi*, 66.

45. Luise White, "Between Gluckman and Foucault: Historicizing Rumor and Gossip," *Social Dynamics* 20, 1 (1994): 75–92; A. L. Epstein, "Gossip, Norms and Social Networks," in J. Clyde Mitchell (ed.), *Social Networks in Urban Situations* (Manchester: Manchester University Press, 1969), 117–27; James Scott, *Weapons of the Weak*, 1–47.

46. Timothy Mitchell, "Everyday Metaphors of Power," *Theory and Society* 19 (1990): 545–77, a critique of James Scott, *Weapons of the Weak*.

47. James Scott, *Domination and the Arts of Resistance* (New Haven: Yale University Press, 1990).

48. George Lipsitz, *Time Passages: Collective Memory and American Popular Culture* (Minneapolis: University of Minnesota Press, 1990), 16–17.

49. Murray Edelman, *From Art to Politics* (Chicago: University of Chicago Press, 1995).

50. Mtoro bin Mwinyi Bakari, *The Customs of the Swahili People: The Desturi za Waswahili of Mtoro bin Mwinyi Bakari and Other Swahili Persons*, ed. and trans. J. W. T. Allen, (Los Angeles: University of California Press, 1981). Mtoro's collection was originally published by Carl Velten as *Desturi za Wasuaheli na Habari za Desturi za Sheria za Wasuaheli* (Göttingen: Dandenhoed and Ruprecht, 1903); Ali bin Hemedi, "Habari za Mrima," *Mambo Leo* (Dar es Salaam), September 1934–35, 141–47; Terrence Ranger, *Dance and Society in Eastern Africa* (Berkeley: University of California Press, 1975); Strobel, *Muslim Women*.

51. Glassman, *Feasts and Riot*, 117–74.

52. Liisa Malkki, *Purity and Exile: Violence, Memory, and National Cosmology among Hutu Refugees in Tanzania* (Chicago: University of Chicago, 1995), 169–70.

53. Although discourses of ethnicity, both as ways of thinking and of talking about social reality, were new to island residents, certain principles reflected long-standing categories of debate among coastal residents. Leroy Vail (ed.), *The Creation of Tribalism in Southern Africa* (London: James Currey, 1989), 1–19; Catherine Newbury, *The Cohesion of Oppression: Clientship and Ethnicity in Rwanda, 1860–1960* (New York: Columbia University Press, 1988); Bravman, *Making Ethnic Ways;* John Iliffe, *A Modern History of Tanganyika* (Cambridge: Cambridge University Press, 1979), 318–341; Willis, *Mombasa*.

54. I thank Chris Walley for encouraging me to think through these connections between ideas of kinship and ethnicity. For her own discussion of the interrelationship of kinship, ethnicity, and community see Christine J. Walley, "Making Waves: Struggles over the Environment, Development and Participation in the Mafia Island Marine Park, Tanzania," (Ph.D. diss., New York University, 1999), esp. 192-262.

55. Willis, *Mombasa*, 12-13, Willis and Meirs, "Becoming and Child of the House;" Glassman, *Feasts and Riot.*

56. Ruschenberger, *Narrative*, 2: 64; Burton, *Zanzibar* 1:81; Guillain, *Documents* 2:81.

57. Mathews, in *Report of the Commission on Agriculture*, 38.

58. AB 4/38 (A): Clove Labour, 1898-1926. Men and women identified as members of the Zaramu ethnic category, many of whom were also brought to the isles as slaves, were the least likely to change ethnic identities in the early decades of the twentieth century. Although some Zaramu were slaves, many others were not, and in the early decades of the century many Zaramu voluntarily immigrated to Zanzibar, thus enhancing the ability of all Zaramu to claim that they were descendants of free ancestors.

59. Nurse and Spear, *Swahili*, 1-31, 80-98; J. Allen, *Swahili Origins*, 1-20, 55-77; Carol Eastman, "Who Are the Waswahili?" *Africa* 41, 3 (1971): 228-36; W. Arens, "The Waswahili: The Social History of an Ethnic Group," *Africa* 45, 4 (1975): 426-38; A. H. J. Prins, *The Swahili-Speaking Peoples of Zanzibar and the East African Coast (Arabs, Shirazi and Swahili)* (London: International African Institute, 1961).

60. Charles New, *Life, Wanderings and Labours in Eastern Africa* (1873; reprint, London: Frank Cass, 1971), 56.

61. Ethel Younghusband, *Glimpses of East Africa and Zanzibar* (London: John Long, 1908), 30, 255-57; W. H. Ingrams, *Zanzibar: Its History and Its People* (London: HF and G Witherby, 1931), 220; Pearce, *Zanzibar*, 235-47; Mervyn Beech, "Slavery on the East Coast of Africa," *Journal of the African Society* 15 (1916): 145-49; Bibi Khole to Wakf Commission, June 1915, and Bibi Khole to Copland, 11 December 1917, HD 6/55: Wakf of Seyyid Hamoud bin Ahmed. Similar process were at work in many coastal towns during this period. See Glassman, *Feasts and Riot*, 25, 95, 117-45; Willis, *Mombasa*, 95-114.

62. AB 4/38: *Clove Labour; Zanzibar Colony Blue Books* (Zanzibar: Zanzibar Government Printer, 1913 and 1916) U3; *Annual Report of the Agriculture Department* (Zanzibar: Government Printer, 1911); AB 36/12: Proposed Ground Rent Decree, 1912-1917.

63. Christie, *Cholera*, 312, 330; Burton, *Zanzibar*, 2:80, 95, 365; Edward Vizetelly, *From Cyprus to Zanzibar, by the Egyptian Delta* (London: Arthur Pearson, 1901), 402; AB 4/38: *Blue Books.*

64. Historically, African women's labor has often been concentrated in the "informal" sector. Susan Geiger, *TANU Women: Gender and Culture in the Making of Tanganyikan Nationalism, 1955-1965* (Portsmouth, N.H.: Heinemann, 1997), 20-44; Deborah F. Bryceson, "A Century of Food Supply in Dar es Salaam," in Jane Guyer (ed.), *Feeding African Cities* (Bloomington: In-

diana University Press, 1987); George Chauncey, "The Locus of Reproduction: Women's Labour in the Zambian Copperbelt, 1927-53," *Journal of Southern African Studies* 7 (1981).

65. By the 1940s, some 90 percent of African women in Zanzibar Town were earning an income separate from their husbands or fathers, compared to less than 5 percent of rural women. Batson, *Social Survey*, vols. 5, 13.

66. List of Deeds Showing Hut Sales on Government Land at Mchangani, 1897-1904, AE 8/10: Land at Mlandege Claimed by Gulamhussein Remtulla Hemani; Deeds of Sale, Zizi la Ng'ombe, AE 8/10; HD 3/28: Collection of Ground Rent, Wakf Department; List of Kiwanja Owners in Arrears to Tharia Topan, 21 December 1928, AB 36/13: Ground Rent Restriction Decree, 1927-33.

67. Interviews with Mwajuma Ali, Shauri Moyo, 26 April 1992; Adija Salum Bakari, Miembeni, 23 March 1992; Nasra Mohamed Hilal, Malindi, 28 July 1991; Fatuma Khamisi, Shauri Moyo, 26 April 1992. This was true not only for the isles, but more generally for the entire African continent. Luise White, "A Colonial State and an African Petty Bourgeoisie: Prostitution, Property and Class Struggle in Nairobi, 1936-40," in Frederick Cooper (ed.), *Struggle for the City: Migrant Labor, Capital and the State in Urban Africa* (Beverly Hills: Sage, 1983), 167-94; Kristin Mann, "Women, Landed Property and the Accumulation of Wealth in Early Colonial Lagos," *Signs* 16, 4 (1991): 682-706.

68. The 1924 census gives the occupational breakdown of men in the isles. Those who were identified in the census as "cultivators," implying no freehold ownership of land, were either Hadimu, who owned land collectively, or members of ethnic categories associated with slavery. Squatters on former owners' plantations were allowed to grow annual crops, but rarely tree crops. The other important "occupational" categories were shamba owners or weeders. Those in the later category were mostly migrant wage laborers, and predominantly Nyamwezi. BA 34/2: Report of the Native Census of Zanzibar Island, 1924. For a discussion of the problematics of interpreting census data, see F. Cooper, *Slaves to Squatters*, 158-164.

69. In general, women were preferred as slaves within the African continent, although the specific gender balances within any given population varied considerably depending on the uses to which slave labor was put. Cooper's work on Zanzibar suggests that overall the gender balance of the island's slave population was fairly equal. Robertson and Klein, "Women's Importance," 3-25; F. Cooper, *Plantation Slavery*, 221-23.

70. Similar appropriations of the Swahili identity occurred throughout the coast. Glassman, *Feasts and Riot*, 25; Captain C. H. Stigand, *The Land of Zinj* (London: Constable and Company, 1913), 115-16; Beech, "Slavery on the East Coast," 146; Peter Lienhardt, Introduction to *The Medicine Man: Swifa ya Nguvumali* by Hasani bin Ismail (Oxford: Clarendon Press, 1968), 11-12.

71. *Report on the Administration of Zanzibar, 1908*; *Medical Reports* 1912-1921, as cited in Kuczynski, *Demographic Survey*, 660-68. These figures lead

successive Medical Officers of Health to conclude that the Swahili—widely regarded among colonial administrators as inherently promiscuous, disease ridden, and generally immoral—were killing off their own race as a result of their fun-loving, pleasure-seeking, and irresponsible lifestyles. Remarks made by W. H. Ingrams about the Swahili in Zanzibar were typical of British perceptions throughout the coast: "These people are utterly detribalized," "they regard their marriage ties very loosely indeed," and "the bulk of the jail population is drawn from this class. . . . Here we have the habitual thieves, gamblers and drunkards." Ingrams, *Zanzibar: Its History,* 220–23. As Willis concluded in his study of the Swahili in Mombasa, however, the negative stereotypes held by administrators were based more on the Swahilis' effective ability to evade colonial tax and labor controls than any precise evidence regarding the prevalence of prostitution, venereal disease, or vagrancy among Swahili urban residents. The Swahili were "bad" because they belied British attempts to reify them as a proper and controllable "tribe." Willis, *Mombasa,* 107–11.

72. Prins, *Swahili-Speaking Peoples,* 11.

73. Beech, "Slavery on the East Coast," 146, n. 2; Lienhardt, introduction to *Medicine Man,* 12.

74. The Shirazi ethnic identity has it roots in the oral tradition of Hasan bin Ali, who is said to have fled Shiraz (Persia/Iran) in 975, because of religious persecution. Hasan and his six sons, each of whom traveled in a separate boat, allegedly arrived at various ports along the East African coast and established themselves as the ruling dynasty of various Swahili city-states, including settlements in Zanzibar and Pemba. Debates about the validity of this tradition have been at the core of both written and oral East African coastal historiography. For various perspectives on this debates, see J. Allen, *Swahili Origins;* Nurse and Spear, *Swahili,* 70–79; Freeman-Grenville, *East African Coast;* J. M. Sir John Gray, "Zanzibar Local Histories," *Swahili* 30 (1959): 24–50; 31 (1960): 111–39; N. Chittick, "The 'Shirazi' Colonization of East Africa," *Journal of African History* 6 (1965): 275–94. This tradition is still widely debated in Zanzibar and throughout the coast. Chizuko Tominaga and Abdul Sheriff have produced an enlightened analysis of these debates, arguing that there is a kernel of truth to this tradition but that "the importance of the tradition does not lie in its genetics but as a socio-historical phenomenon." Tominaga and Sheriff, "The Ambiguity of Shirazi Ethnicity in the History and Politics of Zanzibar," (unpublished manuscript), 5.

75. John Middleton, *Land Tenure in Zanzibar* (London: His Majesty's Stationery Office, 1961), 43, 69–70, 77; C. K. Meek, *Land Law and Custom in the Colonies* (London: Oxford University Press, 1946), 72–75, 230–42; Ingrams, *Zanzibar: Its History,* 274; Prins, *Swahili-Speaking Peoples,* 61–64; AU 3/95: Land Tenure and Leases, 1932–58; AK 13/1: *Siri* (Confidential): Middleton Report on Land Tenure, 1959.

76. Memo to Assistant Collector, 1910, and Notes on a Paper by the Director of Agriculture on Increasing the Hut Tax, Made by the Collector of Zanzibar, 26 June, 1909, AB 36/20: Ground Rents 1898–1912.

77. F. Cooper, *Slaves to Squatters*, 163.

78. Ibid., 69–121; AB 4/38 (A): Clove Labour, 1898–1926; AU 1/13: Labour on Clove Plantations; AU 3/61: Mainland Labour; AB 36/20: Ground Rents, 1901–1912.

79. Among those sold at this time were plantations at Kinaoni, Mbaleni, Bumbwi, Kisauni, Kibweni, Migombani, Chuini, and Bet el-Ras. *Report of the Department of Agriculture, 1910*; *Report of the Commission on Agriculture, 1923*, 15, 17, 21.

80. *Report of the Department of Agriculture, 1910*; *Report of the Commission of Agriculture, 1923*; Craster, *Pemba*, 207–8; R. S. Troup, *Report on Clove Cultivation in the Zanzibar Protectorate* (Zanzibar: Government Printing Office, 1932), 41; *Memorandum on Certain Aspects of the Zanzibar Clove Industry* (Zanzibar: Government Printing Office, 1926); Bartlett and Last, *Report on the Indebtedness of the Agricultural Class* (Zanzibar: Government Printing Office, 1932); HC 8/50, 81, 85: Debates of the Legislative Council; HC 8/81; HC 8/85; Yusufali Esmailjee Jivanje, *Memorandum on the Commission of Agriculture* (Poona, 1923).

81. According to Batson's social survey, conducted in 1948 and 1949, men born before 1909 were generally twice as likely to own farms containing cloves and coconuts as those born between 1910 and 1934. BA 28: Batson, *Social Survey*, vol. 15.

82. The Clove Bonus Scheme was introduced in 1922 in an effort to encourage regeneration of old plantations. Owners of bearing clove trees were paid a "bonus" while those with planted seedlings were paid even more.

83. *Memorandum on the Clove Industry*; Minority Report, *Report of the Commission on Agriculture*, 1923. Ten years later, in 1932, however, the average size of Hadimu holdings on Zanzibar had risen to forty-nine trees. The differential between large-holding Arabs and smallholding indigenous islanders remained, however, with the latter constituting 83 percent of the owners of farms with fewer than 100 clove trees and only 4 percent of the owners of plantations with 1,000 or more trees. Sir Alan Pim, *Report of the Commission Appointed to Consider and Report on the Financial Position and Policy of the Zanzibar Government in Relation to Its Economic Resources* (Zanzibar: Government Printing Office, 1932), as cited in Prins, *Swahili-Speaking Peoples*, 64.

84. According to Bartlett and Last, in the Fumba region in the south of Zanzibar Island, 983 of 1,500 coconut plantations were owned by persons who identified themselves as indigenous Zanzibaris. Bartlett and Last, *Report on Indebtedness*.

85. The physical geography of Unguja island is divided into quite distinctive vegetative zones, based both on soil types and rainfall patterns. The "clove zone" in the central and western parts of the island has dark, rich soils and ample rains for agriculture. The northern and eastern parts of the island, known locally as *wanda* and historically occupied by the Hadimu and Tumbatu, have much rockier soils and receive less rainfall. The Hadimu and Tumbatu raise agricultural crops suitable to the environment, but they also tend to cluster their villages along the coast so they can take advantage of the rich

fisheries off the island. It is highly unlikely that the growth of the "indigenous" peasant smallholder population reflected an effort at economic diversification among those historically identifying as Hadimu and Tumbatu, as the rocky soils and low rainfalls make these areas generally unsuited for clove cultivation. There is also no evidence of large-scale migration from the eastern and northern parts of the isles to the clove belt.

86. Public Lands Decree of 1921 and 10 of 1954, cited in Middleton, *Land Tenure*, 70.

87. *Report of the Commission on Agriculture, 1923.* According to M. A. Ghassany (Mzee Bingwa), a longtime employee of the Ministry of Agriculture in Zanzibar, in 1902 the property of the sultan, including the family's numerous clove plantations, came under control of the Colonial Office. Operating these plantations was not very cost effective, so the administration began selling them off. Interview with M. A. Ghassany, Vuga, 14 July 1992. *Copyhold tenure* is a term borrowed from English land law and is defined by Meek as "tenure of lands being parcel of a manor, 'at the will of the lord according to the custom of the manor' by copy of the manorial court-roll." Meek, *Land Law*, 321. For a complete list of the plantations sold by the state as of 1931 see BA 16/41: Debates of the Legislative Council, 6 January 1938.

88. AP 29/1–4, 17: Clove Bonus Registers, 1924–1928.

89. Craster, *Pemba*, 95; Beech, "Slavery on the East Coast," 145.

90. Abdul Sheriff, "An Outline History of Zanzibar Stone Town," in A. Sheriff (ed.), *The History and Conservation of Zanzibar Stone Town* (Athens: Ohio University Press, 1995), 8–29.

91. Although neither the origins of this song nor the details of how it came to be sung to the tune of "Yankee Doodle" are known, there are wonderful parallels between the common American version and the Zanzibari version. The tune of "Yankee Doodle" is based on an American folk melody and dates from at least 1740. The tune became widely popular among Americans and hundreds of different verses were set to the tune in the eighteenth century. The most widely known verse goes "Yankee Doodle went to town riding on a pony / stuck a feather in his cap and called it macaroni." "Yankee Doodle" has been interpreted by some scholars of American cultural history as a colloquial reference to the allegedly backward and barbaric nature of Americans as perceived by Europeans of the era. In both the American and Zanzibari versions then, a rural bumpkin goes to town with the aim of transforming his or her perceived identity. *Macaroni* was an eighteenth-century term used in reference to self-consciously high-styled English men, whose dress immediately marked them as flamboyant, affected urbanites. It is entirely plausible that in the course of late-evening discussions and entertainment, a nineteenth-century American trader or sailor introduced the tune to a Zanzibari counterpart, who in turn crafted a localized version in which a nice, city house served as the island equivalent of culture and civilization symbolized by the Macaroni's feathered cap. I am grateful to Matthew Dennis, a colleague in the history department at the University of Oregon, for tips on the origin and meaning of "Yankee Doodle." Kenneth Silverman, *A Cul-*

tural History of the American Revolution (New York: Thomas Crowell, 1976), 275, 289–95, 559–61; J. A. Leo Lemay, "The American Origins of 'Yankee Doodle,'" *William and Mary Quarterly* 33, 3 (1976): 435–64; Ona and Peter Opie (eds.), *The Oxford Dictionary of Nursery Rhymes* (Oxford: Oxford University Press, 1997), 528–32; James Fuld, *The Book of World-Famous Music: Classical, Popular and Folk* (New York: Crown, 1966), 659–60.

92. It appears as though the vast majority of men and women in the isles paid little heed to the creation of the Legislative Council. The male coastal elite had always engaged in closed-door discussions of political and economic affairs. In the nineteenth century, the sultans of Zanzibar held regular Friday *baraza* (discussions or meetings), which were attended primarily by key diplomatic, mercantile, landholding, judicial, and religious authorities. Poor men and women were theoretically permitted to present their concerns at these baraza, but in reality few did, preferring less formal, more personalized avenues for addressing their grievances. Presumably then, the majority of the islands' populace, who continued to operate under conceptions of citizenship that centered on consumption, display, and personal networking, initially found little new or threatening in the establishment of the Legislative Council, or the fact that only the most powerful Asian, Arab, and British men were invited to participate in council affairs.

93. AB 8/87: Report of the Committee Appointed to Advise on Matters Relating to Native Administration, 1932–39.

94. Mahmood Mamdani, *Citizen and Subject: Contemporary Africa and the Legacy of Late Colonialism* (Princeton: Princeton University Press, 1996).

95. The Kilwa Chronicle, in Freeman-Grenville, *East African Coast;* Pouwels, *Horn and Crescent,* 2–3, 72–74; Prins, *Swahili-Speaking Peoples,* 40–42.

96. Pouwels, *Horn and Crescent,* 128–31; J. Allen, "Swahili Culture Reconsidered," 105–37; Eastman, "Women, Slaves and Foreigners," 1–20.

97. Glassman provides numerous examples of individuals refashioning their identities during the nineteenth century in such ways and also documents cases of slaves, porters, and other newcomers to coastal towns defining themselves as mwungwana to distinguish themselves from up-country "bumpkins." Glassman, *Feasts and Riot,* 61–64, 117–74; Pouwels, *Horn and Crescent,* 75–80; Prins, *Swahili-Speaking Peoples,* 13.

98. L. W. Hollingsworth, *Zanzibar under the Foreign Office, 1890–1913* (London: MacMillan, 1953); AB 8/87: Report of the Committee Appointed to Advise on Matters Relating to Native Administration, 1932.

99. AB 10/: Records of the sultan and royal family; Pouwels, *Horn and Crescent,* 167–77.

100. Pearce, *Zanzibar,* 214–34; *Memorandum on the Clove Industry,* 1–3.

101. Ed Ferguson, "The Formation of a Colonial Economy, 1915–1945," in A. Sheriff and E. Ferguson (eds.), *Zanzibar under Colonial Rule* (Athens: Ohio University Press, 1991), 36–78; Abdul Sheriff, "The Peasantry under Imperialism, 1873–1963," in Sheriff and Ferguson (eds.), *Zanzibar under Colonial Rule,* 120–33; J. R. Mlahagwa and A. J. Temu, "The Decline of the Landlords, 1873–63," in Sheriff and Ferguson (eds.), *Zanzibar under Colonial*

Rule, 145, 157-60; A. I. Salim notes a similar pattern on the Kenya coast. Salim, *The Swahili-Speaking Peoples of the Kenyan Coast, 1895-1963* (Nairobi: East African Publishing House, 1973).

102. District Commissioner Pemba to Provincial Commissioner, 2 September 1940; Secretary of Shirazi Association, Ali Sharifu, to District Commissioner of Pemba, 29 September 1940; Address by Secretary of the Shirazi Association to Chief Secretary, 8 October 1948; AB 12/2: Shirazi Association, 1940-53; Abdulrahman Ali Saleh to Sheikh Suleiman Othman, 15 December 1990, personal correspondence on the origins of the Shirazi Association, conveyed to the author by Abdulrahman Ali Saleh; Sheriff, "Peasantry," 134-35.

103. It was in light of this "predicament" that Ibuni Saleh, a leading member of the Comorian Association, published his history of the community in Zanzibar, in which some of these arguments were put forth in print. Ibuni Saleh, *A Short History of the Comorians in Zanzibar* (Dar es Salaam: Tanganyikan Standard, 1936), introduction.

104. The provisions of the decree were simply not applied within the limits of the town of Zanzibar, which is where the majority of Comorians resided. BA 16/40: Report of the Select Committee of the Legislative Council Appointed to Consider and Report upon the Native Administration and Authority Bill, 1930, Debates of the Legislative Council, 6 March 1931.

105. PC to Chief Secretary 5 October 1939, AB 8/87: Report of the Committee Appointed to Advise on Matters Relating to Native Administration, 1932-39.

106. The fact that ration cards indicating a family's race were based on the ethnicity of the male head of household, if in fact there was one, again reveals the state's lack of understanding of the ethnic complexity within the islands' families. In one household it would not be uncommon to find a Swahili woman who had children from three previous marriages. These children could perhaps all have different "ethnicities," as the ethnicity of a child often, though not necessarily, followed that of the father. Let us say that the woman's current husband was Comorian. A family classified by the state as Comorian could easily have included family members of Swahili, Hadimu, Shirazi, Arab, and Zaramu descent, although in this instance they too would have probably preferred to be labeled Comorian.

107. Sidney Mintz, *Sweetness and Power: The Place of Sugar in Modern History* (New York: Viking, 1985), 13, 154; Victoria de Grazia (ed.), *The Sex of Things: Gender and Consumption in Historical Perspective* (Berkeley: University of California Press, 1996); Amy Bentley, *Eating for Victory: Food Rationing and the Politics of Domesticity* (Urbana: University of Illinois Press, 1998).

108. Edward Batson, *Report on Proposals for a Social Survey of Zanzibar* (Zanzibar: Government Printing Office Press, 1948), 24; AU 2/59: Record of Mudirs' Meetings, 1944-57.

109. Record of Mudirs' Meeting, 12 May 1944, AU 2/59.

110. Interviews with Ali Makame, CCM Headquarters, Vikokotoni, 13 January 1992; Omar Zahran, Malindi, 31 May 1992; Mbarak Mtubwe, Makunduchi, 25 February 1992; Abdalla Aziz, Makunduchi, 25 February

1992; Abdulrahman Ali Saleh, Saleh Madawa, 26 June 1991; Nunu binti Sa-lum, Kiswandui, 18 March 1992; Pili Jaha Ubwa, Shaangani, 18 February 1991; Mwajuma Ali, Shauri Moyo, 26 April 1992; Mwalim Idd Farhan, 23 December 1991; Ali Haji Muadhini, Makunduchi, 25 February 1992; Adija Haji Simai, Michenzani, 17 January 1992.

111. Provincial Commissioner to District Commissioner, 10 February 1943, AK 17/70: Rationing.

112. Zanzibar Protectorate, *Nutritional Review of the Natives of Zanzibar* (Zanzibar: Government Printer, 1937), as cited in Ferguson, "Formation of a Colonial Economy," n. 54.

113. A. Bentley, *Eating for Victory*, 62, 87.

114. Jamal Ramadhan Nasibu, 19 February 1991.

115. AK 17/70: Rationing; AB 12/2: Shirazi Association; Report on the Zanzibar District for the month of September 1944, BA 30/8; AU 2/59: Record of Mudirs' Meetings, 1944–57; interview with Omar Zahran, Malindi, 31 May 1992.

116. Pierre Bourdieu, *Distinction: A Social Critique of the Judgement of Taste* (London: Routledge and Kegan Paul, 1984); Peter Farb and George Amrelagos, *Consuming Passions: The Anthropology of Eating* (Boston: Houghton Mifflin, 1980); Marvin Harris, *The Sacred Cow and the Abominable Pig: Riddles of Food and Culture* (New York: Simon and Schuster, 1985).

117. Mintz, *Sweetness and Power*, 3–4.

118. African disaffection with the rationing policy was compounded by the imposition of forced food cultivation on the "African" population. In 1939 a food planting campaign was initiated, and by 1942 thousands of African men, many of whom were from town, were being forced, without monetary compensation, to clear and cultivate state-owned land in the countryside in order to feed the islands' population during the war. Memo from the Chief Secretary regarding his meeting with members of the Shirazi Association and the African Association, September 1943, AB 12/2: Shirazi Association, 1940–53; AK 17/70: Rationing; BA 30/8: Record of Mudirs' Meetings, 1944–57; BA 16/41: Debates of the Legislative Council, 1939–45; *Zanzibar Annual Colonial Report* (Zanzibar: Government Printing Office, 1946), 4.

119. Provincial Commissioner to Chief Secretary, 6.30.44, AK 17/70: Rationing.

120. Interviews with Ali Haji Muadhini, Makunduchi, 25 February 1991; Mwajuma Ali, Shauri Moyo, 26 April 1992; Abdulrahman Ali Saleh, Saleh Madawa, 26 June 1992; Ali Makame, CCM Headquarters, Vikokotoni, 13 January 1992; Jamal Ramadhan Nasibu, CCM Headquarters, Vikokotoni, 19 February 1991; Pili Jaha Ubwa, Shaangani, 18 February 1991; Report on the Zanzibar District for the month of September 1944, BA 30/8; Middleton, *Land Tenure*, 7; Shariff Omar, *Kisiwa cha Pemba: Historia na Masimulizi* (Nairobi: Eagle Press, 1951), ch. 4; Juma Aley, *Zanzibar, in the Context* (New Delhi: Lancers Books, 1988); AB 12/2: Shirazi Association, 1940–53.

121. Interview with Jamal Ramadhan Nasibu, CCM Headquarters, Vikokotoni, 19 February 1991.

122. AU 2/59: Record of Mudirs' Meetings; Interviews with Nunu binti Salum, Kiswandui, 18 March 1992; Pili Jaha Ubwa, Shaangani, 18 February 1991; Jamal Ramadhan Nasibu, CCM Headquarters, Vikokotoni, 19 February 1991; Ali Makame, CCM Headquarters, Vikokotoni, 13 January 1992; Abdulrahman Ali Saleh, Saleh Madawa, 26 June 1991; Omar Zahran, Malindi, 31 May 1992; Adija Haji Simai, Michenzani, 17 January 1992.

123. J. P. Farler, "Notes on Labor in Pemba, 1898," J. T. Last, "The Labour Question," Rogers to Hill, 26 February, 1903, AB 4/38: Clove Labour, 1898–1926; *Zanzibar Government Annual Report* (Zanzibar: Government Printing Office, 1911). F. Cooper, *Slaves to Squatters*, 90–110.

124. AU 3/61: Mainland Labour, 1931–41. Ironically, because of their "troublesome" reputation, men from the island even found it difficult to get jobs as musicians in the sultan's band, where "reliable" men from mainland communities were preferred. AB 10/1: His Highness the Sultan's Band, 1913–45.

125. In 1930 unskilled laborers employed by the PWD in Zanzibar earned an average of Sh 30/ per month, compared to Sh 22/ per month paid to men working in Dar es Salaam. Anthony Clayton, *The 1948 Zanzibar General Strike* (Uppsala: Scandinavian Institute of African Studies, 1976), 19, 52 (n. 14).

126. Batson, *Social Survey*, vol. 1; AU 3/47: Organization of Labour, Rates of Pay and Working Hours, 1939–45; Clayton, *General Strike*, 13–22. The number of women as a percent of men was identical for both mainland and indigenous Africans (87%), suggesting little difference in the domestic "stability" of the two communities, or indicating that men from the mainland were in town only temporarily.

127. Jonathon Glassman, "Sorting Out the Tribes: The Creation of Racial Identities in Colonial Zanzibar's Newspaper Wars," *Journal of African History*, 41, 3 (2000): 395–429.

128. Interviews with Nunu binti Salum, Kiswandui, 18 March 1992; Pili Jaha Ubwa, Shaangani, 18 February 1991; Jamal Ramadhan Nasibu, CCM Headquarters, Vikokotoni, 19 February 1991; Ali Makame, CCM Headquarters, Vikokotoni, 13 January 1992; Omar Zahran, Malindi, 31 May 1992; Adija Haji Simai, Michenzani, 17 January 1992; Abdulrahman Ali Saleh, Saleh Madawa, 26 June 1991; Said Mohamed, Mwera, 25 March 1992; Rajab Mzee Ali, Malindi, 5 March 1991; Juma Aley, Kilimani, 15 June 1992.

129. Keith Kyle, "Gideon's Voices," *Spectator*, 7 February 1964; Keith Kyle, "How It Happened," *Spectator*, 14 February 1964; Anthony Clayton, *The Zanzibar Revolution and Its Aftermath* (Hamden, Conn.: Archon Books, 1981); Michael Lofchie, *Zanzibar: Background to Revolution* (Princeton: Princeton University Press, 1965); John Okello, *Revolution in Zanzibar* (Nairobi: n.p, 1967); "The One Hundred Days That Made Tanzania," *Africa Now*, April 1984, 15–21; Amrit Wilson, *U.S. Foreign Policy and Revolution: The Creation of Tanzania* (London: Pluto Press, 1989); A. M. Babu, "The 1964 Revolution: Lumpen or Vanguard?" in A. Sheriff and E. Ferguson (eds.), *Zanzibar under Colonial Rule* (London: James Currey, 1991), 220–47; Esmond Bradley Mar-

tin, *Zanzibar: Tradition and Revolution* (London: Hamish Hamilton, 1978); Catherine Newbury, "Colonialism, Ethnicity, and Rural Political Protest: Rwanda and Zanzibar in Comparative Perspective," *Comparative Politics*, April 1983, 253–80.

130. Much of the existing literature on Zanzibar focuses on the era of party politics, including Lofchie, *Background to Revolution;* Clayton, *Zanzibar Revolution;* E. B. Martin, *Tradition and Revolution.* A number of scholars are once again investigating questions of party and associational politics as well as the development of discourses of race and citizenship. Gary Burgess, "Generational Rebellion in Zanzibar: Students and the ZNP, 1957–64," paper presented at the annual meeting of the African Studies Association, Columbus, Ohio, November 1997; William Cunningham Bissell, "Colonial Constructions: Historicizing Debates on Civil Society in Africa," in John Comaroff and Jean Comaroff (eds.), *Civil Society and Political Imagination in Africa* (Chicago: University of Chicago Press, 1999), 124–59.

131. Strobel, *Muslim Women;* Mirza and Strobel, *Three Swahili Women;* Margaret Strobel, "From Lelemama to Lobbying: Women's Associations in Mombasa, Kenya," in Nancy Hafkin and Edna Bay, *Women in Africa* (Stanford: Stanford University Press, 1976), 183–211.

132. I owe a special word of thanks to Professor Charles (Ben) Pike of the Department of African American and African Studies at the University of Minnesota for reviewing my translations for accuracy and making suggestions on how to improve my English renditions of this material. I would also like to thank Angaluki Muaka, an instructor of Kiswahili at the University of California, Los Angeles, who offered critical assistance in translating certain Arabic phrases found in the songs performed by Siti binti Saad. I, however, accept full responsibility for any inaccuracies in translation.

133. Geoffrey King'ei, "Language, Culture, and Communication: The Role of Swahili Taarab Songs in Kenya, 1963–1990" (Ph.D. diss., Howard University, 1992), 52–99; Askew, *Performing the Nation: Swahili Music and Cultural Politics in Tanzania* (Chicago, University of Chicago, forthcoming).

134. For instance, in the introduction to his recently published book Tapio Nisula mentions how his study of health care and therapy in Zanzibar was fundamentally altered by the residents of the home in which he lived, who introduced him to the importance of spirit induced illness and healing. A study that was originally framed by biomedical literature came to foreground spirit possession, due in large part to the importance of these issues in the lives of those with whom he lived. Tapio Nisula, *Everyday Spirits and Medical Interventions: Ethnographic and Historical Notes on Therapeutic Conventions in Zanzibar Town* (Saarijärvi: Gummerus Kirjapaino Oy, 1999), 10–11.

135. Willis, *Mombasa*, 2; Phyllis Martin, *Leisure and Society in Colonial Brazzaville* (Cambridge: Cambridge University Press, 1995); Frederick Cooper (ed.), *Struggle for the City: Migrant Labor, Capital and the State in Urban Africa* (Beverly Hills: Sage, 1983); Charles Ambler and Jonathan Crush, *Liquor and Labor in Southern Africa* (Athens: Ohio University Press), 1992.

Chapter 2

An earlier version of this chapter was published in *The Journal of African History* 39, 1 (1998): 63–94. The source for the epigraph is H. P. Blok, *A Swahili Anthology* (Leiden: A. W. Sijthoff, 1948), 137. Blok cites the original source as C. Velten, *Prosa und Poesie der Suaheli* (Berlin, 1907). See also Ch. Sacleux, *Dictionnaire Swahili-Français* (Paris: Institute d'Ethnologie, 1941), 2: 740.

1. For a discussion of such practices elsewhere on the African continent see Misty Bastian, "Female '*Alhajis*' and Entrepreneurial Fashions: Flexible Identities in Southeastern Nigerian Clothing Practice" and Deborah James, "'I Dress in This Fashion': Transformations in *Sotho* Dress and Women's Lives in a Sekhukhuneland Village, South Africa," both in Hildi Hendrickson (ed.) *Clothing and Difference: Embodied Identities in Colonial and Post-Colonial Africa* (Durham: Duke University Press, 1996), 97–132 and 34–65; Phyllis Martin, "Contesting Clothes in Colonial Brazzaville," *Journal of African History* 35, 3 (1994): 401–26; Jonathan Friedman, "The Political Economy of Elegance: An African Cult of Beauty," *Culture and History* 7 (1990): 101–25; Donna Klumpp and Corinne Kratz, "Aesthetics, Expertise and Ethnicity: Okiek and Maasai Perspectives on Personal Ornament," in T. Spear and R. Waller (eds.), *Being Maasai* (Athens: Ohio University Press, 1993), 195–221; Timothy Burke, *Lifebuoy Men, Lux Women: Commodification, Consumption, and Cleanliness in Modern Zimbabwe* (Durham: Duke University Press, 1995); Karen Tranberg Hansen, "Second-hand Clothing Encounters in Zambia: Global Discourses, Western Commodities and Local Histories," *Africa* 69, 3 (1999): 343–65.

2. In 1897 the value of cotton cloth imported into Zanzibar was three times as great as the value of any other article, accounting for a quarter of all imports into the isles. *Report for the Year 1897 on the Trade and Commerce of Zanzibar* (London: HM Stationery Office, 1898), 12.

3. See "Sultani Majinuni," "Sultan Darai," and "Kisa cha Kihindi," in Edward Steere, *Swahili Tales as Told by Natives of Zanzibar* (London: Society for Promoting Christian Knowledge, 1922).

4. Strobel, *Muslim Women*, 9, 73–76; Glassman, *Feasts and Riot*, 79–174; Mtoro, *Customs*, 148–53, 169–77.

5. European styles did not become widely popular with island women until the post–World War II era.

6. Dress was in fact the only way that many of them could distinguish between the Omani and Swahili at this time. Rigby, *Zanzibar Dominions*, 8–9; Burton, *Zanzibar*, 1:114, 386, 434; Osgood, *Notes of Travel*, 35; Guillain, *Documents*, 2:78–9; Christie, *Cholera*, 308–10.

7. *Zanzibar: Report for the Year 1897*, 12–14; *Pemba: Report for the Year 1900 on the Trade and Commerce of Zanzibar* (London: HM Stationery Office, 1901), 16.

8. F. Cooper, *Plantation Slavery*, 215–20; Frederick Cooper, "Islam and Cultural Hegemony: The Ideology of Slaveowners on the East African Coast," in Paul Lovejoy (ed.), *The Ideology of Slavery* (Beverly Hills: Sage, 1981), 271–307.

9. Mtoro, *Customs*, 173.

10. Burton, *Zanzibar*, 1: 428; Vizetelly, *Cyprus to Zanzibar*, 401; Guillain, *Documents*, vol. 3. When shown figure D, as part of a clothing survey conducted in 1995, many elderly island residents immediately identified the woman on the left as a slave by her cloth and her shaven head. This survey consisted of an open-ended, seventy-five-part questionnaire regarding various forms of women's clothing. With the assistance of Ally Hassan, Zuhura Shamte, and Maryam Omar, the questionnaire was administered to thirty-one individuals, from a range of class and ethnic backgrounds, living throughout urban Zanzibar. Respondents ranged in age from fifty to one-hundred and six. Unless directly quoting a response given by an informant, results from this survey will hereafter be referred to as Clothing Survey, 1995.

11. Mtoro, *Customs*, 173; Ruete, *Memoirs*, 167–68, 237–38; Guillain, *Documents*, 2:82–85; Burton, *Zanzibar*, 1:386; Rigby, *Zanzibar Dominions*, 9.

12. James Holman, *Travels in Madras, Ceylon, Mauritius, Comoros, Zanzibar and Calcutta* (London: Routledge, 1840), includes drawings; Ruete, *Memoirs*, 83, 237–38; Guillain, *Documents*, 2:84–88; Strobel, *Muslim Women*, 74–76. Clothing Survey, 1995.

13. Ruete, *Memoirs*, 82–83, 146–47, 237–39; Burton, *Zanzibar*, 1:386; Guillain, *Documents*, 2:85.

14. In the case of Seyyid Said, all his children, and therefore all his sons who followed him to the throne were children whose mothers were suria. A child's social position and "official" ethnicity followed the father's line. In Zanzibar it was quite common for a slave concubine to have sons and daughters who ranked among the most elite members of society.

15. Response of Hilal Amour bin Seif to clothing survey, Mwembetanga, 14 July 1995.

16. Ruete, *Memoirs*, 10.

17. While concubines could be forced to change their clothes upon arrival, Ruete and others suggest that such women clung tenaciously to other elements of their cultural heritage, as well as their personal memories of childhood. Women of the harem taught the royal children the customs, traditions, languages, and stories of their homelands. Ruete, *Memoirs*, 5–13, 22, 43–44, 64–67, 210–13. Respect among concubines for the social and cultural traditions of East Africa was also expressed through their participation in female puberty initiation ceremonies, although such participation was sometimes restricted to secret or vicarious involvement through support of slave attendants. Interviews with Fatma binti Baraka, Kisiwandui, 30 September 1991; Bakia binti Juma, Miembeni, 10 July 1992; Amina Seif Othman, Michenzani, 19 July 1995; response of Adija Salum Bakari to clothing survey, Miembeni, 3 July 1995.

18. Ruete, *Memoirs*, 176; Rigby, *Zanzibar Dominions*, 8.

19. Osgood, *Notes of Travel*, 35–39; Burton, *Zanzibar*, 1:433; Christie, *Cholera*, 309; New, *Life*, 57–58; Sir Charles Eliot, *The East Africa Protectorate* (London: Edward Arnold, 1905), 32.

20. Guillain, *Documents*, 2:88; New, *Life*, 58; Burton, *Zanzibar*, 1:434;

J. Ross Browne, *Etchings of a Whaling Cruise* (1846; reprint, Cambridge, Mass.: Belknap Press), 398.

21. Osgood, *Notes of Travel*, 41; Browne, *Etchings*, 397; Burton, *Zanzibar*, 1:434. Guillain, however, argues that by as early as the mid 1840s some Swahili women were covering their heads. Guillain, *Documents*, 2:84–85.

22. New, *Life*, 60; Burton, *Zanzibar*, 1:434; Guillain, *Documents*, 2:78–79, 84–85; Browne, *Etchings*, 397; Osgood, *Notes of Travel*, 42; Mtoro, *Customs*, 173–74.

23. J. P. Farler, "Notes on Labour in Pemba, 1898," J. T. Last, "The Labour Question," and Rogers to Hill, February 26 1903, AB 4/38: Clove Labour; *Report of the Commission of Agriculture;* Robert Lyne, *Zanzibar in Contemporary Times* (New York: Negro Universities Press, 1905), 178–87; F. Cooper, *Slaves to Squatters*, 90–110.

24. Similar processes were long at work along the East African coast. J. Allen, *Swahili Origins*, 240–62; Glassman, *Feasts and Riot*, 62, 95; Justin Willis, *The Making of the Mijikenda* (Oxford: Oxford University Press, 1993), 1–113.

25. Osgood, *Notes of Travel*, 35–39, 70; Browne, *Etchings*, 335; Christie, *Cholera*, 333; New, *Life*, 56; Guillain, *Documents*, 2:74–78; Burton, *Zanzibar*, 1:104, 363, 410–14; Christie, *Cholera*, 333; William Fitzgerald, *Travels in the Coastlands of British East Africa and the Islands of Zanzibar and Pemba* (London: Chapman and Hall, 1898), 549–550; J. Allen, "Swahili Culture Reconsidered," 105–37; Pouwels, *Horn and Crescent*, 76–78.

26. Frederick Johnson notes under his definition of Swahili, "the term Swahili is a very elastic one, and in some places is used for any native who wears a *kanzu* or who is a Muhammadan, even only nominally." F. Johnson, *A Standard Swahili-English Dictionary* (1939; reprint, Nairobi: Oxford University Press, 1987), 442. There is a wealth of evidence from court cases, family property files, and other archival data to suggest that by the First World War a major shift had taken place in local usage of the term *mswahili* (Swahili person), reflecting the recognition that most of those who now identified as Swahili were in fact former slaves.

27. *Pemba: Report for the Year 1900*, 17.

28. *Pemba: Report for the Year 1900*, 15–17.

29. A. C. Madan, *Swahili-English Dictionary* (Oxford: Clarendon Press, 1903), 130; F. Johnson, *Swahili-English Dictionary*, 173; Ingrams, *Zanzibar: Its History*, 221–22, 309; Pearce, *Zanzibar*, 239. The photo collection of F. B. Wilson, housed at the Zanzibar Peace Museum, is filled with pictures of men working both at the port and on the railway dressed in a kanzu and kofia.

30. Virginia Danielson, *The Voice of Egypt: Umm Kulthum, Arabic Song, and Egyptian Society in the Twentieth Century* (Chicago: University of Chicago Press, 1997), 103.

31. Craster, *Pemba*, 153–54.

32. Clothing Survey, 1995; Ingrams, *Zanzibar: Its History*, 226; R. H. Gower, "Swahili Slang," *Tanganyikan Notes and Records* 50 (1958): 250–54; Craster, *Pemba*, 153–54; J. A. K. Leslie, *A Survey of Dar es Salaam* (London:

Oxford, 1963), 147–49. The *beni* ngoma in which African men parodied Europeans by dressing in military-style uniforms and playing in brass marching bands raised the greatest ire of Europeans regarding African appropriations of Western material culture. Ranger, *Dance and Society*.

33. Ingrams, *Zanzibar: Its History*, 221–22.

34. Hansen, "Second-Hand Clothing," 343–45, 352–54; P. Martin, *Leisure and Society*, 161–69; Barber, "Views of the Field," 1–11; Ulf Hannerz, "The World in Creolization," in K. Barber (ed.), *Readings in African Popular Culture* (Bloomington: Indiana University Press, 1997), 12–18.

35. Craster, *Pemba*, 153–54.

36. Ingrams, *Zanzibar: Its History*, 223; Pouwels, *Horn and Crescent*, 189–95; Hansen, "Second-Hand Clothing," 352–54; P. Martin, *Leisure and Society*, 161–69.

37. Clothing Survey, 1995.

38. For similar conflicts between youth and elders in Kenya see Willis, *Mombasa*, 167–83, and Bravman, *Making Ethnic Ways*, 139–82.

39. Shaaban, *Siti binti Saad*, 22; Khatib, *Taarab Zanzibar*, 17–19. Kangas were made of Manchester cotton and subsequently printed in Holland. After World War I, competition developed between the British and the Dutch for control of this lucrative cloth trade in East Africa. Department of Overseas Trade, *Report on the Trade and Commercial Prospects of East Africa* (London: HM Stationery Office, 1923), 19; as cited in Deborah P. Amory, "The Kanga Cloth and Swahili Society: Mke ni Nguo" (unpublished manuscript, 1985), 21; Elisabeth Linnebuhr, "Kanga: Popular Cloths with Messages," in Werner Graebner (ed.), *Sokomoko: Popular Culture in East Africa* (Atlanta: Rodopi, 1992), 81–90.

40. Jeannette Handby, *Kangas, 101 Uses* (Nairobi: Lino Typesetters, 1984), 2–4; Younghusband, *Glimpses*, 34–35; Stigand, *Zinj*, 122; Vizetelly, *Cyprus to Zanzibar*, 395; Craster, *Pemba*, 40; Amory, "Kanga Cloth," 21; Linnebuhr, "Kanga," 87–90.

41. Vizetelly, *Cyprus to Zanzibar*, 395; Craster, *Pemba*, 40; Stigand, *Zinj*, 122; Ingrams, *Zanzibar: Its History*, 309–311; Younghusband, *Glimpses*, 34–35.

42. New, *Life*, 60; Joseph Thomson, *To the Central African Lakes and Back: The Narrative of the Royal Geographical Society's East Central African Expedition, 1878-1880*, 2 vols. (1881; reprint, London: Frank Cass, 1968), 1:20; Linnebuhr, "Kanga," 87–88; Handby, "Kangas," 2–4; Nasra Mohamed Hilal, "Wanawake na Utamaduni," unpublished manuscript, 2.

43. Dept. of Overseas Trade, *Report on Trade*, 1897, 14.

44. Hilal, "Wanawake"; Saida Yahya-Othman, "If the Cap Fits: Kanga Names and Women's Voice in Swahili Society," *Swahili Forum* 4 (1997): 135–49; Mahfoudha Hamid, "Nini Historia na Matumizi ya Kanga," *Jukwaa*, 3–9 July 1995, 5, 10–16 July, 6, 17–23 July, 6 and July 24–30, 6; Handby, *Kangas*; Linnebuhr, "Kanga," 82.

45. *Pemba: Report for the Year 1900*, 15.

46. *Zanzibar Trade Report for 1899*, 14.

47. *Report on Zanzibar for 1897*, 14.

48. *Pemba: Report for the Year 1900*, 15; *Report on Zanzibar for 1897*, 14; *Zanzibar Trade Report for 1899*, 10; Younghusband, *Glimpses*, 34–35.

49. Hilal, "Wanawake," 6; interview with Juma Machano, Malindi, 20 October 1992.

50. In 1899, as a result of drought, the market for merikani largely collapsed. Trade in kangas, however, remained quite strong. During the depression as well, the demand for kangas in Zanzibar remained surprisingly stable. By 1939, 1 million yards of kanga (or half a million pairs) were being imported into Zanzibar annually to meet the needs of the protectorate's women. Supplies of kanga dropped precipitously during the war, yet demand again remained fairly constant, resulting in continuous problems for both shopkeepers and administrators. *Zanzibar Trade Report for 1899*, 10; Batson, *Report on Proposals*, 24; AU 2/59: Record of Mudirs' Meetings.

51. Response of Arafa Salum Ahmed to clothing survey, Malindi, 4 July 1995.

52. Lyne, *Zanzibar*, 183–84; British Anti-Slavery Society, *Anti-Slavery Reporter* (London: British Anti-Slavery Society, June–July, 1901), 92; F. Cooper, *Slaves to Squatters*, 72–84.

53. Clothing Survey, 1995.

54. Interview with Maryam Mohamed, Mwembetanga, 20 July 1995. Frederick Johnson's dictionary from the 1930s similarly identified the kanga as "the common town garment." F. Johnson, *Swahili-English Dictionary*, 172.

55. Response of Fatuma Abdalla to clothing survey, Uwanja wa Farasi, 16 July 1995.

56. Myers, "Eurocentrism."

57. Clothing Survey, 1995.

58. Response of Amina Seif Othman to clothing survey, Michenzani, 14 July 1995.

59. H. E. Lambert, "The Beni Dance Songs," *Swahili* 33, 1 (1962–63), 18–21.

60. The number of individuals who identified themselves as Arabs to census enumerators nearly doubled between 1924 and 1931, from roughly 19,000 to 33,500. *Notes on the Census of the Zanzibar Protectorate, 1948* (Zanzibar: Government Printing office, 1953), BA 34/4: Census of the Entire Population, 4.

61. Response of Adija Saloum Bakari to clothing survey, Miembeni, 3 July 1995.

62. Mirza and Strobel, *Three Swahili Women*, 24; Mary Felice Smith, *Baba of Karo: A Woman of the Muslim Hausa* (1954; reprint, New Haven: Yale University Press, 1981), 22; B. Cooper, "Reflections on Slavery"; Judith Tucker, *Women in Nineteenth-Century Egypt* (New York: Cambridge University Press, 1985); Arlene MacLeod, "Hegemonic Relations and Gender Resistance: The New Veiling as Accommodating Protest in Cairo," *Signs* 17, 3 (Spring 1992): 533–57; Stigand, *Zinj*, 122–23.

63. Mtoro, *Customs*, 173–74.

64. Only two informants, both well past ninety years of age, had any idea

when the buibui was first introduced. Both of them dated it to the reign of Seyyid Ali (1902–1911). Responses to clothing survey of Hilal Amour Seif, Mwembetanga, 14 July 1995, and Arafa Salum Ahmed, Malindi, 4 July 1995. Madan's dictionary, published in 1903, is also the first to include a definition of *buibui* pertaining to women's veils. Neither Edward Steere's *A Handbook of the Swahili Language as Spoken at Zanzibar* (1870; reprint, London: Society for Promoting Christian Knowledge, 1928) nor Krapf's dictionary, published in 1882, include such a definition. Frederick Johnson's dictionary, first published in 1939, defined *buibui* as "a black garment worn by some women when they go out of doors, covering them from head to foot." F. Johnson, *Swahili-English Dictionary*, 40; J. C. Krapf, *A Dictionary of the Swahili Language* (London: Trübner and Co., 1882).

65. Responses to clothing survey of Mwanamvita Mrisho, Kwahani, 16 July 1995, and Mauwa binti Khamis, Daraja Bovu, 24 July 1995.

66. Pearce, *Zanzibar*, 247; Ingrams, *Zanzibar: Its History*, 309–311.

67. Clothing Survey, 1995.

68. Ibid.

69. Response of Fatuma Abdalla to clothing survey, Uwanja wa Farasi, 16 July 1995.

70. Response of Adija Saloum Bakari to clothing survey, Miembeni, 3 July 1995.

71. Nimtz, *Islam and Politics*, 56. This form of Islam spread widely throughout East Africa during the period between the two World Wars. Ibid., 3–15, 55–86; Iliffe, *Modern History of Tanganyika*, 208–16.

72. In the 1910s dhikr rituals in which both men and women participated were a regular occurrence in the isles, while their popularity throughout the coast was also growing at a fast pace. Craster, *Pemba*, 310–11; Pouwels, *Horn and Crescent*, 160; Lienhardt, "Mosque College."

73. Clothing Survey, 1995.

74. BiMkubwa Stadi Fundi, Kisimamajongoo, 8 August 1995.

75. One of the most important branches of the Qadiriyya in East Africa was founded by Sheikh Uways bin Mohammed, who first came to Zanzibar from Somalia in 1884 and initiated many adherents into the brotherhood. Students of his are widely credited with spreading the Qadiriyya throughout mainland Tanzania. Nimtz, *Islam and Politics*, 57–60. Several sources from the mainland coast credit the arrival of the buibui to the efforts of Hadhrami sheriffs, many of whom were also involved in the Qadiriyya brotherhoods. James Allen in fact argues that the buibui was imported into East Africa by men from Shihir. I have found no evidence to substantiate this claim. Available evidence also seems to indicate that the type of veil worn by women in Yemen at this time was distinctly different from the buibui. The Yemeni veil, although black, consisted of two or three separate pieces, whereas the buibui was constructed as a one-piece garment. I would argue that the spread of the buibui was not literally the work of the sheriffs, but was part of a larger process of the spread of Sufi Islam which was occurring during these same years. Additionally, very few women from the Hadhramout or Shihir came to live

in East Africa. While male immigrants from these two areas resident in Zanzibar numbered in the thousands by the 1920s, few of them brought women from their homelands with them. It is therefore even less likely that male immigrants could have had such a dramatic impact on the fashions of women in Zanzibar. Written and oral sources suggest that many of these men married local women, and that many of these women changed their ethnicity after marriage. As G. H. Shelswell-White articulated in a colonial report he authored, " . . . as their women rarely emigrate, Hadhramis who settle in the islands mostly marry local women . . . , so that a large proportion of those included in the census returns as Hadhramis [these women and their children] were by no means of pure stock." Shelswell-White, *Notes on the Hadhrami and Shihiri Community in Zanzibar* (Zanzibar: Government Printing Office, 1935), BA 12/133; *1924 Census;* James Allen in Mtoro, *Customs,* 299, n. 8.

76. Clothing Survey, 1995.

77. Ibid.

78. Response of Salma Halfa to clothing survey, Kisimamajongoo, 29 June 1995.

79. Clothing Survey, 1995. There are also numerous tales of men hiding their identities under the cover of women's veils in order to effect escapes. One such tale is that told by Emily Ruete of Seyyid Barghash's use of the veil to escape from house arrest during his dispute with Seyyid Majid. Ruete, *Memoirs,* 237–39.

80. Clothing Survey, 1995.

81. Response of Fatuma Abdalla to clothing survey, Uwanja wa Farasi, 16 July 1995.

82. Kuczynski, *Demographic Survey,* 660–68.

83. Clothing Survey, 1995.

84. Response of Shemsa Mohammed to clothing survey, Kisimamajongoo, 29 June 1995. The practice of veiling young girls, beginning at the age of five or six years of age, when they begin to attend Qur'anic school, reemerged as "fashion" in Zanzibar in the mid- to late 1990s. During the 1970s, 1980s, and early 1990s girls and young women typically covered their heads with a kanga or scarf while attending Qur'anic school. The gradual adoption of the *hijab,* a head covering wrapped in a particular style, and the buibui by young girls is associated with the growing prominence and influence of fundamentalist scholars from Iran, Sudan, and Saudi Arabia on education and Islamic scholarship in Zanzibar during the 1990s.

85. Response of Adija Saloum Bakari to clothing survey, Miembeni, 3 July 1995. Bibi Adija was being carried on her mother's back during World War I, and estimated that her mother was in her late twenties or early thirties at the time of her birth.

86. Jahadhmy, in Whiteley et al., *Waimbaji wa juzi,* 97; Mgana, *Jukwaa,* 49; Hilal, *Siti binti Saadi;* interviews with Mwalim Idd Abdalla Farhani, Forodhani, 14 October and 23 December 1991; Nasra Mohamed Hilal, Malindi, 28 July 1991. For reasons I do not understand, histories of taarab au-

thored by East Africans have tended to reproduce these arguments about Siti's unappealing physical appearance. This is particularly surprising since most of these histories are written by individuals associated with African nationalist paradigms, and many of their own mothers would have worn their buibuis in the ghubighubi fashion during the author's youth. Nasra Mohammed Hilal is the only Zanzibari historian of taarab who has challenged these representations of Siti.

87. Jahadhmy, in Whiteley et al., *Waimbaji wa juzi*, 97.

88. What is even more surprising is that in this line Jahadhmy is quoting from Shaaban Robert, a Tanganyikan poet and author whose work was widely regarded as a hallmark of African nationalism. Shaaban Robert's biography of Siti, first published in 1958, was generally a glowing portrayal of the intellectual and cultural achievements of a woman who he viewed as doing more for the advancement and international recognition of Kiswahili than anything previously seen. Shaaban Robert described her songs as "the pride of the language" and Siti herself as "the pride of East Africa." In the course of research for a documentary on Siti binti Saad, a Zanzibari scholar of taarab, Nasra Mohamed Hilal, discovered, however, that Shaaban Robert had only personally met Siti once, toward the end of her life, and by the time he returned to begin his research on her in earnest she had passed away. His willingness to accept these descriptions of Siti's physical unattractiveness at face value may therefore have to do with the fact that he met her when she was certainly not looking her best. Although information on Shaaban's sources for his biography are unknown, it is also probable that he gained a good deal of his information from recognized island intellectuals, the majority of whom were Arab and Asian men. Shaaban, *Siti binti Saad.*

89. When asked to explain why certain forms of clothing "went out of fashion" and others became popular both women and men frequently responded as though I was asking the stupidest question imaginable. Change over time was something most people simply took for granted; "the times change and fashions change" or "young people always innovate on the ways of their elders" were the type of response that often followed. When asked to explain why women's fashions appeared to be more mutable than men's, respondents often suggested that clothing and fashion were simply more important to women, though few could offer explanations as to why.

90. Ruete, *Memoirs*, 7; Sheikh Abdalla Saleh Farsy, *Seyyid Said bin Sultan* (New Delhi: Lancers Books, n.d.), 12–14; W. H. Ingrams, *Chronology and Genealogies of Zanzibar Rulers* (Zanzibar: Government Printing Office, 1926); Burton, *Zanzibar*, 1:63–67.

91. The parents of 50 percent of the women interviewed in 1995 were of different ethnic backgrounds. Various forms of census and interview data also suggest that the percentage of women who married more than one man over the course of their life was well over 60 percent. Free women from propertied families also often gave birth to children with several different fathers over the course of their lives. The difference, of course, was that women's involvements were primarily sequential while those of men often were simultaneous. Amur

bin Nasur, "Habari za Amur bin Nasur," in C. G. Büttner (trans. and comp.), *Anthologie aus der Suaheli-Literatur,* 2 vols. (Berlin: Verlag von Emil Felber, 1894), 1:147–75; DJ 1/ Marriage, birth and death registries; AP 28/ Idadi ya Koo, Ex-Sultan's Concubine, 1913–55.

92. AB 10/108: Rusoona binti Tamim; AB 10/116: Surias of the Late Seyyid Ali bin Said, 1923–56; AB 10/200: Royal Marriages Decree, 1940; Browne, *Etchings,* 402.

93. F. Cooper, "Islam and Cultural Hegemony," 271–307; Burton, *Zanzibar,* 1:464; Craster, *Pemba,* 140; Farsy, *Seyyid Said bin Sultan,* 12–14; Robert Lyne, *An Apostle of Empire: Being the Life of Sir Lloyd William Mathews* (London: Allen and Unwin, 1936), 92; Ruete, *Memoirs,* 10, 41–45, 80–82, 111–12.

94. Response of Amina Seif Othman to clothing survey, Michenzani, 14 July 1995; HC 3/549: Noor binti Ali v. Ali bin Omor; HC 3/335: Fatma binti Mohamed v. Shariff Mohammed; HC 3/319: Jena binti Manji v. Hassam Alibhai; HC 3/840: Fatma and Marriam Bakheresa v. Hemed bin Said; HC 8/60: Shariffa binti Barghash v. the government; HC 8/100: Tufaha binti Nusura v. Azan bin Suleiman; HC 8/86 Mgeni binti Salim v. Seif bin Mahomed; AP 28/46: Idadi yo Koo, Ng'ambo; AP 28/2: Idadi ya Koo, Fuoni.

95. *Census of 1924,* 8.

96. Browne, *Etchings,* 402; Burton, *Zanzibar,* 1:393–94; Pouwels, *Horn and Crescent,* 195; AB 10/200: Royal Marriages Decree.

97. Lofchie, *Zanzibar;* Clayton, *Zanzibar Revolution;* Bissell, "Colonial Constructions," 124–59.

98. *Census of 1931;* AB 8/87: Report of the Committee Appointed to Advise on Matters Relating to Native Administration, 1932–39; Saleh, *Comorians in Zanzibar;* Pearce, *Zanzibar,* 214; Prins, *Swahili-Speaking Peoples,* 11.

99. Beginning in the late 1930s it became increasingly rare for women in Zanzibar to be seen working outdoors or even going to shop in the public food market. Leisure activities also became increasingly segregated by sex, as women moved previously public ngoma performances indoors or behind a fence and men became more involved in football clubs, in which women took only marginal interest. Interviews with Abdulrahman Othman, Jang'ombe, 14 June 1991; Mohamed Ali, Malindi, 29 June 1992; Nasra Mohamed Hilal, Malindi, 25 October 1992; Amina Aboud, Zizi la Ng'ombe, 23 December 1991; Bakia binti Juma, Miembeni, 10 July 1992.

100. Fair, "Pastimes and Politics," 284–316; Janet Topp Fargion, "The Role of Women in Taarab in Zanzibar: An Historical Examination of a Process of 'Africanisation,'" *World of Music* 35, 2 (1993): 109–25.

101. Although several elderly Arab respondents, born at or before the turn of the century, recalled their grandmothers or great-grandmothers wearing a barakoa, by the turn of the century "only the *very, very* wealthy wore them, because they were far beyond the means of most women." Responses to clothing survey of Hilal Amour bin Seif, Mwembetanga, 14 July 1995; Ghaniya Said, Malindi, 14 July 1995; Nunu Salum, Kisiwandui, 18 July 1995.

102. Response of Mgeni Ali Hassan to clothing survey, Kisimamajongoo, 14 August 1995.

103. The family history of the sultans is also included in the annual reports of the isles. *Annual Report on Zanzibar for the Year 1946* (London: HM Stationery Office, 1948), 51–57.

104. Kelly Askew, "Female Circles and Male Lines: Gender Dynamics along the Swahili Coast," *Africa Today* 46, 3/4 (1999): 67–102.

105. Interview with Maulid Rehani, Kisimamajongoo, 14 July 1995.

106. Ruete, *Memoirs,* 146.

107. Burton, *Zanzibar,* 1:463, 467–68; Rigby, *Zanzibar Dominions,* 9; Browne, *Etchings,* 402; AB 10/116: Surias of the Late Seyyid Ali bin Said; AB 10/108: Rusoona binti Tamim, Ex-Sultan's Concubine; AB 10/215: Seyyida Sheriffa binti Barghash bin Said and Seyyida Aliya binti Barghash; AB 10/200: Royal Marriages Decree.

108. Ruete, *Memoirs,* 42–44; 223–48; Farsy *Seyyid Said bin Sultan,* 13; Sir John Gray, "Memoirs of an Arabian Princess," *Tanganyika Notes and Records* (July 1954): 49–70.

109. Jahadhmy, in Whiteley et al., *Waimbaji wa juzi,* 63; Farsy, *Seyyid Said bin Sultan,* 28.

110. Response of Rahma Himid to clothing survey, Zizi la Ng'ombe, 19 July 1995.

111. Responses to clothing survey of Amina Seif Othman, Michenzani, 14 July 1995, and Nunu binti Salum, Kiswandui, 18 July 1995. This style of fancy dress also later became popular in *bomu,* a dance frequently sponsored by Comorians in which cross-dressing by gender, class, and ethnicity is encouraged. Bomu is one of the rare female dances in which men are allowed to participate, provided they dress as women.

112. Strobel, *Muslim Women,* 10–12, 196–203; Mtoro, *Customs,* 45–59; Leila Sheikh-Hashim, *Unyago: Traditional Family Life Education among the Muslim Digo, Seguju, Bondei, Shambaa and Sigua of Tanga Region* (Dar es Salaam: Tanzania Media Women's Association, 1989); S. J. Mamuya, *Jando na unyago* (Nairobi: East African Publishing House, 1975); interviews with Fatma binti Baraka (Bibi Kidude), Kiswandui, 30 September 1991; Amani Stadi, Mkamasini, 8 March 1992; Kiboga Bakari, Kwa Alinatoo, 1 August 1995; response of BiMkubwa Stadi Fundi to clothing survey, Kisimamajongoo, 8 August 1995.

113. Interview with Bakia binti Juma, Miembeni, 10 July 1992.

114. Shamsa Muhamad Muhashamy in Mirza and Strobel, *Three Swahili Women,* 98.

115. Laura Fair, "Identity, Difference and Dance: Female Initiation in Zanzibar, 1890–1930," *Frontiers: A Journal of Women Studies* 17, 3 (1996): 146–172.

116. Interview with Adija Salum Bakari, Miembeni, 27 July 1995.

117. Interviews with Kiboga Bakari, Kwa Alinatoo, 1 August 1995; Latifuu Ali Marzuk, Kisimamajongoo, 15 August 1995; Amina Seif Othman, Michenzani, 19 July 1995.

118. Although umbrellas remained the preserve of patricians on the mainland, by the 1880s they were widely carried in Zanzibar, even among well-to-do

slaves. Whether the prominence of umbrellas was a testament of vibarua's (slaves who worked for wages) perceptions of themselves as the equals of mainland Swahili, or whether the sultans encouraged the importation and distribution of umbrellas as a symbol of their power to overturn mainland patricians is a question that needs additional research. Mtoro, *Customs*, 149, 172–73; Glassman, *Feasts and Riot*, 154–57; Ropes, *Zanzibar Letters*, 10, 14. Interestingly enough, when the postrevolutionary ruling Afro-Shirazi Party took control of mkinda (as it did all cultural groups in the isles), they allowed women to retain control over most of their outfits worn during ndege processions, but required them all to now carry umbrellas distributed by the ruling party.

119. Photograph of Seyyida Salme's personal slaves, AV 1/16. Shows her slaves wearing marinda pants and vilemba.

120. Amina Seif Othman (Bi Amina Mapande) 19 July 1995.

121. The involvement of women from the royal family and other members of the aristocracy in the sponsoring of mkinda was doubtlessly influenced as well by pressures from clients whose families' originated along the mainland coast, where elite sponsorship of initiation ceremonies was considered a social and political necessity for all who hoped to maintain a reputation as a capable and benevolent patron. H. E. Lambert, "Habari za Mrima," *Swahili* 1, 3 (1961): 34–59; Mtoro, *Customs*, 58.

Chapter 3

1. Affidavit of Msellem bin Mohammed el-Khalasi, 14 January 1929, and Affidavit of Aradeshir Faredun Almshah, 14 January 1929, AB 28/12: Demonstration by Native Hut Owners against the Payment of Ground Rent on 11 January 1929.

2. Mtoro, *Customs*, 169–77; Mirza and Strobel, *Three Swahili Women*; Rashid bin Hassani, "The Story of Rashid bin Hassani of the Bissa Tribe, Northern Rhodesia" in Margery Perham (ed.), *Ten Africans* (London: Faber and Faber, 1936), 81–119; F. Cooper, *Plantation Slavery*, 213–252; Glassman, *Feasts and Riot*.

3. Abdulaziz Lodhi, *The Institution of Slavery in Zanzibar and Pemba* (Uppsala: Scandinavian Institute of African Studies, 1973), 7–12; Ruete, *Memoirs*, 65–66, 81–82; Christie, *Cholera*, 313, Glassman, *Feasts and Riot*, 85–95; F. Cooper, *Plantation Slavery*, 180–91.

4. Will of Seyyid Barghash in Lyne, *Apostle of Empire*, 91, 161; HD 6/31: Wakf of Bibi ZemZem at Mtoni; HD 5/60: Wakf of Seyyid Hamoud at Saateni; HD 5/43: Wakf of BiMtele binti Said.

5. Craster, *Pemba*, 153–54.

6. Christie, *Cholera*, 312.

7. F. Cooper, *Plantation Slavery*, 252.

8. Ibid., 243.

9. Will of Seyyid Barghash in Lyne, *Apostle of Empire*, 91, 161; Rashid, "Story of Rashid," Guillain, *Documents*, 2:26–27, 51; F. Cooper, *Plantation Slavery*, 243, 252.

10. Guillain noted in the 1840s that as upwardly mobile urban residents began to reinforce their mud and wood homes with lime and stone, they also typically invested in one or two domestic slaves. Being able to keep a domestic slave was as important an indicator of economic and social ability (uwezo) as the power to build in stone. Guillain, *Documents*, 2:136–38.

11. Christie, *Cholera*, 328; Lyne, *Apostle of Empire*, 91–92; Guillain, *Documents*, 2:26–27, 51.

12. Ruete, *Memoirs*, 81.

13. F. Cooper, *Plantation Slavery*, 195–96.

14. *Kibarua* comes from the Arabic root for letter or contract and is used today in Tanzania and Kenya to refer to contract, or day, laborers. Vibarua were widespread throughout the East African coast. For more on the types of jobs they performed as well as their status see Glassman, "Bondsman's New Clothes," 277–312; F. Cooper, *Plantation Slavery*, 184–89.

15. Rashid bin Hassani, "Story of Rashid," 103.

16. On the importance of vibarua wages in sustaining owners, particularly female owners, in times of trouble, see also Amur bin Nasur, "Khabari ya Amur bin Nasur."

17. European observers in Zanzibar regularly remarked, often with some surprise, on the tendency for slaves to purchase a slave or two of their own rather than buy their own freedom. For urban slaves under the protection of a powerful patron, however, "freedom" would have brought little in the way of material benefits, while the labor and wages of one or two of their own vibarua could allow a slave to amass capital needed for other, independent business ventures. It should be noted, however, that not all vibarua were owned by wealthy owners, and their living and working conditions were far less favorable than the slaves of the elite. Although relatively few slaves in Zanzibar bothered to go to court to obtain their freedom papers (only some 5 percent of the total slave population), 64 percent of those who did were city dwellers, the majority of whom were vibarua of poor owners. Lyne, *Zanzibar*, 183–84; Captain Colomb, *Slave-Catching in the Indian Ocean* (London: Dawsons of Pall Mall, 1873), 370; Henry Newman, *Banani: The Transition from Slavery to Freedom in Zanzibar and Pemba* (New York: Negro Universities Press, 1898), 37; Rigby, *Zanzibar Dominions*, 11; Burton, *Zanzibar* 1:380; Vizetelly, *Cyprus to Zanzibar*, 402.

18. Christie, *Cholera*, 303–05.

19. F. Cooper, *Plantation Slavery*, 154–55.

20. Wakf dedication of Seyyid Hamoud bin Ahmed el-Busaidi, Shamba at Saateni for his freed slaves, HD 5/60.

21. Ibid.

22. Rigby, *Zanzibar Dominions*, 5, 8; Sheriff, *Slaves*, 105–09; Burton, *Zanzibar*, 1:270–75.

23. Peter Lienhardt, "Family Waqf in Zanzibar," *Journal of the Anthropological Society of Oxford* 27, 2 (1996): 99. During the reign of Seyyid Said there was no distinction made between the personal property and fortune of the sultan and that of the state. When Seyyid Said died, in 1856, his property—

including the state treasury and even the man-o'-war that comprised the sultan's navy—were divided among his thirty-six living children. His son Majid inherited the throne, but he was required to repurchase the apparatus of state from his brothers and sisters. The division of the estate left the state treasury bare, and as a result he turned to the islands' wealthy merchants for loans. Sheriff, *Slaves*, 109; Ruete, *Memoirs*, 110–13.

24. Rather than overseeing the collection of customs duties themselves, the sultans "farmed out" the collection of duties for five-year intervals to leading Asian merchants and firms in return for a flat annual payment, which in the late 1850s amounted to roughly MT$200,000 (Maria Theresa Dollars, also known as the Austrian Crown or Rial, were current on the East African coast during this period). By 1870 the sultan's debt to the farmer of customs equaled MT$540,000. Sheriff, *Slaves*, 105–9, 126–27; Burton, *Zanzibar*, 1:271; Stanley, *How I Found Livingstone*, 8–9, 37; Garth Myers, "The Early History of the 'Other Side' of Zanzibar Town," in Abdul Sheriff (ed.), *The History and Conservation of Zanzibar Stone Town* (London: James Currey, 1995), 30–45.

25. Abdul Sheriff, "Mosques, Merchants and Landowners in Zanzibar Stone Town," in Abdul Sheriff (ed.), *The History and Conservation of Zanzibar Stone Town* (London: James Currey, 1995), 46–66; F. J. Berg and B. J. Walter, "Mosques, Population and Urban Development in Mombasa," in B. A. Ogot (ed.), *Hadith* (Nairobi: East African Publishing House, 1968), 1:47–100; Muhammed Seif Khatib, "'Siri' ya majina ya Miskiti Unguja," *Mzalendo*, 9 December 1990.

26. HD 5/60: Wakf of Seyyid Hamoud bin Ahmed el-Busaidi, Shamba at Saateni for Freed Slaves; HD 6/55: Wakf of Seyyid Hamoud bin Ahmed, Kiungani; HD 5/76: Wakf of Seyyid Hamoud bin Ahmed; HD 5/64: Wakf of Seyyida Jokha binti Hamoud bin Ahmed; HD 6/128: Wakf of Bibi Khole binti Hamoud at Bungi.

27. HD 3/5: Wakf of Seyyid Suleiman bin Hamed bin Said at Kiungani, Ng'ambo. Similarly, in Turkey, in 1925, it was estimated by colonial authorities that three-fourths of arable land was endowed as wakf, as was one-half of the cultivable land in Algiers. Asaf Fyzee, *Outlines of Muhammadan Law*, 3d ed. (Oxford: Oxford University Press, 1964), 266.

28. From 1905 until 1922 British members of the commission outnumbered Muslim members two to one. In 1922 the composition of the commission was changed to include four Europeans and four Muslims, all of whom were members of leading Arab families, although only two of the later were required to be trained in Muslim law. By 1959, the balance on the commission shifted in favor of a Muslim majority, as part of overall administrative move toward "Zanzibarization." HD 10/14: Appointment of Wakf Commissioners, 1916–1922.

29. Pouwels, *Horn and Crescent*, 177.

30. F. C. McClellan to Ahmed bin Smeit and Ali Mohammed, 2 April 1915, HD 3/5; J. N. D. Anderson, *Islamic Law in Africa* (London: Frank Cass, 1955), 77, 379; Lienhardt, "Family Waqf," 97 and n. 1.

31. Ahmed bin Smeit and Ali bin Mohammed to Acting Secretary of the

Wakf Commission, 16 March 1915, HD 10/9: Law Regarding Kadhi Interpretations; Saleh b. Ali to British Resident Pearce, 12 March 1915, HD 3/5.

32. Ali bin Mohammed to FC McClellan, Acting Secretary of the Wakf Commission, HD 3/5.

33. Ahmed bin Abubakar to F. C. McClellan, HD 3/5.

34. In 1922 the Wakf Commission earned roughly Rs 3000 (£200) from the collection of rent on 1,000 huts built on commission-controlled wakf property. By 1930, the amount of ground rent being collected by the Wakf Commission had nearly doubled and was yielding an annual income of Rs 5,649. By 1957, as a result of increased diligence in the collection of rents and expansion of the number of homes built on wakf property, the Wakf Commission was collecting £45,000 per annum. HD 3/28: Collection of Ground Rent, Wakf Department, 1931–66; Lienhardt, "Family Wakf," 97; HD 6/55. On the importance of Wakf property to urban redevelopment, see Garth Myers, "Reconstructing Ng'ambo: Town Planning and Development on the Other Side of Zanzibar" (Ph.D. diss., UCLA, 1993); HD 10/6: Auditors' Recommendations, 1914–41.

35. HD 6/55: Wakf of Seyyid Hamoud bin Ahmed el-Busaidi, 1915–59.

36. Bibi Khole to Acting Secretary and Wakf Commissioners, 1915, HD 6/55.

37. Copland to British Resident, 23 March 1918, HD 6/55: Wakf of Seyyid Hamoud bin Ahmed, 1917–59.

38. Administrator General to Wakf Commissioners, 9 October 1918, HD 6/55.

39. Shawana binti Seif v. Ali bin Said, case 5 of 1922, *Zanzibar Law Reports, 1923–1927* (London: Waterlow and Sons, 1928); HD 6/55.

40. J. N. D. Anderson, *Islamic Law*, 77; Shawana binti Seif v. Ali bin Said, case 5 of 1922, *Zanzibar Law Reports;* Tatu binti Said v. Wakf Commission, case 57 of 1929, *Zanzibar Law Reports.*

41. Barrister Stephans, on behalf of the Sultan, to the Wakf Commission, 16 December 1924, Wakf Commission to Stephans, 16 May 1925, HD 6/55.

42. British Resident Pearce devoted thirty-one pages of his history of Zanzibar describing "the city of Zanzibar," yet only one paragraph of the total to Ng'ambo. This paragraph begins, "Distinct from the Arab city and European zone is the great conglomerate of wattle and daub houses on the eastern side of the creek where the bulk of the Swahili population dwell. This area is known as Ng'ambo, and it forms in fact a separate town of some 15,000 inhabitants." Pearce, *Zanzibar*, 211; G. H. Shelswell-White, *A Visitor's Guide to Zanzibar* (Zanzibar: Government Printing Office, 1932), 25.

43. AB 36/20: Ground Rents, 1898–1912.

44. Lyne to Clarke, 5 April 1909, AB 36/20.

45. This system was not imposed initially, but only in 1903, after the administration determined that additional "incentives" were needed to encourage peasants to join in the harvest. Ibid.

46. Andrade, *Annual Report of 1911*, 29, 31; PRO/CO/618/26447.

47. Reports of the Assistant Collectors of Mkokotoni, Chwaka and

Mwera in Andrade, "Report of the Collector," in *Annual Report of 1911*, 27–28, 31, 46, 49; Lyne to Clarke, 1909, AB 36/20.

48. Zanzibar, *Report on the Administration and Finance of the Zanzibar Government for the Year 1902* (Zanzibar: Government Printing Office, 1903).

49. Andrade, *Annual Report of 1911*, 31, 46, 56.

50. AB 36/12: Proposed Ground Rent Decree, 1912–17; Unsigned memo to Clarke 6 March 1912, AB 36/20; Andrade, *Annual Report of 1911*.

51. According to one report, as many as two-thirds of the cases initiated by the state against ground rent defaulters were decided by the courts against the state's claims of ownership. Unsigned memo to Captain Barton, 24 January 1910, AB 36/20; Andrade, "Report of the Collector," *Annual Report of 1911*, 2, 26.

52. Andrade, *Annual Report of 1911*, 166.

53. Lyne to Clarke, 6 March 1912, AB 36/20. John Sinclair, *Zanzibar Government, a Report on the Protectorate 1911–1923* (Zanzibar: Government Printing Office, 1923).

54. In 1907, when the state attempted to literally force people from their homes they succeeded in getting only 2,128 pickers to go to Pemba for the harvest. In contrast, in 1911, when the state made no attempts to collect tax or ground rent or enlist forced labor, over 10,000 pickers traveled from Zanzibar to Pemba to assist in the harvest. Andrade, *Annual Report 1911*, 30.

55. Memory of these earlier protests against ground rents were invoked by Afro-Shirazi Party leader Abeid Karume in the 1950s in the course of protests against a proposed increase in ground rents on Wakf Commission property in Ng'ambo. Myers, "Sticks and Stones," 263–64.

56. Seyyid Hamed Thuweni, indebted to the British for his position as sultan, acquiesced in the reduction of his power. During the reign of Thuweni the government was reorganized into four departments, with the heads of all departments appointed by and responsible to the British chief minister. Pouwels has a detailed yet succinct discussion of the political machination involved in the imposition of the civil list in Zanzibar. Thuweni also lost the ten-mile "coastal strip" to the Foreign Office. Pouwels, *Horn and Crescent*, 164–77; Ahmed Hamoud [al-]Maamiry, *Omani Sultans in Zanzibar, 1832–1964* (New Delhi: Lancers Books, 1988), 45–50; Lyne, *Zanzibar*, 190–95; Hollingsworth, *Zanzibar*.

57. AE 8/10: Land Claimed at Mlandege by Gulamhussein Remtulla Hemani.

58. Ingrams, *Zanzibar: Its History*, 174; AB 10: Sultan and Royal Family Records.

59. HD 3/5: Wakf of Seyyid Suleiman bin Hamed bin Said at Kiunga.

60. Shariffa died, in 1880, while in Mecca. Her husband then became the mutawalli of the wakf.

61. Sheikh Saleh bin Ali to Pearce, the British resident, 23 January 1915, HD 3/5.

62. HD 3/5; Maamiry, *Sultans*, 49; Hollingsworth, *Zanzibar*, 82–106. One of the first actions taken by Seyyid Hamed's successor, Seyyid Hamoud

(1896–1902), was to abolish the payment of ground rent by the poor living on his family's wakf land in Ng'ambo. When Seyyid Hamoud died in 1902, however, the Crown Lands Department was established and these rents were once again imposed by the British administration.

63. Myers, "'Other Side' of Zanzibar Town," 38–39.

64. Mohammed Remtulla began collecting rents, in 1908, from tenants on land which had been set aside by Sultan Majid (1856–70) for the occupation of freed slaves of the royal family. In 1912 he used his ability to collect these rents as proof of ownership in a court case brought by Ladi Janbai, the widow of Tharia Topan, to settle disputes over a common boundary. In subsequent cases brought by the government against both Remtulla and Topan the court ruled that the successful collection of rent served as proof of ownership. Memo by Attorney General, 7 January 1927, AE 8/10; AE 8/11: Claim of Land at Ng'ambo by Mohamedhussein Tharia Topan, 1927–28.

65. HD 10/13: Mauli Wakf Mwembetanga.

66. The largest exception to this were the poor and freed slaves who resided on the wakf land of Seyyid Hamoud. As you will recall, it was the refusal of Hamoud's daughters, Khole and Jokha, to demand rent payments from the poor who lived on their land which resulted in attempts by the Wakf Commission to declare them incompetent property managers and to attempt to seize the land from their control.

67. Case of Jambia Ndigo, hut 250, Saateni, and Case of Gabith, hut 88, AB 36/12: Proposed Ground Rent Decree, 1912–17.

68. PRO/CO 68/47/16: Official Commission of Enquiry, Disturbances at the Central Prison, Zanzibar, 1928.

69. The collectors of both private landlords and the government apparently "operated over the whole district indiscriminately" during this period, demanding rent from everyone and taking what they could get. Wiggins to Land Officer, 17 January 1917, AE 8/10. This form of resistance to tax collection is also documented for the mainland in Bagamoyo. Grammar books for German administrators contained examples of frequently encountered dialogues with Africans. One of the examples included in Carl Velten's *Prosa und Poesie der Suaheli* goes like this: "I'm collecting taxes." "I've already paid." "Whom did you pay?" "I paid what's-his-name." "When did you pay?" "Last month." Cited in Charles Pike, "History and Imagination: Swahili Literature and Resistance to German Language Imperialism in Tanzania, 1885–1910," *International Journal of African Historical Studies*, 19, 2 (1986): 201–31.

70. Acting Secretary to the Chief Secretary, 18 August 1917, AB 36/12.

71. AB 36/12: Proposed Ground Rent Decree, 1912–17.

72. Increase in Rent Restriction Decree no. 23 of 1922, *Revised Laws of Zanzibar;* AB 36/22: Ground Rents, 1926–1954; AB 36/13: Ground Rent Restriction Decree, 1927–1932; AB 36/5: Increase of Rent (Restriction) Decree no. 23 of 1922, Amendment Decree no. 16 of 1923; BA 36/21: Restriction of House Rents, 1917–44; Abdulla Saleh and fourteen others of Mlandege to the British resident, 14 September 1926, and Mohammed Remtulla Hemani v. Abdulla bin Mbaruk, case 5047 of 1927, AE 8/10.

73. AB 36/21: Restriction of House Rents, 1917–44; Detailed statement showing the increased rents on tenants of rooms in larger premises (gurfas) in spite of regulations issued on 22 April 1918, AB 36/5: Increase of Rent (restriction) Decree no. 23 of 1922.

74. Letter from Shivlal Dayabhai, Chair of the Mass Meeting of Tenants in Gurfas and President of the Maheta Hit-Vardhak Mandal Zanzibar, 11 September 1922, AB 36/5.

75. The work of Richa Nagar on Asians in Dar es Salaam provides a necessary and very useful corrective to these misperceptions of a monolithic Asian community. Nagar, "The South Asian Diaspora in Tanzania: A History Retold," *Comparative Studies of South Asia, Africa and the Middle East* 16, 2 (1996): 62–80; Nagar, "Communal Places and the Politics of Multiple Identities: The Case of Tanzanian Asians," *Ecumene* 4, 1 (1997): 3–26. A literary depiction of these issues is provided by M. G. Vassanji, *The Gunny Sack* (London: Heinemann, 1989).

76. Many of those who signed the petition were facing eviction because of their inability to pay the increased rent rates. Petition passed at a mass meeting of the Indian National Association, 11 March 1921, AB 36/21: Restriction of House Rents, 1917–44.

77. AB 36/5: Increase of Rent (Restriction) Decree, 1918–23.

78. Ibid. Conditions in many of the houses and flats in Stone Town were extremely bad during these years. According to reports from the municipal officer of health, many shared a single communal toilet which had not been emptied for years, had little or no ventilation, had inadequate and unsafe electricity, had rooms made out of corrugated sheeting, and shared common spaces which were rarely swept. The health officer encouraged the administration to use the Rent Restriction Decree to require that these premises be "cleaned up." Memo from the Municipal Officer of Health, 18 September 1919, AB 36/21; Statement of condensed particulars of Gurfas in Zanzibar, AB 36/5.

79. Anonymous letter to the British resident, 8 October 1924, HD 3/5.

80. Translation of the wakf dedication of Seyyid Suleiman bin Hamed, HD 3/5.

81. Obituary of Varas Mohammed Remtulla Hemani, *Supplement to the Official Gazette,* 17 March 1928.

82. Abdulla Saleh and thirteen others of Mlandege to the British resident, 14 September 1926, and Mohammed Remtulla Hemani v. Abdulla bin Mbaruk, case 5047 of 1927, AE 8/10. Emphasis added.

83. BA 16/37: Debates of the Legislative Council, 11 December 1928; AB 36/22: Government Ground Rent Rates, 1926–54; AB 36/13: Ground Rent Restriction Decree; List of hut owners in arrears to Tharia Topan.

84. On behalf of three hundred people to Your Excellency, Hollis the British resident, 25 April, 1927, AE 8/10. After 1926, there were sixteen annas in a rupee and one rupee exchanged for one shilling sixpence.

85. Mohammed Remtulla Hemani v. Abdulla bin Mbaruk, case 5047 of 1927, AE 8/10.

86. AE 8/11: Claim of Land at Ng'ambo by Mohammedhussein Tharia Topan, 1927–28.

87. Topan to Land Officer, 7 December 1928, Topan to Director of Public Works, 26 November 1928, and Ruling of the Attorney General regarding claim of land at Ng'ambo by Mohamedhussein Tharia Topan, AE 8/11; Topan to Chief Secretary, 14 February 1959, claim over land at Kisimamajongo by M. H. Tharia Topan, AE 8/19.

88. The successful efforts of poor residents to overturn colonial policy through mass collective action figured prominently in the collective social memory of the isles. The successes of the 1910s and 1920s were recalled as a not-so-subtle threat to the administration, by Abeid Karume, in the 1950s, when the Wakf Commission attempted to increase its Ng'ambo rents. Myers, "Sticks and Stones," 264.

89. Tharia Topan and other Kiwanja owners to Chief Secretary, 22 November 1928, AB 36/13: Ground Rent Restriction Decree, 1927–32; Scale of rentals charged by government in Ng'ambo, AB 36/22: Ground Rents, 1926–54.

90. Memo to Chief Secretary, 30 December 1927, Legal report by Attorney General regarding Ground Rent Restriction Decree, 1928, Tharia Topan and other Kiwanja owners to Chief Secretary, 22 November 1928, AB 36/13; On behalf of three hundred people to Your Excellency, Hollis the British Resident, 25 April 1927, and Abdulla Saleh of Mlandege Ng'ambo and others, 14 September 1926, AE 8/10; AB 36/22: Ground Rents, 1926–54.

91. Memo to Land Officer from Chief Secretary, 3 September 1928, Memo from Senior Commissioner to Land Officer, 15 October 1928, Tharia Topan and other Kiwanja owners to Chief Secretary, 22 November 1928, AB 36/13: Ground Rent Restriction Decree, 1927–32; Affidavit of Ardeshir Faredun Alamshah, landowner in Mwembenjugu, 14 January 1928, and Report of Acting Commissioner of Police to Chief Secretary, 19 January 1929, AB 28/12; List of Kiwanja owners in arrears to Tharia Topan, 28 December 1928, AB 36/13: Ground Rent Restriction Decree, 1927–1932; AB 22/12: Demonstration by Native Hut Owners against the Payment of Ground Rent on 11 January 1929; AE 8/10; BA 16: Debates of the Legislative Council, 12 November 1928.

92. Tharia Topan to Chief Secretary, 22 November 1928, AB 36/13.

93. Memo from A. F. Alamshah to the select committee of the Legislative Council considering the Ground Rent Restriction Decree, May 1928, AB 36/13; BA 36/22: Ground Rents.

94. Interviews with Said Mohammed, 14 January 1992; Adija Haji Simai, 3 February 1992; Amina Aboud, 17 January 1992.

95. There are several other instances in which major anticolonial protests within the sultan's domain coincided with Islamic holidays, including the expulsion of the Germans from Pangani, in 1888, and the 1948 general strike in Zanzibar. Glassman, *Feasts and Riot; Tanganyikan Standard,* 21 August 1948.

96. Rahman, *Islam,* 21–22; Affidavit of Juma bin Omar, detective,

Zanzibar Police, 14 January 1929, AB 28/12. The book al-Badr commemorates fourteen of the Prophet's disciples who lost their lives in the course of the battle. By invoking their names, it is believed that one's prayers are accorded additional power. Al-Badr was also used the course of other confrontations with the colonial state, including the *Vita vya Ng'ombe* Cattle Inoculation War of 1951, to reaffirm unity of participants. As with all medicine based on the use of the Qur'an, al-Badr should theoretically only be used for positive purposes such as strengthening communal unity and resolve. Frequently, however, the power of al-Badr is invoked to bring misfortune to enemies, including rival football teams, defectors from popular movements, or colonial administrators. Interviews with Omar Zahran, Malindi, 31 May 1992; Ali Juma Mwinyi, Kiembe Samaki, 6 January 1992; BA 108/7: A. M. Juma, "Cattle Riot (Vita vya Ng'ombe): A Case Study of a Peasant Rising, Zanzibar, 30 July 1951" (M.A. thesis, University of Dar es Salaam, 1982), 16.

97. Affidavit of Paul Sheldon, 14 January 1929, AB 28/12.

98. Sheryl McCurdy, "'Storm in a Tea Cup': Islam and Identity Politics in Tabora and Ujiji, Tanganyika, 1880–1934," unpublished seminar paper; Nimtz, *Islam and Politics*, 58, 77–81.

99. Nimtz, *Islam and Politics*, 73–74; Carl Becker, "Islam in German East Africa," 31–61; John Iliffe, *Tanganyika under German Rule, 1905–1912* (Cambridge: Cambridge University Press, 1969), 189–200.

100. The following persons were deported to Pemba: Faraji Mpira, Mohammed Athman, Akida Maftaha, Mzee bin Wayo, Ulimwengu Abdala, Mwinyi Kondo Mwinyi, Juma Khamis, Jumane Juma, Rehani Sudi, Athman Pongwa, Selemani Abdalla, Mjike Machano, Sheikh Zahor, Juma Sururu, Songoro Juma, Pesa Songoro. Memo to Chief Secretary, 14 January 1929, and Affidavit of Paul Sheldon, Senior Commissioner, 14 January 1929, AB 28/12: Demonstration by Native Hut Owners against the Payment of Ground Rent on 11 January 1929.

101. Interviews with Said Mohamed, Mwera, 25 March 1992; Adija Haji Simai, Michenzani, 3 February 1992; Amina Aboud, Zizi la Ng'ombe, 17 January 1992.

102. Interview with Said Mohamed, Mwera, 25 March 1992.

103. List of hut owners in arrears to M. H. Tharia Topan, AB 36/13.

104. Throughout colonial Africa, British officials persistently arrested, questioned, and deported men whom they assumed were behind political actions being taken by women. For other cases of this see Judith Van Allen, "'Aba Riots' or Igbo 'Women's War'?" in Nancy Hafkin and Edna Bay (eds.) *Women in Africa: Studies in Social and Economic Change* (Stanford: Stanford University Press, 1976), 59–85; Isaria Kimambo, *Mbiru: Popular Protest in Colonial Tanzania* (Nairobi: East African Publishing House, 1971); Jean O'Barr, "Pare Women: A Case of Political Involvement," *Rural Africana* 29 (1975): 121–34; Helen Bradford, "'We Are Now the Men': Women's Beer Protests in the Natal Countryside, 1929" in B. Bozzoli (ed.), *Class, Community and Conflict* (Johannesburg: Ravan Press, 1987), 292–323; Susan Geiger, "Anti-Colonial Protest in Africa: A Female Strategy Reconsidered," *Heresies* 13, 1

(1980): 22–25; Margaret Strobel, "African Women," *Signs* 8, 11 (1982): 109–31.

105. Affidavit of Juma bin Omar, detective, Zanzibar Police, 14 January 1929, Affidavit of Suleiman bin Khamis, detective, Zanzibar Police, 14 January 1929, Affidavit of Ardeshir Faredun Alamshah, Zanzibar landlord, 14 January 1929, Report from the Acting Commissioner of Police to Chief Secretary regarding the 11 January demonstration by hut owners against the payment of rent, 19 January 1929, Affidavit of Brian Wardle, Superintendent in Charge of CID, Zanzibar Police, 14 January 1929, Report submitted to Your Excellency, 19 January 1929, regarding the 11 January demonstration by hut owners against the payment of rent, Report of Acting Commissioner of Police to Chief Secretary, 19 January 1929, AB 28/12.

106. List of hut owners brought to court by Tharia Topan for rent in arrears, 21 December 1928, AB 36/13: Ground Rent Restriction Decree, 1927–32.

107. Interviews with Fatuma Hamis, Shauri Moyo, 26 April 1992; Mwajuma Ali, Shauri Moyo, 26 April 1992; Adija Salum Bakari, Miembeni, 23 March 1992; Nasra Mohamed Hilal, Malindi, 28 July 1991; Shaaban, *Siti binti Saad*, 7; Khatib, *Taarab Zanzibar*, 15.

108. List of deeds showing hut sales on government land at Mchangani and List of rents collected by government collectors in Mchangani and Zizi la Ng'ombe, AE 8/10.

109. HD 3/28: Collection of Ground Rent, Wakf Department, 1931–66.

110. This figure is based on an analysis of clove tree ownership and does not include women who identified as Arab, nor those who owned no trees. According to Batson's social survey, by 1948 less than 6 percent of the rural population lived in female-headed households, compared to 20 percent in the city. Batson, *Social Survey*, vol. 4; AP 29/17: Clove Bonus Registers, Southern District; AB 29/2: Clove Bonus Registers, Northern District.

111. AB 28/12: Demonstration by Native Hut Owners against the Payment of Ground Rent on 11 January 1929.

112. Affidavit of Salim bin Khamis, 14 January 1929, and Affidavit of Msellem bin Mohammed, 14 January 1929, AB 28/12.

113. Affidavit of Salim bin Khamis, 14 January 1929, AB 28/12. Although Rehani was watched by the CID after being broken out of court, he was not among those eventually arrested or deported as "ringleaders" of the strike.

114. Affidavit of Salim bin Khamis, 14 January 1929, Affidavit of Khamis bin Ali, 14 January 1929, Affidavit of Brian Wardle, Superintendent in charge of CID, Zanzibar Police, 14 January 1929, AB 28/12.

115. Interview with Said Mohamed, Mwera, 25 March 1992.

116. Affidavit of Ardeshir Faredun Alamshah, 14 January 1929, and Affidavit of Msellem bin Mohammed el-Khalasi, 14 January 1929, AB 28/12.

117. Affidavit of Sultan bin Ahmed el-Mugheri, Senior Inspector of CID, 14 January 1929, AB 28/12.

118. Interviews with Said Mohamed, Mwera, 25 March 1992; Adija Haji

Simai, Michenzani, 3 February 1992; Amina Aboud, Zizi la Ng'ombe, 17 January 1992.

119. Popular protests and community intervention on behalf of prisoners "unjustly" prosecuted by the state has a long historical tradition in Zanzibar. In 1911 the assistant collector of Mkokotoni reported a "riot" as a result of government attempts to impose a *sheha* (local administrator) not of their own choosing on the people of Mkokotoni. Four persons were arrested for contempt of court for not agreeing to accept the authority of the appointee. When the police came to make the arrests, however, hundreds of villagers came to their rescue, overpowered the police, and freed the prisoners. The tradition of hundreds attending court in order to register their dissent against the state continues today. The trials of Seif Sheriff Hamad, Zanzibar's former chief minister and current leader of the main opposition party in the isles, illustrate that this tradition is still alive and well. Seif Sheriff was removed from his position as chief minister and expelled from the ruling party, Chama Cha Mapinduzi, in 1988 for allegedly supporting islanders' demands for a referendum on the union with Tanganyika which was created in 1964. In the late 1980s calls for a referendum, combined with demands for government respect for the rights of citizens to freedom of association, freedom of speech, and a right to legal council during trial were increasingly heard in both Zanzibar and Pemba. Seif Sheriff's support of these demands led him to be labeled "a threat to national security." In 1989, Seif Sheriff was arrested and charged with illegal possession of state security documents, charges that many believed were false. He was held without bail, without trial, and without the right to legal counsel for well over three years. In the early 1990s, his case was taken up by both Amnesty International and the Lawyers' Committee on Africa. Many people in Zanzibar and Pemba respected Seif for his support of their demands for legal and political reform in the isles. While I was living in Zanzibar from 1990 through 1992, each time Seif Sheriff was brought to the court building, hundreds of men and women would gather outside. Tempered by their fear that the security forces guarding Seif would in fact use their guns, the crowd never attempted to intervene or to break him out of court. The large and vocal presence of those gathered outside nonetheless reminded both Seif and the ruling powers that the popular will was on the side of the accused. Assistant Collector of Mkokotoni, *Annual Report 1911*, 49.

120. Report of the Acting Commissioner of Police, 19 January 1929, AB 28/12.

121. BA 16/39: Debates of the Legislative Council, 26 November 1928; BA 106/15: Report of the Commission of Enquiry Concerning the Riot in Zanzibar on the 7th of February, 1936; Juma Aley, *Zanzibar, in the Context*, 76, BA 16/39; PRO CO 618/45/2: Disturbances at the Central Prison, 1928; PRO CO 68/47/16: Official Commission of Enquiry, Disturbances at the Central Prison, Zanzibar, 1928.

122. Interview with Said Mohamed, Mwera, 25 March 1992. Perceptions that the courts were biased in favor of the wealthy were not new. In the nine-

teenth century similar complaints were leveled against the legal system throughout the sultan's domain. Pouwels, *Horn and Crescent;* Strobel, *Muslim Women,* 93; Susan Hirsch, *Pronouncing and Persevering: Gender and the Discourses of Disputing in an African Islamic Court* (Chicago: University of Chicago, 1998), 117–19.

123. Interview with Ali Juma Mwinyi, Kiembe Samaki, 6 January 1992.

124. Affidavit of Salim bin Khamis, 14 January 1929, AB 28/12; also PRO CO 618/45/2; PRO CO 68/47/16.

125. Commissioner of Police to Chief Secretary, 17 October 1922, Commissioner of Police to Chief Secretary, 3 August 1925, Commissioner of Police to Chief Secretary, 22 April 1939, AB 10/1: His Highness the Sultan's Band. Recruits from mainland Tanganyika increased significantly later in the colonial era as the administration attempted to consciously undermine this apparent affinity between its police force and the local population. Clayton, *Zanzibar Revolution,* 22, 63–65. See also Garth Andrew Myers for an elaboration on conflicts regarding "custom and tradition" (*desturi*) as they relate to urban housing during this era. Myers, "Sticks and Stones," 252–68.

126. Interview with Said Mohamed, Mwera, 25 March 1992. Also PRO CO 618/45/2; PRO CO 68/47/16.

127. Chief Secretary to Land Officer, 3 September 1928, Tharia Topan, on behalf of Kiwanja owners, to Chief Secretary, 11 March 1928, Tharia Topan to Chief Secretary, 22 November 1928, AB 36/13: Ground Rent Restriction Decree, 1927–32.

128. Memo to Land Officer for Chief Secretary, 3 September 1928, and Legal report by Attorney General regarding Ground Rent Restriction (Amendment) Decree no. 14 of 1928, AB 36/13.

129. Memo from Land Officer to Chief Secretary, 3 September 1928, and Memo from the Chief Secretary, AB 36/13.

130. AB 36/22: Ground Rent, 1926–54. The schedule of Standard Ground Rents set rates as follows: up to 70 square yards, 4 annas per month; 70–120 square yards, 8 annas; 120–150 square yards, 12 annas; 150–200 square yards, 1 rupee; 200–300 square yards, 1 rupee, 8 annas. AB 36/13: Ground Rent Restriction Amendment Decree, 1928; Memo submitted by Tharia Topan and 10 Kiwanja owners to Land Officer, 1953, AE 8/19: Claim over land at Kisimamajongoo by M. H. Tharia Topan, 1959–1962. These rates were subsequently altered to provide an additional category charging 6 annas for plots measuring 50–70 square yards, but this still meant that the bulk of Ng'ambo tenants continued to pay only 4 annas in rent.

131. Judgment, High Court Civil Appeal no. 9, 1931. M. H. Tharia Topan v. Zhazeta Mohammed, AB 36/23: Procedure Regarding Compensation Paid to Hut Owners in Ng'ambo in Relation to Ground Rent Due by Them, 1932–38.

132. Other tactics were used, however, by landlords, including the British administration and Wakf Commission, to increase the income derived from these plots. See Myers, "Sticks and Stones," 262–65.

133. Topan to Chief Secretary, a petition to the government to raise the

Kiwanja rates, 12 July 1954, AB 36/22: Ground Rents, 1926–54; Topan to Ministry of Works, 4 January 1962, AE 8/19: Claim of Land at Kisimamajongoo by M. H. Tharia Topan, 1959–62.

134. Affidavit of Paul Sheldon, Senior Commissioner, 14 January 1929, AB 28/12.

135. PRO CO 618/45/2: Disturbances at the Central Prison, 1928; PRO CO 68/47/16: Official Commission of Enquiry, Disturbances at the Central Prison, Zanzibar, 1928.

136. PRO CO 68/47/16; PRO CO 618/45/2.

137. List of men deported as ringleaders in the ground rent resistance and memo to the Chief Secretary regarding the deportation of Fajari Mpira, Sheik Zahor, Juma Sururu, and Songoro under the 1923 Deportation Decree, 14 January, 1929, AB 28/12.

138. Affidavit of Brian Wardle, superintendent in charge, CID, 14 January 1929, Report submitted to Your Excellency, 19 January 1929, regarding the 11 January demonstration by hut owners against the payment of rent, AB 28/12.

139. Report of Acting Commissioner of Police to Chief Secretary, 19 January 1929, and Report submitted to Your Excellency, AB 28/12.

140. Report submitted to Your Excellency, AB 28/12.

141. Van Allen, "Aba Riots"; Cheryl Johnson, "Grass Roots Organizing: Women in Anticolonial Activity in Southwestern Nigeria," *African Studies Review* 25, 2–3 (1982): 137–57; O'Barr, "Pare Women"; Bradford, "We Are Now the Men"; Geiger, "Anti-Colonial Protest."

142. A few of these female rulers were Mwana Mkisi of Mombasa, Mwana Khadija of Pate, Mwana Mwema of Zanzibar, and Queen Fatuma of Zanzibar. Edward Alpers, "'Ordinary Household Chores': Ritual and Power in a Nineteenth Century Swahili Women's Spirit Possession Cult," *International Journal of African Historical Studies* 17, 4 (1984): 677–702; Patricia Caplan, "Gender Ideology and Modes of Production on the Coast of East Africa," *Paideuma* 28 (1982): 29–43; Ingrams, *Zanzibar: Its History,* 148–50, 160; Sir John Gray, *History of Zanzibar from the Middle Ages to 1856* (London: Oxford, 1962), 51–54, 83; Askew, "Female Circles and Male Lines," 102.

143. Memo on the collection of Ground Rents by Wakf Commissioners, 30 June 1930, HD 3/28: Collection of Ground Rent, Wakf Department, 1931–66.

144. Secretary of Commission to Commissioners, 21 July 1934, HD 3/28.

145. Secretary to Commissioners, 11 September 1934, HD 3/28. Private ground landlords fared little better in their attempts to collect in the 1930s and 1940s, as demonstrated by the number of court cases they were forced to initiate in order to receive their rents. HC 13/: Ground Rent Cases.

146. BA 16/37: Debates of the Legislative Council, 5 December 1935; Native Hut Tax Decree, no. 22 of 1932, PRO/CO 618/55/16; AB 28/17: Abolition of Hut Tax and consequent Alteration in Tariff Duties, 1937.

147. BA 16/37: Debates of the Legislative Council, 2 December 1937.

148. BA 16/37: Debates of the Legislative Council, 5 December 1935; 11 December 1928.

149. Municipal Officer to Chief Secretary, 20 October 1937, AB 28/17: Abolition of Hut Tax, 1937; BA 16/37: Debates of the Legislative Council, 2 December 1937. This tax on food raised prices in local shops, thus effectively making Asian shopkeepers the scapegoats of African ire. Zanzibar Police Criminal Investigation Department, Police Information Bulletin, 13 December 1937, AB 28/17.

Chapter 4

1. *Tarab* is an Arabic word which translates as delight, pleasure, entertainment, or to excite and please through the means of sound. It is generally used throughout the Arabic speaking world to describe music or musical events, but it was only in late-nineteenth-century Zanzibar that the term came to be associated with a specific musical genre. Lois Ibsen al-Faruqi, *An Annotated Glossary of Arabic Musical Terms* (Westport, Conn.: Greenwood Press, 1981), 350; Stanley Sadie (ed.), *The New Grove's Dictionary of Music and Musicians*, 20 vols. (London: MacMillan, 1980), 18:569; Janet Topp Fargion, "Women and the Africanization of Taarab in Zanzibar" (Ph.D. diss., School of Oriental and African Studies, 1992), 41–47.

2. After the death of Seyyid Said, in 1856, a series of disputes regarding succession to the throne erupted among Said's numerous sons. In 1859, Barghash attempted to overthrow his brother, Seyyid Majid, who was then the reigning sultan. After losing this battle Barghash was exiled until Majid's death. Pearce, *Zanzibar*, 262–69; Ruete, *Memoirs*, 223–48; Maamiry, *Omani Sultans*, 18–22.

3. Barghash built numerous monuments to his own wealth and power, including the palace Beit al-Ajaib (House of wonders), so named because of its flamboyant style.

4. Mwalim Idd Farhan, "History of Taarab Music in Zanzibar," paper presented at the International Conference on the History of Stone Town, December 1992; manuscripts of Shaib Abeid Barajab, in the possession of Mwalim Idd Farhan; Seif Salim Saleh, "Historia na Muundo wa Taarab," *Lugha na Utamaduni* 1 (July 1988): 9–11 and 2 (August 1988): 9–11, 24; Khatib, *Taarab Zanzibar*, 1–7. Interviews with Mwalim Idd Farhan, 24 September 1991; Mohamed Seif Khatib, Michenzani, 24 February 1991.

5. Laura Fair, "Pastimes and Politics: A Social History of Zanzibar's Ng'ambo Community, 1890–1950," (Ph.D. diss., University of Minnesota, 1994), 162–68.

6. In the early years of their training these young men operated in fear of the sultan's retribution if they were discovered stealing "his music." Although some members of the sultan's own band provided secret lessons to the young men, other members of the sultan's band are reputed to have demanded hush money from the young men to keep the sultans ignorant of these developments. Interview with Mwalim Idd Farhan, 24 September 1991; manuscripts of Shaib Abeid Barajab.

7. Manuscripts of Shaib Abeid Barajab. Shaib Abeid was one of the founding members of Nadi Ikhwan Safaa, formed in 1905.

8. Commercial recordings were available in Egypt as early as 1890 and their popularity grew enormously by 1910. Many recording companies were active in Egypt at the turn of the century, and by 1910 the Gramophone Company alone had released over 1,100 Egyptian recordings. Danielson, *Voice of Egypt*, 27.

9. As early as the 1860s Rigby noted that the majority of members of the island's Arab community no longer used Arabic in daily life. By 1900, even the sultan used Kiswahili as the common language within his home. Arabic retained an important symbolic power, however, demarcating status, education, and religious training. Interview with M. A. Ghassany, Vuga, 14 May 1992; Rigby, *Zanzibar Dominions*, 5; Sir Charles Eliot, *East African Protectorate*, 114; Saleh, *History of the Comorians*, 11–13.

10. Manuscripts of Shaib Abeid Barajab, one of the founding members of Ikhwan Safaa, in the possession of Mwalim Idd; Kelly Askew, "Performing the Nation: Swahili Musical Performance and the Production of Tanzanian National Culture" (Ph.D. diss., Harvard University, 1997), 157–66.

11. Interviews with Fatma binti Baraka (Bibi Kidude), Kiswandui, 30 September 1991; Amina Aboud, Zizi la Ng'ombe, 13 January 1992.

12. Debates about the alien or indigenous character of taarab were resurrected in the postindependence era. President Karume (1964–72) attempted to ban taarab for a while due to what he perceived as its affinity with Arab domination. However, Karume was quickly convinced by taarab fans, island musicians, and supporters within his own Ministry of Culture to change his tune. Until the early 1990s, taarab continued to be defined as an "alien" musical style by the Ministry of Culture on the Tanzanian mainland. Interviews with Machano Mtwana Haji, Kariakoo, 8 July 1992; Masoud Mohammed Rashid, Forodhani, 20 January 1992; Mwajuma Ali, Shauri Moyo, 26 April 1992. Askew, "Performing the Nation," 335–98.

13. Janet Topp Fargion, "A History of Taarab Music in Zanzibar: A Process of Africanisation," in David Parkin (ed.), *Continuity and Autonomy in Swahili Communities* (London: School of Oriental and African Studies, 1994), 153–65.

14. Although many coastal residents had long emphasized the importance of this intermediary position between polar extremes, because many of the principal informants utilized by scholars of the Swahili coast, particularly in the case of Kenya, came from elite patrician families these distinctions often appeared much more concrete and exclusive in the scholarship than they did in the homes and neighborhoods of most Swahili. Zanzibar, being a place populated largely by recent immigrants, had a much more fluid sense of status than Swahili city-states like Lamu or Mombasa, which date to a much earlier period.

15. Christopher Waterman, *Juju: A Social History and Ethnomusicology of an African Popular Music* (Chicago: University of Chicago Press, 1990), 6.

16. The majority of Zanzibar's Omani aristocracy were members of the

puritan Ibadhi sect, while Sunnis dominated the population at large in the nineteenth century. The distinctions between Ibadhis and Sunnis were often minimized in daily practice, however. Ibadhis and Sunnis in Zanzibar often studied under the same scholars and prayed at the same mosques. Wealthy Ibadhi merchants and landlords also endowed a number of mosques in urban Zanzibar for use by Sunnis. By the mid-twentieth century, in fact, many individuals whose grandparents had been Ibadhi now identified themselves as Sunni. Sheriff, "Mosques, Merchants and Landowners," 46–66; According to the 1948 Social Survey, 86 percent of the islands' Muslims were Sunni, including 100 percent of those identified as African, 57 percent of those identified as Arab, and 29 percent of those identified as Indian. Batson, *Social Survey*, Vol. 3.

17. Lois Ibsen al-Faruqi, "The Cantillation of the Qur'an," *Asian Music* 19, 1 (1987): 2–25; Danielson, *Voice of Egypt*, 21–24.

18. Danielson, *Voice of Egypt*, 128.

19. E. J. Collins, "Ghanaian Highlife," *African Arts* 10, 1 (1976): 62–68; David Coplan, *In Township Tonight! South Africa's Black City Music and Theatre* (New York: Longman, 1985), 3; Sandra Lieb, *Mother of the Blues: A Study of Ma Rainey* (Boston: University of Massachusetts Press, 1981); Bruno Nettl (ed.), *Eight Urban Musical Cultures* (Urbana: University of Illinois Press, 1978); Martin Stokes (ed.), *Ethnicity, Identity, and Music: The Musical Construction of Place* (Oxford: Berg, 1994), 17; Waterman, *Juju*.

20. Coplan, *In Township*, 232.

21. For reasons which are not entirely clear, Jahadhmy begins his life history of Mbaruku by stating explicitly that Mbaruku had no father. He later returns to this same point, suggesting that Mbaruku's mother, Bibi Mishi, and her master, Abdukarim Talsam, had one child together, but that Abdukarim later released Mbaruku's mother from her position as a slave concubine (suria) and that she became pregnant with Mbaruku only after this point. Jahadhmy's own position as a son of Lamu patricians becomes evident here and elsewhere in this book, where he often goes to great lengths attempting to establish the "immorality" of coastal slaves and their descendants as well as the magnanimity of former slave owners. In this particular case, Jahadhmy then discusses the numerous ways in which the Talsams treated Mbaruku as "one of their own," despite the fact that Mbaruku was "illegitimate." Mbaruku's experience illustrates the variance between legal and social interpretations of identity, paternity, and belonging as well as the variations within them throughout the Swahili coast. The patricians of Lamu were some of the most conservative when it came to awarding paternity and inheritance to the children of masuria. Elsewhere on the coast, however, desire to build a large following of clients often resulted in much more open interpretation of paternity. According to many interpretations of Islamic law, any child born within two years of divorce is legally considered the former husband's child. Jahadhmy, in Whiteley et al., *Waimbaji wa juzi*, 61–62; El-Zein, *Sacred Meadows;* J. N. D. Anderson, *Islamic Law*, 75–76; Hirsch, *Pronouncing and Persevering*, 133.

22. Jahadhmy, in Whiteley et al., *Waimbaji wa juzi*, 61; Ranger, *Dance and Society*.

23. Batson, *Social Survey*, vols. 10, 11.

24. The Roman alphabet was officially adopted as the script for Kiswahili in 1905, yet many island residents, particularly the elderly, continued to use the Arabic script for decades to come.

25. Jahadhmy, in Whiteley et al., *Waimbaji wa juzi*, 1–7.

26. Ibid., 67–69; Susan Geiger, personal communication.

27. Leslie, *Survey of Dar es Salaam*, 217. According to Leslie, the consumption of alcohol by Muslims in Dar es Salaam was also so common that it generally went without comment, except by those who were very strict in their observance of religion (210–11).

28. Unni Wikan, "Man Becomes Woman: Transsexualism in Oman as a Key to Gender Roles," *Man* 12, 3 (1977): 304–19. Wikan made these remarks in regard to the overwhelming tolerance of *xanith* (which she defines as transsexual, but which is more accurately rendered in Kiswahili as cross-dressers or gay men who exhibit "feminine" behaviors) in Oman, an acceptance which is generally found in Zanzibar as well. Wikan's own assessment of xanith was, however, much less tolerant than that of Omanis.

29. Interviews with Suleiman Ali and Chief Msabila Lugusha, Tabora, 25 July 1992; Hamza Omar Khatib, Amani, 2 September 1992; Clayton, *General Strike*, 15. J. A. K. Leslie made similar observances during a survey conducted in 1963 in Dar es Salaam: " . . . the vast majority of the population are Muslims, but many of these are really pagans in Muslim clothes . . . in any case the observances of Islam are strikingly absent here; this is not confined to town, but is true, to a large extent, of the whole coast, though in town the rules of religion, like all rules, are more than usually evaded. Most take usually only to the social aspects of Islam. . . . The attraction of Islam in Dar-es-Salaam is that it is the religion of the majority, and the donning of a kanzu is a simple but effective membership card enabling the country bumpkin to be accepted as a civilized man. . . . It is undemanding and has no unwelcome organization for the supervision of its adherents' private life." Leslie, *Dar es Salaam*, 11–12.

30. Luise White, *The Comforts of Home: Prostitution in Colonial Nairobi* (Chicago: University of Chicago, 1990); Iliffe, *Modern History of Tanganyika*, 208–16, 267–70; Geiger, *TANU Women*.

31. Although such names as Mtumwa, Kijakazi, and Kitwana, all of which refer to individuals of servile and subordinate status, are today said to indicate an individual's position as a servant of God, they are names which were previously reserved for socially marginal, unfree members of coastal society. Sheriffa Zawawi, *Unaitwaje? A Swahili Book of Names* (Trenton, N.J.: African World Press, 1993); Shafi Adam Shafi, *Kasri ya Mwinyi Fuad* (Dar es Salaam: Tanzania Publishing House, 1978); F. Cooper, *Plantation Slavery*, 217.

32. The sources available on Siti binti Saad's life history are numerous by Zanzibar standards. In fact, with the exception of the sultans, there has been more written about her life than any other island resident. Although

there are many biographies of Siti this is the first textual and historical analysis of her songs. Shaaban, *Siti binti Saad*, 1–7; Khatib, *Taarab Zanzibar*, 15–20; Sheikh-Hashim, "Siti's Voice," 3; Hilal, *Siti binti Saadi;* Mgana, *Jukwaa*, 34–60.

33. Shaaban, *Siti binti Saad*, 7.

34. Khatib, *Taarab Zanzibar*, 15.

35. Al-Faruqi, "Cantillation of the Qur'an."

36. His Qur'anic school, later known as the Mosque College, became a center of Islamic scholarship where individuals born outside the small circle of elite families were able to study. Lienhardt, "Mosque College"; Alan Boyd, "To Praise the Prophet: A Symbolic Analysis of Maulidi, a Muslim Ritual in Lamu, Kenya" (Ph.D. diss., Indiana University, 1980).

37. The *Maulid Barzanji* was composed by Sayyid Abu Bakr, popularly known as Sayyid Mansab (1829–1922), the kadhi of Zanzibar under Seyyid Majid (1856–70) and later kadhi of Lamu. Sayyid Mansab also translated a number of works of Islamic law and theology into Kiswahili in order to meet the growing demand for Islamic knowledge in late-nineteenth-century East Africa. Godfrey Dale, *The Peoples of Zanzibar* (1920; reprint, New York: Negro University Press, 1969), 65, 71–72; L. Harries, *Swahili Poetry*, 102–18; Ibrahim, "Islam and Secularity," 52.

38. AB 39/339: Rules under the Ngoma Regulation Decree.

39. Craster, *Pemba*, 310–11; Ingrams, *Zanzibar: Its History*, 419–20; Trimingham, *Islam in East Africa*, 85–102; Pouwels, *Horn and Crescent*, 192–200; Nimtz, *Islam and Politics*, 98, 121–30.

40. Sheikh-Hashim, "Siti's Voice," 3.

41. Interviews with Mwalim Idd Farhan, 14 October 1991; Nasra Mohamed Hilal, Malindi, 14 July 1992.

42. The title Siti later became a common form of reference to female performers along the coast.

43. "Siti," video; Mgana, *Jukwaa*, 36–39. Interviews with Mwalim Idd Farhan, 24 September 1991 and 23 December 1991; Fatma binti Baraka (Bibi Kidude), Kiswandui, 30 September 1991; Mwajuma Ali, Shauri Moyo, 26 April 1992; Said Mohamed, Mwera, 25 March 1992; Amina Aboud, Zizi la Ng'ombe, 13 January 1992.

44. Fair, "Music, Memory, and Meaning," 2–16.

45. Interviews with Mohamed Salum, Kizimbani, 26 June 1992; Said Mohamed, Mwera, 25 March 1992; Fatma binti Baraka (Bibi Kidude), Kiswandui, 30 September 1991; Amina Aboud, Zizi la Ng'ombe, 13 January 1992; Suleiman, "Swahili Singing Star," 89.

46. Interviews with Mwalim Idd Farhan, 24 September 1991 and 23 December 1991; Fatma binti Baraka (Bibi Kidude), Kiswandui, 30 September 1991; Nasra Mohamed Hilal, Malindi, 28 July 1991 and 14 July 1992; Mohamed Seif Khatib, Michenzani, 24 February 1991.

47. Fatma Alloo, "Umuhimu wa Kuwa na Gazeti la Wanawake Nchini," *Sauti ya Siti* 1, 1 (1988): 1; Sheikh-Hashim, "Siti's Voice"; interviews with Nasra Mohamed Hilal, Malindi, 28 July 1991 and 14 July 1992.

48. "Reading" is often done collectively and out loud for the benefit of those who cannot read themselves, cannot afford the paper, or are otherwise too engaged to read themselves but can listen while doing other chores. Reading in this context is filled with debate, not only of the "news" being presented, but also that which is being ignored.

49. Interviews with Fatma binti Baraka (Bibi Kidude), Kiswandui, 30 September 1991; Nasra Mohamed Hilal, Malindi, 28 July 1991 and 14 July 1992; Mohamed Seif Khatib, Michenzani, 24 February 1991; Said Mohamed, Mwera, 25 March 1992; Mwajuma Ali, Shauri Moyo, 26 April 1992; Adija Salum Bakari, Miembeni, 25 May 1992.

50. Aili Mari Tripp, "Rethinking Civil Society: Gender Implications in Contemporary Tanzania," in John Harbeson, Donald Rothchild, and Naomi Chazan (eds.), *Civil Society and the State in Africa* (Boulder: Lynne Rienner, 1994), 149–68; Myers, "Sticks and Stones," 258.

51. White, "Genealogies of Gossip," 3.

52. The performance culture of taarab was doubtlessly one of the elements which accounted for the consolidation of neighborliness, consensus, and interdependence identified by Myers as part of the "disorderly order" of Ng'ambo, often overlooked by colonial administrators. Myers, "'Other Side' of Zanzibar Town."

53. Transcriptions for 100 of the 160 songs I have translated came from Whiteley et al., *Waimbaji wa juzi.* Lyrics to other songs were either given to me by friends in Zanzibar, transcribed by me with their assistance from tapes, or taken from HMV/Gramophone Catalogues. A fuller history of the politics of the recording industry at this time remains to be done. None of the following songs were among those originally recorded by HMV in 1928 or 1929. Several, however, were subsequently recorded by Columbia. British Library. EMI Music Archives, HUS 016.78, Microfilm Reels Nos. 520, 535, 536, 539, 541, 543.

54. Leroy Vail and Landeg White, "Forms of Resistance: Songs and Perceptions of Power in Colonial Mozambique," *American Historical Review* 88, 4 (1983): 883–919; Leroy Vail and Landeg White, *Power and the Praise Poem* (Charlottesville: University Press of Virginia, 1991); Thomas Hale, "Griottes: Female Voices from West Africa," *Research in African Literature* 25, 3 (1994): 71–92; Graham Furniss and Liz Gunner (eds.), *Power, Marginality and African Oral Literature* (Cambridge: Cambridge University Press, 1995).

55. Nasra, *Siti binti Saadi;* Jahadhmy, in Whiteley et al., *Waimbaji wa juzi,* 59; interviews with Mohamed Seif Khatib, 24 February 1991; Nasra Mohammed Hilal, 28 July, 1991.

56. Mwalim Shaaban in Whiteley et al., *Waimbaji wa juzi,* 59. For more on the importance of audiences in shaping the meaning of talk in general, and particularly when speech is intentionally indirect, see Donald Brennis, "Shared Territory: Audience, Indirection and Meaning," *Text* 6, 3 (1986): 339–47.

57. Khatib, *Taarab Zanzibar,* 21–23; Hilal, *Siti binti Saadi.*

58. F. Cooper, *Plantation Slavery,* 1–6, 213–42.

59. Numerous songs in the late 1890s contained refrains that celebrated the conviction of Ali bin Abdulla, one of the largest slaveholders on Pemba, for abuse of a slave. Ali was apparently renowned for his cruelty. One refrain recorded in 1898 included the lines "We use to beg for mercy / But there was no mercy. / Now he that had no mercy on us / He is shut up in the European's stone house [prison] in Zanzibar." Newman, *Banani*, 37; Lyne, *Apostle of Empire*, 150–57; Vizetelly, *Cyprus to Zanzibar*, 401.

60. Interviews with Nasra Mohamed Hilal, 14 July 1992; Said Mohamed 25 March 1992; Mwalim Shaaban in Whiteley et al., *Waimbaji wa juzi*, 101.

61. Batson, *Social Survey*, vol. 10.

62. Abdulla Saleh and thirteen others of Mlandege to the British resident, 14 September 1926, AE 8/10: Land at Mlandege Claimed by Gulamhussein Remtulla Hemani; Tuna binti Abdalla v. Said bin Nassor, HC 8/81; Mgeni binti Salim v. Seif bin Mohamed, HC 8/86; Maryam binti Dalwash v. Mohamed bin Abbas, HC 3/2955.

63. Siti and her band were surrounded by the larger discussions and debates leading up to the ground rent strike and kept informed of its daily progress by Faraji Mpira, who not only served as the leading orator at the mass meetings called to further the strike, but also as Siti's bodyguard and the head of crowd control at some of her shows. None of the band's published material that I have collected specifically addressed the ground rent strike. Whether this is due to the fact that I have only managed to collect about half of their recorded material, censorship on the part of company executives, or the fact that the band left the isles for Bombay just as the strike began to move into high gear, I do not know. Records dealing specifically with the recording sessions of Siti's band and decisions about publication of her material are unavailable. More general evidence regarding the policies of EMI and other recording companies in East Africa do indicate, however, that the companies exercised considerable caution in terms of who and what they recorded and what was ultimately released for marketing in East Africa. EMI, "Vernacular Trade," 7–10, 12; Graebner, "First Thirty-Five Years," 10, 15–16; Mgana, *Jukwaa*, 45.

64. Interview with Said Mohamed, Mwera, 25 March 1992.

65. Hirsch, *Pronouncing and Persevering*, 117–19; Sandra Burman, "Fighting a Two-Pronged Attack: The Changing Legal Status of Women in Cape-Ruled Basutoland, 1872–1884," and Phil Bonner, "Desirable or Undesirable Basotho Women? Liquor, Prostitution and the Migration of Basotho Women to the Rand, 1920–1945," both in Cheryl Walker (ed.), *Women and Gender in Southern Africa to 1945* (Cape Town: David Philip, 1990), 48–75 and 221–50, respectively; Martin Chanock, *Law, Custom, and Social Order: The Colonial Experience in Malawi and Zambia* (Cambridge: Cambridge University Press, 1985).

66. Chukwani and Sharifmsa refer to two rural areas outside town. The latter is where the woman's violently assaulted body was found.

67. Interviews with Nasra Mohamed Hilal, Malindi, 28 July 1991; Mwajuma Ali, Shauri Moyo, 26 April 1992; Sheikh-Hashim, "Siti's Voice," 4.

68. Andrade to Clarke, 1912, in Seyyida Sheriffa binti Barghash and Seyyida Aliya binti Barghash, 1911–1947, AB 10/215; Andrade to First Minister, 3 March 1913, and Andrade to Chief Secretary, 6 April 1914, AB 10/108: Rosuna binti Tamim, Ex-Sultan's Concubine, 1913–1955; HC 8/86; HC 8/100; HC 8/60; HC 3/2895; AB 30/18.

69. AB 10/108; AB 10/215.

70. Interviews with Mwajuma Ali, Shauri Moyo, 26 April 1992; Nasra Mohamed Hilal, Malindi, 28 July 1991; Adija Salum Bakari, Miembeni, 23 March 1992; Adija Haji Simai, Michenzani, 2 March 1992; Amina Aboud, Zizi la Ng'ombe, 17 January 1992. HC 3/2895; HC 4/91; HC 4/42; HC 3/2955; HC 3/335; HC 8/67; HC 8/60; HC 8/55; HC 3/1344.

71. HC 4/: High Court Criminal Cases, 1908–1937.

72. Chanock, *Law, Custom;* Strobel, *Muslim Women,* 93; Bonner, "Desirable or Undesirable," 226–41.

73. Such legal transformations were by no means unique to Zanzibar, however, as the confluence of European and African patriarchies systematically undermined the position of female property holders across the continent during the first half of the twentieth century. Martin Chanock, "Paradigms, Policies, and Property: A Review of the Customary Law of Land Tenure," in Kristin Mann and Richard Roberts (eds.), *Law in Colonial Africa* (London: James Curry, 1991), 61–84; Martin Chanock, "Making Customary Law: Men, Women and Courts in Colonial Northern Rhodesia," in *African Women and the Law: Historical Perspectives,* Margaret Jean Hay and Marcia Wright (eds.), Boston University Papers on Africa, no. 7 (Boston: Boston University Press, 1982), 53–67; Judith Carney, "Struggles over Land and Crops in an Irrigated Rice Scheme: The Gambia," in Jean Davidson (ed.), *Agriculture, Women and Land* (Boulder: Westview Press, 1988), 59–78; Mann, "Women, Landed Property."

74. Craster, *Pemba,* 209; Khalfan, Salima, Shamsa, and Saada, children of Said bin Salim el-Barwani v. Khalfani bin Mohamed el-Barwani, 1913, HC 8/83; Shariffa binti Hamed v. Farhan Babe Panya, 1913, HC 8/85; Mgeni binti Salim bin Abdulla el-Marhubi v. Seif bin Mohamed bin Abdulla el-Marhubi, 1913, HC 8/86; Khole binti Hamoud el-Busaidi, guardian of the children of Seif bin Hamoud v. Issa bin Mossa, 1916, HC 8/108; Rehema binti Mohamed bin Rashid el-Shaksia v. Nassor bin Salem bin Nassor el-Batshi, 1921, HC 3/123; Fatumbai Issa v. Murji Khoja, 1930, HC 3/2947; Zem Zem binti Salem v. Said Mohamed and Ayesha binti Hassan, 1930, HC 3/2915; Bibiye binti Salem v. Khalfan bin Hassan, 1918, HC 3/73; Shinuna v. Wakf Commission, no. 48 of 1934, *Zanzibar Law Reports, 1935–38.*

75. Byrne to Cunliffe-Lister, 9 July 1934, CO 533/422/23030/452 and Kenya Colony and Protectorate, *Native Affairs Department Annual Report* (1934), 143, as cited in Karim Janmohamed, "A History of Mombasa, c. 1895–1939: Some Aspects of Economic and Social Life in an East African Port Town during Colonial Rule" (Ph.D. diss., Northwestern University, 1977), 231.

76. HC 8/86; HC 8/60; HC 3/2895; AB 30/18: Zanzibar Native Divorce Decree, 1915–52.

77. J. N. D. Anderson, *Islamic Law,* 64–75; Patricia Caplan, "Cognatic Descent, Islamic Law and Women's Property on the East African Coast," in Renée Hirschon (ed.), *Women and Property, Women as Property* (London: Croom Helm, 1984), 23–43; Hirsch, *Pronouncing and Persevering,* 4, 85–88, 96, 127.

78. A man can easily divorce his wife, either by informing a kadhi of his wish to do so, or by repudiating his wife by repeating *talaka,* three times in succession. Divorce for a woman is much more difficult to initiate under Muslim law. Whereas a husband need not provide any reason or evidence to a judge for divorce, a woman must prove her husband's failure to fulfill one of his duties. The difficulties of obtaining a divorce also intensify for higher-status women, whose families might also have a financial and social stake in perpetuating the marriage. As there are typically fewer property issues at stake, a poor woman can often receive a divorce either by repaying her husband the bridewealth that had been transferred to her family, known as *khuluu,* or simply annoying her husband until he initiates the divorce himself. Middleton, *World of the Swahili,* 124–27; Prins, *Swahili-Speaking Peoples,* 79–89; Hirsch, *Pronouncing and Persevering,* 119–27; interviews with Adija Haji Simai, Michenzani, 17 January 1992; Mwajuma Ali, Shauri Moyo, 26 April 1992; Hawa Pili Pandu, Amani, 2 September 1992.

79. Mgeni binti Salim bin Abdulla el-Marhubia v. Seif bin Mohamed bin Abdulla el-Marhubi, 1913, HC 8/86.

80. Strobel, *Muslim Women,* 54–64.

81. For a concise description of the power of British legal control even in Islamic courts, see Pouwels, *Horn and Crescent,* 176.

82. Pouwels and others suggest that bribery of Islamic judges had been a common complaint in the isles since the nineteenth century. Pouwels, *Horn and Crescent,* 176, 180; Hirsch, *Pronouncing and Persevering,* 118–20.

83. Mwalim Shaaban in Whiteley et al., *Waimbaji wa juzi,* 41.

84. Ruete, *Memoirs,* 206; Mtoro, *Customs,* 60–62; Craster, *Pemba,* 324–26; Peter Lienhardt, introduction to *The Medicine Man: Swifa ya nguvumali* by Hasami bin Ismail (Oxford: Clarendon Press, 1968), 48–80.

85. Alpers, "Ordinary Household Chores"; Linda Giles, "Possession Cults on the Swahili Coast: A Re-Examination of Theories of Marginality," *Africa* 57, 2 (1987): 234–57; Lienhardt, intro. to *Medicine Man,* 51–80; Mtoro, *Customs,* 60–62, 98–113.

86. Mwalim Shaaban and Jahadhmy in Whiteley et al., *Waimbaji wa juzi,* 30, 67, 70, 102; Shaaban, *Siti binti Saad,* 17, 26–27; Khatib, *Taarab Zanzibar,* 20.

87. Interviews with Mwajuma Ali, 26 April 1992; Fatma binti Baraka (Bibi Kidude) 15 September 1991; Mwalim Shaaban in Whiteley et al., *Waimbaji wa juzi,* 102.

88. Ezekiel Mphahlele, *Down Second Avenue* (London: Faber and Faber, 1959); Kristin Mann, *Marrying Well: Marriage, Status and Social Change among the Educated Elite in Colonial Lagos* (Cambridge: Cambridge University Press, 1985); Belinda Bozzoli, *Women of Phokeng: Consciousness, Life Strategy,*

and Migrancy in South Africa, 1900–1983 (Portsmouth, N.H.: Heinemann, 1991), 81–121; Caleb Prichard, "The Perceptions and Standards of Courtship and Mate Selection among Johannesburg's Educated Elite," unpublished manuscript.

89. P. Martin, *Leisure and Society,* 127–36; Christopher John Ballantine, *Marabi Nights: Early South African Jazz and Vaudeville* (Johannesburg : Ravan Press, 1993); Waterman, *Juju,* 27–54, Ranger, *Dance and Society;* Lambert, "Beni Dance Songs."

90. Fair, "Pastimes and Politics," 300–316.

91. Interview with Mwajuma Ali, Shauri Moyo, 28 April 1992.

92. Vail and White, *Power and the Praise Poem,* 231–77; Janice Boddy, *Wombs and Alien Spirits: Women, Men, and the Zar Cult in Northern Sudan* (Madison: University of Wisconsin Press, 1989); Steven Friedson, *Dancing Prophets: Musical Experience in Tumbuka Healing* (Chicago: University of Chicago Press, 1996); Victor Turner, *The Drums of Affliction: A Study of Religious-Processes among the Ndembu of Zambia* (Oxford: Clarendon Press, 1968); Middleton, *World of the Swahili,* 170–78; Sheryl McCurdy, "Transforming Associations: Fertility, Therapy, and Ethnicity in Urban Kigoma, Tanzania c. 1850–1993." (Ph.D. diss., Columbia University, 2000).

93. As Caplan found on Mafia Island, one of the most common times for a woman to become possessed was when her husband took a second wife. Frequently the prescribed cure offered by the spirits was divorce. A. Patricia Caplan, *Choice and Constraint in a Swahili Community: Property, Hierarchy, and Cognatic Descent on the East African Coast* (Oxford: Oxford University Press, 1975), 118–20; Leroy Vail and Landeg White, "The Possession of the Dispossessed," in Vail and White, *Power and the Praise Poem,* 231–77.

94. J. N. D. Anderson, *Islamic Law,* 76.

95. Lodhi, *Slavery in Zanzibar and Pemba,* 13; Ingrams, *Zanzibar: Its History,* 205. The term *besar* is included in none of the standard dictionaries, including Steere, Sacleux, and Johnson, suggesting either that its use became common only after the 1930s, when the last of these dictionaries was published, or that it is a Swahili-ized version of the English word *bastard.*

96. *Njiwa* translates literally as dove, but is often used as an idiom for a woman, particularly a young and attractive one. *Mnara* is also frequently translated as lighthouse or minaret.

97. White, "Colonial State"; Claire Robertson, "Traders and Urban Struggle," *Journal of Women's History* 4, 3 (1993): 9–42; Marjorie Mbilinyi, "'This Is an Unforgettable Business': Colonial State Intervention in Urban Tanzania," in Jane Parpart and Kathleen Staudt (eds.), *Women and the State in Africa* (Boulder: Lynne Rienner, 1990), 111–29; Karen Tranberg Hansen, "The Black Market and Women Traders in Zambia," in Parpart and Staudt (eds.), *Women and the State,* 143–60; J. C. Wells, "The History of Black Women's Struggle against Pass Laws in South Africa, 1900–1960," (Ph.D. diss., Columbia University, 1982).

98. Shaaban in Whiteley et al., *Waimbaji wa juzi,* 9–60.

99. Paisley Harris, "I'm as Good as Any Woman in Your Town: The

Blues of Ma Rainey and Bessie Smith as a Counter-Narrative of Black Womanhood and Respectability in the Early Twentieth Century," paper presented at the Berkshire Conference on the History of Women, Chapel Hill, N.C., June 1996; Hazel Carby, "'It Jus Be's Dat Way Sometime,': The Sexual Politics of Women's Blues." in E. C. DuBois and V. Ruíz (eds.), *Unequal Sisters: A Multicultural Reader in U.S. Women's History* (New York: Routledge, 1990), 238–49; Lieb, *Mother of the Blues;* Angela Davis, *Blues Legacies and Black Feminism* (New York: Pantheon, 1998), 42–65.

100. Carby, "'It Jus Be's,'" 339.

101. In Mombasa and Lamu extramarital relationships were sometimes referred to as *ndoa ya siri* (secret marriage), which were agreed upon by the parties involved but often kept from in-laws and other spouses. Middleton, *World of the Swahili,* 123–26; El-Zein, *Sacred Meadows,* 84–86, 156–59; Prins, *Swahili-Speaking Peoples,* 87–89; Stigand, *Zinj,* 128.

102. Interviews with Nasra Mohamed Hilal, Malindi, 28 July 1991; Fatma binti Baraka (Bibi Kidude), Raha Leo, 9 October 1991; Adija Salum Bakari, Miembeni, 23 March 1992.

103. James Scott, *Weapons of the Weak.*

104. Interviews with Mwalim Idd Farhan, 24 September 1991 and 23 December 1991; Fatma binti Baraka (Bibi Kidude), Kiswandui, 30 September 1991; Nasra Mohamed Hilal, Malindi, 28 July 1991 and 14 July 1992.

Chapter 5

An earlier version of this chapter appeared in *Africa* 67, 2 (1997): 224–51.

1. C. L. R. James, *Beyond a Boundary* (1963; reprint, Durham: Duke University Press, 1993), 65.

2. James Scott, *Domination.*

3. Frederick Cooper, "Urban Space, Industrial Time, and Wage Labor in Africa," in F. Cooper (ed.), *Struggle for the City: Migrant Labor, Capital and the State in Urban Africa* (Beverly Hills: Sage, 1983), 7–50; Patrick Harries, *Work, Culture and Identity: Migrant Laborers in Mozambique and South Africa, 1860–1910* (Portsmouth, N.H.: Heinemann, 1994); White, *Comforts of Home;* Hortense Powdermaker, *Copper Town: Changing Africa, the Human Situation on the Rhodesian Copperbelt* (New York: Harper, 1962), 105–19, 151–305; Ambler and Crush, *Liquor and Labor;* Tim Couzens, *The New African: A Study in the Live and Work of H. I. E. Dhlomo* (Johannesburg: Ravan Press, 1995); Phyllis Martin, "Colonialism, Youth and Football in French Equatorial Africa," *International Journal of the History of Sport* 8, 1 (1991): 56–71.

4. Kamati Maalum ya Kuchunguza Historia ya Michezo ya Riadha na Mipira Visiwani, "Taarifa ya Kamati ya Kuchunguza Historia ya Michezo ya Riadha na Mipira Visiwani: Historia ya Michezo, Hali Halisi ya Michezo na Mapendikezo," unpublished confidential report, Zanzibar, 1981: 2; Lyne, *Zanzibar,* 71.

5. David Anthony, "Culture and Society in a Town in Transition: A People's History of Dar es Salaam, 1865–1939," (Ph.D. diss., University of

Wisconsin, Madison, 1983); J. A. Mangan, "Ethics and Ethnocentricity: Imperial Education in British Tropical Africa," in W. Baker and J. A. Mangan (eds.), *Sport in Africa: Essays in Social History* (New York: Africana Publishing, 1987), 138–77.

6. E. P. Thompson, *The Making of the English Working Class* (New York: Vintage, 1966), 401–47; E. P. Thompson, "Time, Work Discipline and Industrial Capitalism," *Past and Present* 38 (1967): 59–96; Gary Cross, *A Social History of Leisure since 1600* (State College, Pa.: Venture, 1990), 86–104; D. A. Reid, "The Decline of St. Monday, 1776–1876" *Past and Present* 71 (1976): 76–101; Ian Henry, *The Politics of Leisure Policy* (London: Macmillan, 1993), 6–12; Anthony Delves, "Popular Recreation and Social Conflict in Derby, 1800–1850," in E. Yeo and S. Yeo (eds.), *Popular Culture and Class Conflict, 1590–1914* (Atlantic Highlands, N.J.: Humanities, 1981), 89–127.

7. P. Martin, *Leisure and Society;* Tim Couzens, "An Introduction to the History of Football in South Africa," in Belinda Bozzoli (ed.), *Town and Countryside in the Transvaal* (Johannesburg: Ravan Press, 1983), 198–214; Anthony Clayton, "Sport and African Soldiers: The Military Diffusion of Western Sport throughout Sub-Saharan Africa," in W. Baker and J. A. Mangan (eds.), *Sport in Africa: Essays in Social History* (New York: Africana Publishing, 1987), 114–37.

8. *Annual Report of the Watoto Club of Zanzibar* (Zanzibar: UMCA Press, 1936).

9. BA 104/33: *Supplement to the Zanzibar Official Gazette,* 7 February 1920.

10. Interview with Juma Aley, Kilimani, 15 June 1992. Juma Aley captained the Zanzibar National Cricket Team for ten years and also played for London University while studying in England from 1946 to 1948.

11. *Report of the Watoto Club.*

12. Interview with Khamis Fereji, Malindi, 19 September 1991.

13. Interview with Abdulrahman Othman, Jang'ombe, 5 July 1991.

14. BA 104/49: *Supplement to the Zanzibar Official Gazette,* 3 November 1928; BA 104/43: 22 August 1925; AB 12/24 (B): Minutes of the Annual Meeting of the Sports Association of Zanzibar 1952–55; Kamati Maalum, "Taarifa ya Kamati"; interviews with Abdulrahman Othman, Jang'ombe, 14 June 1991; Hamidi Feruz, Mlandege, 16 September 1991; Rajab Mzee Ali, Malindi, 5 March 1991.

15. Interviews with Nasra Mohamed Hilal, Malindi, 25 October 1992; Abdulrahman Othman, Jang'ombe, 14 June 1991; Hamidi Feruz, Mlandege, 16 September 1991; Rajab Mzee Ali, Malindi, 5 March 1991; Juma Aley, Kilimani, 15 June 1992; Omar Said (Kidevu), Kikwajuni, 23 July 1991; Seif Rashid, Ministry of Agriculture, Kokoni, 27 July 1991; Said (Nyanya) Mohamed, Dar es Salaam, 17 September 1991.

16. Interviews with Juma Aley, Kilimani, 30 May and 15 June 1992; Omar Said (Kidevu), Kikwajuni, 23 July 1991; Ali Makame, V. I. Lenin Hospital, 27 August 1991; Abdulrahman Othman, Jang'ombe, 14 June and 5 July 1991.

17. BA 104/33: *Supplement to the Zanzibar Official Gazette,* 7 February 1920.

18. BA 104/43: *Supplement to the Zanzibar Official Gazette,* 17 October 1925; BA 104/45: 17 April 1926; BA 104/53: *Supplement to the Zanzibar Official Gazette,* 15 February 1930.

19. Myers, "Eurocentrism."

20. Interviews with Abdulrahman Othman, Jang'ombe, 14 June 1991; Omar Said (Kidevu), Kikwajuni, 23 July 1991; Hamidi Feruz, Mlandege, 16 September 1991; Said (Nyanya) Mohamed, Dar es Salaam, 17 September 1992; Rajab Mzee Ali, Malindi, 5 March 1991; Mohamed Salum, Vikokotoni, 16 June 1991; Seif Rashid, Ministry of Agriculture, Kokoni, 27 July 1991.

21. Interviews with Hamidi Feruz, Mlandege, 16 September 1991; Abdulrahman Othman, Jang'ombe, 5 July 1991.

22. Younghusband, *Glimpses,* 218.

23. BA 104/43: *Supplement to the Zanzibar Official Gazette,* 5 January 1925; BA 104/43: *Supplement to the Zanzibar Official Gazette,* 22 August 1925.

24. It appears as though the willingness of Zanzibar's colonial administrators to play against African teams may have been unique. In the case of South Africa and colonial Brazzaville colonial officials and other members of white society consciously denied Africans the ability to beat them by restricting matches along racial lines. P. Martin, "Colonialism, Youth and Football," 61; Couzens, "Football in South Africa," 202–12. In a few instances Europeans also played with African teams.

25. In 1929 there were sixty-two matches that pitted island teams against the men employed on HMS ships. BA 104/51.

26. C. James, *Beyond a Boundary,* 55.

27. Interviews with Abdulrahman Othman, Jang'ombe, 14 June 1991; Omar Said (Kidevu), Kikwajuni, 23 July 1991; Abaas Mirza, Mambo Msiige, Forodhani, 27 August 1991.

28. BA 104/*Supplement to the Zanzibar Official Gazette,* 26 November 1927 and 3 November 1928.

29. The European team took as the name for their team Mnazi Moja, which was also the name of the sports grounds on which football matches were played. In *Beyond a Boundary,* C. L. R. James also makes note of the fact that the Queen's Park Club cricket team, which was composed of white wealthy men, controlled the Queen's Park Oval, which is where all the major matches on the island were held. It would be interesting to know how common such practices of naming the colonizers team after the field on which matches were held were, and if this represented an intentional attempt by the colonizers to symbolically assert their ownership and control over the fields, and thus the game, on which sports competitions were held.

30. Interviews with Omar Said (Kidevu), Kikwajuni, 23 July 1991; Hamidi Feruz, Mlandege, 16 September 1991; BA 104/43: *Supplement to the Zanzibar Official Gazette,* 5 January 1925.

31. BA 104/43: *Supplement to the Zanzibar Official Gazette,* 22 August 1925.

32. Interviews with Abdalla Seif, Mbarouk Mzee, and Mtumwa Juma, Ng'ambo Station, 31 January 1992; Ranger, *Dance and Society;* Steve Martin, "Brass Bands and the *Beni* Phenomenon in Urban East Africa," *African Music* 7, 1 (1991): 72–81.

33. Juma Aley, unpublished handwritten manuscript and interview, Kilimani, 15 June 1992.

34. See Robert Whiting, *The Chrysanthemum and the Bat: Baseball Samurai Style* (New York: Avon, 1977), for a wonderfully readable description and analysis of the ways in which the Japanese took the "American" game of baseball and infused it with their own distinctive cultural values.

35. AB 12/24 (A): Minutes of the First Annual Meeting of the Recreation Park Sports Fund, 12 February 1927; AB 12/24 (A): Annual Report of the Sports Control Board, 1928; BA 104/49: *Supplement to the Zanzibar Official Gazette,* 17 March 1928.

36. P. Martin, "Colonialism, Youth and Football," 62–65; P. Martin, *Leisure and Society,* 104–12; Couzens, "Football in South Africa," 205–9; Robert Archer, "An Exceptional Case: Politics and Sport in South Africa's Townships," in W. Baker and J. A. Mangan (eds.), *Sport in Africa: Essays in Social History* (New York: Africana Publishing, 1987); Hyder Kindy, *Life and Politics in Mombasa* (Nairobi: East African Publishing House, 1972), 97; Anthony, "Culture and Society," 125; Remi Clignet and Maureen Stark, "Modernization and Football in Cameroon," *Journal of Modern African Studies* 12, 3 (1974): 409–21; Cecil Badenhorst and Charles Mather, "Tribal Recreation and Recreating Tribalism: Culture, Leisure and Social Control on South Africa's Gold Mines, 1940–1950," *Journal of Southern African Studies* 23, 3 (1997): 473–89.

37. Interview with Seif Rashid, Ministry of Agriculture, Kokoni, 27 July 1991.

38. AB 12/24 (A): Annual Report of the Sports Control Board, 1928.

39. AB 12/24 (A); President of Sports Control Board to Chief Secretary, 19 March 1932, AB 12/183; Wheatley to Chief Secretary, 6 November 1948, AB 85/4.

40. AB 85/4: Extract from the *Samachar,* 25 November 1956. Similar letters also appeared in another newspaper, *Adal Insaf,* around the same time.

41. Anthony, "Culture and Society," 125; AB 12/183; AB 85/4; AB 12/24 (A).

42. Vice president of Arab Sports Club to president of Sports Association, 1 February 1932, and secretary of the Sports Control Board to chief secretary, 19 March 1932, AB 12/183.

43. Wheatley to chief secretary, 6 November 1948, AB 85/4.

44. Attempts by postcolonial African governments, including that of Zanzibar, to capitalize on the power of football in support of political objectives have continued to be less than successful. As John Hargreaves argues, the ability of subordinate groups to evade and subvert control should come as little surprise. Power is a relationship between agents and is never exclusively possessed by any single agent nor generated at any single location. The sub-

altern are equally adept at engaging in discourses of practice and attributing their own meaning to daily experience. John Hargreaves, *Sport, Power and Culture: A Social and Historical Analysis of Popular Sports in Britain* (Cambridge: Polity Press, 1986), 3–4; Dean McHenry Jr., "The Use of Sports in Policy Implementation: The Case of Tanzania," *Journal of Modern African Studies* 18, 2 (1980): 237–56.

45. BA 104/45: *Zanzibar Official Gazette*, 3 April 1926.

46. AB 10/1: His Highness the Sultan's Band, 1913–1945; AB 10/218: Sultan's Dinner Party Cards, 1930–58.

47. BA 104/47: *Supplement to the Zanzibar Official Gazette*, 29 November 1927.

48. Commissioner of Police to Chief Secretary, 10 January 1927, AB 10/2; AB 10/1: His Highness the Sultan's Band; interviews with Abdalla Seif and Mtumwa Juma, Ng'ambo Station, 31 January 1992.

49. Interviews with Omar Said (Kidevu), Kikwajuni, 24 July 1991; Hamidi Feruz, Mlandege, 16 September 1991; Abdalla Seif and Mbarouk Mzee, Ng'ambo Station, 31 January 1992.

50. Juma Aley, personal manuscripts.

51. BA 104/45; BA 104/49.

52. Cross, *History of Leisure*; Henry, *Politics of Leisure*, 6–12; C. James, *Beyond a Boundary;* Delves, "Popular Recreation and Social Conflict"; Mangan, "Ethics and Ethnocentricity"; Anthony Kirk-Greene, "Imperial Administration and the Athletic Imperative: The Case of the DO in Africa," in Baker and Mangan (eds.) *Sport in Africa*, 81–113.

53. Juma Aley, personal manuscript; interview with Rajab Mzee Ali, Malindi, 5 March 1991.

54. AB 12/183: Correspondence of the Sports Association of Zanzibar.

55. BA 104/49: *Supplement to the Official Gazette*, 5 May 1928; AB 12/183.

56. Presidential report of Sports Association for the season 1945–46, AB 12/24.

57. R. H. Gower, "Swahili Borrowings from English," *Africa* 50 (1952); reprinted in *Tanganyikan Notes and Records* 50 (1958): 118–20.

58. Interviews with Seif Rashid, Ministry of Agriculture, Kokoni, 27 July 1992; Said (Nyanya) Mohamed, Dar es Salaam, 17 September 1992; Abdulrahman Othman, Jang'ombe, 5 July 1991.

59. AB 12/183; BA 104/57; interviews with Abdulrahman Othman, Jang'ombe, 14 June 1991; Juma Aley, 30 May 1992; Omar Said (Kidevu), Kikwajuni, 23 July 1991.

60. Interview with Omar Said (Kidevu), Kikwajuni, 23 July 1991.

61. Interview with Abdulrahman Othman, Jang'ombe, 14 June 1991.

62. From his earliest days in Zanzibar, Wheatley was avidly involved in the organization of football. During his twenty-eight years of residence in the isles he oversaw the formation of the PWD team, played with African employees on the PWD team, served the Sports Control Board in many capacities, including president, and oversaw the construction of Zanzibar's first enclosed stadium in 1949. Wheatley, who came to Zanzibar as a mechanic,

was later decorated as a Member of the British Empire (MBE) in recognition of his role in developing sports in Zanzibar. AB 12/24 (B); Juma Aley, personal manuscript. Nearly every Zanzibari man I spoke to mentioned Mr. Wheatley and the enthusiasm he brought to sports on the island.

63. AB 12/24 (A).

64. Ibid.

65. Interviews with Abdulrahman Othman, Jang'ombe, 5 July 1991; Omar Said (Kidevu), Kikwajuni, 23 July 1991; Hamidi Feruz, Mlandege, 16 September 1991.

66. Interview with Mohamed Ali (Mzee Jahare), Malindi, 29 June 1992.

67. AB 12/24(B); AB 85/4.

68. Eugene Genovese, *Roll Jordan Roll: The World the Slaves Made* (New York: Vintage, 1972), 295–309; F. Cooper, *African Waterfront*, 13–25, 142–58.

69. Interviews with Abdulrahman Othman, Jang'ombe, 5 July 1991; Hamidi Feruz, Mlandege, 16 September 1991; Omar Said (Kidevu), Kikwajuni, 23 July 1991; Mohamed Ali (Mzee Jahare), Malindi, 29 June 1992.

70. As Charles Ambler has argued, studies of leisure need to be attentive not simply to the activities being pursued, but to the enjoyment and satisfaction that individuals get from participating in such activities. Similar conflicts emerged between mine managers and player-workers on the Copperbelt, where players refused to show up for matches unless they were paid overtime for their "work." Ambler, "A History of Leisure in Colonial Urban Africa," paper presented at the annual meeting of the African Studies Association, Toronto, 1994, 16–18.

71. Interview with Hamidi Feruz, Mlandege, 16 September 1991.

72. Afro-Shirazi Party, *The History of Zanzibar Africans and the Formation of the Afro-Shirazi Party* (Zanzibar: Afro-Shirazi Headquarters, n.d.); R. K. Mwanjisi, *Ndugu Abeid Amani Karume* (Nairobi: East African Publishing House, 1967), 14–16; interview with Juma Aley, Kilimani, 15 June 1992.

73. Mwanjisi, *Abeid Amani Karume*, 20.

74. Afro-Shirazi, *History of Zanzibar Africans*. The administration estimated the membership of the African Association at 2,500 in 1937. Provincial Commissioner to District Commissioner, Zanzibar, 26 April 1937, AB 12/180: African Association.

75. Mwanjisi, *Abeid Amani Karume*, 14–16.

76. Interview with Abdulrahman Othman, Jang'ombe, 14 June 1991.

77. Interview with Hamidi Feruz, Mlandege, 16 September 1991.

78. Interviews with Hamidi Feruz, Mlandege, 16 September 1991; Abdulrahman Othman, Jang'ombe, 14 June 1991; Omar Said (Kidevu), Kikwajuni, 23 July 1991.

79. Kamati Maalum, "Taarifa ya Kamati," 17; Annual Report of the President of the Sports Control Board, 1941 (AB 12/24 (A); interviews with Rajab Mzee Ali, Malindi, 5 March 1991; Abdulrahman Othman, Jang'ombe, 5 July 1991; Abaas Mirza, Mambo Msiige, Forodhani, 27 August 1991. Suspicions regarding the administration's motivations for inaugurating the reserve league were also fueled by the fact that the sports of hockey and

cricket—which were dominated by the elite—continued to be organized along ethnic lines.

80. Interview with Khamis Fereji, Malindi, 19 September 1991.

81. Work and ethnic clubs were also allowed to enter the elimination tournaments for the Zanzibar Cup.

82. Interview with Mohamed Salum, Vikokotoni, 16 June 1991.

83. Interview with Abdulrahman Othman, Jang'ombe, 14 June 1991.

84. Personal communication, 26 September 1991. Wilson was stationed in Zanzibar from 1933 to 1948.

85. Interviews with Khamis Fereji, Malindi, 19 September 1991; Abdulrahman Othman, Jang'ombe, 5 July 1991.

86. Interview with Said (Nyanya) Mohammed, Dar es Salaam, 17 September 1992.

87. Interview with Rajab Mzee Ali, Malindi, 5 March 1991.

88. Interviews with Said (Nyanya) Mohamed, Dar es Salaam, 17 September 1992; Rajab Mzee Ali, Malindi, 5 March 1991; Ali Makame, CCM Headquarters, Vikokotoni, 27 August 1991; Abdulrahman Othman, Jang'ombe, 14 June 1991.

89. Interview with Ali Makame, CCM Headquarters, Vikokotoni, 27 August 1991.

90. Interviews with Mohamed Salum, Vikokotoni, 16 June 1991; Said (Nyanya) Mohamed, Dar es Salaam, 17 September 1992; Abdulrahman Othman, Jang'ombe, 14 June 1991; Ali Makame, Vikokotoni, 27 August 1991.

91. Interview with Khamis Fereji, Malindi, 19 September 1991.

92. Interview with Abdulrahman Othman, Jang'ombe, 14 June 1991.

93. Saleh, *History of the Comorians,* 18–19.

94. AK 14/10: Ngoma; Saleh, *History of the Comorians.*

95. DC urban and DC rural to Senior Commissioner, 31 January 1956, AK 14/10: Ngomas.

96. Interviews with Mohamed Ali (Mzee Jahare), Malindi, 29 June 1992; Amani Stadi, Mkamasini, 4 August 1992.

97. Interview with Abdulrahman Othman, Jang'ombe, 14 June 1991.

98. Interviews with Omar Said (Kidevu), Kikwajuni, 23 July 1991; Idirisa Baraka, CCM Headquarters, Vikokotoni, 14 January 1992; Abdulrahman Othman, Jang'ombe, 14 June 1991.

99. Interviews with Hamidi Feruz, Mlandege, 16 September 1991; Abdulrahman Othman, Jang'ombe, 14 June 1991.

100. Interview with Rajab Mzee Ali, Malindi, 5 March 1991.

101. See Fair, "Pastimes and Politics," 284–300.

102. Interview with Nasra Mohamed Hilal, Malindi, 25 October 1992.

Chapter 6

1. P. Martin, *Leisure and Society,* 99.

Glossary

Swahili nouns typically consist of a root and a prefix, which indicates whether the noun is singular or plural. I have listed both forms in the glossary to aid those unfamiliar with the Swahili noun class system in finding the term they are looking for. However, in an attempt to make the text more accessible to non-Swahili-speaking readers, the singular form of nouns followed by an *s* has been used whenever possible for the plural. For example, the plural form of Islamic judge (*kadhi*) has been given as kadhis, rather than *makadhi*. In the text, most references to people are made using the root of the word only. For example, *Swahili* refers both to an individual of that culture (rather than the proper *mswahili*) and to the people as a group (*waswahili*). Arabic spellings of Islamic terms, rather than their Swahili variants, have been used in the text, with the exception of the term *waqf,* which appears frequently and is spelled in Zanzibar as *wakf.*

al-Busaidi: the ruling clan in Zanzibar, descended from Arabs from Oman.

ASP (Afro-Shirazi Party):   the political party that ruled Zanzibar from the 1964 revolution until 1977, when ASP merged with the Tanganyikan party, TANU (Tanganyikan African National Union) to form CCM (Chama cha Mapinduzi), which rules all of Tanzania.

barakoa: face masks worn by female members of Omani clans in nineteenth-century Zanzibar. A form of veil (figs. 2.4, 2.5).

baraza: stone seats built along the front of Swahili buildings used as neighborhood meeting and gossip spots.

beni: dance societies that feature a big side-drum, brass instruments, and European-style military uniforms.

Bibi: a term of respect given to women, formerly reserved for women of the aristocracy, now commonly used for grandmother or any elderly or respected woman; Madam, lady, mistress of a household.

buibui: a black garment worn by Swahili women to cover their bodies, heads, and sometimes faces while in public (figs. 2.13, 2.14).

Bwana: a term of respect used when addressing men; Sir. Formerly used to signify a master or owner.

ghubighubi: one fashion of wearing a buibui (fig. 2.14).

kadhi: Islamic judge.

kanga: colorful cloths, sold in pairs, worn by women in East Africa (figs. 2.11, 2.12).

kaniki: dark blue or black cloths worn by poor and slave women (fig. 2.3).

kibarua (**pl.** *vibarua*): a slave who was hired out and paid wages, a portion of which he or she was allowed to keep.

Kiswahili: the Swahili language.

kiunga (**from** *-unga*): to join together, connect or unite; patron-client ties.

Kiungani: the nineteenth-century term used for Ng'ambo.

kunguiya: one of a pair of dances performed as part of female puberty initiation. The other dance is *ndege*.

masuria: see "suria."

maulid: Islamic religious celebrations involving the performance of poetry or Qur'anic verse often to the accompaniment of tambourines and drums. Originally performed in celebration of the birth of the Prophet Muhammad.

mitaa: see "mtaa."

mkinda: a particular form of female puberty initiation created in Zanzibar Town at the turn of the twentieth century. Mkinda included the public performance of two particular dances, *kunguiya* and *ndege*.

mshamba: a person from the countryside. Frequently used to deride someone as uncouth, a lout, or a country bumpkin.

mstaarabu: a person possessing Arab or civilized customs and habits.

mtaa (pl. *mitaa*): neighborhood.

mwungwana (pl. *waungwana*): a freeborn, well-bred, refined urban person. A person of high social standing or rank.

mzalia (pl. *wazalia*): a coastal slave born in an owner's household. An mzalia would frequently be awarded rights and responsibilities not granted to individuals who were enslaved as adults.

ndege (literally "bird"): a dance performed as part of the *mkinda* puberty initiation ceremonies. Elaborately and expensively dressed, bejeweled, and coiffed women paraded through the streets of town carrying parasols or umbrellas (fig. 2. 18).

Ng'ambo (literally "the other side" of a creek, road; "the opposite side"): the part of urban Zanzibar inhabited largely by working-class women and men.

ngoma (sing. and pl.): drum. Dance, music, and poetry performance or competition.

PWD (Public Works Department): one of the largest employers of men in Zanzibar Town during the colonial era.

qasida: Islamic religious poetry performed at either sacred or secular events.

Seyyid/Seyyida: a title given to male and female members of the Royal Family.

shamba (pl. *mashamba*): farm, plantation, or countryside.

suria (pl. *masuria*): slave concubine.

tariqa **(literally "the path" or "the way" to communication with God):** a mystical tradition in Sunni Islam, associated with Sufi brotherhoods; devotional groups that involve both women and men.

ukaya: a long, frequently sheer, cloth used by women to cover their heads or faces (figs. 2.6, 2.10, 2.13, 2.14).

Unguja: the coastal term for one of the two main islands commonly referred to collectively as Zanzibar; the island on which Zanzibar Town is located. Pemba is the other major island.

uwezo: social and economic ability; power, competence, capacity.

ustaarabu: civilized, like an Arab.

vibarua: see "kibarua."

wakf: endowments of property held in trust under Islamic law for religious or charitable purposes.

waungwana: see "mwungwana."

wazalia: see "mzalia."

zikiri: an Islamic ritual that involves repetitive recitation of the names of God. A form of religious service practiced by mystical brotherhoods.

Bibliography

The Swahili do not have family or "last" names in the Western sense. Individual names have been alphabetized by first name, followed by the father's name, as this is how they would be known in Zanzibar. Published works are listed as found in OCLC.

Interviews

All interviews were conducted by the author, in Kiswahili. Most were recorded on cassette tape and were then transcribed by Amour Khalid Andrew, to whom I am eternally indebted. In addition to interviews conducted with the persons listed below, I conducted additional interviews with persons who requested that their anonymity be preserved. Individuals who are more commonly known by their nickname than their given name have been listed with their nickname in parentheses, for example: Amina Seif Othman (Bibi Amina Mapande). In quotes from the interviews I have added italics to indicate verbal emphasis.

Abaas Mirza. Mambo Msiige, Forodhani, 27 August 1991.
Abdalla Aziz. Makunduchi, 25 February 1992.
Abdalla Ibrahim. Kama, 11 June 1992.
Abdalla Seif. Ng'ambo Station, 31 January 1992.
Abdulrahman Ali Saleh. Saleh Madawa, 26 June 1991; Malindi, 14 August 1991.
Abdulrahman Othman. Jang'ombe, 14 June, 5 July 1991.
Adam Mzee. Makunduchi, 26 February 1992.

Adija Haji Simai. Michenzani, 17 January, 3 February 1992.

Adija Salum Bakari. Miembeni, 23 March, 25 May 1992; 27 July 1995.

Ali Haji Muadhini. Makunduchi, 25 February 1992.

Ali Juma Mwinyi. Kiembe Samaki, 1 June 1992.

Ali Makame. V. I. Lenin Hospital, 27 August 1991; CCM Headquarters, Vikokotoni, 13 January 1992.

Ali Sultan Issa. Chuini, 15 June 1992.

Amani Stadi. Mkamasini, 23 July, 3 August, 4 August 1992.

Amina Aboud. Zizi la Ng'ombe, 23 December 1991; 13 January, 15 January, 17 January 1992; 28 August 1995.

Amina Mohamed Musa. Amani, 2 September 1992.

Amina Seif Othman (Bibi Amina Mapande). Michenzani, 19 July, 25 July, 26 July 1995.

Arafa Salum Ahmed. Malindi, 9 July 1995.

Bakari Jabu. Mbweni, 30 December 1991.

Bakia binti Juma. Miembeni, 10 July 1992.

Fatma binti Baraka (Bibi Kidude). Kisiwandui, 30 September 1991; Raha Leo, 9 October 1991, 15 September 1992; Haile Selassie School, 16 January 1992.

Fatma Toti. Kokoni, 18 January 1992.

Fatuma Khamis. Shauri Moyo, 26 April 1992.

Ghaniya Said. Malindi, 14 July 1995.

M. A. Ghassany (Mzee Bingwa). Vuga, 14 May, 14 July, 28 July 1992.

Hamed Ali Suleiman. Tabora, 25 July 1992.

Hamidi Feruz. Mlandege, 16 September 1991.

Hamza Omar Khatib. Amani, 2 September 1992.

Hawa Pili Pandu. Amani, 2 September 1992.

Idirisa Baraka. CCM Headquarters, Vikokotoni, 14 January 1992.

Jamal Ramadhan Nasibu. CCM Headquarters, Vikokotoni, 19 February, 20 February 1991.

Juma Aley. Kilimani, 30 May, 10 June, 15 June 1992.

Juma Machano. Malindi, 20 October 1992.

Joyti Raj. Dar es Salaam, 14 July 1989.

Khamis Fereji. Malindi, 19 September 1991.

Kiboga Bakari. Kwa Alinatoo, 29 July, 1 August 1995.

Latifuu Ali Marzuk. Kisimamajongoo, 15 August 1995.

Machano Mtwana Haji. Kariakoo, 8 July 1992.

Mariam Mohamed Ali. Kariakoo, 10 August 1995

Maryam Mohamed. Mwembetanga, 20 July 1995.

Masoud Mohamed Rashid (Dr. Ayoubu). Forodhani, 20 January 1992.

Maulid Rehani. Kisimamajongoo, 14 July, 8 August 1995.

Mbarak Mtubwe. Makunduchi, 25 February 1992.

Mbarouk Mzee. Ng'ambo Station, 31 January 1992.

Mchangani Shopkeepers' Survey. Mchangani, 16 December 1991.

R. F. Medon. Shangani, 27 May 1992.

Mkubwa Stadi Fundi. Kisimamajongoo, 8 August 1995.

Mohamed Abdallah. Kizimbani, 26 June 1992.

Mohamed Ali (Mzee Jahare). Malindi, 29 June, 6 September 1992.

Mohamed Salum. Vikokotoni, 16 June 1991.

Mohamed Salum. Kizimbani, 26 June 1992.

Mohamed Seif Khatib. State House, Mnazi Moja, 11 February 1991; Michenzani, 24 February 1991.

(Chief) Msabila Lugusha. Tabora, 25 July 1992.

Mtumwa Juma. Ng'ambo Station, 31 January 1992.

Mwajuma Ali. Shauri Moyo, 26 April, 28 April, 30 November 1992.

Mwalim Idd Farhan. Forodhani, 24 September, 29 September; Kokoni, 5 October, 14 October, 23 December 1991.

Mwalim Salum Pandu. Makunduchi, 25 February 1992.

Mwapombe. Uwanja wa Ndege, 7 January 1992.

Mwinyi Khatib Hamedi. Tabora, 26 July 1992.

Mzee Ali. Kwahani, 19 March 1992.

Mzee Ramadhani. Kizimbani, 26 June 1992.

Nasra Mohamed Hilal. Malindi, 14 July 1991; 28 July, 25 October 1992.

Nunu binti Salum (Bibi Raba). Kiswandui, 18 March 1992.

Omar Said (Kidevu). Kikwajuni, 23 July 1991.

Omar Shah. Kizimbani, 26 June 1992.

Omar Zahran. Malindi, 31 May 1992.

Pili Jaha Ubwa. Shaangani, 18 February 1991.

Rajab Mzee Ali. Malindi, 5 March 1991.

Ramadhani Mshandete. Kizimbani, 26 June 1992.

Said Mohamed. Michenzani, 18 July 1991; Mwera, 14 January, 25 March 1992.

Said (Nyanya) Mohamed. Dar es Salaam, 17 September 1992.

Salum Baraka Said. Miembeni, 13 July 1992.

Seif Rashid. Ministry of Agriculture, Kokoni, 27 July, 6 December 1991.

Seif Salim. Vuga, 28 December 1992.

Shaaban Ali Suleiman. Tabora, 25 July 1992.

Subira Mzee. Kwa Hani, 17 July 1995.

Suleiman Ali. Tabora, 25 July 1992.

Suleiman Mpakira Suleiman. Amani, 2 September 1992.

Suleiman Salum Mohamed. Malindi, 12 December 1991.

Clothing Survey, 1995

A survey on clothing and fashion was administered from June through August 1995 by the author and the following research assistants: Maryam Suleiman Omar, Zuhura Shamte, and Ally Hassan. In addition to the respondents listed, ten other women also participated in the survey but preferred that their names not be mentioned.

Adija Salum Bakari. Miembeni, 3 July.

Amina Seif Othman. Michenzani, 14 July.

Arafa Salum Ahmed. Malindi, 4 July.

Asha Feruz. Mwembeladu, 4 July.
BiMkubwa Stadi Fundi. Kisimamajongoo, 25 July, 8 August.
Fatma Hafidh. Mtendeni, 24 July.
Fatuma Abdalla. Uwanja wa Farasi, 16 July.
Hilal Amour Seif. Mwembetanga, 14 July.
Kairi Mohammed. Kisiwandui, 25 July.
Kijakazi Hamisi. Kwahani, 16 July.
Latifuu Ali Marzuk. Kisimamajongoo, 16 August.
Mauwa binti Khamis. Daraja Bovu, 24 July.
Mgeni Ali Hassan. Kisimamajongoo, 14 August.
Mwanaidi Adi. Mwembetanga, 27 July.
Mwanamvita Mrisho. Kwahani, 16 July.
Nunu Salum. Kisiwandui, 18 July.
Rahma Himid. Zizi la Ng'ombe, 19 July.
Salma Halfa. Kisimamajongoo, 29 June.
Shemsa Mohammed. Kisimamajongoo, 29 June.
Subira Mzee. Kwahani, 17 July.
Zaina Omari. Kwahani, 16 July.

Archival Sources

Zanzibar National Archives

Secretariat: Agriculture, 1908–64
AB 4/38 (A): Clove Labour, 1898–1926.
AB 4/38 (B): Clove Labour, 1926–.
AB 4/39: Boycott of Clove-Picking Contracts.

Secretariat: Provisional and District Administration, 1921–64
AB 8/87: Report of the Committee Appointed to Advise on Matters Relating to Native Administration, 1932–39.

Secretariat: Social Welfare
AB 9/70: Brothels, 1917–27.

Secretariat: Sultan and the Royal Family
AB 10/1: His Highness the Sultan's Band, vol. 1, 1913–45.
AB 10/2: His Highness the Sultan's Band, Private Performances, 1920–50.
AB 10/3: His Highness the Sultan's Band, 1945–62.
AB 10/89: Alia binti Mohamed, 1920–35.
AB 10/105: Loan to Seyyida Meya.
AB 10/106: Affairs of Seyyida Meya.
AB 10/107: Seyyida Nunu binti Ali, 1924–30.
AB 10/108: Rusoona binti Tamim, Ex-Sultan's Concubine, 1913–55.
AB 10/109: Recognition of Mr. R. Said Ruete as a Member of the Royal Family.

AB 10/112: Sakina binti Abdula, 1927.
AB 10/113: Bibi Sakina, Second Wife of the Late Sultan, 1930–56.
AB 10/116: Surias of the Late Seyyid Ali bin Said, 1923–56.
AB 10/118: Affairs of Seyyida Zeana, 1926–56.
AB 10/195: Sultan's Christmas Card List, 1950–54.
AB 10/198: Legal Proceedings against Members of the Aulad Iman.
AB 10/199: Royal Family, General, 1931–55.
AB 10/200: Royal Marriages Decree, 1940.
AB 10/215: Seyyida Sheriffa binti Barghash bin Said and Seyyida Aliya binti Barghash, 1911–47.
AB 10/218: Sultan's Dinner Party Cards, 1930–58.

Secretariat: Clubs and Associations
AB 12/2: Shirazi Association, 1940–53.
AB 12/3: Non-European Civil Servants Association, 1948–56.
AB 12/11: Youth Movement in Zanzibar.
AB 12/22: Arab Hadhramout Association, 1937–54.
AB 12/24 (A): Sports Association of Zanzibar, 1926–45.
AB 12/24 (B): Minutes of the Annual Meeting of the Sports Association of Zanzibar, 1952–55.
AB 12/28: Arab Association, 1934–54.
AB 12/30: Manyema Union, 1933–40.
AB 12/31: Young Arab Union, 1933–56.
AB 12/32: Young Muslim League, 1938.
AB 12/33: African Youth Union.
AB 12/67: Cosmopolitan Club, 1947–63.
AB 12/74: Comorian Social Club.
AB 12/128: Joining of Political Associations by Government Employees.
AB 12/180: African Association.
AB 12/183: Correspondence of the Sports Association of Zanzibar, 1932.
AB 85/4 (A): Sports Control Board, 1943–56.
AB 85/4 (B): Sports Control Board Appointments, 1943–56.

Secretariat: Income Tax
AB 28/12: Demonstration by Native Hut Owners against the Payment of Ground Rent on 11 January 1929.
AB 28/13: Native Tax Decree, 1932.
AB 28/14: Rules under the Native Tax Decree, 1932–37.
AB 28/15: Rules under the Native Tax Decree, 1933.
AB 28/16: Collection of Native Hut Tax in Town.
AB 28/17: Abolition of Hut Tax and consequent alteration of tariff duties, 1937.

Secretariat: Rent Records Series
AB 36/1: Rent Boards, 1944–54.
AB 36/5 (A): The Increase of Rent (restriction) Decree no. 23 of 1922.
AB 36/5 (B): Statement of Condensed Particulars of Gurfas in Zanzibar.

AB 36/12: Proposed Ground Rent Decree, 1912–17.

AB 36/13–19: Ground Rent Restriction Decree.

AB 36/20 (A): Ground Rents, 1898–1912.

AB 36/21: Restriction of House Rents, 1917–44.

AB 36/22: Ground Rents, 1926–54.

AB 36/23: Procedure Regarding Compensation Paid to Hut Owners in Ng'ambo in Relation to Ground Rent Due by Them, 1932–38.

Secretariat: Municipal and Town Council

AB 39/151: Stone Town Town Council Minutes, 1940.

AB 39/152: Ng'ambo Town Council Minutes, 1944–48.

AB 39/153: Joint Town Council Minutes, 1948–50.

AB 39/154: Zanzibar Town Council, 1948–49.

AB 39/155: Ng'ambo.

AB 39/156–61: Zanzibar Township Council.

AB 39/177: Town Planning Decree, 1925–47.

AB 39/207: Minutes of the Joint Building Authority.

AB 39/337: Rules under the Ngoma Regulation Decree, 1929–53.

AB 39/338: Ngoma Prohibition and Regulation Decree no. 35 of 1934 and Amendment no. 19 of 1935.

AB 39/339: Rules under the Ngoma Regulation Decree.

Secretariat: Miscellaneous

AB 14/67: Moneylenders Decree, 1927–55.

AB 14/68: Native Mortgages to Moneylenders, 1930–31.

AB 26/65: Status of Half-Castes.

AB 30/14: African Marriage Customs, 1947.

AB 30/18: Zanzibar Native Divorce Decree, 1915–52.

AB 30/22: Campaign amongst the Arabs and Africans against Extravagant Expenditure on Marriage Feasts, Funeral Feasts, etc.

AB 34/1: Confidential: Reorganization of Wakf Department, 1913.

Land Office

AE 8/10: Land Claimed at Mlandege by Gulamhussein Remtulla Hemani.

AE 8/11: Claim of land at Ng'ambo by Mohamedhussein Tharia Topan, 1927–28.

AE 8/19: Claim over land at Kisimamajongoo by M. H. Tharia Topan, 1959–62.

Medical Department

AJ 1/9: Age of Consent, 1934.

AJ 3/24: Child Marriages.

AJ 6/1: Family Planning.

AJ 11/30: Living and Housing Conditions, 1935–42.

AJ 14/1: Opium Habits, 1930–56.

AJ 21/5: Venereal Disease, 1928–45.

AJ 22/10: Workmen's Compensation, 1938–57.

AJ 24/1: Yaws, 1935–56.

Provincial Administration
AK 1/72: African Music Society, 1948–59.
AK 1/104: Confidential: Land Alienation.
AK 13/1: Siri Confidential: Middleton Report on Land Tenure, 1959–62.
AK 13/11 (A): Coffee Shop Gossip Reports, 1962.
AK 14/10: Ngomas, 1936–69.
AK 17/70: Rationing.
AK 18/1. Confidential: Squatters.
AK 18/13: Seasonal Dhow Visits, 1939–60.
AK 18/26: Squatters, 1958–63.
AK 20/1: Confidential: Unrest: Zanzibar Town, 1948–60.
AK 20/2: Unrest: Mainland Labour, 1948–60.

Clove Growers' Association
AP 28/5, 12–15, 22, 41, 46, 51: Census of Rural Plantation Ownership.
AP 29/1–4, 9, 17: Clove Bonus Registers.
AP 38/12: Alienation at Kiembe Samaki, 1930–58.

Agricultural Department
AU 1/13: Labour on Clove Plantations.
AU 1/56: Coir Making, 1939–50.
AU 2/12: Monthly Reports, Kizimbani, 1933–34.
AU 2/29: Riot Enquiry Commission, 1936–52.
AU 2/54: Report on Peasant Agriculture, 1940–47.
AU 2/59: Record of Mudirs' Meetings, 1944–57.
AU 2/129: Monthly Reports from District Agriculture Officers, 1947–50.
AU 3/9: Cultivation by Squatters, 1958–61.
AU 3/30: Small-Holdings, 1936–39.
AU 3/47: Organization of Labour, Rates of Pay, and Working Hours, 1939–45.
AU 3/61: Mainland Labour, 1931–41.
AU 3/91: Theft of Agricultural Produce, 1927–48.
AU 3/95: Land Tenure and Leases, 1932–58.
AU 9/2: Applications for Employment, Kizimbani, 1936–60.
AU 13/5: Land Tenure and Land Usage.
AU 17/164: Squatters on Government Plantations, 1939–61.
AU 17/166: Pengeles and Daily Tasks, 1941–65.

Maps
AW 2/24: Government, Private, Public Land, 1910.
AW 2/26: Map of Ng'ambo, 1892.
AW 2/27: Map of Ng'ambo, 1910.
AW 2/100: Ng'ambo Area Folder, 1938.
AW 2/106: Map of Racial Districts, 1946.

AW 2/133: Map of Town, 1928.
AW 7/4: Mudiras.

Birth, Death, and Marriage Certificates
DJ 1/2: Christian Marriage Registers, 1935–59.
DJ 1/3: Marriage and Divorce Registers, 1956–57.
DJ 2/1–10: Hati ya Kujulisha Ufutaji wa Ukabila [Certificates announcing the abolition of (shirazi) ethnicity], 1970–73.
DJ 3/1–10: Hati ya Kujulisha Ufutaji wa Ukabila, 1970–73.
DJ 4/1–7: Hati ya Kujulisha Ufutaji wa Ukabila, 1970–73.

Court Records
HC 3/ High Court Civil Cases.
HC 4/ High Court Criminal Cases.
HC 8/ Sultan's Court Cases.
HC 13/ Ground Rent and Hut Tax Cases.
HC 14/ Lunacy Cases.
HC 22/ Juvenile Court Cases.

Wakf Commission
HD 3/5: Wakf of Seyyid Suleiman bin Hamed bin Said at Kiunga, Ng'ambo.
HD 3/28: Collection of Ground Rent, Wakf Department, 1931–66.
HD 3/31: Wakf of Fatma binti Amber, Freed Slave of Said bin Masud al-Barwani.
HD 5/17: Wakf of Hammoud bin Seif, Gulioni.
HD 5/42: Procedures for Sale of Wakf Houses.
HD 5/43: Wakf of BiMetle binti Said.
HD 5/55: Wakf of Jokha binti Ahmed bin Nassor.
HD 5/60: Wakf of Seyyid Hamoud bin Ahmed al-Busaidi, Shamba at Saateni for Freed Slaves.
HD 5/64: Wakf of Seyyida Jokha binti Hamoud bin Ahmed.
HD 5/66: Wakf of Seyyid Hamoud bin Ahmed.
HD 5/76: Wakf of Seyyid Hamoud bin Ahmed.
HD 6/23: Wakf of Aysha binti Juma at Kiungani.
HD 6/31: Wakf of ZemZem binti Said at Mtoni.
HD 6/55: Wakf of Seyyid Hamoud bin Ahmed al-Busaidi, 1915–59.
HD 6/60: Wakf of Seyyid Hamoud bin Ahmed.
HD 6/128: Wakf of Khole binti Hamoud at Bungi.
HD 6/154: Wakf of Seyyida Khole binti Hamoud al-Busaidi.
HD 10/6: Auditors' Recommendations.
HD 10/7: Circulars, Agendas, and Minutes of Wakf Commission Meetings, 1915–43.
HD 10/13: Mauli Wakf Mwembetanga.
HD 10/14: Appointment of Wakf Commissioners, 1916–62.
HD 10/17: Minutes of Commission Meetings, 1915–43.
HD 10/19: Law Regarding Kadhi Interpretations, 1915–63.

HD 10/32: General Correspondence.
HD 10/61: Sale of Wakf Properties, 1951–52.
HD 10/90: Deeds of Dedication, 1914–26.

Official Government Reports and Publications
BA 3/11: Report of the Department of Agriculture for 1910.
BA 3/19: Report on the Indebtedness of the Agricultural Classes, 1933.
BA 3/20: Report on the Indebtedness of the Agricultural Class, 1935.
BA 4/16: Rationalization of the Clove Industry.
BA 4/17: Clove Cultivation, 1931.
BA 5/30: Labour Conciliation Committee, 2 September 1948.
BA 12/133: G. H. Shelswell-White. *Notes on the Hadhrami Community in Zanzibar.* Zanzibar: Government Printing Office, 1935.
BA 16/36–41: Debates of the Legislative Council, 1926–38.
BA 19/1–15: *Labour Reports.* Zanzibar: Government Printer, 1946–61.
BA 30/5: Annual Report of the DC Urban, 1937.
BA 30/8: Record of Mudirs' Meetings, 1944–57.
BA 34/1: Non-Native Census, 1921.
BA 34/2: Report of the Native Census of Zanzibar, 1924.
BA 34/3: Report of the Census Enumeration for the Entire Zanzibar Protectorate, 1931.
BA 34/4: Census of the Entire Population, 1948.
BA 34/5: Draft Report on the 1948 Census.
BA 34/6: Census Report, 1958.
BA 36/21: Restriction of House Rents, 1917–44.
BA 106/15: Report of the Commission of Enquiry Concerning the Riot in Zanzibar on the 7th of February, 1936.

Afro-Shirazi. *The History of Zanzibar Africans and the Formation of the Afro-Shirazi Party.* Zanzibar: Afro-Shirazi Headquarters, n.d.
Annual Report of the Agriculture Department. Zanzibar: Government Printer, 1911.
Annual Report of the Watoto Club of Zanzibar. Zanzibar: UMCA Press, 1936.
C. A. Bartlett and J. S. Last. *Report on the Indebtedness of the Agricultural Class.* Zanzibar: Government Printing Office, 1933.
Batson, Edward. *Report on Proposals for a Social Survey of Zanzibar.* Zanzibar: Government Printing Office, 1948.
———. *Social Survey of Zanzibar Protectorate.* 21 vols. Cape Town: School of Social Sciences and Social Administration at the University of Cape Town, 1960.
Department of Overseas Trade. *Report on the Trade and Commercial Prospects of East Africa* (London: HM Stationery Office, 1923).
Memorandum on Certain Aspects of the Zanzibar Clove Industry. Zanzibar: Government Printing Office, 1926.
Muhtasari wa Riporti ya Tume ya Kuchunguza Taratibu na Mfumo wa Utoaji wa Nyaraka za Serikali. Zanzibar: Government Printer, 1992.

Pemba: Report for the Year 1900 on the Trade and Commerce of Zanzibar. London: H.M. Stationery Office, 1901.

Pim, Sir Alan. *Report of the Commission Appointed to Consider and Report on the Financial Position and Policy of the Zanzibar Government in Relation to Its Economic Resources.* Zanzibar: Government Printing Office, 1932.

Report for the Year 1897 on the Trade and Commerce of Zanzibar. London: H.M. Stationery Office, 1898.

Report of the Labour Conciliation Committee, 2 September 1948. Zanzibar: Government Printer, 1948.

Report of the Commission on Agriculture. Zanzibar: Government Printer, 1923.

Report on Labour for the Zanzibar Protectorate. Zanzibar: Government Printer, 1943.

Report on the Administration and Finance of the Zanzibar Government for the Year 1902. Zanzibar: Government Printing Office, 1903.

Shelswell-White, G. H. *A Visitor's Guide to Zanzibar.* Zanzibar: Government Printing Office, 1932.

Sinclair, John. *Zanzibar Government, a Report on the Protectorate, 1911–23.* Zanzibar: Government Printing Office, 1923.

Troup, R. S. *Report on Clove Cultivation in the Zanzibar Protectorate.* Zanzibar: Government Printing Office, 1932.

Wilson, F. B. "A Note on Adult Literacy amongst the Rural Population of the Zanzibar Protectorate." Zanzibar: Government Printing Office, 1939.

Zanzibar Blue Books.

Zanzibar Government Annual Reports.

Tanzanian National Archives
Provincial and District Books for Coast and Tabora Regions.

Public Records Office, London
PRO/CO 68/47/16: Official Commission of Enquiry, Disturbances at the Central Prison, Zanzibar, 1928.

PRO/CO 618: Zanzibar Correspondence, 1913–40.

PRO/CO 859/35/7: Report on the Zanzibar Prisons, 1939.

British Library, EMI Music Archives
His Master's Voice, Black Label Catalogues: August 1928; December 1928; 1929; Second Supplement 1929; Second Supplement 1930.

His Master's Voice, Black and Blue Catalogues: Third Supplement 1930; Fourth Supplement 1931; [Fifth] Supplement May 1931; [Sixth] Supplement August 1931.

Newspapers Cited

The Express, 1991–93.
Kweupe, 1970.
Maarifa, 1953.

Mwongozi, 1948.
Nuru, 1992–93.
The Samachar, 1956.
Tanganyika Standard, 1948.
Zanzibar Official Gazette, 1890–1932.

Legal Documents

Law Reports of Zanzibar, 1951–56. London: Waterlow and Sons, 1957.
Zanzibar Law Reports, 1868–1918. London: Waterlow and Sons, 1920.
Zanzibar Law Reports, 1923–27. London: Waterlow and Sons, 1928.
Zanzibar Law Reports, 1935–38. London: Waterlow and Sons, 1939.

Secondary Sources and Published Primary Sources

Abdulaziz, Mohamed. *Muyaka, Nineteenth-Century Swahili Popular Poetry.* Nairobi: Kenya Literature Bureau, 1979.

Abu-Lughod, Leila. "The Romance of Resistance: Tracing Transformation of Power through Bedouin Women." *American Ethnologist* 1, 1 (1990): 41–51.

Aley, Juma. Manuscript on Organized Sport in Zanzibar, Conveyed to the author on 10 June 1992.

———. *Zanzibar, in the Context.* New Delhi: Lancers Books, 1988.

———. "The Zanzibar Town: Continuity of Urban Tradition." Paper presented at the Zanzibar Stone Town Workshop, Zanzibar, 19–20 November 1990.

al-Faruqi, Lois Ibsen. *An Annotated Glossary of Arabic Musical Terms.* Westport, Conn.: Greenwood Press, 1981.

———. "Cantillation of the Qur'an." *Asian Music* 19, 1 (1987): 2–25.

Allen, James de Vere. "Swahili Culture and the Nature of East Coast Settlement." *International Journal of African Historical Studies* 14, 2 (1981): 306–34.

———. "Swahili Culture Reconsidered: Some Historical Implications of the Material Culture of the Northern Kenya Coast in the Eighteenth and Nineteenth Centuries." *Azania* 9 (1974): 105–37.

———. *Swahili Origins.* London: James Currey, 1993.

Allen, Miss. "Glimpses of Harem Life." *Central Africa* (1883): 147–49.

Allina, Eric. "Fallacious Mirrors: Colonial Anxiety and Images of African Labor in Mozambique, ca. 1929." *History in Africa* 24 (1997): 9–52.

Alpers, Edward. *Ivory and Slaves in East Central Africa.* Berkeley: University of California Press, 1975.

———. "'Ordinary Household Chores': Ritual and Power in a Nineteenth-Century Swahili Women's Spirit Possession Cult." *International Journal of African Historical Studies* 17, 4 (1984): 677–702.

———. "The Story of Swema: Female Vulnerability in Nineteenth-Century East Africa," in C. Robertson and M. Klein (eds.), *Women and Slavery in Africa*, 185–219. Madison: University of Wisconsin Press, 1983.

Altorki, Soroya. "Milk Kinship in Arab Society: An Unexplored Problem in the Ethnography of Marriage." *Ethnography* 19, 2 (1980): 233–44.

Ambler, Charles. "A History of Leisure in Colonial Urban Africa." Paper presented at the annual meeting of the African Studies Association, Toronto, 1994.

————. *Kenyan Communities in the Age of Imperialism: The Central Region in the Late Nineteenth Century.* New Haven: Yale University Press, 1988.

Ambler, Charles, and Jonathan Crush (eds). *Liquor and Labor in Southern Africa.* Athens: Ohio University Press, 1992.

Amur bin Nasur. "Habari za Amur bin Nasur." In C. G. Büttner (trans. and comp.), *Anthologie aus der Suaheli-Literatur,* 2 vols., 1:147–75. Berlin: Verlag von Emil Felber, 1894.

Anderson, J. N. D. *Islamic Law in Africa.* London: Frank Cass, 1955.

Anderson, Jon. "Social Structure and the Veil." *Anthropos* 77, 2 (1982): 397–420.

Anthony, David. "Culture and Society in a Town in Transition: A People's History of Dar es Salaam, 1865-1939." Ph.D. diss., University of Wisconsin, Madison, 1983.

Archer, Robert. "An Exceptional Case: Politics and Sport in South Africa's Townships." In W. Baker and J. A. Mangan (eds.), *Sport in Africa: Essays in Social History.* New York: Africana Publishing, 1987.

Arens, W. "The Waswahili: The Social History of an Ethnic Group." *Africa* 45, 4 (1975): 426–38.

Asante-Darko, Nimrod, and Sjaak van der Geest. "The Political Meaning of Highlife Songs in Ghana." *African Studies Review* 25, 1 (1982): 27–35.

Askew, Kelly. "Female Circles and Male Lines: Gender Dynamics along the Swahili Coast." *Africa Today* 46, 3/4 (1999): 67–102.

————. "Performing the Nation: Swahili Musical Performance and the Production of Tanzanian National Culture." Ph.D. diss., Harvard University, 1997.

————. *Performing the Nation: Swahili Music and Cultural Politics in Tanzania.* Chicago: University of Chicago Press, forthcoming.

Baba of Karo and Mary Felice Smith (transcriber). *Baba of Karo: A Woman of the Muslim Hausa.* 1954. Reprint, New Haven: Yale University Press, 1981.

Babu, A. M. "The 1964 Revolution: Lumpen or Vanguard?" In A. Sheriff and E. Ferguson (eds.), *Zanzibar under Colonial Rule,* 220–47. London: James Currey, 1991.

Badenhorst, Cecil, and Charles Mather. "Tribal Recreation and Recreating Tribalism: Culture, Leisure, and Social Control on South Africa's Gold Mines, 1940-50," *Journal of Southern African Studies* 23, 3 (1997): 473–89.

Bader, Zinnat Kassamali. "The Social Condition of the 1964 Land Reform in Zanzibar." Ph.D. thesis, University of London, 1984.

Baker, William, and J. A. Mangan (eds.). *Sport in Africa: Essays in Social History.* New York: Africana Publishing, 1987.

Banerjee, Sumanta. "Marginalization of Women's Popular Culture in Nineteenth Century Bengal." In K. Sangari and S. Vaid (eds.), *Recasting Women*, 127-79. New Delhi: Kali for Women, 1989.

Baramia, Salma. "Iwapi ngoma ya Kunguiya Unguja?" *Nuru*, 16 July 1992, 11.

Barber, Karin. "Views of the Field." In K. Barber (ed.), *Readings in African Popular Culture*, 1-12. Bloomington: Indiana University Press, 1997.

————, (ed.). *Readings in African Popular Culture*. Bloomington: Indiana University Press, 1997.

Barth, Frederick (ed.). *Ethnic Groups and Boundaries*. London: George Allen and Unwin, 1969.

Bastian, Misty. "Female '*Alhajis*' and Entrepreneurial Fashions: Flexible Identities in Southeastern Nigerian Clothing Practice." In Hildi Hendrickson (ed.), *Clothing and Difference: Embodied Identities in Colonial and Post-Colonial Africa*, 97-132. Durham: Duke University Press, 1996.

Baumann, Oscar. *Die Insel Sansibar*. Leipzig: Dunker and Humbolt, 1897.

Becker, C. H. "Materials for the Understanding of Islam in German East Africa." Ed. and trans. B. G. Martin. 1911. Reprinted in *Tanzania Notes and Records* 68 (1968): 31-61.

Beech, Mervyn. "Slavery on the East Coast of Africa." *Journal of the African Society* 15 (1916): 145-49.

Bender, Wolfgang. *Sweet Mother: Modern African Music*. Chicago: University of Chicago Press, 1991.

"Beni Society of Tanganyika." *Primitive Man* 3 (1938): 74-81.

Bentley, Amy. *Eating for Victory: Food Rationing and the Politics of Domesticity*. Urbana: University of Illinois Press, 1998.

Bentley, G. C. "Ethnicity and Practice." *Comparative Studies in Society and History* 29 (1987): 24-55.

Berg, F. J. "The Coast from the Portuguese Invasion to the Rise of the Zanzibar Sultanate." In B. A. Ogot and J. A. Kieran (eds.), *Zamani: A Survey of East African History*, 119-41. Nairobi: East African Publishing House, 1968.

Berg, F. J., and B. J. Walter. "Mosques, Population, and Urban Development in Mombasa," in B. A. Ogot (ed.), *Hadith* 1:47-100. Nairobi: East African Publishing House, 1968.

Binsbergen, W. Van "The Unit of Study and the Interpretation of Ethnicity." *Journal of Southern African Studies* 8, 1 (1981): 51-81.

Bissell, William Cunningham. "Colonial Constructions: Historicizing Debates on Civil Society in Africa." In John Comaroff and Jean Comaroff (eds.), *Civil Society and the Political Imagination in Africa*, 124-59. Chicago: University of Chicago Press, 1999.

Blok, H. P. *A Swahili Anthology with notes and glossaries*. Leiden: A. W. Sijthoff, 1948.

Boddy, Janice. *Wombs and Alien Spirits: Women, Men, and the Zar Cult in Northern Sudan*. Madison: University of Wisconsin, 1989.

Boer, Gabriel. *A History of Landownership in Modern Egypt*. London: Oxford Press, 1962.

Bonner, Phillip. "'Desirable or Undesirable Basotho Women?' Liquor, Prostitution, and the Migration of Basotho Women to the Rand, 1920-1945."

In Cheryl Walker (ed.), *Women and Gender in Southern Africa to 1945*, 221-250. Cape Town: David Philip, 1990.

Bourdieu, Pierre. *Distinction: A Social Critique of the Judgement of Taste.* London: Routledge and Kegan Paul, 1984.

Bowles, B. D. "The Struggle for Independence, 1946-1963." In A. Sheriff and E. Ferguson (eds.), *Zanzibar under Colonial Rule*, 79-106. London: James Currey, 1991.

Boyd, Alan. "To Praise the Prophet: A Processual Symbolic Analysis of Maulidi, a Muslim Ritual in Lamu, Kenya." Ph.D. diss., Indiana University, 1980.

Bozzoli, Belinda. "Marxism, Feminism, and South African Studies." *Journal of Southern African Studies* 9, 2 (1983): 39-171.

———, (ed.). *Class, Community, and Conflict.* Johannesburg: Ravan Press, 1987.

Bozzoli, Belinda, and Mmantho Nkotsoe. *Women of Phokeng: Consciousness, Life Strategy, and Migrancy in South Africa, 1900-1983.* Portsmouth, N.H.: Heinemann, 1991.

Bradford, Helen. "'We Are Now the Men': Women's Beer Protests in the Natal Countryside, 1929." In B. Bozzoli (ed.), *Class, Community, and Conflict*, 292-323. Johannesburg: Ravan Press, 1987.

Bravman, Bill. *Making Ethnic Ways: Communities and Their Transformations in Taita, Kenya, 1800-1950.* Portsmouth, N.H.: Heinemann, 1988.

British Anti-Slavery Society. *Anti-Slavery Reporter.* London: British Anti-Slavery Society, 1901.

Browne, J. Ross. *Etchings of a Whaling Cruise.* 1846. Reprint, Cambridge, Mass.: Belknap Press 1968.

Bryceson, Deborah F. "A Century of Food Supply in Dar es Salaam." In Jane Guyer (ed.), *Feeding African Cities.* Bloomington: Indiana University Press, 1987.

Burke, Timothy. *Lifebuoy Men, Lux Women: Commodification, Consumption, and Cleanliness in Modern Zimbabwe.* Durham: Duke University Press, 1995.

Burman, Sandra. "Fighting a Two-Pronged Attack: The Changing Legal Status of Women in Cape-ruled Basutoland, 1872-1884." In Cheryl Walker (ed.), *Women and Gender in Southern Africa to 1945.* Cape Town: David Philip, 1990.

Burton, Richard F. *Zanzibar: City, Island, and Coast.* 2 vols. London: Tinsley Brothers, 1872.

Büttner, C. G. (trans. and comp.). *Anthologie aus der Suaheli-Literatur.* 2 vols. Berlin. Verlag von Emil Felber, 1894.

Calhoun, Craig. "Community." In R. S. Neale (ed.), *History and Class: Essential Readings in Theory and Interpretation*, 86-110. Oxford: Basil Blackwell, 1983.

Campbell, Carol. "Nyimbo za Kiswahili: A Socio-Ethnomusicological Study of a Swahili Poetic Form." Ph.D. diss., University of Washington, 1983.

Caplan, A. Patricia. *Choice and Constraint in a Swahili Community: Property, Hierarchy, and Cognatic Descent on the East African Coast.* Oxford: Oxford University Press, 1975.

———. "Cognatic Descent, Islamic Law, and Women's Property on the East

African Coast." In Renée Hirschon (ed.) 23–43. *Women and Property, Women as Property.* London: Croom Helm, 1984.

———. "Gender Ideology and Modes of Production on the Coast of East Africa." *Paideuma* 28 (1982): 29–43.

Carby, Hazel. "'It Jus Be's Dat Way Sometime': The Sexual Politics of Women's Blues." In E. C. DuBois and V. Ruíz (eds.), *Unequal Sisters: A Multicultural Reader in U.S. Women's History*, 238–49. New York: Routledge, 1990.

Carey, James. "Changing Courtship Patterns in the Popular Song." *American Journal of Sociology* 74 (1969): 720–31.

Cashman, Richard. "Cricket and Colonialism: Colonial Hegemony and Indigenous Subversion? " in J. A. Mangan (ed.), *Pleasure, Profit, and Proselytism: British Culture and Sport at Home and Abroad, 1700–1914*, 258–59. London: Frank Cass, 1988.

Cassanelli, Lee. "The Ending of Slavery in Italian Somalia: Liberty and the Control of Labor, 1890–1935." In Susan Miers and Richard Roberts (eds.), *The End of Slavery in Africa*, 308–31. Madison: University of Wisconsin Press, 1988.

Chanock, Martin. "Paradigms, Policies, and Property: A Review of the Customary Law of Land Tenure." In Kristin Mann and Richard Roberts (eds.), *Law in Colonial Africa*, 61–84. London: James Curry, 1991.

———. "A Peculiar Sharpness." *Journal of African History* 32 (1991): 65–88.

Chittick, N. "The 'Shirazi' Colonization of East Africa." *Journal of African History* 6 (1965): 275–94.

Christie, James. *Cholera Epidemics in East Africa.* London: Macmillan, 1876.

Clayton, Anthony. *The 1948 Zanzibar General Strike.* Uppsala: Scandinavian Institute of African Studies, 1976.

———. "Sport and African Soldiers: The Military Diffusion of Western Sport throughout Sub-Saharan Africa." In W. Baker and J. A. Mangan (eds.), *Sport in Africa: Essays in Social History*, 114–37. New York: Africana Publishing Company, 1987.

———. *The Zanzibar Revolution and Its Aftermath.* Hamden, Conn.: Archon Books, 1981.

Clignet, Remi, and Maureen Stark. "Modernization and Football in Cameroon," *Journal of Modern African Studies* 12, 3 (1974): 409–21.

Collins, E. J. "Ghanaian Highlife." *African Arts* 10, 1 (1976): 62–68.

———. "Post-War Popular Band Music in West Africa." *African Arts* 10, 3 (1977): 53–60.

———. *West African Pop Roots.* Philadelphia: Temple University Press, 1992.

Colomb, Captain. *Slave-Catching in the Indian Ocean.* London: Dawsons of Pall Mall, 1873.

Constantine, François. "Social Stratification on the Swahili Coast: From Race to Class? " *Africa* 59, 2 (1989): 145–60.

Conzen, Kathleen, et al. "The Invention of Ethnicity: A Perspective from the USA." *Altreitalie* (April 1990): 37–62.

Cooper, Barbara. "Reflections on Slavery, Seclusion, and Female Labor in the Maradi Region of Niger in the Nineteenth and Twentieth Centuries." *Journal of African History* 35, 1 (1994): 61–78.

Cooper, Frederick. *From Slaves to Squatters: Plantation Labor and Agriculture in Zanzibar and Coastal Kenya, 1890–1925.* 1980. Reprint, Portsmouth, N.H.: Heinemann, 1997.

———. "Islam and Cultural Hegemony: The Ideology of Slaveowners on the East African Coast." In Paul Lovejoy (ed.), *The Ideology of Slavery,* 271–307. Beverly Hills: Sage, 1981.

———. *On the African Waterfront: Urban Disorder and the Transformation of Work in Colonial Mombasa.* New Haven: Yale University Press, 1987.

———. *Plantation Slavery on the East Coast of Africa.* New Haven: Yale University Press, 1977.

———. "Urban Space, Industrial Time, and Wage Labor in Africa." In F. Cooper (ed.), *Struggle for the City: Migrant Labor, Capital, and the State in Urban Africa,* 7–50. Beverly Hills: Sage, 1983.

Coplan, David. "Eloquent Knowledge: Lesotho Migrants' Songs and the Anthropology of Experience." *American Ethnologist* 14, 3 (1987): 413–33.

———. "Go to My Town, Cape Coast! The Social History of Ghanaian Highlife." In Bruno Nettl (ed.). *Eight Urban Musical Cultures,* 96–114. Urbana: University of Illinois Press, 1978.

———. *In Township Tonight! South Africa's Black City Music and Theatre.* New York: Longman, 1985.

Cordell, Dennis. "Blood Partnership in Theory and Practice: The Expansion of Muslim Power in Dar al-Kuit." *Journal of African History* 20, 3 (1979): 379–94.

Coupland, R. *East Africa and Its Invaders.* 1935. Reprint, New York: Russell and Russell, 1965.

Couzens, Tim. "An Introduction to the History of Football in South Africa." In Belinda Bozzoli (ed.), *Town and Countryside in the Transvaal,* 198–214. Johannesburg: Ravan Press, 1983.

———. *The New African: A Study of the Life and Work of H. I. E. Dhlomo.* Johannesburg: Ravan Press, 1995.

Craster, Captain J. E. E. *Pemba, the Spice Island of Zanzibar.* London: T. Fisher Unwin, 1913.

Craton, Michael. "The Passion to Exist: Slave Rebellions in the British West Indies." *Journal of Caribbean History* 13 (1980): 1–20.

———. "Proto-Peasant Revolts? The Late Slave Rebellions in the British West Indies, 1816–1832." *Past and Present* 85 (1979): 99–125.

Cross, Gary. *A Social History of Leisure since 1600.* State College, Pa.: Venture Publishing, 1990.

Dale, Godfrey. *The Peoples of Zanzibar.* 1920. Reprint, New York: Negro University Press, 1969.

Daniels, Douglas. "Taarab Transformations: Culture and Political Innovations in Swahili Popular Music and Culture," *Elimu,* Department of Black Studies Newsletter University of California, Santa Barbara, Winter/Spring 1994, 3–6.

Danielson, Virginia. *The Voice of Egypt: Umm Kulthum, Arabic Song, and Egyptian Society in the Twentieth Century.* Chicago: University of Chicago, 1997.

Davis, Angela. *Blues Legacies and Black Feminism.* New York: Pantheon, 1998.

Davis, Natalie Zemon. *Society and Culture in Early Modern France.* Stanford: Stanford University Press, 1975.

Delves, Anthony. "Popular Recreation and Social Conflict in Derby, 1800–1850." in E. Yeo and S. Yeo (eds.), *Popular Culture and Class Conflict, 1590–1914,* 89–127. Atlantic Highlands, N.J.: Humanities Press, 1981.

Denzer, LaRay. "Domestic Science Training in Colonial Yorubaland." In Karen Hansen (ed.), *African Encounters with Domesticity,* 116–39. New Brunswick, N.J.: Rutgers University Press, 1992.

Depelchin, Jacques. "The Transition from Slavery, 1873–1914." In A. Sheriff and E. Ferguson (eds), *Zanzibar under Colonial Rule.* London: James Currey, 1991.

Desan, Suzanne. "Crowds, Community, and Ritual in the Work of E. P. Thompson and Natalie Davis." In Lynn Hunt (ed.), *The New Cultural History.* Berkeley: University of California Press, 1989.

Dourado, W. "The Consolidation of the Union: A Basic Re-Appraisal." Paper presented at the Tanzanian Law Society Seminar, 27–29 July 1983.

Eastman, Carol. "Who Are the Waswahili?" *Africa* 41, 3 (1971): 228–36.

———. "Women, Slaves, and Foreigners: African Cultural Influence and Group Processes in the Formation of the Northern Swahili Coastal Society." *International Journal of African Historical Studies* 21, 1 (1988): 1–20.

Edelman, Murray. *From Art to Politics.* Chicago: University of Chicago Press, 1995.

Eliot, Sir Charles. *The East African Protectorate.* London: Edward Arnold, 1905.

El-Zein, A. H. M. *The Sacred Meadows: A Structural Analysis of Religious Symbolism in an East African Town.* Evanston: Northwestern University Press, 1974.

EMI. "Review of the Present Vernacular Record Trade." Unpublished manuscript, 1931.

Epstein, A. L. "Gossip, Norms, and Social Networks." In J. Clyde Mitchell (ed.), *Social Networks in Urban Situations,* 117–27. Manchester: Manchester University Press, 1969.

———. *Politics in an Urban African Community.* Manchester: Manchester University Press, 1958.

Fabian, Johannes. *Moments of Freedom: Anthropology and Popular Culture.* Charlottesville: University Press of Virginia, 1998.

———. "Popular Culture in Africa." *Africa* 48, 4 (1978): 315–34.

Fage, J. "Music and History." In Klaus Wachsmann (ed.), *Essays on Music and History in Africa,* 257–66. Evanston: Northwestern University Press, 1971.

Fair, Laura. "Identity, Difference, and Dance: Female Initiation in

Zanzibari, 1890–1930." *Frontiers: A Journal of Women Studies* 17, 3 (1996): 146–72.

———. "Music, Memory and Meaning: the Kiswahili Recordings of Siti Binti Saad," *Swahili Forum* (September 1998): 1–16.

———. "Pastimes and Politics: A Social History of Zanzibar's Ng'ambo Community, 1890–1950." Ph.D. diss., University of Minnesota, 1994.

Farsy, Sheik Abdallah Salih. *Seyyid Said bin Sultan: Joint Ruler of Oman and Zanzibar (1804–1856).* New Delhi: Lancers Books, n.d.

———. *Ada za harusi katika unguja.* Dar es Salaam: East African Literature Bureau, 1956.

Ferguson, Ed. "The Formation of a Colonial Economy, 1915–1945." In A. Sheriff and E. Ferguson (eds.), *Zanzibar under Colonial Rule,* 36–78. Nairobi: Heinemann Kenya, 1991.

Fitzgerald, William. *Travels in the Coastlands of British East Africa and the Islands of Zanzibar and Pemba.* London: Chapman and Hall, 1898.

Fluehr-Lobban, Carolyn. *Islamic Law and Society in the Sudan.* London: Frank Cass, 1987.

Franken, Marjorie. "Anyone Can Dance: A Survey and Analysis of Swahili Ngoma Past and Present." Ph.D. diss., University of California, Riverside, 1986.

Freeman-Grenville, G. S. P. *The East African Coast: Select Documents from the First Century to the Early Nineteenth Century.* Oxford: Oxford University Press, 1962.

French-Sheldon, M. *Sultan to Sultan.* London: Saxon and Company, 1892.

Friedman, Johathan. "The Political Economy of Elegance: An African Cult of Beauty." *Culture and History* 7 (1990): 101–25.

Friedson, Steven. *Dancing Prophets: Musical Experience in Tumbuka Healing.* Chicago: University of Chicago Press, 1996.

Furniss, Graham, and Liz Gunner (eds.). *Power Marginality and African Oral Literature.* Cambridge: Cambridge University Press, 1995.

Fyzee, Asaf. *Outlines of Muhammadan Law.* 3d ed. Oxford: Oxford University Press, 1964.

Geertz, Clifford. *The Interpretation of Cultures.* New York: Basic Books, 1973.

Geiger, Susan. "Anti-Colonial Protest in Africa: A Female Strategy Reconsidered." *Heresies* 13, 1 (1980): 22–25.

———. *TANU Women: Gender and Culture in the Making of Tanganyikan Nationalism, 1955–1965.* Portsmouth, N.H.: Heinemann, 1997.

———. "Women in Nationalist Struggle: TANU Activists in Dar es Salaam." *International Journal of African Historical Studies* 20, 1 (1987): 1–26.

Genovese, Eugene. *Roll Jordan Roll: The World the Slaves Made.* New York: Vintage, 1972.

Giles, Linda. "Possession Cults on the Swahili Coast: A Re-Examination of Theories of Marginality." *Africa* 57, 2 (1987): 234–57.

Glassman, Jonathon. "The Bondsman's New Cloths: The Contradictory Consciousness of Slave Resistance on the Swahili Coast." *Journal of African History* 32 (1991): 277–312.

———. *Feasts and Riot: Revelry, Rebellion, and Popular Consciousness on the Swahili Coast, 1856–1888*. Portsmouth, N.H.: Heinemann, 1995.

———. "Sorting Out the Tribes: The Creation of Racial Identities in Colonial Zanzibar's Newspaper Wars." *Journal of African History* 41 (2000): 395–429.

Gower, R. H. "Swahili Slang." *Tanganyikan Notes and Records* 50 (1958): 250–54.

Graebner, Werner. "The First Thirty-Five Years of Commercial Recording in East Africa, 1928–1953." Paper delivered at the Institute of African Studies, University of Nairobi, 1989.

———. (ed.). *Sokomoko Popular Culture in East Africa*. Atlanta: Rodopi, 1992.

Gray, Sir John. *History of Zanzibar from the Middle Ages to 1856*. London: Oxford, 1962.

———. "Memoirs of an Arabian Princess." *Tanganyika Notes and Records*, July 1954, 49–70.

———. "Zanzibar Local Histories." *Swahili* 30 (1959): 24–50; 31 (1960): 111–39.

Guillain, Charles. *Documents sur l'histoire, la géographie et le commerce de l'Afrique Orientale*. 3 vols. Paris: Librarie de la Société de Géographie, 1856.

Hadjivayanis, George, and Ed Ferguson. "The Development of a Colonial Working Class." In A. Sheriff and E. Ferguson (eds.), *Zanzibar under Colonial Rule*, 188–219. London: James Currey, 1991.

Hale, Thomas. "Griottes: Female Voices from West Africa." *Research in African Literature* 25, 3 (1994): 71–92.

Handby, Jeannette. *Kangas, 101 Uses*. Nairobi: Lino Typesetters, 1984.

Hannerz, Ulf. "The World in Creolization." In K. Barber (ed.), *Readings in African Popular Culture*, 12–18. Bloomington: Indiana University Press, 1997.

Hansen, Karen Tranberg. "The Black Market and Women Traders in Zambia." In Jane Parpart and Kathleen Staudt (eds.), *Women and the State in Africa*, 143–160. Boulder: Lynne Rienner, 1990.

———. "Second-Hand Clothing Encounters in Zambia: Global Discourses, Western Commodities, and Local Histories." *Africa* 69, 3 (1999): 343–65.

Hargreaves, John. *Sport, Power, and Culture: A Social and Historical Analysis of Popular Sports in Britain*. Cambridge: Polity Press, 1986.

Harries, Lyndon. *Swahili Poetry*. Oxford: Clarendon Press, 1962.

Harries, Patrick. *Work, Culture, and Identity: Migrant Laborers in Mozambique and South Africa, 1860–1910*. Portsmouth, N.H.: Heinemann, 1994.

Harris, Paisley, "'I'm as Good as Any Woman in Your Town': The Blues of Ma Rainey and Bessie Smith as a Counter-Narrative of Black Womanhood and Respectability in the Early Twentieth Century." Paper presented at the Berkshire Conference on the History of Women, Chapel Hill, N.C., June 1996.

Harkema, R. C. "De stad Zanzibar in de tweede helft van de negentiende eeuw" [The town of Zanzibar in the latter half of the nineteenth century]. Ph.D. diss., University of Groningen, 1967.

Hélie-Lucas, Marie-Aimée. "Women, Nationalism and Religion in the Algerian Liberation Struggle." In Margot Badran and Miriam Cooke (eds.),

Opening the Gates: A Century of Arab Feminist Writing, 105–14. Blooming-
   ton: Indiana University Press, 1990.
Henry, Ian. *The Politics of Leisure Policy*. London: Macmillan, 1993.
Hilal, Nasra Mohamed. *Siti binti Saad*. Dar es Salaam: Tanzanian Media
   Women's Association, 1990. Videocassette.
————. "Wanawake na Utamaduni," unpublished manuscript.
Hino, Shunya. "The Costume Culture of the Swahili People." *Kyoto Univer-
   sity African Studies* (1968): 109–45.
Hirsch, Susan. *Pronouncing and Persevering: Gender and the Discourses of Disput-
   ing in an African Islamic Court*. Chicago: University of Chicago Press, 1998.
Hoffman, Valerie. *Celebrating the Prophet in the Remembrance of God: Sufi Dhikr
   in Egypt*. Urbana: University of Illinois, Office of International Pro-
   grams and Studies, 1997. Videocassette.
————. *Sufism, Mystics, and Saints in Modern Egypt*. Columbia: University of
   South Carolina Press, 1998.
Hollingsworth, L. W. *Zanzibar under the Foreign Office, 1890–1913*. London:
   Macmillan, 1953.
Horowitz, Donald. *Ethnic Groups in Conflict*. Berkeley: University of Califor-
   nia Press, 1985.
Hove, Chanjerai. *Shebeen Tales*. Harare: Baobab, 1994.
Iliffe, John. *A Modern History of Tanganyika*. Cambridge: Cambridge Univer-
   sity Press, 1979.
Ingrams, W. H. *Chronology and Genealogies of Zanzibar Rulers*. Zanzibar: Gov-
   ernment Printing Office, 1926.
————. *A Report on the Social, Economic, and Political Condition of the Hadhra-
   maut*. London: Colonial Office, 1936.
————. *Zanzibar: An Account of its People, Industry and History*. Zanzibar: Gov-
   ernment Printer, 1924.
————. *Zanzibar: Its History and Its People*. London: H. F. and G. Witherby,
   1931.
Jabir, Mohammed Hemeid. "The Plantation Economy during the Protector-
   ate Period in Zanzibar, 1890–1964." Master's thesis, University of Dar es
   Salaam, 1977.
James, C. L. R. *Beyond a Boundary*. 1963. Reprint, Durham: Duke University
   Press, 1983.
————. *The Black Jacobins: Toussant L'Ouverture and the San Domingo Revo-
   lution*. New York: Random House, 1963.
James, Deborah. "'I Dress in This Fashion': Transformations in *Sotho* Dress
   and Women's Lives in Sekhukhuneland Village, South Africa." In Hildi
   Hendrickson (ed.), *Clothing and Difference: Embodied Identities in Colonial
   and Post-Colonial Africa*, 34–65. Durham: Duke University Press, 1996.
Janmohamed, Karim. "A History of Mombasa, c. 1895–1939: Some Aspects
   of Economic and Social Life in an East African Port Town during Colonial Rule." Ph.D. diss., Northwestern University, 1977.
Jeffrey, Ian. "Street Rivalry and Football in Sharpville." *African Studies* 15, 1
   (1992): 70–76.

Johnson, Cheryl. "Grass Roots Organizing: Women in Anticolonial Activity in Southwestern Nigeria." *African Studies Review* 25, 2–3 (1982): 137–157.

Johnson, Frederick. *A Standard Swahili-English Dictionary.* 1939. Reprint, Nairobi: Oxford University Press, 1987.

Kamati Maalum ya Kuchunguza Historia ya Michexo ya Riadha na Mipira Visiwani. "Taarifa ya Kamati ya Kuchunguza Historia ya Michexo ya Riadha na Mipira Visiwani: Historia ya Michexo, Hali Halisi ya Michexo na Mapendikezo." Unpublished confidential report, Zanzibar, 1981.

Kaplan, Temma. "Class Consciousness and Community in Nineteenth Century Andalusia." In Maurice Zeitlin (ed.), *Political Power and Social Theory,* vol. 2. Greenwich, Conn.: JAI Press, 1981.

———. "Female Consciousness and Collective Action: The Case of Barcelona, 1910–1918." *Signs* 7, 3 (1982): 545–66.

Khatib, Muhammed Seif. "'Siri' ya majina ya Miskiti Unguja." *Mzalendo,* 12 September 1990.

———. *Taarab Zanzibar.* Dar es Salaam: Tanzania Publishing House, 1992.

Kimambo, Isaria. *Mbiru: Popular Protest in Colonial Tanzania.* Nairobi: East African Publishing House, 1971.

Kindy, Hyder. *Life and Politics in Mombasa.* Nairobi: East African Publishing House, 1972.

King'ei, Geoffrey. "Language, Culture, and Communication: The Role of Swahili Taarab Songs in Kenya, 1963–1990." Ph.D. diss., Howard University, 1992.

Kirk-Greene, Anthony. "Imperial Administration and the Athletic Imperative: The Case of the DO in African." In W. Baker and J. A. Mangan (eds.). *Sport in Africa: Essays in Social History,* 81–113. New York: Africana Publishing Company, 1987.

Klein, Alan. *Sugarball: The American Game, the Dominican Dream.* New Haven: Yale University Press, 1991.

Klumpp, Donna, and Corinne Kratz. "Aesthetics, Expertise, and Ethnicity: Okiek and Maasai Perspectives on Personal Adornment." In T. Spear and R. Waller (eds.), *Being Maasai,* 195–221. Athens: Ohio University Press, 1993.

Knappert, Jan. *An Anthology of Swahili Love Poetry.* Berkeley: University of California Press, 1972.

———. *Four Centuries of Swahili Verse.* London: Heinemann, 1979.

———. "Swahili Tarabu Songs." *Afrika and Übersee* (1977): 116–55.

Krapf, J. L. *A Dictionary of the Swahili Language.* London: Trübner and Co., 1882.

Kuczynski, Robert. *Demographic Survey of the British Colonial Empire.* 2 vols. London: Oxford University Press, 1949.

Kyle, Keith. "Gideon's Voices." *Spectator,* 7 February 1964.

———. "How It Happened." *Spectator,* 14 February 1964.

Lambert, H. E. "The Beni Dance Songs." *Swahili* 33, 1 (1962–63): 18–21.

Larson, Pier. *History and Memory in the Age of Enslavement: Becoming Merina in Highland Madagascar, 1770–1822.* Portsmouth, N.H.: Heinemann, 2000.

Last, Murray. *The Sokoto Caliphate.* London: Longman, 1965.

Leslie, J. A. K. *A Survey of Dar es Salaam.* London: Oxford, 1963.

Lieb, Sandra. *Mother of the Blues: A Study of Ma Rainey.* Boston: University of Massachusetts Press, 1981.

Lienhardt, Peter. "Family Waqf in Zanzibar." Paper presented at the East African Institute of Social Research, Makerere, June 1958. Published in *Journal of the Anthropological Society of Oxford* 27, 2 (1996): 95–106.

———. Introduction to *The Medicine Man: Swifa ya nguvumali,* by Hasani bin Ismail. Oxford: Clarendon Press, 1968.

———. "The Mosque College of Lamu and Its Social Background." *Tanganyikan Notes and Records* 52 (1959): 228–42.

Linnebuhr, Elisabeth, "Kanga: Popular Cloths with Messages." In W. Graebner (ed.), *Sokomoko: Popular Culture in East Africa.* 81–90. Atlanta: Rodopi, 1992.

Lipsitz, George. *Time Passages: Collective Memory and American Popular Culture.* Minneapolis: University of Minnesota Press, 1990.

Lodhi, Abdulaziz. *The Institution of Slavery in Zanzibar and Pemba.* Uppsala: Scandinavian Institute of African Studies, 1973.

Lofchie, Michael. *Zanzibar: Background to Revolution.* Princeton: Princeton University Press, 1965.

Lovejoy, Paul. "Concubinage and the Status of Women Slaves in Early Colonial Northern Nigeria." *Journal of African History* 29 (1988): 245–66.

Low, John. "A History of Kenyan Guitar Music, 1948–1980." *African Music* 6, 2 (1982): 17–36.

Lugard, F. D. *The Dual Mandate in British Tropical Africa.* London: Blackwood and Sons, 1922.

Lyne, Robert. *An Apostle of Empire: Being the Life of Sir Lloyd William Mathews.* London: George Allen and Unwin, 1936.

———. *Zanzibar in Contemporary Times: A Short History of the Southern East in the Nineteenth Century.* 1905. Reprint, New York: Negro Universities Press, 1969.

[al-]Maamiry, Ahmed Hamoud. *Omani Sultans in Zanzibar, 1832-1964.* New Delhi: Lancers Books, 1988.

MacClancy, Jeremy. "Sport, Identity and Ethnicity." In J. MacClancy (ed.), *Sport, Identity, and Ethnicity,* 1–20. Oxford: Berg, 1996.

MacLeod, Arlene Elowe. "Hegemonic Relations and Gender Resistance: The New Veiling as Accommodating Protest in Cairo." *Signs* 17, 3 (Spring 1992): 533–57.

Madan, A. C. *Swahili-English Dictionary.* Oxford: Clarendon Press, 1903.

Maini, Krishan. *Land Law in East Africa.* Nairobi: Oxford University Press, 1967.

Malkki, Liisa. *Purity and Exile: Violence, Memory, and National Cosmology among Hutu Refugees in Tanzania.* Chicago: University of Chicago Press, 1995.

Mamuya, S. J. *Jando na unyago.* Nairobi: East African Publishing House, 1975.

Mangan, J. A. "Ethics and Ethnocentricity: Imperial Education in British Tropical Africa." In W. Baker and J. A. Mangan (eds.), *Sport in Africa: Essays in Social History.* New York: Africana Publishing Company, 1987.

Mani, Lata. "Contentious Traditions: The Debate on SATI in Colonial India." *Cultural Critique* 7 (1987): 119–56.

Mann, Kristin. *Marrying Well: Marriage, Status, and Social Change among the Educated Elite in Colonial Lagos.* Cambridge: Cambridge University Press, 1985.

———. "Women, Landed Property, and the Accumulation of Wealth in Early Colonial Lagos." *Signs* 16, 4 (1991): 682–706.

Manning, Patrick. *Slavery and African Life.* New York: Cambridge University Press, 1990.

Martin, Esmond Bradley. *Zanzibar: Tradition and Revolution.* London: Hamish Hamilton, 1978.

Martin, Phyllis. "Colonialism, Youth, and Football in French Equatorial Africa." *International Journal of the History of Sport* 8, 1 (1991): 56–71.

———. Contesting Clothes in Colonial Brazzaville." *Journal of African History* 35, 3 (1994): 401–26.

———. *Leisure and Society in Colonial Brazzaville.* Cambridge: Cambridge University Press, 1995.

Martin, Steve. "Brass Bands and the *Beni* Phenomenon in Urban East Africa." *African Music* 7, 1 (1991): 72–81.

McCurdy, Sheryl. "'Storm in a Tea Cup': Islam and Identity Politics in Tabora and Ujiji, Tanganyika, 1880–1934." Unpublished paper.

———. "Transforming Associations: Fertility, Therapy and Ethnicity in Urban Kigoma, Tanzania c. 1850–1993." Ph.D. diss. Columbia University, 2000.

McHenry, Dean. "The Use of Sports in Policy Implementation: The Case of Tanzania." *Journal of Modern African Studies* 18, 2 (1980): 237–56.

Meek, C. K. *Land Law and Custom in the Colonies.* London: Oxford University Press, 1946.

Meillassoux, Claude. *Anthropologie de l'esclavage: Le ventre de fer et d'argent.* Paris: PUF, 1986.

Menon, R. "Zanzibar in the Nineteenth Century: Aspects of Urban Development in an East African Coastal Town." M.A. thesis, University of California, Los Angeles, 1978.

Mernissi, Fatima. *Beyond the Veil.* 1975. Reprint, Bloomington: Indiana University Press, 1987.

Mgana, Issa. *Jukwaa la Taarab Zanzibar.* Helsinki: Mradi wa Medafrica, 1991.

Middleton, John. *Land Tenure in Zanzibar.* London: His Majesty's Stationery Office, 1961.

———. *The World of the Swahili: An African Mercantile Civilization.* New Haven: Yale University Press, 1992.

Miers, Suzanne, and Igor Kopytoff. "African 'Slavery' as an Institution of Marginality." In S. Miers and I. Kopytoff (eds.), *Slavery in Africa,* 3–81. Madison: University of Wisconsin Press, 1977.

———, (eds.). *Slavery in Africa.* Madison: University of Wisconsin Press, 1977.

Miller, Joseph. "Lineages, Ideology and the History of Slavery in Western

Central Africa." In Paul Lovejoy (ed.), *The Ideology of Slavery in Africa.* Beverly Hills: Sage, 1981.

Mintz, Sidney. *Caribbean Transformations.* Chicago: Aldine, 1974.

———. *Sweetness and Power: The Place of Sugar in Modern History.* New York: Viking, 1985.

Mirza, Sarah, and Margaret Strobel. *Three Swahili Women: Life Histories from Mombasa, Kenya.* Bloomington: Indiana University Press, 1989.

Mitchell, J. Clyde. *The Kalela Dance.* Manchester: Manchester University Press, 1956.

Mitchell, Timothy. "Everyday Metaphors of Power," *Theory and Society* 19 (1990): 545–77.

Mphahlele, Ezekiel. *Down Second Avenue.* London: Faber and Faber, 1959.

Mtoro bin Mwinyi Bakari. *The Customs of the Swahili People: The Desturi za Waswahili of Mtoro bin Mwinyi Bakari and Other Swahili Persons.* Ed. and trans. James Allen. Los Angeles: University of California Press, 1981.

Mwalim Idd Farhan. "History of Taarab Music in Zanzibar." Paper presented at the International Conference on the History and Culture of Zanzibar, Zanzibar, December 1992.

———. Manuscripts on life histories of taarab performers in Zanzibar.

Mwanjisi, R. K. *Ndugu Abeid Amani Karume.* Nairobi: East African Publishing House, 1967.

Myers, Garth Andrew. "The Early History of the 'Other Side' of Zanzibar Town." In A. Sheriff (ed.), *The History and Conservation of Zanzibar Stone Town*, 30–45. London: James Currey, 1995.

———. "Eurocentrism and African Urbanization: The Case of Zanzibar's Other Side." *Antipode* 26, 3 (1994): 195–215.

———. "Reconstructing Ng'ambo: Town Planning and Development on the Other Side of Zanzibar." Ph.D. diss., University of California, Los Angeles, 1993.

———. "Sticks and Stones: Colonialism and Zanzibari Housing," *Africa* 67, 2 (1997): 252–72.

Nagar, Richa. "Communal Places and the Politics of Multiple Identities: The Case of Tanzanian Asians." *Ecumene* 4, 1 (1997): 3–26.

———. "The South Asia Diaspora in Tanzania: A History Retold." *Comparative Studies of South Asia, Africa, and the Middle East* 16, 2 (1996): 62–80.

———. "Social Identities and Their Reconstructions among South Asians in Post-Colonial Dar es Salaam." Ph.D. diss., University of Minnesota, 1995.

New, Charles. *Life, Wanderings and Labours in Eastern Africa.* 1873. Reprint, London: Frank Cass, 1971.

Newman, Henry. *Banani: The Transition from Slavery to Freedom in Zanzibar and Pemba.* New York: Negro Universities Press, 1898.

Nicholls, C. S. *The Swahili Coast: Politics, Diplomacy, and Trade on the East African Littoral, 1798–1856.* New York: Africana Publishing Corporation, 1971.

Nimtz, August. *Islam and Politics in East Africa: The Sufi Order in Tanzania.* Minneapolis: University of Minnesota Press, 1980.

Nisula, Tapio. *Everyday Spirits and Medical Interventions: Ethnographic and Historical Notes on Therapeutic Conventions in Zanzibar Town.* Saarijärvi: Gummerus Kirjapaino Oy, 1999.

Nurse, Derek, and Thomas Spear. *The Swahili: Reconsidering the History and Language of an African Society, 800–1500.* Philadelphia: University of Pennsylvania Press, 1985.

O'Barr, Jean. "Pare Women: A Case of Political Involvement." *Rural Africana* 29 (1975): 121–34.

Okello, John. *Revolution in Zanzibar.* Nairobi: n.p., 1967.

Omari, H. H. "Zanzibar Administrative History: 1840 to the Post-Revolutionary Period." M.A. thesis, University of London, 1985.

Osaghae, Egosha. "Redeeming the Utility of the Ethnic Perspective in African Studies: Towards a New Agenda." *Journal of Ethnic Studies* 18, 2 (1990): 37–58.

Osgood, Joseph. *Notes of Travel or Recollections of Majunga, Zanzibar, Muscat, Aden, Mocha and other Eastern Ports.* 1854. Reprint, Freeport, N.Y.: Books for Libraries Press, 1972.

Parkin, David (ed.). *Continuity and Autonomy in Swahili Communities: Inland Influences and Strategies of Self-Determination.* London: School of Oriental and African Studies, 1994.

Parpart, Jane. "Working-Class Wives and Collective Labor Action on the Northern Rhodesian Copperbelt, 1926–1964." Boston University African Studies Center Working Papers, no. 98, 1985.

Patterson, Orlando. *Slavery and Social Death: A Comparative Study.* Cambridge, Mass.: Harvard University Press, 1982.

Pearce, Major F. B. *Zanzibar: The Island Metropolis of Eastern Africa.* London: TF Unwin, 1920.

Pike, Charles. "History and Imagination: Swahili Literature and Resistance to German Language Imperialism in Tanzania, 1885–1910." *International Journal of African Historical Studies* 19, 2 (1986): 201–31.

Pouwels, Randall. *Horn and Crescent: Cultural Change and Traditional Islam on the East African Coast, 800–1900.* Cambridge: Cambridge University Press, 1987.

Powdermaker, Hortense. *Copper Town: Changing Africa, the Human Situation on the Rhodesian Copperbelt.* New York: Harper and Row, 1962.

Prichard, Caleb. "The Perceptions and Standards of Courtship and Mate Selection among Johannesburg's Educated Elite." Photocopy.

Prins, A. H. J. *The Swahili-Speaking Peoples of Zanzibar and the East African Coast (Arabs, Shirazi and Swahili).* London: International African Institute, 1961.

Rahman, Fazlur. *Islam.* Chicago: University of Chicago Press, 1966.

Ramazani, Nesta. "The Veil: Piety or Protest." *Journal of South Asian and Middle Eastern Studies* 7, 2 (1983): 20–36.

Ranger, Terrence. *Dance and Society in Eastern Africa.* Berkeley: University of California Press, 1975.

Rashid bin Hassani. "The Story of Rashid bin Hassani of the Bisa Tribe,

Northern Rhodesia." In Margery Perham (ed.), *Ten Africans*, 81–119. London: Faber and Faber, 1936.

Reid, D. A. "The Decline of Saint Monday, 1766–1876." *Past and Present* 71 (1976): 76–101.

Rigby, C. P. *Report on the Zanzibar Dominions*. Bombay: Education Society Press, 1861.

Roberts, Andrew. "Review Article: Photographs and African History." *Journal of African History* 29 (1988): 301–11.

Roberts, Richard, and Suzanne Miers. "The End of Slavery in Africa." in Miers and Roberts (eds.), *The End of Slavery in Africa*, 3–68. Madison: University of Wisconsin Press, 1988.

Robertson, Claire. "Post-Proclamation Slavery in Accra: A Female Affair?" In C. Robertson and M. Klein (eds.), *Women and Slavery in Africa*, 220–45. Madison: University of Wisconsin Press, 1983.

Robertson, Claire, and Martin Klein. "Women's Importance in African Slave Systems." in C. Robertson and M. Klein (eds.), *Women and Slavery in Africa*, 3–28. Madison: University of Wisconsin Press, 1983.

———, (eds.). *Women and Slavery in Africa*. Madison: University of Wisconsin Press, 1983.

Ropes, Edward D. *The Zanzibar Letters of Edward D. Ropes Jr., 1882–1892*. Ed. Norman Bennett. Boston: Boston University, African Studies Center, 1973.

Rosaldo, Renato. *Culture and Truth: The Remaking of Social Analysis*. Boston: Beacon Press, 1989.

Rude, G. *The Crowd in History: A Study of Popular Disturbances in France and England, 1730–1848*. New York: Wiley, 1964.

———. *The Face in the Crowd: Studies in Revolution, Ideology and Popular Protest*. Atlantic Highlands, N.J.: Humanities Press International, 1988.

———. *Ideology and Popular Protest*. New York: Pantheon Books, 1980.

Ruete, Emily [Seyyida Salme]. *Memoirs of an Arabian Princess from Zanzibar*. 1888. Reprint, New York: Markus Weiner, 1989.

Ruschenberger, W. S. W. *Narrative of a Voyage around the World in 1835, 1836, and 1837*. 1838. Reprint, 2 vols., London: Dawsons of Pall Mall, 1970.

Sacleux, Ch[arles]. *Dictionnaire Swahili-Français*. 2 vols. Paris: Institut d'Ethnologie, 1941.

Sadie, Stanley (ed). *The New Grove's Dictionary of Music and Musicians*. 20 vols. London: MacMillan, 1980.

Salamone, Frank. "Becoming Hausa: Ethnic Identity Change and Its Implications for the Study of Ethnic Pluralism and Stratification." Africa 45, 4 (1975): 410–24.

Saleh, Ibuni. *A Short History of the Comorians in Zanzibar*. Dar es Salaam: Tanganyika Standard, 1936.

Salim, A. I. "Native or Non-Native? The Problem of Identity and the Social Stratification of the Arab-Swahili of Kenya." In B. A. Ogot (ed.), *History and Social Change in East Africa*, 65–85. Nairobi: East African Literature Bureau, 1976.

————. *The Swahili-Speaking Peoples of the Kenyan Coast, 1895-1963*. Nairobi: East African Publishing House, 1973.

Schildkrout, Enid. "Dependence and Autonomy: The Economic Activities of Secluded Hausa Women in Kano." In Christine Oppong (ed.), *Female and Male in West Africa*, 107-126. London: George Allen and Unwin, 1983.

Scott, James. *Domination and the Arts of Resistance*. New Haven: Yale University Press, 1990.

————. *The Moral Economy of the Peasant*. New Haven: Yale University Press, 1976.

————. *Weapons of the Weak: Everyday Forms of Resistance*. New Haven: Yale University Press, 1985.

Scott, Joan. *Gender and the Politics of History*. New York: Columbia University Press, 1988.

Scully, Pamela. *Liberating the Family? Gender and British Slave Emancipation in the Rural Western Cape, South Africa, 1823-1853*. Portsmouth, N.H.: Heinemann, 1997.

Seif Salim Saleh. "Historia na Muundo wa Taarab." *Lugha na Utamaduni* 1 (July 1988): 9-11; 2 (August 1988): 9-11, 24.

Sewell, William. "Narratives and Social Identities." *Social Science History* 16, 3 (Fall 1992): 479-88.

Shaaban Robert. *Wasifu wa Siti binti Saad*. 1958. Reprint, Dar es Salaam: Mkuki na Nyota Publishers, 1991.

Shaib Abeid Barajab. Personal manuscripts on the history of Nadi Ikhwan Safaa, in the possession of Mwalim Idd Farhan.

Shao, Ibrahim Fokas. "Land Tenure and Land Reform in Zanzibar, 1830-1978." Master's thesis, University of Dar es Salaam, 1978.

Shariff, Omar. *Kisiwa cha Pemba: Historia na Masimulizi*. Nairobi: Eagle Press, 1951.

Sheikh-Hashim, Leila. "Siti's Magnetic Voice." *Sauti ya Siti* 1, 1 (March 1988), 3-4.

————. *Unyago: Traditional Family Life Education among the Muslim Digo, Seguju, Bondei, Sambaa and Sigua of Tanga Region*. Dar es Salaam: Tanzania Media Women's Association, 1989.

Sheriff, Abdul. "Mosques, Merchants, and Landowners in Zanzibar Stone Town." In A. Sheriff (ed.), *The History and Conservation of Zanzibar Stone Town*. London: James Currey, 1995.

————. "The Peasantry under Imperialism, 1873-1963." In A. Sheriff and E. Ferguson (eds.), *Zanzibar under Colonial Rule*, 109-40. London: James Currey, 1991.

————. *Slaves, Spices, and Ivory in Zanzibar*. London: James Currey, 1987.

————, (ed.). *The History and Conservation of Zanzibar Stone Town*. London: James Currey, 1995.

Sheriff, Abdul, and Ed Ferguson (eds.). *Zanzibar under Colonial Rule*. London: James Currey, 1991.

Silverman, Kenneth. *A Cultural History of the American Revolution*. New York: Thomas Crowell, 1976.

Skene, R. "Arab and Swahili Dances and Ceremonies." *Journal of the Royal Anthropological Institute of Great Britain and Ireland* (1917): 413–34.

Smith, Maynard. *Frank Bishop of Zanzibar: The Life of Frank Weston, 1871–1924*. London: Society for Promoting Christian Knowledge, 1926.

Sollors, Werner (ed.). *The Invention of Ethnicity*. New York: Oxford University Press, 1989.

Spear, Thomas, and Richard Waller (eds.). *Being Maasai*. Athens: Ohio University Press, 1993.

Stanley, Henry Morton. *How I Found Livingstone*. New York: Scribner, Armstrong and Company, 1872.

———. *Stanley's Dispatches to the New York Herald, 1871–1872, 1874–1877*. Ed. Norman Bennett. Boston: Boston University Press, 1970.

Steere, Edward. *A Handbook of the Swahili Language as Spoken at Zanzibar*. 1870. Reprint, London: Society for Promoting Christian Knowledge, 1928.

———. *Swahili Tales, as Told by the Natives of Zanzibar*. 1869. Reprint, London: Society for Promoting Christian Knowledge, 1922.

Stewart, Gary. *Breakout: Profiles in African Rhythm*. Chicago: University of Chicago Press, 1992.

Stigand, Captain C. H. *The Land of Zinj*. London: Constable and Company, 1913.

Stoddart, Brian. "Cricket and Colonialism in the English Speaking Caribbean to 1914: Towards a Cultural Analysis." In J. A. Mangan (ed.), *Pleasure, Profit, and Proselytism: British Culture and Sport at Home and Abroad, 1700–1914*, 231–57. London: Frank Cass, 1988.

Stokes, Martin (ed.). *Ethnicity, Identity, and Music: The Musical Construction of Place*. Oxford: Berg, 1994.

Strandes, Justus. *The Portuguese Period in East Africa*. Trans. J. F. Wallwork. 1899. Reprint, Nairobi: East African Literature Bureau, 1961.

Strobel, Margaret. "African Women." *Signs* 8, 11 (1982): 109–31.

———. "From Lelemama to Lobbying: Women's Associations in Mombasa, Kenya." In Nancy Hafkin and Edna Bay (eds.), *Women in Africa: Studies in Social and Economic Change*, 183–211. Stanford: Stanford University Press, 1976.

———. *Muslim Women in Mombasa, 1890–1975*. New Haven: Yale University Press, 1979.

———. "Slavery and Reproductive Labor in Mombasa." In C. Robertson and M. Klein (eds.), *Women and Slavery in Africa*, 111–29. Madison: University of Wisconsin Press, 1983.

Stuart, Ossie. "Players, Workers, Protestors: Social Change and Soccer in Colonial Zimbabwe." In Jeremy MacClancy (ed.), *Sport, Identity, and Ethnicity*, 167–80. Oxford: Berg, 1996.

Suleiman, A. A. "The Swahili Singing Star Siti binti Saad." *Swahili* 39, 1 (1969): 87–90.

Swartz, Marc. *The Way the World Is: Cultural Processes and Social Relations among the Mombasa Swahili*. Berkeley: University of California Press, 1991.

Thompson, E. P. "Eighteenth Century English Society: Class Struggle without Class?" *Social History* 3, 2 (1978): 133-65.

———. *The Making of the English Working Class.* New York: Vintage, 1966.

———. "The Moral Economy of the English Crowd in the Eighteenth Century." *Past and Present* 50 (1971): 76-136.

———. "Patrician Society, Plebeian Culture." *Journal of Social History* 7, 4 (1974): 382-405.

———. "Time, Work Discipline, and Industrial Capitalism." *Past and Present* (1967): 59-96.

Tilly, Louise. "The Food Riot as a Form of Political Conflict in France." *Journal of Interdisciplinary History* 2 (1971): 23-58.

Tominaga, Chizuko, and Abdul Sheriff. "The Ambiguity of Shirazi Ethnicity in the History and Politics of Zanzibar." Photocopy.

Topp Fargion, Janet. "A History of Taarab Music in Zanzibar: A Process of Africanisation." In D. Parkin (ed.), *Continuity and Autonomy in Swahili Communities*, 153-65. London: School of Oriental and African Studies, 1994.

———. "The Role of Women in Taarab in Zanzibar: An Historical Examination of a Process of 'Africanization.'" *World of Music* 35, 2 (1993): 109-25.

Trimingham, J. Spencer. *Islam in East Africa.* Oxford: Clarendon Press, 1964.

Tripp, Aili Mari. "Rethinking Civil Society: Gender Implications in Contemporary Tanzania." In John Harbeson, Donald Rothchild, and Naomi Chazan (eds.), *Civil Society and the State in Africa*, 149-68. Boulder: Lynne Rienner, 1994.

Turner, Patricia. *I Heard It Through the Grapevine: Rumor in African-American Culture.* Berkeley: University of California Press, 1993.

Turner, Victor. *The Drums of Affliction: A Study of Religious Processes among the Ndembu of Zambia.* Oxford: Clarendon Press, 1968.

Vail, Leroy, and Landeg White. "Forms of Resistance: Songs and Perceptions of Power in Colonial Mozambique." *American Historical Review* 88, 4 (1983): 883-919.

———. *Power and the Praise Poem.* Charlottesville: University Press of Virginia, 1991.

———. " 'Tawani Machambero!': Forced Cotton and Rice Growing on the Zambezi." *Journal of African History* 19, 2 (1978): 239-63.

Vail, Leroy (ed.). *The Creation of Tribalism in Southern Africa.* London: James Curry, 1989. Reprint, Berkeley: University of California Press, 1991.

Van Allen, Judith. "'Aba Riots' or Igbo 'Women's War'?" In Hafkin and Bay (eds.), *Women in Africa: Studies in Social and Economic Change*, 59-85. Stanford: Stanford University Press, 1976.

Velten, C. *Desturi za Wasuahili.* Göttingen: Dandenhoed and Ruprecht, 1903.

———. *Prosa und Poesie der Suaheli.* Berlin: C. Velten, 1907.

———. *Safari za Wasuaheli.* Göttingen: Dandenhoed and Ruprecht, 1901.

Vernon, Paul. "Feast of East." *Folk Roots* (1995): 26-28.

Vizetelly, Edward. *From Cyprus to Zanzibar, by the Egyptian Delta.* London: Arthur Pearson, 1901.

Walker, Cheryl. "Gender and the Development of the Migrant Labour System, c. 1865-1930." In C. Walker (ed.), *Women and Gender in Southern Africa to 1945,* 168-96. Cape Town: David Philip, 1990.

Walley, Christine J. "Making Waves: Struggles over the Environment, Development and Participation in the Mafia Island Marine Park, Tanzania." Ph.D. diss, New York University, 1999.

Ware, Naomi. "Popular Music and African Identity in Freetown, Sierra Leone." In Bruno Nettl (ed.), *Eight Urban Musical Cultures,* 296-320. Urbana: University of Illinois Press, 1978.

Waterman, Christopher. *Juju: A Social History and Ethnomusicology of an African Popular Music.* Chicago: University of Chicago Press, 1990.

Weule, Karl. *Native Life in East Africa.* Trans. Alice Werner. 1909. Reprint, Westport, Conn.: Negro Universities Press, 1970.

White, Luise. "Between Gluckman and Foucault: Historicizing Rumor and Gossip." *Social Dynamics* 20, 1 (1994): 75-92.

———. "A Colonial State and an African Petty Bourgeoisie: Prostitution, Property, and Class Struggle in Nairobi, 1936-1940." In Frederick Cooper (ed.), *Struggle for the City,* 167-94. Beverly Hills: Sage, 1983.

———. *The Comforts of Home: Prostitution in Colonial Nairobi.* Chicago: University of Chicago Press, 1990.

Whiteley, Wilfred H. *Swahili: The Rise of a National Language.* London: Methuen, 1969.

Whiteley, Wilfred H., A. A. Jahadhmy, S. Matola, and Mw. Shaaban. *Waimbaji wa juzi.* Dar es Salaam: Chuo cha Uchunguzi wa Lugha ya Kiswahili, 1966.

Whiting, Robert. *The Chrysanthemum and the Bat: Baseball Samurai Style.* New York: Avon, 1977.

Williams, Raymond. "Analysis of Culture." In Tony Bennett (ed.), *Culture, Ideology, and Social Process,* 43-52. London: Batsford Academic and Educational, 1981.

Willis, Justin. *Mombasa, the Swahili, and the Making of the Mijikenda.* Oxford: Clarendon Press, 1995.

Willis, Justin, and Suzanne Miers. "Becoming a Child of the House: Incorporation, Authority, and Resistance in Giryama Society." *Journal of African History* 38 (1997): 470-95.

Wilson, Amrit. *U.S. Foreign Policy and Revolution: The Creation of Tanzania.* London: Pluto Press, 1989.

Wright, Marcia. *Strategies of Slaves and Women: Life-Stories from East/Central Africa.* New York: Lilian Barber, 1993.

Yahya-Othman, Saida. "If the Cap Fits: Kanga Names and Women's Voice in Swahili Society." *Swahili Forum* 4 (1997): 135-49.

Younghusband, Ethel. *Glimpses of East Africa and Zanzibar.* London: John Long, 1908.

Zawawi, Sheriffa. *Unaitwaje? A Swahili Book of Names.* Trenton, N.J.: African World Press, 1978.

Index

abolition, 3, 7, 14, 53, 74, 82. *See also*
    emancipation
and labor, 129–33, 134, 186–88
African Association, 52–53, 99, 249–
    54, 261
Africans, 47–51, 83, 94–96, 230–31,
    233, 241–42, 244, 250, 253, 262,
    269, 287 n. 118. *See also* Had-
    imu; patron-client ties; Shirazi;
    Swahili; Tumbatu
Afro-Shirazi Party (ASP), 51, 55, 88,
    99, 250–52
Arab Association, 42–47, 99, 248–54
Arabs, 41–47, 94–96, 170–74, 189–
    94, 230–31, 233, 241–42, 253,
    262, 268–69, 315 n. 21. *See also*
    Omanis; patron-client ties
aristocracy, 37–38, 65, 68–71, 100–
    108, 114, 117–22, 128–29, 187–
    88, 236. *See also* Arabs; Omanis
Asians, 237–38, 241, 269. *See also*
    landlords

barakoa, 69, 96, 100–102
beni, 84, 176, 238, 243

Bibi Jokha binti Hamoud, 109, 125–
    29. *See also* Seyyid Hamoud bin
    Ahmed
Bibi Khole binti Hamoud, 109,
    125–29. *See also* Seyyid
    Hamoud bin Ahmed
buibui, 18, 85–96, 266, 294 n. 64,
    295 n. 75
Busaid dynasty, 10–12, 70, 109,
    110–29, 134–36, 145–46. *See also*
    Omanis

capitalism, 4, 110–68 passim, 186.
    See also gender and waged la-
    bor; gramophone recordings;
    kanga; waged labor
citizenship, 27, 55, 111–13, 148,
    164–67, 239
and consumption, 41–47. *See also*
    buibui; kanga; kanzu
and ethnicity 26–28, 41–47, 55,
    99–102, 267–68
and gender, 96–108, 164
civil servants, 78, 159, 186, 189–95,
    236

civil society, 8–9, 22, 26–27, 62, 111–
13, 164, 169–71, 183–85, 194,
214, 223–24, 236, 240–46, 270.
See also collective action; justice
civilization, 6, 36, 40, 43–44, 46, 105,
173–74
class, 1–8, 16, 18, 20, 22, 33–36, 64–
74, 81–84, 85–86, 98, 105, 111,
149, 159, 169, 171–73, 185, 186–
88, 229–31, 233, 236, 241–42,
244. *See also* football and; property ownership; women, class
divisions among
clothing, 64–109
cloves, 13–15, 37–39, 45, 65, 130,
129–33
collective action, 129–33, 139, 141–
68 passim, 214, 245
collective memory, 133, 166, 183
colonial politics, 8, 26, 41–47, 99–
100, 110–68 passim, 231, 263.
See also Legislative Council;
Siti binti Saad, critiques of colonial authority; Sports Control
Board
colonialism, 62–63, 112, 163, 167,
185–86, 189–96, 199, 207, 223–
24, 226, 240–46, 270–71
economic aspects of, 129, 246–48.
See also colonial politics; law;
Protectorate; Siti binti Saad,
critiques of colonial authority;
taxes
community, 20–22, 105–9, 150–51,
159, 167, 176–79, 200, 207–8, 238
cultural components of, 20–25, 105–
6, 227–28, 235–37, 247–48, 254–
59, 270–71
Comorian Association, 45–46, 50,
236–37, 248–49, 260–61
concubines, 18, 70, 97–99, 101–5,
115, 120, 176, 215–17, 315n. 21
Cooper, Frederick, 14, 116, 118
cricket, 226, 230, 238

dance. *See ngoma; kunguiya*

dress. *See* clothing

emancipation, 8, 14–15, 103–8, 179,
186, 207, 210, 234, 265–69
and consumerism, 64–65, 74–85,
266
cultural components of, 2–8, 27,
34, 64–109 passim, 170, 207,
210, 232–34
and ethnicity, 29–30, 32, 34–36,
44–45, 157, 266–69
and Islam, 18–19, 85–96, 179–81,
266
and labor, 53, 129–33
and property ownership, 34–38,
82, 110–13, 153–55, 265–66,
268–69
and urbanization, 3, 15–17, 32, 82,
103–8, 153–55, 179, 265–66
See also abolition; ethnicity,
changes in; gender; women
ethnicity, 22, 28, 269–70
British conceptions of, 28–29,
41–55, 99, 231, 267–69, 287n.
118
and census returns, 28, 30–31,
268–69
changes in, 28–38, 41–51, 99, 267–
69
and clothing, 64–109 passim
coastal conceptions of, 28–29, 97–
99, 262, 267–69
and rationing, 46–52
See also Africans; Arabs; emancipation and; football and; gender
and; Manyema; Nyasa; Swahili;
Shirazi; Yao; Zanzibari

fashion. *See* style
femininity, 18, 93, 170. *See also buibui; gender; kanga; women*
football, 23–24, 226–64
and class, 227, 235–36, 246–49,
261–63
and colonial administration, 26,
240–48

competitions and leagues, 227, 239, 242, 247, 252, 255
and ethnicity, 231, 233–34, 236, 248–56, 262–63
fans, 236–39, 241, 243, 256, 260–61
and nationalism, 240–64 passim
and *ngoma,* 227, 232–34, 239, 254–55
origins, 227–40

gender
and citizenship, 26–27, 42, 99–101, 106–8, 164–66, 183–84
and clothing, 66, 67, 96–102
and collective action, 130, 133, 153–55, 158, 162
and ethnicity, 33–35, 96–99
and Islam, 19, 120, 125–29, 212
and law, 125–29, 195–209
and leisure, 23–24, 102–8, 170, 180–85, 227–28, 257–61, 262–63
and patron-client ties, 20–22, 102–8, 113–29, 232–34
and property ownership, 33–35, 98, 117–29, 150, 153–55, 201–4, 265–66
and slavery, 5, 8, 16–17, 105, 115. *See also* concubines
and waged labor, 17, 33–34, 109, 118, 150
See also femininity; masculinity; women
gossip, 177, 182, 184, 188–89, 213, 224, 235
gramophone recordings, 1–2, 60, 169, 318n. 53, 319n. 63
ground rent, 111, 133–34, 137

Hadimu, 31, 36, 51, 132
His Master's Voice (HMV), 1–2
housing. *See* gender and property ownership

initiation, 19–20, 103–8, 259, 268
Islam, 17–19, 74, 112, 174–82, 199, 206–7

and clothing, 68–69, 72–75, 85–96, 108, 316n. 29. *See also* veil
and community, 151–52, 176–79, 224
and local custom, 19, 135, 143, 152
and ritual, 174–75, 179–81, 267, 270, 278n. 38, 307n. 96
See also law, Islamic; Muhammad; sufism

James, C. L. R., 226, 236
justice, 8, 25–26, 130, 136, 143, 151–53, 156, 159, 195–201, 203–6, 208–9, 224

kanga, 46–47, 68, 79–86, 190, 266
kaniki, 67, 72
kanzu, 71, 75
kilemba, 64–66, 68, 72
kinship, 20–22, 44, 97–98, 114–15, 134, 256, 262
kiunga. See patron-client ties
kofia, 72, 75
kunguiya, 19, 103–8, 233

labor. *See* gender and waged labor; waged labor
landlords, 110–13, 121–22, 136–48. *See also* Topan, Muhammed-hussein Tharia; Topan, Tharia; Wakf Commission
law
colonial, 25, 110–68 passim, 170, 192–93, 195–209
and courts, 131, 139–40, 146, 156, 157–59, 163, 167, 207
Islamic, 113, 115–16, 124–25, 202, 204, 212. *See also wakf*
colonial changes to, 123–29, 170, 201–6, 216–17
and concubines, 70, 97–99, 216–17, 315n. 21
and inheritance, 70, 97–99, 115–17, 120
and land, 37, 39, 119, 131, 136–37, 139, 157,

Legislative Council, 26, 41–43, 99, 241, 249, 285n. 92
leisure, 8, 23–25, 62–63, 99, 103–8, 150–52, 156, 270–71
  aesthetics of, 235–37, 247–48, 254–55, 262–63
  and moral reform, 229–32, 244, 247–48
  and social mobility, 1–9, 173–75, 179–82, 233–34, 246–47, 266–67
literacy, 78, 144–45, 189–92, 244
lovers, 92, 97, 101–2, 115, 209–23

Manyema, 29–31, 35, 157, 234, 268
marinda, 71, 89, 102–8
masculinity, 8, 21, 23–24, 26, 33–34, 41–42, 46, 56, 64–68, 70, 75–78, 96–102, 114, 118–20, 125, 143, 151, 155–58, 164–65, 177–78, 185–89, 200, 203–7, 209–12, 226–28, 236, 257–61
Muhammad, the Prophet, 19, 143, 151
mwungwana. See civilization

ndege. See initiation
Ng'ambo, 15, 20–24, 105–8, 110–68 passim, 233–34, 242, 251, 253–59, 262, 269, 270. *See also* community; Stone Town; urbanization
ngoma, 23, 103–8, 172–73, 176, 181, 190, 200, 232–37, 260, 270. *See also beni; kunguiya*
Nyasa, 29–31, 34, 176

Omanis, 10–12, 43, 54, 100, 107, 111, 114–29, 171
  and dress, 64–65, 68–71, 96–108
  See also patron-client ties

patron-client ties, 20–22, 44, 102–8, 110–29, 128, 134–36, 186–89, 232–43, 269–70
Pemba, 36, 37, 51, 64, 81
poetry, 1, 4, 172. *See also* Siti binti Saad
politics, 26, 41–52, 55, 99. *See also*

civil society; class; collective action; colonialism; justice
Pouwels, Randall, 108–9, 123
property ownership, 36–38, 110–29, 131
  titles to, 34, 37–39, 119–20, 131, 136–37
  See also gender; emancipation and; *wakf*
Protectorate, 13, 110. *See also* colonialism
public sphere. *See* civil society
purdah, 16, 70, 101–2. *See also buibui;* veil; women

rationing, 46–51
Remtulla bin Hema, 122, 136
Remtulla, Gulamhussein, 122, 142
Remtulla Mohammed, 122, 142, 144
rent control, 140–41, 146, 160–62
Royal Navy, 77, 236, 262–63
Ruete, Emily, 70, 101, 103, 117

sexuality, 101–8, 170, 197–201, 207, 209–23, 260–61, 166–67, 316n. 28. *See also* concubines; law, Islamic; lovers
Seyyid Barghash, 117, 171
Seyyid Hamoud bin Ahmed, 119–20, 122–29
Seyyid Khalifa, 3, 100–101, 162–65, 186, 242–43
Seyyid Said bin Sultan, 12, 97, 100, 119–21. *See also* Omanis
Seyyid Suleiman bin Hamed, 119, 125, 135–37, 143–46
Seyyida Salme. *See* Ruete, Emily
Shirazi, 36, 51, 282n. 74
Shirazi Association, 45, 51–52
Siti binti Saad, 94–96, 169–225
  and African-American parallels, 2, 222
  audience, 1–3, 182–87
  and band, 175–82, 211
  and the community, 24–26, 153, 177, 182, 184, 188–89

critiques of colonial authority, 25,
    78, 189–209
  early life, 179–80
  and emancipation, 2–8, 94–96
  and parenting, 211
  and recording, 1–2, 60, 169, 318 n.
    53, 319 n. 63
  and the veil, 94–96
slave labor, 12, 16–17, 107, 115
slave trade, 11–12
slavery, urban, 16, 68, 106–8, 115–
    18. *See also* patron-client ties;
    concubines; gender and slavery
slaves, 29–30, 107. *See also* concu-
    bines; emancipation; Siti binti
    Saad
  and manumission, 116–17
  status among, 115–20
soccer. *See* football
Sports Control Board, 240–48
Stone Town, 13, 16–17, 20–22, 105–
    8, 128, 140–42, 172, 215–16,
    232–34, 253, 262–70. *See also*
    civilization; Ng'ambo; patron-
    client ties; urbanization
Strobel, Margaret, 57, 105
style, 75–77, 83, 237, 243. *See also*
    buibui; kanga; kanzu
sufism, 19, 90, 152, 179–81
suria. See concubines
Swahili
  clothing, 72–85, 102–8
  detribalization of, 35, 76–79,
    281 n. 71
  as euphemism for "slave," 35–36,
    104–6, 126
  identity, 29–30, 32–33, 35, 39,
    102–8, 233, 267–68
Swahili culture, 3, 6–7, 15, 40–41, 82
  and community, 25, 177–79, 233
  sources and the construction of,
    56–57, 60–62, 184–85, 277 n. 27
  See also Islam; Siti binti Saad; lei-
    sure

taarab, 1–8, 24, 58, 101, 171, 173,

    262–63, 270. *See also* Siti binti
    Saad
tariqa. See sufism
taxes, 37, 129–33, 167. *See also*
    ground rent
Topan, Muhammedhussein Tharia,
    121, 136, 147, 150, 154, 160–61
Topan, Tharia, 121
Tumbatu, 31, 36, 51, 132

urbanization, 13, 16–17, 32–34, 40–
    41, 53, 112, 237, 266, 270–71. *See
    also* Ng'ambo; Stone Town
ustaarabu. See civilization

veil, 85–96. *See also barakoa; buibui;
    kanga*

waged labor, 17, 32–34, 109
  and ethnic stereotypes, 53
  See also gender and waged labor
wages, 33–34, 53
wakf, 119–29, 138–40, 144
Wakf Commission, 123–29, 134,
    139, 143–44, 150, 166, 201–2,
    241
winda, 64–67
women, 195–223
  class divisions among, 16, 67, 69–
    70, 82–84, 86, 91, 96–108, 155,
    281 n. 65
  and emancipation, 3–5, 209–23,
    265–68. *See also buibui;* gender
    and property ownership; *kanga*
  and political participation, 26–27,
    99–101, 103–8, 113, 139, 142,
    149–50, 153–55, 158, 162–66,
    183–84. *See also* civil society
  and slavery, 16, 82, 101
  violence against, 196–200, 203–6
  and work, 33–34, 82, 179, 181,
    218–21, 265–66, 278 n. 44, 281 n.
    65
  See also concubines; femininity;
    gender; Seyyida Salme; Siti
    binti Saad

World War II, 46–51, 252, 262
    as a war over rice, 48–51

Yao, 29–31, 34

Zanzibar
    compared to other Swahili towns,
        15–16, 177, 180, 190, 240
    and East Africa, 2, 10–11, 123
    immigration to, 10–13, 53–55, 93.

See also Busaid dynasty; Omanis
    as the Paris of the Indian Ocean,
        80, 102, 103
    revolution, 51, 263. *See also* Afro-
        Shirazi Party
    and slave trade, 3, 10–11
Zanzibari, 38–40, 48, 103–8, 112,
    148, 156–57, 163, 167, 170–75,
    266, 268